The Invisible Element:

A Practical Guide for the Human Dynamics of Innovation

A Practical Guide for the Human Dynamics of Innovation

by

Robert B. Rosenfeld

& Gary J. Wilhelmi

with

Andrew Harrison

The Invisible Element: A Practical Guide for the Human Dynamics of Innovation

www.TheInvisibleElement.com

ISBN: 978-0-9839812-0-6

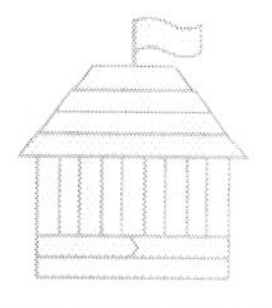

Table of Contents

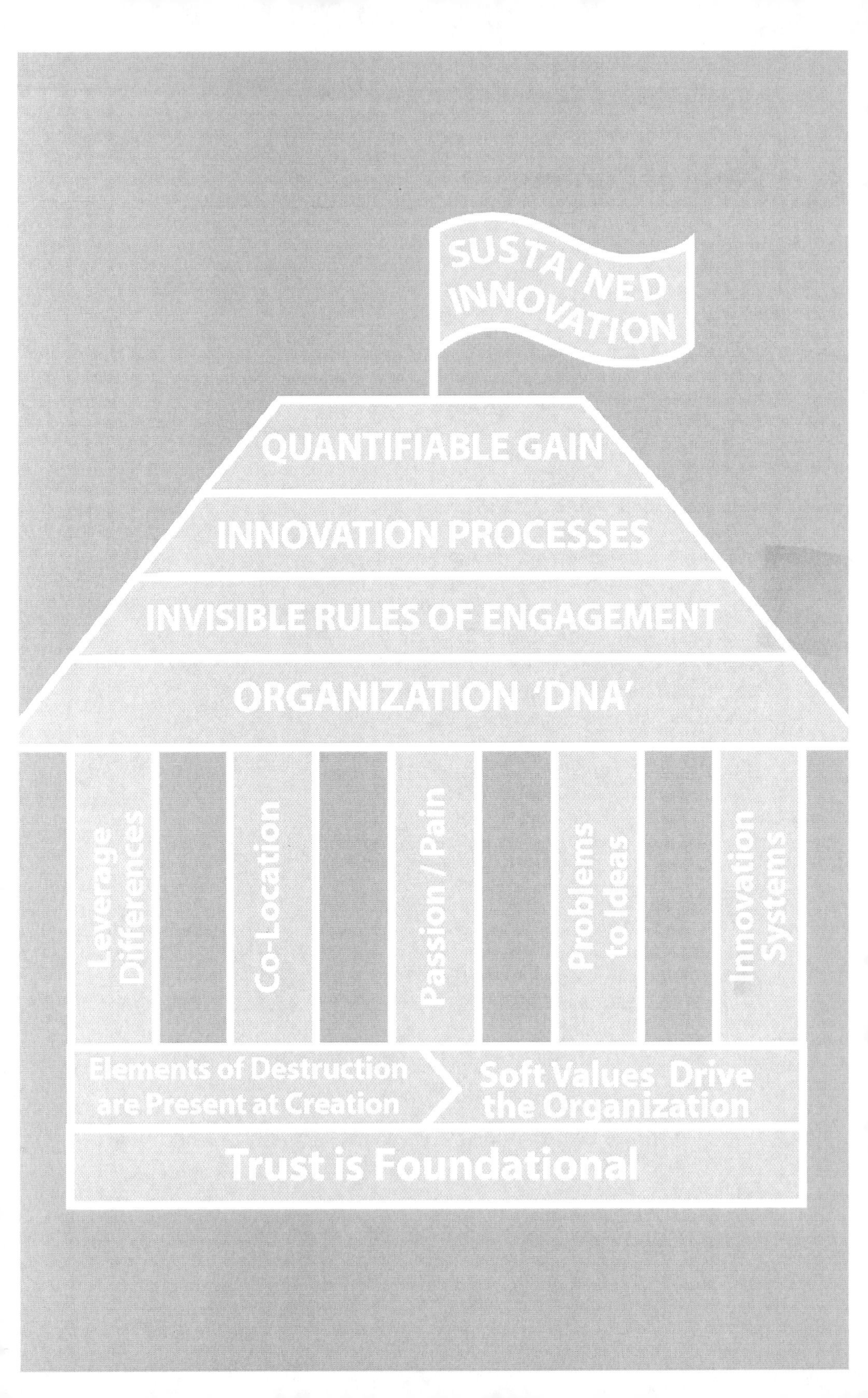
SUSTAINED INNOVATION
QUANTIFIABLE GAIN
INNOVATION PROCESSES
INVISIBLE RULES OF ENGAGEMENT
ORGANIZATION 'DNA'
Leverage Differences
Co-Location
Passion / Pain
Problems to Ideas
Innovation Systems
Elements of Destruction are Present at Creation
Soft Values Drive the Organization
Trust is Foundational

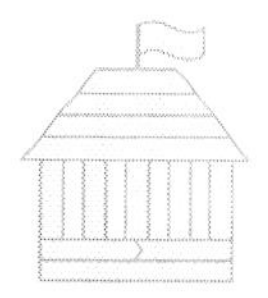

Endorsements

"Innovation has been the holy grail of technology-driven companies, where hit and miss has been more the norm than the exception. Yet, in this book, Rosenfeld and Wilhelmi give the reader an inner view of the necessary albeit hidden human chemistry of innovation. They masterfully combine three critical dimensions to creating innovation: in-depth leanings of textbook, actionable steps of a how-to guidebook and the priceless wealth of over 40 years of hands-on experience. I highly recommend this book to any executive who wants to take innovation from fuzzy trial-and-errors to success by design."

Dr. Francois Nader, President and Chief Executive Officer, NPS Pharmaceuticals

"Change agents take notice! You need to put Bob Rosenfeld and Gary Wilhelmi's new book, *The Invisible Element: A Practical Guide for the Human Dynamics of Innovation*, on your 'must read' list. As anyone who has tried to affect change in an organization will tell you, it's one thing to know something; it's quite another thing to apply it. Those who've tried to make a difference in an organization know from experience that application is everything. Stated another way, it's what you do with what you know that makes a difference. *The Invisible Element* is the practical guide you've been waiting for -- it will help you apply all the innovation principles that are nicely summarized here."

Mary Margaret Evans, Vice President for Government Relations & Strategy, Insitu

"I found this book to be much more than a how-to book on the human aspects of innovation, it is an insightful guidebook on optimizing the human power element of any organization. A must read for anyone who believes in the value of an empowered and engaged workforce. I highly recommend it to anyone in serious pursuit of sustained innovation in their business."

Dennis Duke, Director of Advanced Programs, Rolls-Royce Naval Marine Inc.

"*The Invisible Element: A Practical Guide for the Human Dynamics of Innovation* is an essential read for anyone trying to establish or lead an effort to drive innovation throughout an organization. Sustained innovation requires both a good process and the right culture. Much has been written about process, but no one has addressed the human side of innovation as thoroughly and insightfully as this book."

Gary Einhaus, Retired General Manager, CTO and New Business Development Director at Eastman Kodak

"Rosenfeld and Wilhelmi crystallize new aspects of human innovation in this latest book."

Pierre Legualt, President and CEO, Prosidion Ltd.

"Innovation in an organization often creates an alpha and omega relationship between innovators and their bosses. Desired but often misunderstood and rejected, the dynamics of this complex and often contentious interaction has baffled and eluded all involved for many years. Using 40 years of experience, Bob and Gary create practical approaches to unlock this paradox, reduce the friction of change, and clearly illustrate what actually happens as new ideas are broached, developed and implemented. This 'how to' manual is a must read for innovators and leadership teams wishing to maximize the return on their innovative investment!"

Peter Engstrom, Co Founder and Board President of At Home Chesapeake and former Vice President for Federal Knowledge Business, Science Applications International Corporation (SAIC)

"*The Invisible Element* is a persuasive, practical and insightful book dedicated to helping firms, institutions, and individuals unleash their hidden creativity. Teamwork is only as good as the team itself, and the specific and innovative techniques in this wide-ranging book will be essential to helping leaders build the right team for the right job. In the process, they will also come to understand one of the keys to *The Invisible Element*: that the constants of human behavior transcend cultures and unite civilizations."

Charles King, Professor of International Affairs and Government at Georgetown University

"Bob and Gary have provided a unique business guide to innovation. This is not a recipe, which presumes consistent results from standard ingredients, but rather a detailed discussion of the key human characteristics that need to be gently nudged and nurtured in order to create an environment in which innovation can flourish. Too often books of this type focus on one or two pieces of the puzzle. From the Innovation House, through the various frameworks, tools, and assessments, to the epilogue, the authors effectively use models, diagrams, analogies and examples to explain the breadth of the human aspects (the hidden elements) of the innovation challenge. For individuals and organizations willing to make the necessary investment, the authors' recommendations payoff could be significant."

Allison F. Dolan, Privacy Specialist, MIT and former Innovation Facilitator at Eastman Kodak

"Bringing creative ideas to life requires not only brilliant thoughts, but considered, insightful, and principled actions. You need trust; you need principles; you need some analytical tools and facts on hand; and you need a profound respect—and, ideally, affection—for the diversity of human beings. In *The Invisible Element: A Practical Guide for the Human Dynamics of Innovation*, Robert Rosenfeld and Gary Wilhelmi demonstrate their deep understanding of the social dynamics behind the realization of great ideas. Their work draws on decades of practical experience and reveals how to transform organizations into more productive, more innovative, and more humane places."

Margaret Paxson, PhD, Senior Associate, Kennan Institute, Woodrow Wilson International Center for Scholars and Visiting Scholar, Institute for European, Russian, and Eurasian Studies, Elliott School of International Affairs, George Washington University

"*The Invisible Element: A Practical Guide for the Human Dynamics of Innovation* is an inescapable part of our individual, community and institutional lives. Being part of positive sustainable change or innovation is an immense challenge in our chaotic and complex societies. If you want greater coherence and cohesion in the innovations that you are a part of, then *The Invisible Element* is an excellent road map for navigating your journey. Whether you are involved in incremental, expansionary or revolutionary innovation, this detailed and thoughtful book is a must-have operating manual. Along with Rosenfeld's previous book, *Making the Invisible Visible: The Human Principles for Sustaining Innovation*, we are using *The Invisible Element* to realize our vision of 'advancing prosperity by fostering sustainable cultures of innovation.'"

Johann S. Wong, CFA, serial entrepreneur and founder, London Innovation Centre and InnovationPi

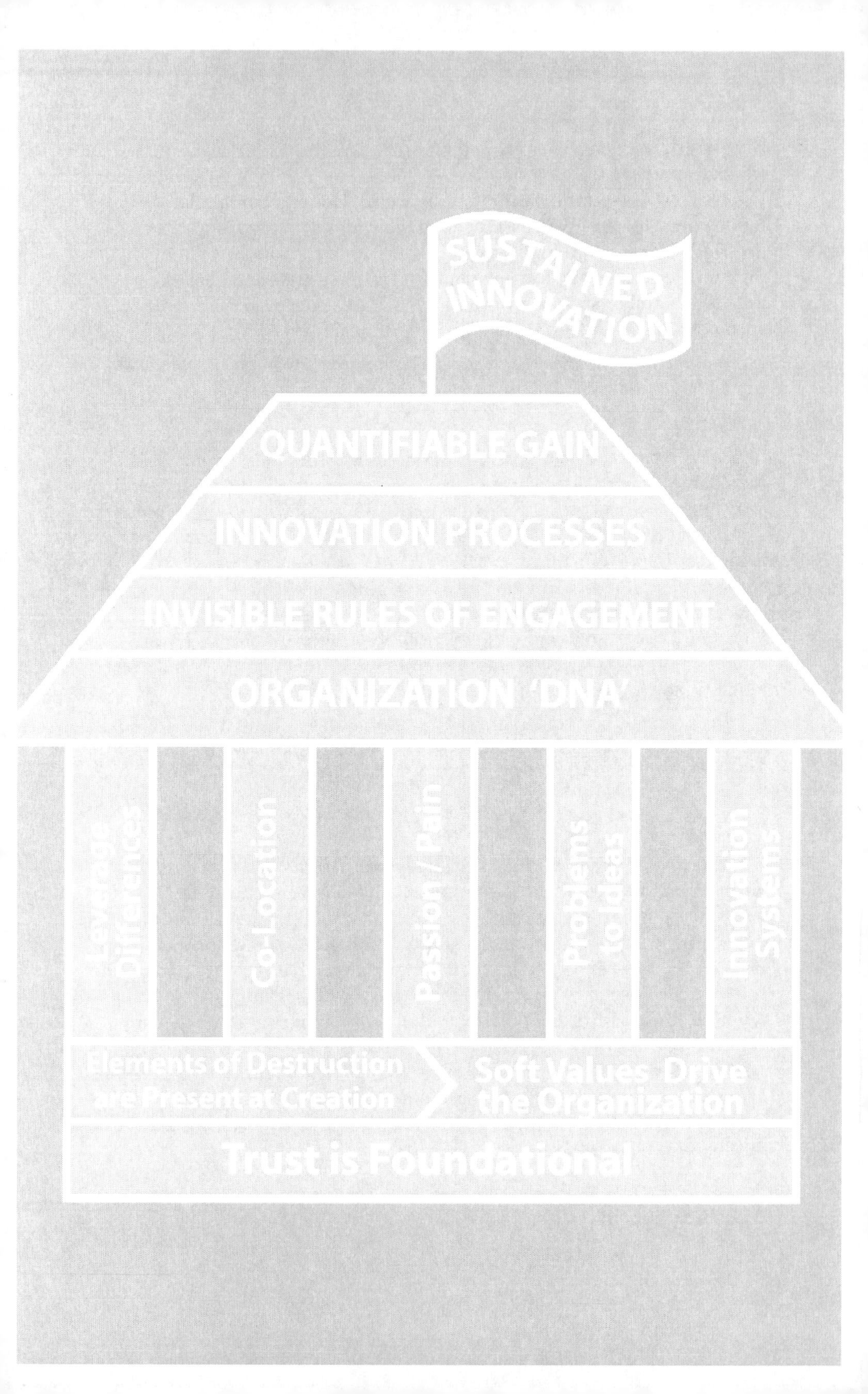
SUSTAINED INNOVATION
QUANTIFIABLE GAIN
INNOVATION PROCESSES
INVISIBLE RULES OF ENGAGEMENT
ORGANIZATION 'DNA'
Leverage Differences
Co-Location
Passion / Pain
Problems to Ideas
Innovation Systems
Elements of Destruction are Present at Creation
Soft Values Drive the Organization
Trust is Foundational

Acknowledgements

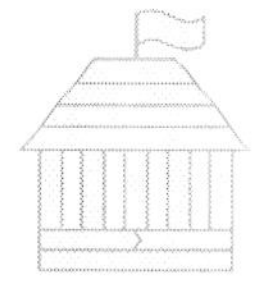

There is no way that we could ever acknowledge all of the individuals who helped shape this book. It is truly an integration of all of the interactions we have had with different colleagues/innovators throughout our careers. It is through these interactions that we have been able to shape our thoughts and insights into the world of innovation. To all of you, we sincerely thank you and hope that each of you can see a little of yourselves in this book.

We want to thank our colleagues at Idea Connection Systems, Inc. for the many hours of idea sharing and shaping as well as valuable suggestions and critique of the material in this book. In particular we want to thank Larry VanEtten for putting up with our "Pingging" and keeping us somewhat grounded. Without his insights and support, we would have never completed construction of our Innovation House™.

To Andrew Harrison, the writer of this book, it has been our pleasure to watch your evolution in the field of innovation. At our introductory lunch, it was apparent you were a social innovator and truly understood the value of people. But as our relationship grew, you moved well beyond "just our writer." You have fully grasped the concepts in this book and added a flavor that brings our work a more understood way of application. By working with us and at Idea Connection Systems over the past three years, we are pleased to call you a peer in the human dynamics of innovation.

The friendship and support of the Center for Creative Leadership was an invaluable catalyst in pulling this book together. In particular, Barbara Demarest and David Horth's support and assistance in developing the "Making the Invisible Visible" short course provided the impetus for us to put all of the pieces together in what we hope is a coherent model.

We are especially grateful to our friends and colleagues who read early drafts of the book and provided valuable insights and suggestions that helped shape the final manuscript.

We'd like to thank our editor, Martha Whalen. Your efforts helped focus our thoughts. To our proofreaders Margaret Tash, Sarah Williams and Marco De-Moor Bey, thank you for your attention to detail. To our cover designer, David Royka, we appreciate your vision. To our book layout designer, Kim Wood, thank you for your flexibility. To our book production specialist, Matthew Bernius, thanks for your expertise.

Finally, to our wives, Debbie and Leeann; without your encouragement, endless hours of editing and your "constructive" critiques, this book would never have been finished. We are eternally grateful and to you, we dedicate this book.

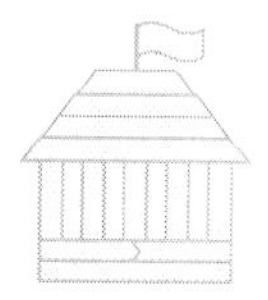

Biographies

Robert Rosenfeld

Robert "Bob" Rosenfeld is the Founder and CEO of Idea Connection Systems, Inc. (*www.innovating.com*). For over 40 years, he has been a leader and practitioner in the human dynamics that make innovation happen inside organizations. Along with co-authoring this book, Bob is the author of *Making the Invisible Visible: The Human Principles for Sustaining Innovation* (2006).

Bob created the first Office of Innovation ever to be successfully implemented in Corporate America in 1978 at Eastman Kodak. In 1985, he co-founded the Association for Managers of Innovation (AMI).

After working with many diverse people and organizations, in 2001, Bob and his ICS team developed Mosaic Partnerships™—an innovative process for breaking down barriers between races that has been implemented in cities around the United States and organizations around the world.

Because of Bob's innovation experience, in May 2006, he was named the Center for Creative Leadership's (CCL) first "Innovator in Residence" and in 2008, he was awarded Innovator in Residence Emeritus status.

In 2008, he and his ICS team created the ISPI® (Innovation Strengths Preference Indicator®), an innovation tool used to highlight how people prefer to innovate as well as how they prefer to innovate with others. The ISPI® is used to make the invisible elements of innovation visible to individuals, teams, departments and organizations.

Bob's efforts in the human dynamics of innovation continue to impact organizations around the globe with clients in the U.S., India, Brazil, Singapore, South Africa, Canada and Europe.

Bob and his wife Debbie have been married for over 30 years. They have seven children, five of whom are adopted, and six grandchildren who live in Rochester, New York. The diversity of their family is a true reflection of the world today and inspires Bob to continue to understand humankind and find ways to cope with the struggles facing modern society.

Gary Wilhelmi

Gary Wilhelmi has consistently been recognized by his peers as an agent of change. As an innovation leader, he has focused on the critical role that people play in the innovation process. He recognized early in his career that "organizations don't innovate...people do". As a result, he has developed pioneering approaches and unique tools that allow employers and their employees to understand the role that they play in driving successful innovation.

As an electrical engineer, his experience includes innovative work in such areas as high tech laser and optical systems, first generation fiber optics communication systems, biotechnology, consumer products resulting in hundreds of millions of dollars in sales, sensory research, packaging materials, and more. He has successfully implemented innovation breakthroughs using both internal teams as well as virtual R&D organizations.

Over his 35 years of experience he has worked for McDonnell Aircraft Company, ITT Electro-Optics Products Division, and PepsiCo. Currently he is Vice President of Idea Connection Systems (*www.innovating.com*) where he is working with various governmental agencies and Fortune 100 companies. This broad range of experience has provided Gary with a unique insight into what is required to create and sustain innovation. It has led to the development of several proprietary tools focusing on the human dynamics critical to the innovation process including the ability to assess an organization's culture, level of trust, invisible decision making processes, level of motivation, and ability to deal with "wicked" problems.

Gary and his wife, Leeann, have four children and live in the Dallas/Fort Worth area.

Andrew Harrison

Andrew Harrison is the writer of *The Invisible Element: A Practical Guide for the Human Dynamics of Innovation*. The experience of writing this book alongside two industry experts allowed him a rare and exciting opportunity to explore what it takes to spark and sustain innovation within organizations and working groups. The book process also saw Andrew become part of Idea Connection Systems (*www.innovating.com*) and evolve into the role of Innovation Ambassador.

Andrew's unique background as a social innovator, author and researcher of human motivation began in 2004 when he exchanged his master's degree and high paying sales job for a year on the road—traveling the United States interviewing people from varied walks of life about how they came to discover passion from their work; a passion which inevitably spilled over into the remaining aspects of their lives (*www.iamontheroad.com*).

His study of human motivation now spans many industries and fields. Andrew's debut book entitled, *Love Your 84,000 Hours at Work: Stories on the Road from People with Purpose and Passion* (Dotted Lines Press, 2010), chronicles the inspiring journeys of a select number of people who have mastered one of the core ingredients to maintaining a happy life—loving what you do (*www.84000hours.com*).

An understudy to Bob Rosenfeld since 2008, Andrew has been an instrumental part of the team responsible for developing the Innovation Strengths Preference Indicator® (ISPI®). He is certified in the ISPI® for delivering feedback to individuals and groups, in analyzing and forming teams, as well as conducting organizational ISPI® analyses.

Andrew designs and delivers keynote presentations and leads workshops on the human principles that create a culture of innovation. He also instructs and inspires people on how to marry purpose and passion into their work. Andrew has a passion for teaching the tools of the innovation and career trades; a byproduct from his days as a former adjunct college professor.

Andrew's work has been featured in the Miami Herald, Charlotte Observer, Rochester Democrat and Chronicle, as well as on local ABC, CBS, Fox, and Time Warner TV news programs, NPR radio, and a number of business journals and national magazine publications. He is currently based in Rochester, NY and is both purposeful and passionate about writing, traveling, meeting new people, speaking to groups, cooking and eating, playing golf and watching sports.

Foreword

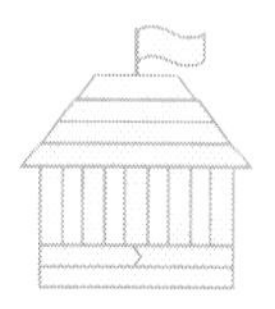

We believe that everybody has the potential to be innovative. Some are more adept at innovation towards the **evolutionary** (or Six Sigma) end of the innovation continuum while others may be more suited for the **revolutionary** (or breakthrough) end, or somewhere in between. The real question is not whether a person is innovative. The question is how to unlock the innovation potential in all of us.

Through our almost 20 years of working together, we have seen organizations that brought out this innovative spirit in their employees. We have also seen too many that held their innovators "hostage." They were prevented from turning their potential into a reality by largely invisible characteristics imbedded in the organization. Human dynamics rather than the business or technological aspects drive most of these. For example, when trust within the organization declines, there is a corresponding increase in risk aversion. This is a result of the innovators no longer feeling that their managers will support them if they are not successful. They start making decisions based on their internal fear of failure filter. The net result is that the company's innovation shifts significantly to the lower risk, evolutionary end of the continuum.

In *Making the Invisible Visible: The Human Principles for Sustaining Innovation* (Rosenfeld, 2006), eight fundamental principles were defined which are foundational for understanding these invisible hurdles. The book provided great understanding, but not the full practical application. Applying them was up to the innovation leader.

In this book, we are moving beyond theory and are providing a practical guide for how to put these principles into action. In the first part of the book, we expand on the human principles and provide tools to better understand them. While it is not required that you have read the first book to be able to understand this book, we encourage you to do so at some point to get a more in-depth exposure to the principles themselves.

The second part of the book is about the application of the principles within your organization to create a sustainable culture of innovation, one that "unshackles your innovators."

When we first talked about the need for this book and whether or not we wanted to write it, several conflicting thoughts emerged. The biggest reason for not writing it was that we would be giving the world a significant portion of our intellectual property. Yet, when we weighed that against our deep-rooted desire to help current and future innovation leaders create the world of tomorrow, the answer was obvious. We wrote this book to help with the evolution of innovation, of work, and of how organizations work with people.

If reading this book changes or reinforces your beliefs and values relative to being an innovation leader, then we have more than accomplished our goal. If you read it and at least think about what we are saying, then we are still moving innovation in the right direction. If you read it and disagree, we want to hear from you.

Today's world has been created through innovation. So will tomorrow's. What role do you want to play in shaping that future? Don't allow your innovation to be shackled. Set it free. After all:

Organizations Don't Innovate, People Do™

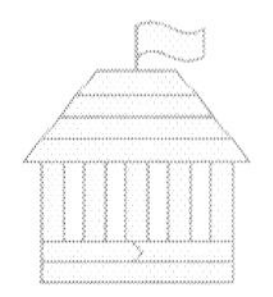

Introduction

Globally, the need for innovation has never been stronger. In 2009, United States President Barack Obama introduced the "Strategy for American Innovation."[1] In India, their government dedicated 2010 - 2020 as the "Decade of Innovation."[2] In addition, if you were to poll leaders of organizations around the globe, most would list innovation as a top priority. Yet, if you were to ask those same leaders how they were going to make innovation happen, they would not be able to explain how to do it.

The need for innovation is clear; yet understanding how to do it is not. The reason we wrote this book is to help the world understand how to make innovation happen inside an organization.

To start, we need to understand the world we live in today and the implications of that world on the future of innovation. In this book, you will learn more about the eight fundamental human principles for sustaining innovation and how they can be applied to today's world. We will describe the principles and make them more visible and then assist you, the innovation leader, in using them to **help navigate ideas into innovations**.

What Is Innovation?

At this point, it makes sense to clearly define what we mean by innovation. Unfortunately, innovation is one of those words that has come to mean different things to different people. One area of confusion is the belief that innovation and **creativity** are synonymous. We see these two activities as complementary but very distinct. The following are definitions of creativity and innovation that we will use throughout this book:

- Creativity is the generation of new and/or novel ideas.
- Innovation is a creative act or solution that results in a **quantifiable gain**.

Many organizations do a good job of focusing on creativity and the tools necessary to produce creative thought. Yet, the key to success is to understand how to take people's creative ideas and turn them into a quantifiable gain.

A quantifiable gain is determined by the **currency of the realm** or, in other words, "what matters." A quantifiable gain is a measure that defines the value of exchange between individuals or companies in the marketplace. The currency of the realm might be return on investment (ROI) for one company, the number of new products for another, or the number of publications or students for a university, and so forth.

Many times, organizations get stuck on their own concepts of innovation. They associate innovation only with new ideas that are **revolutionary** or breakthrough (e.g., the iPod®). Yet, there is much more to innovation than popular innovations publicized in magazines.

A breakthrough **idea** or product is just one end of the **innovation continuum**. Tweaking a process may also be considered innovation. Innovation is any change, be it large or small, which leads to a quantifiable gain. We look at the end goals of innovation on a continuum, ranging from **Revolutionary** (e.g., breakthrough) to **Evolutionary** (e.g., **Kaizen Teian**, **Six Sigma**) (Figure I.1, see next page).

When we talk about product development or new product life cycles, we will look at the continuum from revolutionary to evolutionary. In contrast, when we talk about human or organizational characteristics, we generally reverse the continuum. The reason for doing so is simply to mirror the way most people think about innovation in the different contexts. We will refer to the innovation continuum throughout the book.

Revolutionary ideas redefine problems, break boundaries, and create new paradigms – they provide completely new and sometimes **disruptive** ideas. The first flight and the personal computer are examples of revolutionary ideas.

Expansionary ideas tackle challenges. They answer the question, "How can we do things differently?" An example here is a product line extension (e.g., different flavor, color, or shape) that uses the same technology and pulls in new customers or expands the market.

Evolutionary ideas seek solutions by using existing concepts. They answer, "How can we do things better?" These ideas are very process-driven, such as **Lean Six Sigma**, which uses the "Define, Measure, Analyze, Improve, and Control" (or DMAIC) methodology.[3]

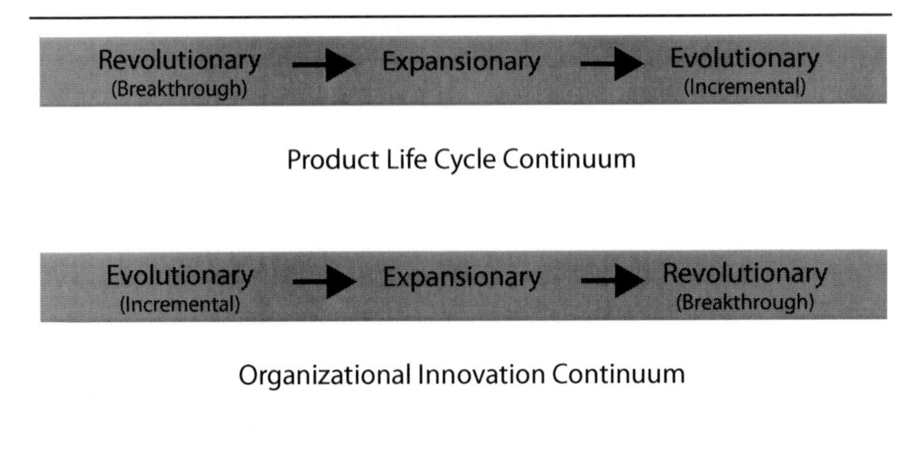

Revolutionary	Redefines the problem definition to break boundaries and create new paradigms
Expansionary	Challenges the problem definition to do things differently
Evolutionary	Seeks solutions based on existing concepts to do things better

Figure I.1
The Innovation Continuum™

Innovation is tied into all activities of an organization, including leadership, operations, sales, marketing, and research and development (R&D), among others. In all of these activities, there is the need to innovate somewhere along the innovation continuum.

Operations may focus more on Lean Six Sigma programs, which align more often with the evolutionary end. In contrast, R&D may align better with expansionary or **revolutionary innovation**. The key is that for any organization to sustain growth, innovation is required somewhere along this continuum – and it generally translates into activities across all three categories. The dilemma facing **innovation leaders** in today's world is how to make such innovation happen. Their organizations need to shift focus in order to expand their innovation portfolio, but how? What are their innovation objectives? How do they identify where to focus their innovation efforts? And finally, how do they create an environment conducive to innovation and how can they assist employees?

Business and Innovation – Past, Present and Future

Drafts of this book were all written using computers – not a surprise in today's world. One of the devices that is used constantly is one that we have grown to take for granted: the mouse.[4,5] This device has been instrumental in making the human interface with computers significantly easier and opened up the frontier of personal computers.

We will now show our age: For some of us, early in our careers, computers were the size of buildings and we interfaced with them primarily through punch cards.[6] We would walk to the computer center with stacks of these cards, wait in line to feed them into the reader (or oftentimes, the card eater), hope we hadn't mistyped a card (or worse, mixed up the order of the cards), and then wait to see if the program ran correctly. The advent of the modern age of computing has changed all of that. The introduction of the graphical user interface (a symbolic world with little pictures of folders and other icons on our desktops) and the use of the mouse to allow the user to easily navigate through these icons has changed computing forever.

The mouse took almost 20 years to go through its initial development. It started from what Douglas Engelbart invented in the 1960s at the Stanford Research Institute and was later refined by the engineers and scientists at the Xerox Palo Alto Research Center (PARC) in the 1970s. In 1979, Steve Jobs saw the mouse at PARC and, based upon what he saw, a decision was made to bring it into Apple and create a version that could be a commercial success.

The **problem** for Jobs and Apple was that in 1979, the mouse itself cost about $400, and it required an additional interface module at a cost of $300. Jobs wanted a mouse that could be manufactured for $10 to $35, but it was far from obvious that it could be done. Jobs went to Hovey-Kelly, a small start-up design company (that later became known as IDEO) to redesign the mouse.[7] Starting with a Ban Roll-On ball and some Teflon dishes, they were able to overcome myriad technical issues, and, as we know, the rest is history. While the story of the design effort at Hovey-Kelly is interesting in itself, the main focus of thinking about the evolution of the mouse in this book is more about the "why" rather than the "how" or "what."

The real question is why it took almost 20 years to go from the invention of the mouse in the 1960s to having the version that Jobs saw in 1979 to having 25 prototypes of the "modern" mouse by the end of 1980. There were brilliant scientists and engineers working on it from the beginning. The value of the interface was obvious to the people involved. So what made the difference?

We believe a major part of the answer is that Jobs wanted to build Apple rather than create a new computer. He wanted to grow Apple and have a distinct, competitive advantage over other computer manufacturers.

Think of the countless examples of companies not wanting to take risks to grow. Instead, they were more focused on maintaining their current markets, improving productivity, and extending current product lines, i.e., basically focusing on evolutionary and some expansionary innovation. Why is it that Kodak invented the digital camera but was a late entry into the world of digital photography? Why did the Swiss not capitalize on digital watches? Why did it take 3M years to introduce Post-it® Notes? And so on.

For sustained growth, you need to create a dynamically balanced innovation portfolio and focus efforts to meet the ongoing growth needs of your organization. To successfully do this, you need to also understand the world around you.

While the understanding of today's world will date this part of the book, the methodology of looking at and understanding the implications of current events, both political and commercial, can be utilized at any point in time. So, how do we view the landscape of the current world and what are the implications for innovation?

We have seen that innovation has been cyclical throughout generations, shifting from revolutionary to evolutionary and back again. The current cycle appears to have its beginnings in the early 1990s, with a number of large organizations going through significant reorganizations, downsizings, and reduction in forces (RIFs). Organizations reduced staff predominantly to improve overall bottom-line performance. These reductions have had a profound effect on organizations, impacting their ability to keep up with innovation demands and, in particular, on revolutionary innovation.

First of all, these RIFs tended to shatter the psychological contract between the employee and the company. Any idea of an implied employment contract was eliminated. People felt far less secure in their jobs. Along with this shift came an erosion of **trust** between employees and the organization. Individual decisions shifted to include a major component of "looking out for myself." Many innovation decisions are now based on an individual's fear of failure assessment because employees no longer feel that the innovation leaders or the organization will support them if the innovation is unsuccessful. This has forced the innovation portfolio to shift significantly towards the lower risk, evolutionary end.

Another unintended (and far less visible) consequence of the RIFs was that a disproportionate number of strong pioneers (out-of-the-box thinkers and doers) were included in staff reductions. Pioneers tend to be viewed by organizations as undisciplined, disruptive, and unconventional – basically as "nice to have" but not required. Consequently, in difficult times this group is viewed as the least critical element for immediate success. Eliminating these people has resulted in organizations no longer having the ability to generate the **paradigm**-pioneering ideas required for breakthrough innovation.

The final, unintended consequence from the RIFs that we want to mention impacts the innovation leaders of today. Many current leaders were trained and developed their innovation leadership skills during the 1990s. They have become very adept at leading Lean Six Sigma or line extension innovations. However, few of them have ever had the opportunity to lead the complicated process of a revolutionary or breakthrough innovation. They have never had to grow something new.

All of these combined circumstances help explain why so many organizations are currently struggling with the need for more revolutionary innovation to re-energize their top and bottom lines.

Through the focus on productivity over the past 20 years, organizations have lost sight of the need to balance their portfolios for both short- and long-term growth. As the short-term growth engine slows down, companies are trying to understand why they no longer have the pipeline of new ideas to fuel their continued growth. They are now trying to instantaneously jump-start the breakthrough innovation engine. Unfortunately, most breakthrough innovation does not occur that way. Large organizations are now trying to look for innovations and technologies that they can bring inside to accelerate the restarting of the innovation engine.

Also during this period, companies shifted a significant amount of their manufacturing and some of their development efforts offshore. A somewhat invisible consequence of this is that the innovation leaders in these countries are getting firsthand experience in developing and growing organizations with the ability for successful breakthrough innovation. These managers are developing the technical, business, and human understanding required to start competing globally with innovation breakthroughs. If you are in the United States, what are the implications of this consequence for your organization?

The final two elements that are shaping the innovation landscape of the world today are terrorism and the economic crisis of 2008. We won't go into detail on either one of these elements. However, we want to point out that both are obviously having a significant, visible impact. Just as important, and somewhat less visible, is the impact they are having on trust around the world. We are becoming less trusting of those who are different from us. People have become less trusting of the leadership of financial institutions. Overall, trust in political leaders is at an all-time low. The bottom line is that the innovation leader in today's world is faced with a combination of consequences from the:

- Erosion of trust within organizations and around the world
- Reduction or elimination of the pioneers within larger organizations
- Focus on evolutionary/expansionary innovation, to the detriment of continued development of breakthrough innovations

The impact of each of these consequences has directly affected innovators. Therefore, it is more critical than ever before that the innovation leader takes into consideration the eight human principles in designing and implementing the innovation organization for the future.

Now Is the Time

This is a great time to be an **innovator**. The world is now seeing the need for innovation in how to conduct business, utilize technology, and deal with people.

The recent emphasis on innovation may be attributed to many factors, but the main reason is that organizations now need to grow in highly competitive markets. They no longer compete with businesses down the street; rather, they compete all across the globe.

We have heard from many innovation leaders who say their organization talks about innovation but does not allow it to happen: "We've been pretty successful with our current processes. We're growing at X% per year, we only have 15% of the market, and we are still growing. We've done this by being fairly autocratic and ensuring everyone is working on exactly what we want them working on. Why would we want to change? At some point, yes, but we're a long way from being at that point."

We tell them, "If you are interested only in quarterly results as opposed to sustaining that growth for a long period, we agree – you don't need to change. But at what point in the future would you like to go out of business? How many minicomputer manufacturers are still thriving today? What happened to the big TV sets that used vacuum tubes?" The examples go on and on.

If you simply compare the Fortune 100 lists from 1968 to 2007, there are only 10 companies from the top 50 that showed up on both lists. This means that 40 companies doing great in 1968 were replaced on the 2007 Fortune list. What happened? Why did 80% of the list change over this timeframe?

The Fortune 100 list changes because innovation evolves over time. Based on our combined 80 years in the field, for organizations to succeed in today's world, they must grow both the top and bottom lines concurrently. More than ever, it has become much more complicated to get the job done on both sides. Our message is clear and simple: If organizations don't innovate, they're not going to be around. Your organization can do one of two things – **Innovate or die.**

People Make Innovation Happen

If you Google the term, "innovation books," the list is massive. Many of these books talk about the business aspects of innovation. Books such as Christensen and Raynor's *The Innovator's Solution*[8] or Kim and Mauborgne's *Blue Ocean Strategy*[9] help answer the question of how to identify where to focus innovation efforts. They primarily focus on the business aspects. However,

---

Organizations Don't Innovate, People Do™

If managers don't understand the people side of innovation, they can have the latest advancements in technology and appropriate business processes, but they will still be left wondering why they cannot generate innovative ideas and translate them into business successes.

Therefore, this book is intended to offer guidance on the human element as it pertains to innovation. It will walk you through the human dynamics required for innovation to take place. This book will not tell you where to look for innovation; rather, it will tell you what it's going to take for your organization to be innovative. This book will not tell you where to innovate; instead, this book will tell you how to innovate.

Robert Rosenfeld's book, titled *Making the Invisible Visible: The Human Principles for Sustaining Innovation*, provides a solid philosophical understanding of how to make innovation work.[10] Our book expands on that foundation with a primary focus on how to transform understanding into action within an organization. It goes into greater detail on the eight underlying human principles of innovation and, more importantly, describes how to put these principles into practice. This book is not about theory;

rather, it is about how to put theory into practice to create a sustainable **culture** of innovation.

We will explain how to sustain innovation by implementing an approach that can be replicated. We go beyond the foundational principles and give you tips and tools for generating innovation in both the short and long term. The model that we will use throughout the book is based on **information** conveyed in the Innovation House™[11] (Figure I.2).

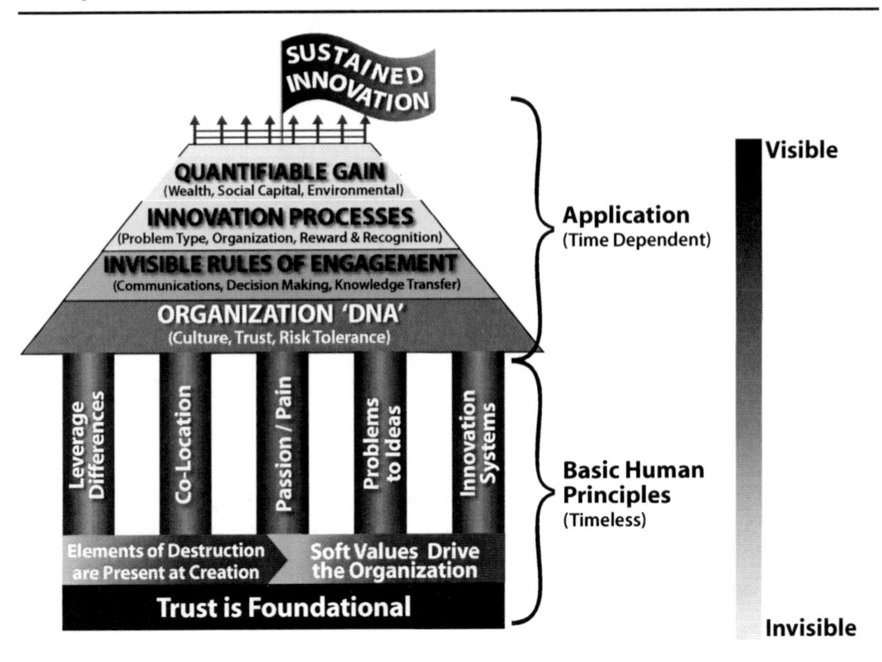

Figure I.2
The Innovation House™. *This house is a schematic that represents how key human principles (depicted in the lower portion of the house) can be applied to create a culture conducive to sustaining innovation.*

As indicated via this model, we will explore innovation in numerous ways. To begin with, we will briefly discuss the principles defined by Rosenfeld, which form the bottom of the Innovation House.[12] These include:

- Three principles of an Innovative Environment:
    1. Trust Is Foundational
    2. Elements of Destruction Are Present at Creation
    3. Soft **Values** Drive the Organization

- Five principles for the Essence of Innovation (or the five "pillars")
    1. Leveraging Differences
    2. Co-Locate For Effective Exchange
    3. **Passion** Is the Fuel and **Pain** Is the Hidden Ingredient
    4. Innovation Starts When Problems Are Converted Into Ideas
    5. Innovation Needs a System

We will also explain how these principles are integrated to create the time-dependent applications depicted at the top of the house. These include: Organization DNA, Invisible Rules of Engagement, Innovation Process, and Quantifiable Gain. By moving from the principles through the application portions of the Innovation House, we also move from the invisible to the more visible aspects of innovation.

In this book, we will show you how all of the individual elements of the house link to each other to form a whole, how they work synergistically, and why leaving one out can be deadly. We will also help you understand the implications of defining each of the elements in relation to your organization's goals and objectives.

To apply the Innovation House at a very high level, follow these two strategies:

1. If you are creating a new organization, culture, or team, start from the base of the house and work your way up.
2. If you are doing long-range planning, conducting an end-of-year review, or initiating a major innovation strategy, start at the top of the house and work your way down. If you are not getting the quantifiable gain you are hoping for at the top of the house, chances are there is an issue with the bottom of the house.

Appendix I provides a glossary of terms to help you understand and apply the principles in this book.

It is now time to start building your organization's Innovation House.

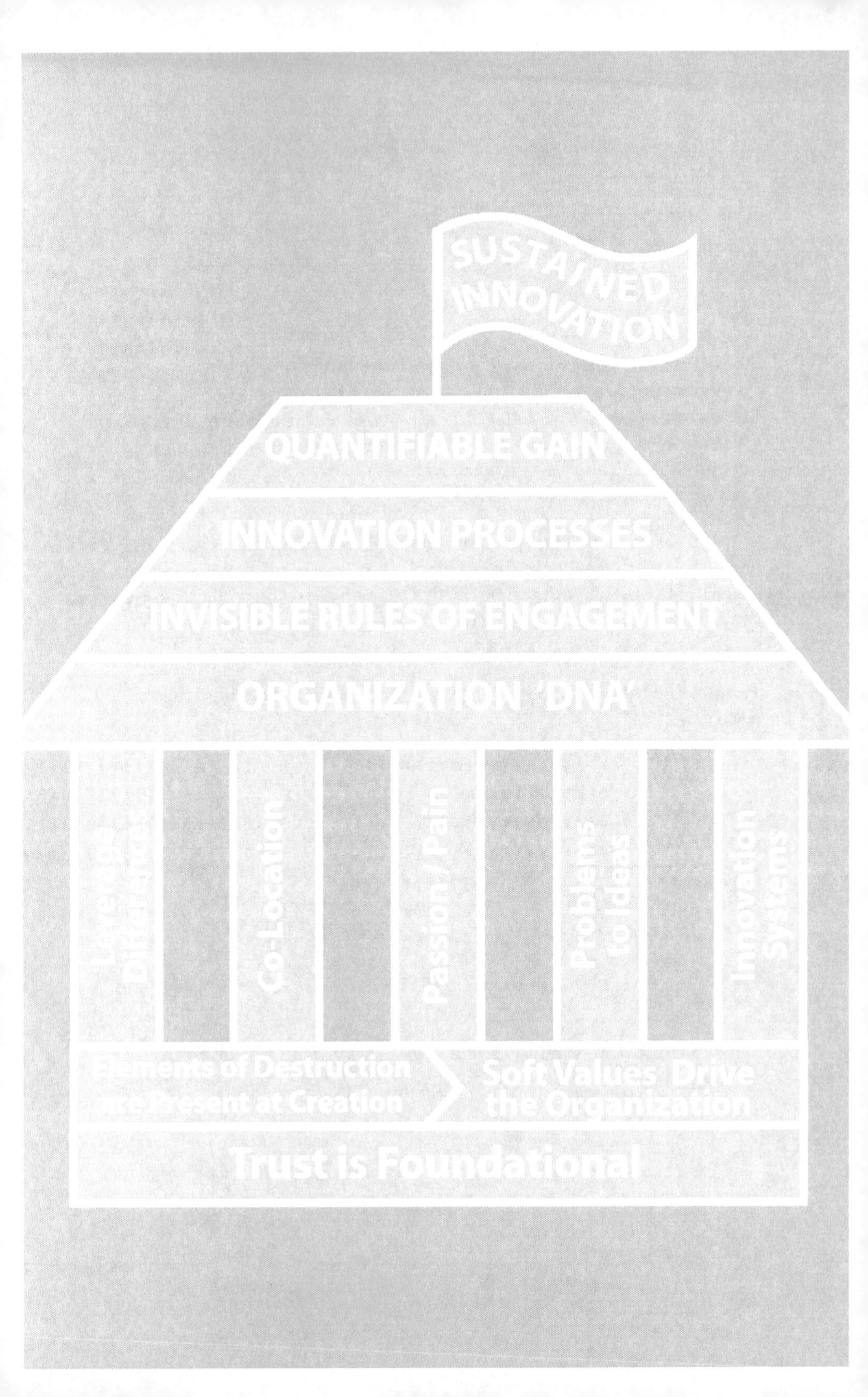
SUSTAINED INNOVATION
QUANTIFIABLE GAIN
INNOVATION PROCESSES
INVISIBLE RULES OF ENGAGEMENT
ORGANIZATION 'DNA'
Leverage Differences
Co-Location
Passion / Pain
Problems to Ideas
Innovation Systems
Elements of Destruction are Present at Creation
Soft Values Drive the Organization
Trust is Foundational

Part One

The Eight Human Principles

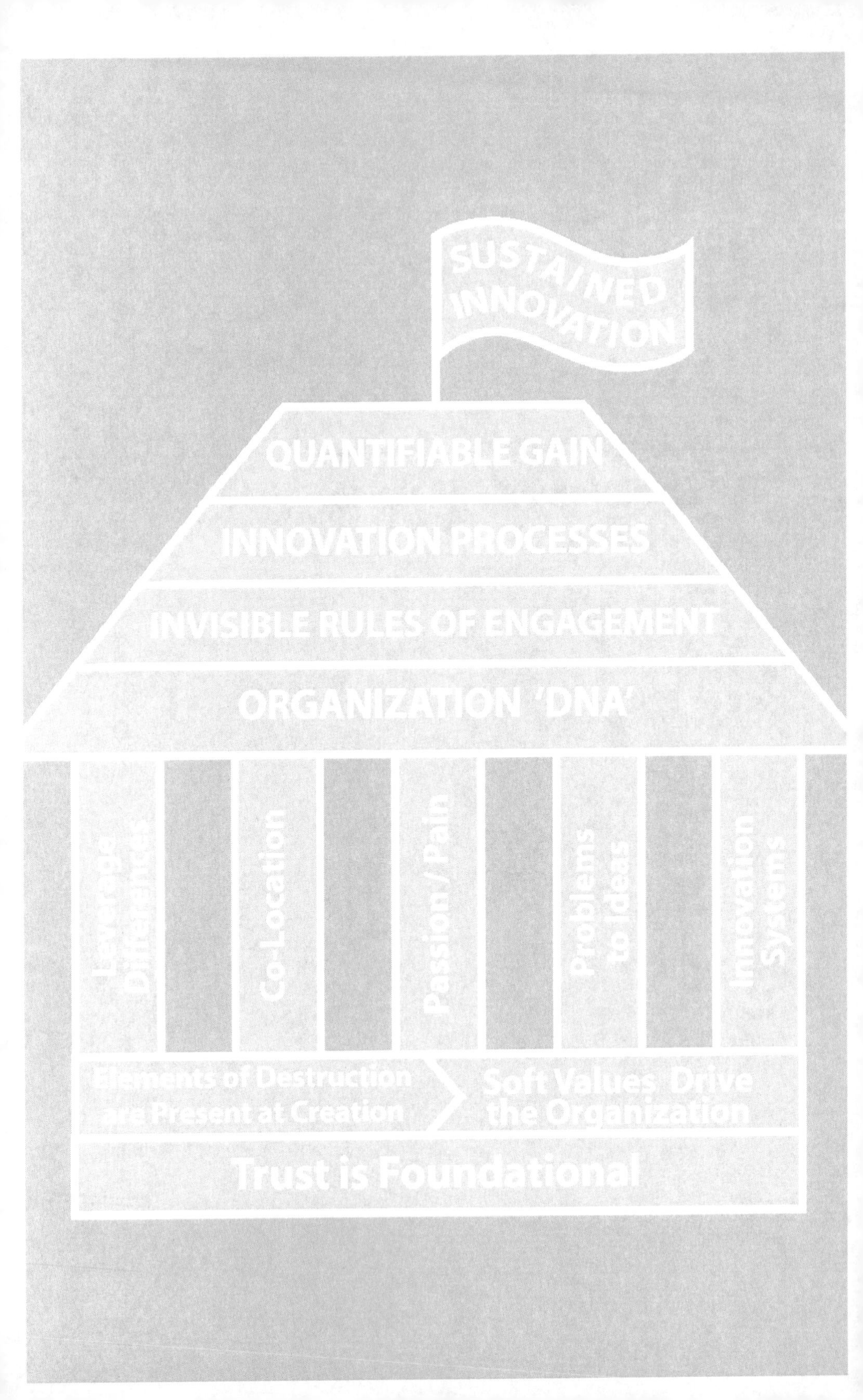

SUSTAINED INNOVATION
QUANTIFIABLE GAIN
INNOVATION PROCESSES
INVISIBLE RULES OF ENGAGEMENT
ORGANIZATION 'DNA'
Leverage Differences
Co-Location
Passion / Pain
Problems to Ideas
Innovation Systems
Elements of Destruction are Present at Creation
Soft Values Drive the Organization
Trust is Foundational

Part I

Chapter One

Innovation Starts With People, Principles, and Lexicon

In the 1920s, it took 17 days to paint a Buick and 34 days to paint a Cadillac. At that time, Charles "Boss" Kettering was made a Vice President of United Motor Company (which later became known as General Motors, or GM).[1,2,3] At a division manager's meeting, Kettering explained the problem. He pointed out that GM could put together a car in minutes but that it took anywhere from 17 to 34 days to paint it. If GM was going to produce thousands of cars a day, then storage was going to become a major issue.

Kettering called a meeting of some of GM's paint suppliers, paint chemists, and internal paint experts. After explaining the problem, he asked for ideas about what could be done. Following considerable discussion, somebody asked Kettering how long he thought it should take. To this he replied, "One hour should be about right." The group responded that his timeframe was unrealistic, since the paint would not have time to dry. Kettering asked if anything could be done to make the paint dry faster. The group responded, "Not a thing in the world."

One day in New York, Kettering saw a wooden tray in a jewelry shop with a lacquer on it that he did not recognize. He bought the tray, tracked down the manufacturer and, eventually, learned the source of the lacquer. He went and talked to the man who was making the lacquer in his backyard and asked to buy a quart. The man replied that he had never made that much before and then asked Kettering, "What are you going to do with it?"

Kettering answered, "Paint a car door." The man said that Kettering wouldn't be able to do so because the lacquer would dry almost immediately. He said, "If you put the lacquer in one of your spray guns, it would dry and blow away as dust before it reached the door." So Kettering asked, "Can't you do anything to slow down the process?" The man replied, "Not a thing in the world."

Here was the dilemma: Kettering had one lacquer that dried too fast and another that dried too slow. So he continued to work with both lacquers and, with the help of DuPont and others, they eventually created a new kind of lacquer called Pyroxylin. It dried in an hour.

Developing the technical solution, however, was only part of actually reducing the time to paint a car from 17 to 34 days down to one hour. Getting the technical solution tried and proven within GM (and ultimately accepted by one or more of the division managers) proved to be a significant challenge for Kettering. When he asked if the primer coat could be altered to allow the new lacquer to adhere to the car, Kettering received a somewhat typical bureaucratic response: "No sir – we have adopted it [our current primer], and it is our standard."

Overcoming bureaucratic opposition required taking significant risk, driven by passion and commitment to making GM successful. At one point, Kettering went so far as to get one of the general managers to give his paint manager a six-week vacation to go fishing. During that time, they were able to prove that the alternative primer successfully helped the new DuPont Pyroxylin paint to stick. Prior to a lunch meeting, Kettering asked one of the paint suppliers what color he would like to have his car painted. While at lunch, without telling the supplier, Kettering had the car repainted that color. Upon leaving the meeting, the supplier said that somebody had stolen his car. To this, Kettering replied, "That's your car. That's the color you selected, isn't it?"

In the end, Kettering was successful in getting all of the division managers to accept the new paint and primer. He reduced the time to paint a car to one hour – his goal in the first place. His comment on the success was, "We don't have the perfect paint yet. But reducing the time it takes to paint a car from 17 days to one hour is a good first step."

Charles Kettering was one of the legendary innovators of the early twentieth century. He was responsible for innovations ranging from selective ringing for the telephone industry to the electric cash register and the electric car starter. He helped create what became the *Memorial Sloan-Kettering Cancer Center*. And on January 1, 1998, the former *General Motors Institute* changed its name to *Kettering University*, to honor Kettering as a founder.

A few quotes from Kettering provide a glimpse into how he viewed innovation:[4]

> *"An* ***inventor*** *fails 999 times, and if he succeeds once, he's in. He treats his failures simply as practice shots."*
>
> *"If you have always done it that way, it is probably wrong."*
>
> *"We often say that the biggest job we have is to teach a newly hired employee to fail intelligently, to experiment over and over again and to keep trying and failing until he learns what works."*

The question to ask yourself is, if Charles Kettering came into our organization as a young engineer from Ohio State University, would he be encouraged to develop into one of our greatest innovators, or would our organization attempt to squelch his innovative nature just because it's "not the way we do things"?

The Human Element

How many times have you heard about an organization or company being innovative, or about an organization that is not as innovative as it used to be? Since Organizations Don't Innovate, People Do™, what people are really saying is, "Our organization's culture sponsors innovation," or "Our organization used to have an innovative culture." An organization's culture can unlock the innovative potential of its people or keep it suppressed via an attitude of, "That is not how we do things here." Upon reflection, what kind of culture does your organization have?

To diagnose issues that may be associated with a less than optimal level of innovation, it is imperative to understand that innovation does not occur in a vacuum. Innovation occurs in the real world with all of its complications, problems, and setbacks. Human beings, much like innovation, thrive best in nurturing environments. Innovation cannot be forced, but it can be fostered. Organizations cannot mandate innovation. They can only provide the environment, resources, and focus that will allow it to flourish.

Creating and sustaining innovation is very complex because of the human element. Until now, we did not have a universally accepted set of core principles that emphasized the importance of the human element. Nor did we have a common language for innovators to use. As such, innovation leaders would strive toward reaching similar goals, but up until now they were unable to learn from each other's experiences through use of standard terminology. Herein, we provide such principles and language.

There are three interconnected dimensions of a successful innovation organization: business, technical, and human. We call this the "Innovation DNA" (Figure 1.1).

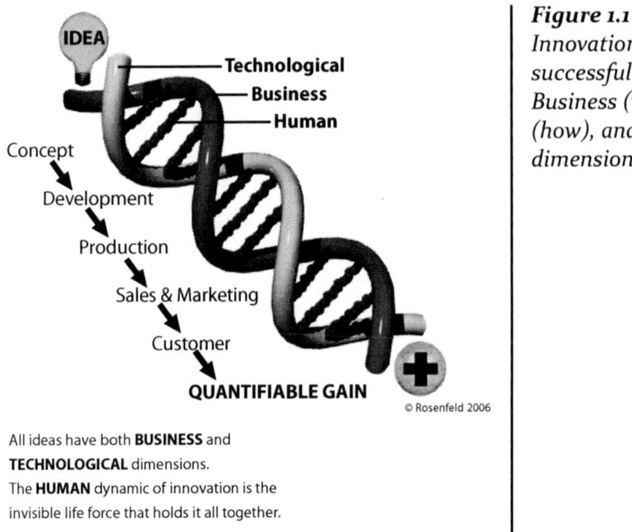

Figure 1.1
Innovation requires the successful integration of Business (what), Technical (how), and Human (who) dimensions.

All ideas have both business and technological dimensions. The business dimension is made up of typical factors associated with bringing ideas to fruition: development costs, venture capital, promotion, market acceptance, production costs, break-even points, etc. In contrast, the technological dimension encompasses **methods** used in the development of an idea into a final product. The business and technological dimensions vary between different organizations. However, the human dimension does not vary – in fact, it is the life force that can bind business and technology dimensions together to make the whole system work. But when the human dimension breaks down, the system implodes on itself or splinters and breaks apart.

You can take advantage of technology and have great business systems, but if you don't have a successful human dimension, your organization will never reach peak innovation potential. Human dynamics provide a positive, but invisible, life force. They consist of the principles, values, methods/**actions**, and behaviors that help organizations generate positive results.

Principles, Methods and Actions, Values and Behaviors[5]

We define a "**principle**" as a fundamental truth used as the basis for:

- Understanding a natural or scientific phenomenon

Reasoning or action

- Conducting our personal lives

Specifically, **a principle is a fundamental truth** that:

- Offers insight into why and how people try to solve specific problems or make decisions
- Provides a solid foundation upon which to build new ideas and innovations
- Is universally applicable to a broad spectrum of problems
- Allows for **enhancement** and modification of ideas, as well as increased understanding

Examples of principles include:

- Gravity – Law of Nature
- Family is foundational – Law of Society
- Innovation requires people – Law of Innovation

The world of innovation is continuously changing. As such, it requires that we understand and embrace fundamental principles in order to design and implement the systems and/or processes needed to support innovation. And without this understanding, we will not gain the **knowledge** we need to continuously update and improve these systems or processes so that we can generate the desired results.

Principles are tools we rely on and use knowing that they are timeless. They may evolve over time, but they represent generally accepted fundamental truths and understandings of the world as it exists.

As with all tools, only those principles that we actively employ will impact results. In order for principles to be translated into results, we need methods and actions through which to apply them. Principles are timeless, whereas methods and actions are situational. Methods answer the question, "What should we do?" And actions answer the question, "How should we do it?"

Here are two examples that will help paint the picture:

- *Example 1:* Say you want to pick up a pallet of merchandise. The fundamental principle involved here is that lifting the pallet requires overcoming gravity. Some of the methods and actions include using an overhead hoist, a forklift, or lever and fulcrum.

- *Example 2:* With innovation, you often strive to reduce time required for the innovation process. The key principle here is that innovation does not occur without motivating people to use appropriate methods and take appropriate actions. Some of the methods and actions you might use include making innovation a strategic priority, establishing an appropriate reward and recognition system, creating a culture of innovation within your organization, and so forth.

In the examples provided above, it is important to note that the same results could be achieved for some time without ever truly understanding the key principles involved. However, principle-based development illuminates the knowledge required to modify methods and actions over time. This allows organizations to repeatedly generate (and replicate) desired results. It sustains innovation.

Think about the Wright Brothers and the development of aviation following their first flight. If the principle of air flowing over the wing, generating lift, was not identified, could others have duplicated and advanced the initial designs of the Wright Brothers as quickly? Only by understanding the underlying principles can we modify what works today to meet needs in the future without relying strictly on luck.

Consider that principles are tools, whereas methods and actions define what and how the tools should be implemented. Regardless, a fundamental concept is still missing: the source of energy (or **motivation**) for implementing methods and actions. Values are the impetus for generating results. Values provide the source of energy (or fuel) for turning a principle into action.

Said another way, there exists a tremendous number of principles in the universe that are widely accepted but most of which we do not really care about. We will only expend time and energy to apply those principles that we truly value. For example, if you are not trying to lift a pallet of merchandise, how much time would you actually spend thinking about the weight of the pallet (gravity)? And if you're not into aeronautics, how much energy would you put into studying aerodynamics and, specifically, the lift associated with airflow over a wing?

Simply put: If you don't value something, you won't value its principles. If you don't value the positive human dynamics that make innovation happen, and if you don't value the people inside your organization, then it doesn't matter if there is a poster on your company's wall that states, "People are our most important asset." **Principles and values drive actions, not posters.**

One way to determine what is valued by your organization is to examine key behaviors. What are your senior leaders interested in, where do they spend their time, and what questions do they ask? Answers to these questions provide a window into what is valued. Many years ago, Frito-Lay had a serious accident in one of the labs. Rocco Papalia[6] (Senior Vice President of R&D) and the rest of his leadership team agreed that the accident was unacceptable and that, going forward, the whole organization would be committed to creating and sustaining a safe place to work. Indeed, they put their words into actions and told employees that their safety was to be valued. From then on, every senior staff meeting started with a safety update. Every accident (whether or not it resulted in lost time) was reviewed, and action plans were implemented to ensure that the causes of the accident were eliminated. Engineers, scientists, and technicians completed safety training programs, and employees were not allowed to operate equipment without implementing the required safety practices. Attention to safety became an important part of annual performance reviews. Home safety was even addressed. The net result was a virtual elimination of accidents. And even better: Employees understood that senior management valued their safety.

What does your organization value? Where are leaders spending their time and energy? Do they value people as a crucial element in the innovation process? The model in Figure 1.2 (next page) provides a way to identify the principles driving your organization via an examination of observable behaviors and business performance. In addition, the model allows the innovation leader to work forward from fundamental principles, to design the methods and actions necessary to encourage appropriate behaviors, and (consequently) to achieve the desired results.

As indicated in Figure 1.2, key stakeholders[7] drive the current set of principles and values within an organization. In turn, their principles and values drive the organization's response. Because key stakeholders have control and influence over the organization, the way they think and behave impacts employees' behavior in lower levels of the organization.

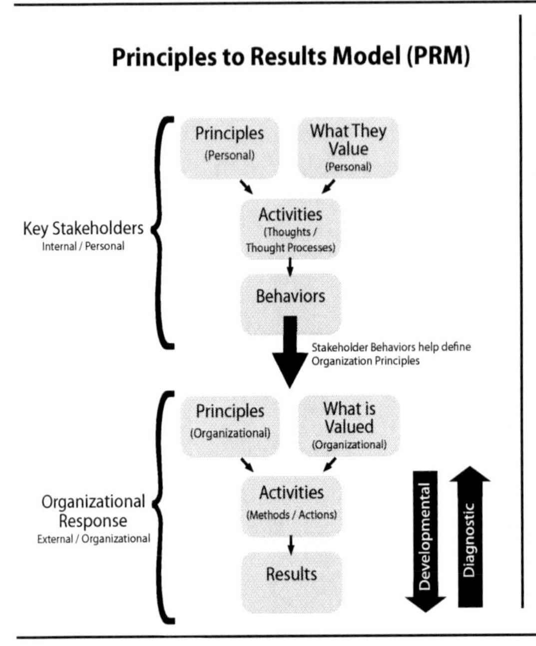

Figure 1.2
Start with the principles in this book and work forward to identify the desired organizational behaviors and subsequent results. In contrast, if you begin by analyzing behaviors and results and work backward, then you will be able to identify the principles that drive the organization.

To make innovation happen, the key stakeholders must first identify and understand the principles and values in this book and then implement them. This will drive the overall methods and actions within their organizations. As part of this, the stakeholders' behaviors must be consistent with what they say are the company's values for the organization to believe them.

Here is a summary of the **Principles to Results Model (PRM)**:

- Principles are fundamental truths.
- What you value determines which principles you and/or your organization will utilize.
- Methods and actions dictate how the principles are applied.
- Behaviors leading to results are the visible outcomes from the methods and actions.

If you create an organization without knowing the principles upon which you are building a foundation, you will have no idea where your organization is headed or how it will get there. Therefore, to be sustainable, your Innovation House must be constructed on identified and valued principles. You must also understand the different focuses of innovation within your organization, i.e., Where does your organization require revolutionary innovation?

Expansionary? Evolutionary? By examining current and future innovation portfolios, the desired innovation focus should become apparent. This will help you articulate the long-term vision required to construct your Innovation House.

Innovation Portfolio

An innovation leader must have a clear understanding of both the type of innovation required and how to generate it. Having a well-planned business strategy without the human or organizational systems to execute it will produce "hit and miss" results. It will also be unclear as to what worked or didn't work and why. In the same way, having an ideal organizational system without a clear innovation focus is like driving a car blindfolded; you will be expending energy but not arriving at the desired destination, with potentially disastrous results.

Part of the learning that must occur should be geared toward understanding the desired innovation portfolio and the level of effort needed to move along the innovation continuum. What percent of your organization's innovation effort should be directed toward revolutionary, expansionary, and evolutionary innovation? There must be a clear understanding of the innovation portfolio and the level of effort devoted to business as usual, new products for existing customers, existing products for new customers, and new ventures as addressed in Figure 1.3 (see next page). The purpose of this book is not to go into what this portfolio should look like for your particular organization. Instead, we only want to emphasize that developing this portfolio for your organization must be done in conjunction with understanding and applying the human principles for innovation.

As we begin to use the innovation portfolio, it is important to understand each of the quadrants and how they relate to **the Innovation Continuum.**

- **Quadrant I is called business as usual.** It is primarily associated with those slight modifications or improvements to the product to improve quality, reduce cost, or meet an existing market need (e.g., a different flavor). Innovation in this quadrant represents the evolutionary end of the continuum.

- **Quadrant II is called platforms.** The focus of activity in this quadrant is to expand the company's market through application of its existing technology. This might include moving into a different geography or market segment. An

Figure 1.3
One approach for looking at the distribution of innovation effort. Upon completion of this analysis, an innovation leader can begin to build the required innovation culture and apply the human principles for sustained innovation.

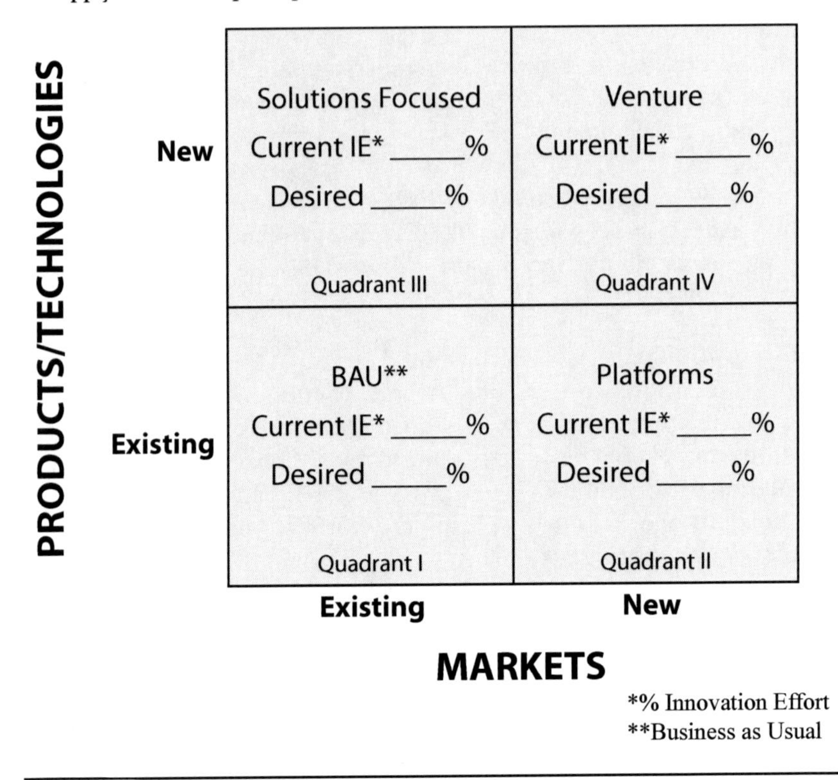

*% Innovation Effort
**Business as Usual

example might be taking a product that has been successful in one country and moving it into a different one. Innovation in this quadrant falls within the expansionary portion of the continuum.

- **Quadrant III is called solutions focused.** The primary focus is to provide products to meet a current customer or market need. As an example, consider the development of a new system to allow unmanned aircraft vehicles (UAV) to operate in a civilian airspace for an existing customer. Innovation in this quadrant is in the expansionary portion of the continuum.

- **Quadrant IV is called venture.** Activities in this quadrant are focused on developing new products for new markets.

Developing the personal computer for general use in the home and inventions such as cell phones, **GPS** systems in cars, and the Internet are good examples. Innovation in this quadrant is toward the revolutionary end of the continuum.

By understanding your organization's current and desired portfolios and the types of innovation required, you will be able to define the types of **innovation systems** you'll need, the people (skill sets) you'll need, and the overall culture you'll need to foster in order to succeed.

Summary

Every idea has both a business and technological dimension, but it is the human dimension that translates an idea into a valuable innovation. There are eight human principles for sustaining innovation, which comprise the lower portion of the Innovation House (see page xx).

The impact of key stakeholders on your organization cannot be overestimated, as their principles and values will impact their behaviors and, subsequently, determine how innovation will be viewed, encouraged, acted upon, and so forth. Employees will attempt to mimic behaviors of these key stakeholders – which will ultimately impact business performance. Therefore, it is critical to understand how principles and values are adopted by your organization and, consequently, how they influence the methods and actions that can drive results. This is the way key behaviors are adopted and, in turn, how they become part of the culture.

In the remainder of Part One, we will examine each of the eight human principles for sustaining innovation and address how to apply them.

At the beginning of this chapter, we said innovation cannot be forced, but it can be fostered. This brings us to our first human principle: For innovation to be fostered, there must be trust.

Part I

Chapter Two

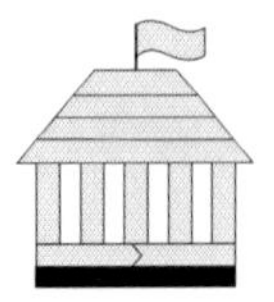

Trust Is Foundational[1]

The Innovation House lays the groundwork for the most fundamental, yet often most misunderstood, concept in creating and sustaining innovation: **Trust is the foundation.** We have seen many of our clients try to glaze over the idea of trust. "We know about trust, we have it, let's move on..." Our work has shown us that trust is a paradox – the obvious is not so obvious. We realize that trust is a basic concept, yet organizations do not fully comprehend what trust means and the significant positive or negative effects it has on long-term success. Trust is the oil that keeps the innovation engine functioning.

Trust takes a long time to build and a short time to break down. As human beings, we typically remember and talk about our bad experiences. As an example, one of the authors used the United States Postal Service (USPS) to mail car payments. For 99 times in a row, the USPS delivered the check on time and to the appropriate location. On the 100th time, the car payment check got lost in the mail. Even though the USPS was successful 99 out of 100 times, the author now uses the Internet to make his payments. He has also voiced the one-time error to other people.

The same thing happens in our organizations. When our organization, leaders, or peers break our trust, it takes a long time for our psychological pain to dissipate. And those who have been hurt typically tell others in the organization about what has happened. A trust breakdown sends ripples throughout the organization. People remember – and they share.

It doesn't matter if an organization is made up of three people or 30,000; a high level of trust encourages imagination, allows people to take risks, and spurs on the passion that makes difficult problems solvable. As the foundation for any group of people working toward a common goal, trust has an impact on productivity, quality, turnover, absenteeism, motivation, innovation, and (ultimately) the generation of quantifiable gains.

This chapter is vital for understanding the rest of the book. Many of the concepts reinforced in subsequent chapters are introduced here. We will first look at what we mean by trust, how our individual **filter** systems impact our communications, and how head and heart trust directly impact results. We will then examine the importance of trust relative to **Creativity Partners**™, the Mosaic Partnerships™ Model, and the **Relationship Spectrum**™.

Understanding Individual Trust

We could share a lot of stories about trust. However, as trust is an individual experience, we feel it is better to let you examine your own trust experiences as a starting point.

Think about a project you've worked on with a group or a person you trusted. How did you feel? Were you motivated? What were your actions like? How was your performance? And how well did the team perform?

Now think about a person or team you didn't trust. How did you feel? Were you motivated to work with them? What were your actions like? How was your performance? Overall, how well did the person or team perform?

Now think about a risky project. Make a list of the people you might want on your team. How did you choose the people? Do you trust the people on your list? How might these people impact the project?

When we think about trust, it is not just about job security, salaries, benefits, company stability, stock price, and work-life balance. Trust within an organization and between people is individually driven. It includes not only what is happening around us today, but it is also an accumulation of our prior experiences.

Working in a trusting environment allows people to use their talents and abilities. They feel that their interests are valued. They feel their ideas and concerns are asked for and listened to. They feel respected. They feel recognized for their efforts on a regular basis – not just when they complete their annual reviews.

Trust between individuals is about caring for others personally and professionally. It is showing genuine interest and concern for other people's lives. It is not demonstrated by being self-absorbed.

Organizational trust is about having a common goal and not worrying about hidden agendas, politics, or backstabbing. It is about feeling free to think independently and share ideas with others. It is also about being motivated to think and act beyond a job description. Trust empowers people to work both harder and smarter.

A culture built on trust allows people to care about their organization, jobs, co-workers, and customers. It also allows them to be more creative and innovative because the fear of individual failure has been dramatically reduced. Communication is open and less filtered. Energy is devoted to achieving results rather than examining the motivation of others and searching for hidden agendas.

As we will discuss later, trust has both an intellectual component and an emotional component. The intellectual component tends to be objective based. The emotional component tends to be far more personal and far less objective. It is both very emotional and personal. Yet, most organizations in the United States have tried to separate work from home and personal life. This is not the norm globally. It means American workers have been taught to become emotionally detached at work. Being labeled "emotional" about our work often comes with a negative connotation. So, we check our feelings at the door. We often don't ask about other people's home life. We steer clear of "passionate" people. We either avoid or think twice about comforting a co-worker in need. However, emotion is the very fuel that drives people to put their time, passion, and energies into innovative ideas that may or may not come to fruition.

The concept of trust is tied to the Innovation Continuum™ defined in the Introduction. The more revolutionary the innovation, the greater the amount of trust that is needed. As the focus of an innovation program moves along the continuum from evolutionary to revolutionary, the probability of success declines exponentially. Thus, the probability of success for a truly revolutionary idea is very low (one in 100 or worse). For this reason, the risk associated with undertaking a revolutionary idea is much greater than that of a corresponding evolutionary idea – where success probability can be one in two or greater.

So where does trust come in? As the innovation risk goes up, the corresponding requirement for trust also increases. Without trust, the level of interaction and open communication required to maximize the probability of success goes down. At the evolutionary end, it is entirely possible to successfully innovate with relatively low levels of trust. However, as trust decreases, the efficiency of evolutionary innovation also decreases – and, unfortunately, a loss of efficiency in development and execution is difficult to observe or measure.

Think about the performance differences between high-performance teams with high levels of trust and dysfunctional teams with significantly lower levels of trust. Both teams can successfully implement evolutionary innovations but at different levels of performance. As an innovation moves along the continuum toward revolutionary, only the high-trusting team will have a reasonable probability of success.

Communication

In any organization, trust begins with the way we interact with each other. **People problems are usually due to trust issues that are evident in the way people communicate.**

With regard to innovation, there are two main types of communication: **Generative** and **Destructive** (Figure 2.1).[2] Generative communication comes from listening to learn or understand. We get truth, ideas, and creation from generative communication – a type of communication ideal for innovation (e.g., the comment, "Very interesting. Let's see how we can make this idea workable.").

Destructive communication occurs when listening to and responding strictly for one's self-interests. It is biased by one's ego and spun in an attempt to "win." It often contains phrases such as, "You know we can't do that," or, "That idea will never work."

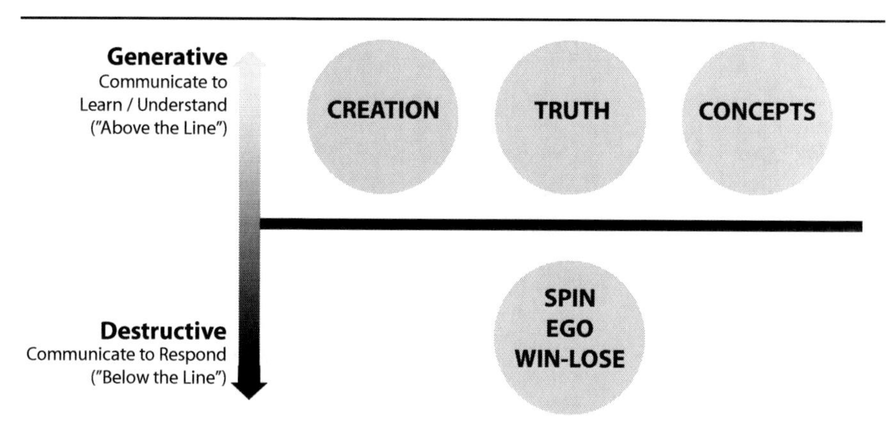

Figure 2.1
Communicating to Learn/Understand allows the possibility for innovation to be enhanced. Communicating to Respond generally shuts down possibilities and diminishes innovation potential.

In order to have generative conversations (as opposed to destructive ones), it is necessary to understand the mental process associated with communicating between individuals. Our internal biases and level of trust for other individuals dramatically impacts the degree of potential "above the line" communication (generative). We must understand our own internal filtering systems used for talking and listening. We must also appreciate that the persons with whom we are communicating have their own filters that are invisible to us. By understanding these filtering systems, we can begin to shift a greater percentage of the conversation above the line and maximize innovation potential.

Filtering System

People need to trust each other in order to form partnerships that will lead to positive results. However, fostering the human contact that brings about trust is easier said than done. During a conversation, each person utilizes a unique input and output filtering system to communicate with a fellow worker, team, and/or organization. The filtering system determines what that person hears, how they act, and what information they will subsequently share with the group.

All trust is related. This means that individual filters go beyond the control of the organization. These filters result from the individual's entire life experiences. If anyone has been hurt or gets hurt, it will reflect on the whole group.

If someone has been cheated, it will take time to rebuild a working trust with that person. If someone believes (via their filtering system) that everyone is out to get them, then they see everything that anyone is doing to them as destructive. We all carry baggage. The question is, how do you overcome group baggage? First, you must recognize that it is baggage. Afterward, try to have as much **patience** as possible to allow group members to work through their problems. Meet people at their level of trust.

If a person is not trusting of a group because of personality differences, it is the job of the leader to facilitate building trust. If a person is not trusting because of previous betrayals, it may be hard for anyone to get them to trust again. Ultimately, the innovation leader cannot let one person derail the development of the group's trust, so that person may need to be replaced or reassigned to activities that require very little group trust.

Open communication is made up of trust, **personal sensitivity**, motivation, and preconceived notions. The more open we are with each other, the greater the likelihood that the conversation will be above the line and generative in nature. When people within a group feel comfortable enough to openly share their knowledge and **wisdom**, they will facilitate generative communication. Then, the foundation is set for innovation to occur. When trust is absent, however, people tend to significantly filter their communications. The conversation tends to be below the line and innovation is dramatically limited. As an example of filtering, think of something very sensitive to you. Now think about how you would share this with:

- Your spouse
- A trusted friend
- A peer
- Your boss
- Somebody you distrust

Is there any difference in what you would share? The filtering process we are talking about is depicted in Figure 2.2. When we want to communicate, our thoughts travel through four primary filters: 1) Trust, 2) Sensitivity, 3) Motivation, and 4) Preconceived Notions. Similarly, when listening we use the same filters.

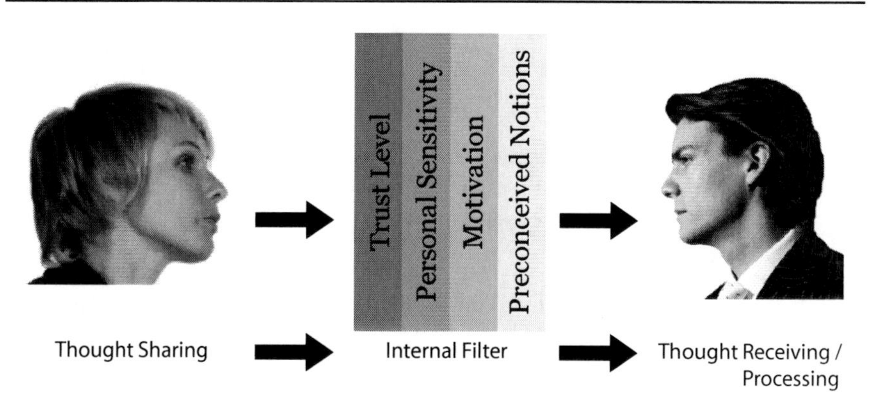

Sharing and internalization of new thoughts is a function of Personal **Sensitivity**, Degree of **Trust**, Personal **Motivation**, and **Preconceived Notions**.

Figure 2.2

Communication involves filtering of both what is being said or transmitted and what is being heard or received. Trust is the dominant element of both filtering systems.

Take a moment to think about filters. Have you experienced yourself filtering what you want to say? What did you do? Have you seen other people filtering their input to you? If you observed others filtering their communications, were you able to identify why? Being able to identify when significant filtering is taking place (by yourself and others) is key to being able to open up the filters and keep the communications above the line. Generally, trust is the most restrictive of the filters. The following steps detail how to calibrate trust for yourself and how to increase trust between individuals.

Head and Heart Trust

We've talked about how trust is necessary to make innovation happen. Now we will move a step further and say that trust is always a blend of two components: **Head Trust** and **Heart Trust**.

Head (Intellectual) Trust answers the question, "Do I trust a person's competence, skills, knowledge, etc.?" This type of trust is always situation-specific and exemplified by statements such as:

- I trust that this person is knowledgeable, given the situations that may arise in our relationship.
- I trust that this person is competent.

Examples of Head Trust include:

- You call the IT Department with a computer issue and are confident that it will be resolved.
- You call marketing for sales numbers, knowing they will be accurate.

Alternatively, **Heart (Emotional) Trust** answers the question, "Do I trust a person's motivation and emotional maturity?" This kind of trust is always person-specific, but it may also depend on the situation and is exemplified by statements such as:

- I trust that this person will not do anything to cause me harm.
- I trust that this person will do everything possible to help me when needed.
- I trust that this person is not overly selfish or self-centered and has the maturity necessary to put his or her needs aside to help me when needed.

Some examples of Heart Trust include:

- You share something personal about yourself, knowing that it will be held confidential with that person.
- You take a risk with someone, knowing that the information will not be used against you.

Head trust is needed for basic problem solving. In contrast, heart trust is needed for making major decisions, forming partnerships, and generating revolutionary ideas.

Without heart trust, we ask ourselves, "What is the hidden agenda? Should I really share this? Maybe I should try this on my own." With high levels of heart trust, when someone asks a question, you do not feel attacked or defensive. You don't ponder the motivation and wonder whether or not something is wrong.

Heart trust is the foundation of a bond between individuals. That bond is what gets us through the tough times – and it can get tough in the world of innovation! As soon as the risk or difficulty level increases, people tend to behave differently – i.e., they instinctively shut down and think of themselves first. That's where heart trust comes in. You truly believe that your peer or team will not harm you intentionally because you are "in it together" – so you press on toward solving the problem. Head trust gets you started, whereas heart trust propels you to the finish line.

Where have you seen head and heart trust succeed within your organization? Where have you seen it break down?

Calibrating Trust

For you to better understand the idea of head and heart trust, we'd like to walk you through a trust calibration. On a separate sheet of paper, create one line scale for Head Trust and one for Heart Trust (see Figure 2.3, page 23).

Identify an individual from these four groups of people:

1. Relative = R
2. Your best friend (not a relative) = F
3. A manager = M
4. A co-worker = CW

Rate each person on both scales of 1 - 9:

"9" means your trust in them is near total or absolute.
"1" means you have little trust in them.

Next, plot them similarly to the example in Figure 2.3.

Now list four people within your work group that you would confide in during the early stages of generating an innovative idea:

1.
2.
3.
4.

As was done with the first group, rate each person on the Head Scale and Heart Scale. Plot the ratings on two lines.

Now create a grid with an X-axis and Y-axis. Label the X-axis: Head/ Intellectual Trust. Label the Y-axis: Heart/Emotional Trust. (See Figure 2.4, next page) Plot both groups of people on the grid. What does this information tell you?

Generally, the people who are sought out in the early stage of a higher risk innovation are the ones for whom we have a high level of both head and heart trust. As an innovation evolves, we start to bring in individuals in whom we have a high level of head trust and at least a moderate level of heart trust. We normally do not seek out those individuals for whom we do not have at least a moderate level of heart (or emotional) trust, unless we are required to do so for other reasons (political and/or organizational).

Individuals who fall into the high-high (upper right) quadrant are candidates for Creativity Partners. We will use this term throughout the book. Creativity Partners are described as:

> Two or more people committed to exploring innovative ideas, growing and expanding these ideas into exceptional new concepts, and creating the excitement and ownership required to gain organizational support.

Ways to Develop Trust

Creativity Partners

We need Creativity Partners because partnerships are required to turn dreams into realities. There are numerous examples of accomplished Creativity Partners, including: Henry Ford and Thomas Edison, the Wright Brothers, Walt and Roy Disney, and Paul Allen and Bill Gates. In order for any partnership to succeed, the prerequisite is trust.

Creativity Partners share a very close relationship. These partners can call each other at 3:00 a.m. to discuss a problem, a success or anything else. Their relationships allow them to argue with each other and deal with the animosity, because the end goal is the search for truth.

Creativity Partners understand each other and foster creativity and innovation within each other. They use each other's brain almost as part of their own. They leverage the other person's skills and disposition in multiple ways.

How much do I trust: R, F, M, CW

9 means your trust in them is near total or absolute
1 means you have little trust in them

Head Rating:

Example

		R		F	CW	M		
1	2	3	4	5	6	7	8	9

Heart Rating:

Example

		M		CW	R	F		
1	2	3	4	5	6	7	8	9

Figure 2.3
Example of a trust calibration worksheet looking at the Head and Heart Trust for a relative (R), friend (F), manager (M), and co-worker (CW)

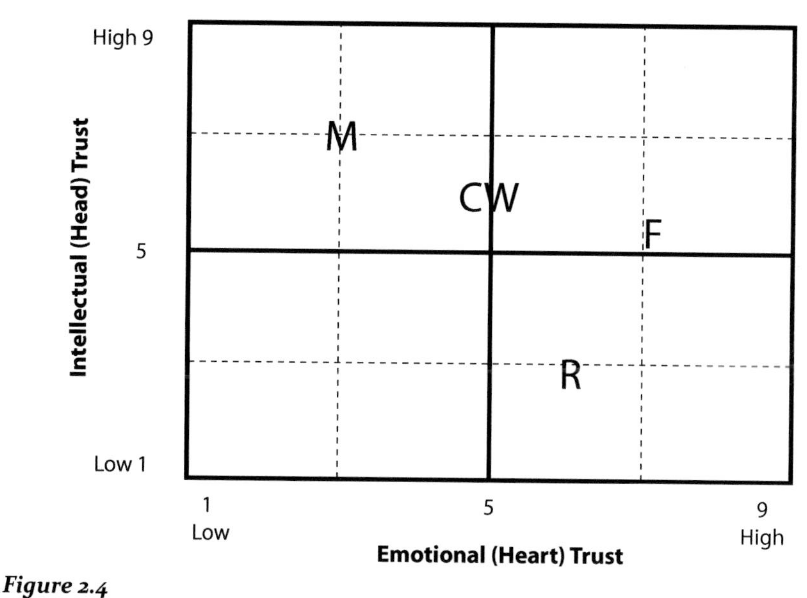

Figure 2.4
Example plot of Head and Heart Trust

There are two guiding principles for a successful Creativity Partnership:

1. Each **partner** must have a prevailing attitude of trust, wonder, and fascination comparable to that of the other.
2. Partners must trust each other. They must attend to, respect, and enjoy their relationship and mutual ideation process.

Personal creativity and innovation usually do not occur because we tend to self-filter and stifle our ideas before they have a chance to grow and mature. We talk ourselves out of many of our ideas before we do anything with them. Enter Creativity Partners: individuals who free us up to bounce around any and all ideas. They listen to an idea on its own merit. They play around with it to see if there is something there. And they are not "Yes" people. They candidly point out hurdles that must be overcome.

Creativity Partners help us understand how we might do something, not why we can't.

The common theme here is that Creativity Partners are people you can go to without the slightest bit of hesitation about how they might react or whether or not they will have your best interests at heart. Basically, a Creativity Partner is someone who creates a very safe, non-judgmental environment for idea generation and evaluation. As such, they can potentially add great value to the innovation dialogue.

It helps to utilize different Creativity Partners for different stages of innovation. For ideas in the early stages, the best partners are those who tend to not be constrained by the problem definition. (More about this is presented in Chapter 5: Leveraging Differences.) As the innovative idea matures and takes root, we need partners to help ground the idea in reality. These partners tend to be bond by the problem statement and are more pragmatic in their problem-solving style. The bottom line: For innovation within an organization to flourish and be sustainable, there must be a variety of Creativity Partners at work simultaneously.

The role of the innovation leader is to recognize the value of these partnerships and to encourage and support them. Generally, the development of these partnerships requires co-location for the trust to be developed. However, once both head and heart trust have been established, they do not need to communicate every day or every week. Time in these relationships is not linear. Once the trust is there, they can reconnect and rekindle very quickly. Like friends who haven't seen each other for a year or more, once they start talking, it's just like yesterday. Time is on a different dimension with trust.

Go back to your trust calibration chart (Figure 2.4). The trust level for Creativity Partners should be high on both axes. Do you already have one or more Creativity Partners? The more your organization has, the more productive your innovation will become.

Building Trust: The Mosaic Partnerships Model

Problems are solved through interactions between people. We have found the most effective innovation teams are made up of diverse groups of people. This means the differing personalities of a scientist, engineer, marketer, and salesperson may be trying to tackle the same idea. For all of these personalities to mesh, you must build partnerships. As with Creativity Partners, trust is a prerequisite. The result of these partnerships is the social capital they will create within an organization. According to the World Bank, social capital is the glue that holds societies together and without which there can be no economic growth or human well-being.[3]

To improve social networks, at Idea Connection Systems (ICS) we created the Mosaic Partnerships Model.[4] It was first created to reduce racial polarization in a mid-sized city. Based on its success, the model has been expanded and at the time of this writing, has been implemented in Rochester, NY, Greensboro, NC, and Milwaukee, WI, along with numerous organizations around the globe.

The purposes of the Mosaic Partnerships Model are to:

- Promote the essential building blocks of a community or organization by creating trusting relationships between people who are not necessarily from the same domain (e.g. different races, religions, ethnic backgrounds, or people from different stereotypical business groups such as marketing and R&D).
- Serve as a catalyst to appreciate, embrace, and leverage human differences, in order to move an organization down a path toward connectedness.

To expand social networks, we start with two people at a time and focus on creating strong and weak ties. (See Figure 2.5, next page)

- A strong tie is a bond of trust and friendship between two people.
- A weak tie is a relationship that is created with a third person from this strong tie.

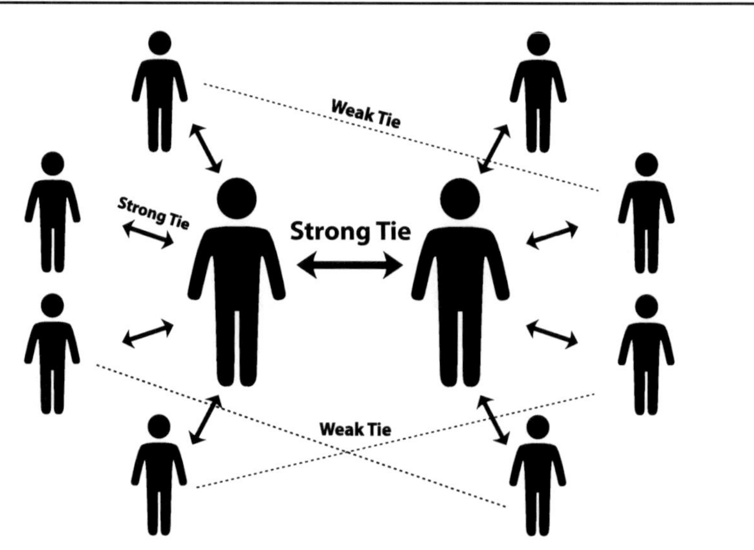

Figure 2.5
Strong ties between two individuals help create social capital to allow networks of weak ties to grow and flourish within organizations.

Creativity Partners are an excellent example of strong ties. Referrals and networking show the linkage between strong and weak ties. The online community LinkedIn™ is about strong and weak ties – your network may be comprised of strong ties but, when you tap into somebody else's network, a weak tie is created.

We live among strong and weak ties every day. If you were to call a colleague and say, "I think you'd enjoy talking to my close friend about your problem. I'm going to connect the two of you," you are using the strong tie with your colleague to create a weak tie between your colleague and friend. Because the strong ties existed, it allowed for a weak tie to be initiated. If you don't have strong ties, you can't create weak ties.

Think about what would have happened if your colleague directly called your friend without your help connecting the two together. The conversation may have never taken place or, if it did, the knowledge sharing would have been very different and closed. The conversation would have been highly filtered by both parties. Without having the transferral of trust that is generated when a strong tie introduces someone else, it takes a long time for the trust to develop so something productive can happen.

You solve problems through networks and by creating social capital. Mosaic Partnerships is a model that will assist in developing the strong ties that facilitate weak ties. It expands social capital within your organization. Ties are an absolute must for allowing interactions between individuals to effectively take place.

The doctoral thesis of Dr. Melody Cofield focused on Mosaic Partnerships and its results.[5] Her findings said that the primary social outcomes included:

- Access to people, information, and resources
- Interracial sensitivity, competence and confidence
- Bridging network expansion
- Social bonding

All of these outcomes will aid your innovation (and/or social) efforts.

To put the Mosaic Partnerships Model into action, start with two people and have them meet one-on-one. The ideal candidates for initial partnerships are those within your organization who are natural opinion leaders and trusted by others.

During one-on-one meetings, partners will get to know each other as individuals. They begin to share personal information in order to facilitate creation of trust. Through use of the process and sample questions in Appendix II (page a18), partners are focused on learning and talking about personal topics rather than impersonal ones (such as the weather, news, sports, etc.). Only by sharing information about themselves (thereby taking incrementally greater and greater risks) will lasting emotional trust be developed.

It is critical that individuals treat any information that is shared as confidential. As trust is created, questions will follow a slow progression – from fairly benign (such as, "Where were you born?") to quite intimate (such as, "How have you been affected by a divorce or death?") The speed of progression of trust is different for each individual and respect for each other's privacy must be maintained. However, the need for progress is required in order for trust to continue to grow.

Sustained innovation is about solving problems via leveraging social capital by creating strong ties that facilitate weak ties.

Relationship Spectrum

The amount of trust between workers in your organization dictates the levels of commitment and the strength of relationships. Our Relationship Spectrum™[6] connects the dots (Figure 2.6).

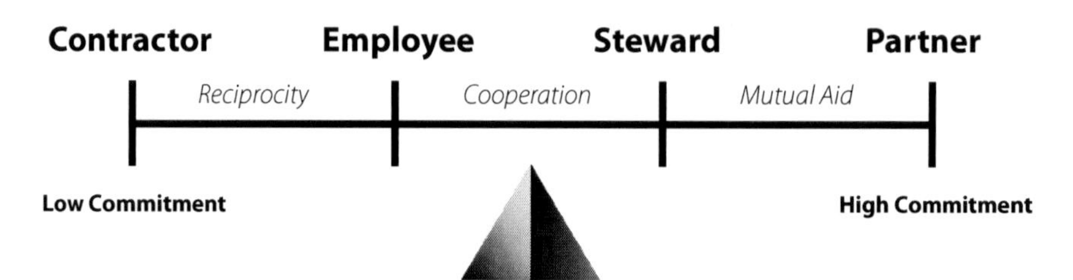

Figure 2.6

As the trust level between workers in an organization increases, the relationship between them shifts away from reciprocity and toward mutual aid. Increasing organizational trust also shifts commitment to the organization from contractor to a partner mindset.

Along the spectrum, there are specific behavior patterns. We won't name each point, but suffice it to say that the stronger the trust, the stronger the commitment, effort, and performance.

There are three main ways in which people relate to each other in organizations[7]:

- **Reciprocity**: occurs when two people do something for each other in exchange for like consideration.
- **Cooperation**: occurs when two people work together toward a common objective.
- **Mutual Aid**: occurs when one person comes to the aid of another with no expectation of a returned favor.

All three of these have their place in organizations. Reciprocity relationships are the easiest to create, whereas mutual aid requires the greatest degree of commitment and comes with the highest level of trust.

At the top of the chart, we define an individual's commitment level. We ask ourselves, "Why am I doing this?" The answers we come up with will help determine how we work, how we interact, and how we produce. These answers also help determine our commitment level. Organizations need to examine their people and determine where each falls in the four categories of commitment orientation.

Partners demonstrate the most productive long-term relationships between organizations and individuals. They are stars, in terms of effort. They feel ownership in the company and their work gives meaning to their lives. The company's and the partner's identities are intertwined.

On the other end of commitment are **Contractors**. They fulfill their job description and may achieve great results, but their loyalty is to the project and/or their profession, not the organization.

We have seen CEOs acting as contractors and people sweeping the floors acting as partners. The commitment mindset comes down to what role the organization plays in a person's life. If a person feels strong ownership for the organization and has a high level of trust for people in the organization, they will likely have the mindset of a partner or **steward**. In contrast, if they are not committed to the organization and do not necessarily trust the people in the organization, they will have more of a contractor or employee mindset. Think about your work group. Can you name someone for each commitment level? How does each act and perform?

Take a moment to analyze your group. Where does each person fall on the different levels of the relationship spectrum? Put the initials of your group members on the spectrum. Then think about your innovation focus. If it is toward the revolutionary end, are most of the group members more towards the partner/mutual aid end of the spectrum? If so, you have the overall group commitment required for this type of innovation. If not, higher risk innovation will be more difficult. It is important for you to see where your group is and to ensure that it is aligned with the type of innovation required. Later on, we will help you understand how to shift your employees more to the right.

Advice for the Innovation Leader

When thinking about trust, the following pieces should be taken into account:

- Type of Communication and Filtering Systems
- Head and Heart Trust
- Creativity Partners
- Mosaic Partnerships Model
- The Relationship Spectrum

As an innovation leader, part of your role is to foster the creation of Creativity Partners internal to the organization and to connect people externally. You are often required to be the catalyst. You need to bring people together in the right environment that allows partnerships to form and grow. In a sense, you are a matchmaker. This requires that you understand how to look at trust between individuals and how to foster an environment that will allow it to grow. We will discuss more about trust as it applies to your organization in Chapter 13.

Remember

A high level of trust encourages imagination, allows people to take risks, and spurs on the passion that makes difficult problems solvable. Trust takes a long time to build and a short time to break down.

Part I

Chapter Three

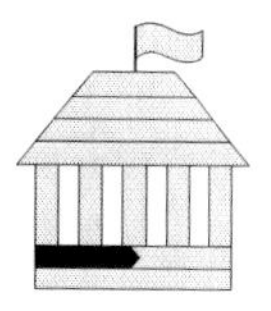

Elements of Destruction Are Present at Creation

The moment something is born, it begins the process of dying. This is not uplifting news, but it is true of people, ideas, products, and organizations. All innovations have a life cycle: birth, growth, vigor, decline, and death. Within organizations, the principles and processes that are established in the womb and at birth can either cause great good or great harm.

For some, this is a difficult concept to grasp. They say, "We've been innovative. We've been successful. We don't get it." But what they don't get is that elements of destruction typically don't start as destructive forces. When you start an organization or work group, or try to implement a new idea, it becomes pretty clear when the rules don't work. Since you are the one establishing the rules, when you find they are not working, you can readily change them.

But this is where it gets very complicated: The rules may start off as an asset, but over time they can turn into a negative. In most organizations, if some action taken turns out to be positive, then it is repeated again and again because, "That is the way it has always been done." Over time, then, we lose track of why we do something. This is the element of destruction that is present at creation. Here, we are going to focus on elements present at creation which may have helped make an organization successful, but end up being destructive down the road.

Monkey Business

There is a story called "Monkey Business" (author unknown) which illustrates our point. It is about a cage that has five monkeys in it. In the cage is a stepladder leading to a cluster of bananas. Next to the cage is a hose connected to ice cold water. One of the monkeys walks up the ladder for a banana. When the monkey nears the banana at the top of the ladder, all of the monkeys not on the ladder get sprayed with ice-cold water.

Monkeys don't like ice water. Later, another monkey decides to go for a banana. Again, the ice water is sprayed on those monkeys on the ground.

After a few rounds of being sprayed, the process changes the way the monkeys act. Now, when one monkey goes up the ladder, the other monkeys pull him down and attack. They don't want to get sprayed.

Soon, the hose is turned off and a new monkey replaces a veteran in the cage. The new monkey climbs the ladder for a banana and, to his shock and horror, the other monkeys attack him.

Another veteran is replaced with a new monkey. Again, the newcomer goes for the banana and is attacked. This time, the previous newcomer takes part in the punishment with enthusiasm. Soon, all of the original five monkeys have been replaced. No one has been sprayed with the ice water. Yet, because the rules have been passed on, no monkeys go up the ladder anymore.

In the end, none of the monkeys have any idea why they are pulling each other down from the ladder, but they have accepted that it's the way things are and the way they always will be. In many organizations, that's how policies and procedures are developed. Those "rules" that were present at the beginning stay with the organization longer than the creators could have ever imagined.

"Why can't we try it?" "Because that's the way we've always done it."

Ask yourself: In your company, are there policies or procedures that spray ice water and keep your innovators from climbing up the ladder?

When told of the monkey story, one of our colleagues had this illustration. A daughter was talking to her mother in the kitchen and asked, "Why do you always cut off the end of the roast before cooking it?" Her mother responded, "Because that's the way I learned it from your grandmother."

Later in the day, she spoke to her grandmother and said, "Mom says you taught her to always cut off the end of the roast. Why?" Her grandmother laughed and said, "Because the roasts were too big for my roasting pan."

The reason we share these stories is to show you that what was defined many years ago (or even yesterday) will have a profound impact on the way people think and act in the future. People don't always know why they do something; they just do it. And that type of thinking and doing typically hinders innovation along the entire continuum.

For organizations to succeed, they need freedom to reinvent ideas, products, policies and procedures. Yet, many organizations have built-in safeguards to fight reinvention. They keep doing the same thing over and over again.

As an example, for hundreds of years, the prevailing notion was that the world was flat. Only until an innovator proved that idea wrong did a new idea become accepted. In science, many ideas go against the prevailing wisdom of the day and are originally rejected because they don't conform to current thinking. Therefore, it is often very difficult to get people to look at things differently because doing so goes against what they've always known. The following are just a few noteworthy, timeless quotes:

> "I think there's a world market for maybe five computers." (Thomas Watson, chairman of IBM, 1943)

> "This 'telephone' has too many shortcomings to be seriously considered as a means of communication. The device is inherently of no value to us." (Western Union memo, 1876)

> "Who the hell wants to hear actors talk?" (HM Warner, Warner Bros, 1927)

> "Heavier than air flying machines are impossible." (Lord Kelvin, president, Royal Society, 1895)

Here are three other phrases that show how things change over time:

> "In the United States, no one will buy a foreign-made car."

> "Digital pictures will never replace film."

> "Why in the world would someone want to carry a phone with them?"

Tail Winds and Head Winds

Within every organization, there are numerous positive/driving and negative/opposing forces that help or hinder solving problems. In our work, we call the positive forces **Tail Winds.**

- **Tail Winds:** The driving energy that supports solving a problem or moves innovation forward.

We call the negative forces **Head Winds.**

- **Head Winds:** Opposing forces that make solving a problem more difficult and, therefore, hinders innovation.

As in aviation, tail winds can speed you toward your goals, while head winds can slow, stop, or reverse progress. Some head and tail winds are visible and easy to detect. Others are invisible and much more difficult to identify.

Destructive elements fall on a continuum from invisible to visible. It's the invisible elements that often create the most significant and unexpected opposing forces (Figure 3.1).

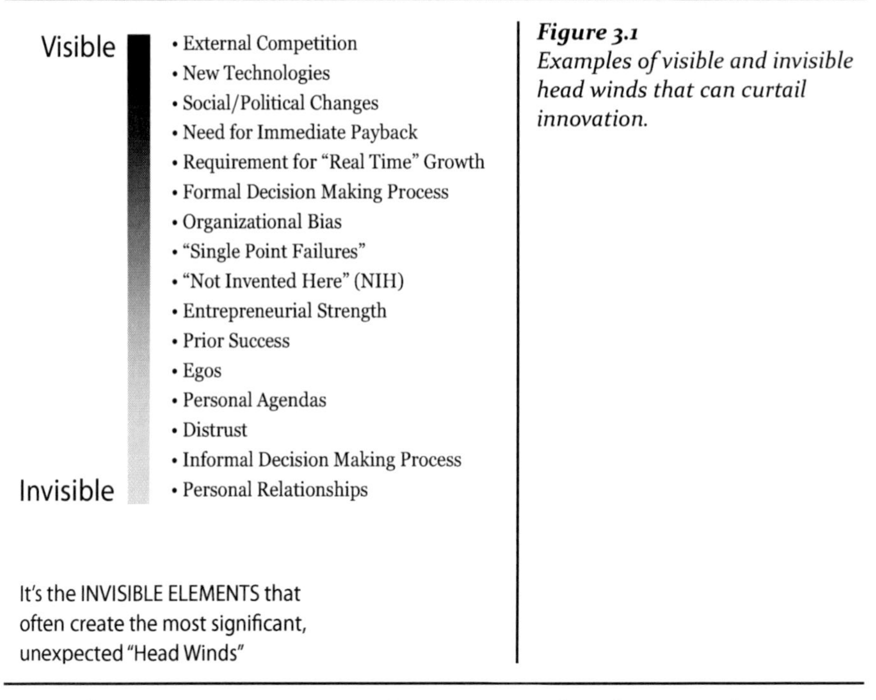

Figure 3.1
Examples of visible and invisible head winds that can curtail innovation.

External competition is easy to analyze, gauge, and track. Personal relationships are much more difficult to study and understand.

They say, "Hindsight is always 20/20." Yet, we don't often look back to analyze why something occurred. Think about your organization. In the following force field diagram, list some of your tail winds and head winds. What are some actions that have worked? How were they successful? What elements of destruction were present (positive and negative)? When looking at the elements of destruction, think about the ones that are part of the **genetic** DNA code of your company. It is likely that they go back to the formation of the company (or at least as far back as 10 years). They are the ones most deeply rooted and have the greatest potential for employees to misunderstand their origin or how to handle them. Now, think about some

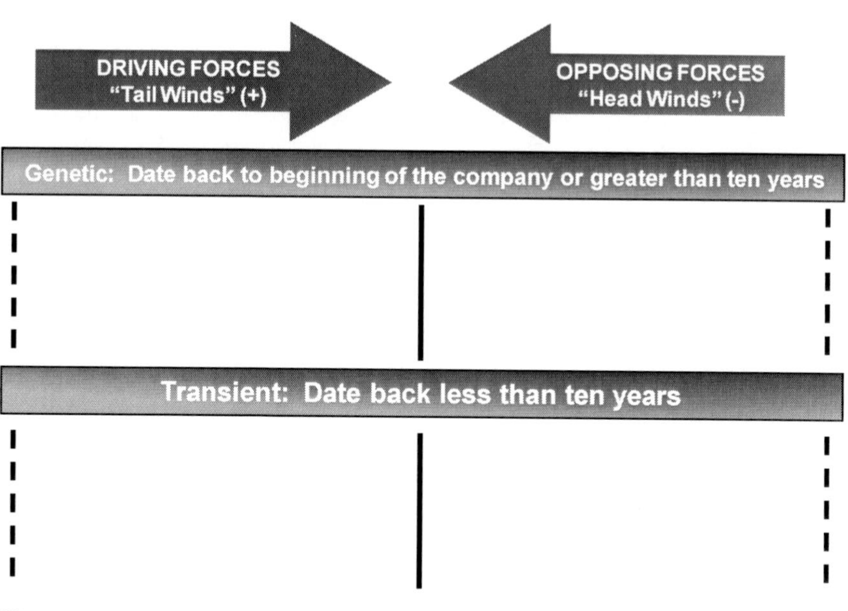

Figure 3.2
Tail and head winds force field diagram. Tail winds need to be leveraged, while head winds need to be overcome.

that have developed more recently. The **transient** ones are newer and are usually based on the values, preferences, and ways of thinking of individuals currently in leadership positions. Can you identify some of these in your organization? How would you leverage them or work around them? (Figure 3.2)

It is important to understand tail winds in order to leverage them effectively. Yet, head winds are also critical to identify, understand, and overcome so as to avoid stalling the innovation process. Think about it: An airplane can fly backward with enough opposing force or head wind. So can innovation. Organizational opposing forces can be strong enough to not only halt innovation, but to make it appear that they are moving backwards.

It is important to point out that tail and head winds are dependent on the application. As an illustration, look at the utilization of a sales force. If a sales force is given a new innovation that fits within their "sweet spot" for making money for themselves, then the actions of the sales force will serve as a positive tail wind. However, if an innovation given to the same group is not believed to be beneficial for maximizing income potential, then their actions will become a significant head wind. In the first case, the new innovation has the greatest probability of success. In the second case, the innovation is virtually doomed before it is ever launched. Thus, the innovation leader must identify their head winds and tail winds, understand their impact, determine how to leverage the positive ones, and redirect the negative ones appropriately. Remember: The invisible elements are the ones that can kill an organization.

There are many examples of destructive forces that are not normally thought of in this context. Some of these include:[1]

- Disruptive technologies and business practices
- Success
- Personal relationships
- Product life cycles
- New processes
- **Entrepreneurial** strengths (not focusing on the business)

Think back to the story of Kettering's experience in Chapter 1. Can you identify the elements of destruction that created significant head winds? Can you also see examples that expose an attitude of, "That's not how we do things," throughout the story?

What became a huge innovative success for GM almost didn't happen because of prior successes, personal agendas, and risk aversion. Whether you are the monkey going for a banana or the person with a new idea, it is necessary to understand the underlying principles behind your actions. Otherwise, you will fall into the trap of, "That's not how we do things," and create significant head winds and unnecessary obstacles for new innovation.

Kettering's story is a good example of how (and why) innovation does not usually go smoothly. Indeed, Kettering was tenacious in driving it. He didn't stop. And he used all of the tools at his disposal to overcome organizationally induced barriers to make it happen. In innovation, nothing happens simply. Frequently, the business and technology components are the easiest parts.

Kettering stepped over the lines to make things happen. He didn't see the boundaries as a permanent roadblock. He saw them merely as obstacles to overcome. Innovation doesn't occur unless someone is willing to take that risk.

To make it fair and balanced, sometimes it is good to cut off the end of the roast. Many times, it is appropriate to hold to current standards. It makes it easier for everyone to function and improves efficiencies. But following the status quo is not good if and when it hinders progress and undermines innovation.

The key is to determine whether or not a system is broken. The challenge for the innovation leader is to know and balance the risk associated with going against, "This is how we've always done it," versus the potential rewards of a new idea. When the innovation leader doesn't know where to draw the line and address the pitfalls of the status quo, a disaster can ensue.

With innovation, we often set up systems and policies that block progress and find that we don't know how to get around them. In circumstances where people can't choose between staying the course and taking a risk, it is the job of the innovation leader to help everyone understand the implications of either choice. Kettering was an innovation leader. He saw the lines and stepped over them to make things happen. He didn't see the boundaries as something that blocked him. He weighed the options, took risks, and innovated successfully.

It is critical to identify and understand the elements of destruction that are present from the beginning. As soon as an organization forms, the elements begin to sprout. Nothing new within your organization is immune to their potential impact – not new management, new business strategies, new funding, or new business endeavors. The elements of destruction grow at various rates, depending upon the length of time your organization has existed. Some elements have sprouted and your organization has conquered them. Some are just beginning to grow, while others have yet to grow. The point is, the elements cannot be ignored.

It can be very scary for organizations to acknowledge the potential harm these elements can do. It may be assumed that leaders don't like it when the "Emperor has no clothes." Similarly, an elephant can be in the room, but no one will talk about it. If we can't tell the emperor they have no clothes on, then the elements of destruction will continue to sprout and grow and eventually cause harm, much like the story of the monkeys in the cage.

Let's consider two companies that learned a product's life cycle has a definite endpoint: Kodak and IBM. Kodak ruled the world of photographic film for many years until the world went digital, and it faced a huge reduction in its consumer base. Even though Kodak invented the digital camera, the company was unwilling to introduce it to the marketplace for fear of undermining its film business. And before computers, IBM made huge revenues from the sale of typewriters. Now, a typewriter is a relic of the past and IBM has reinvented numerous aspects of their business offerings since computers were introduced.

Entrepreneurial strength can also be a destructive force. An entrepreneur who starts a company from scratch has to be a jack-of-all-trades. The founder, whose passion and energy contributes to the growth and success of the company, runs every idea, decision, and process.

With this growth, more people are hired. As more people become involved, however, the element that started out as a positive (i.e., the owner's passion) can eventually becomes an element of destruction. The owner can't be a part of every idea, decision, and process any more but may still try to be. This hinders the growth process. For the organization to innovate, the owner has to let go and trust other people to make decisions. Some founders can do it; some can't. Knowing those elements are there and adapting to them are what separate the good entrepreneurs from the great ones.

As an illustration, Steve Jobs and Steve Wozniak founded Apple Computer, Inc., in 1977. Apple grew quickly and, by 1980, the board of directors decided to make it a public company – a move that Jobs feared would cause him to lose control of the business. Apple has since gone through turbulent times in which Jobs has been replaced and left the company, only to return again.[2,3] Jobs has been at the forefront of driving much of Apple's innovation, yet at times, he has also been an obstacle to helping the company realize potential gains from innovation. This is a critical flaw of many entrepreneurs: They don't understand how vital a role their strengths play in their company's success and, at the same time, how their weaknesses (or blind spots) can lead to corporate downfall.

In many organizations, the decision criteria currently used are based upon a success model that worked very well in the past. Unfortunately, the model may no longer be valid because the world changes – and does so very rapidly today. Therefore, it is imperative to understand the origins of the model and why it was valid – otherwise, it makes it very difficult to know the degrees of freedom that exist for changing it in order to be successful in the future.

Here are some circumstances to think about:

- Have prior successes laid the foundation for success in the future? If so, how have they influenced current strategies and decision making?
- In looking at your top management, do you see any elements of destruction in terms of their values, current ways of thinking, and/or skills?
- By reviewing your most recent new products, what elements of destruction do you see? And what is the expected life of each of these new products?
- What are the potential disruptive forces that could put your company out of business (e.g., new technology, business changes, laws, etc.)? How ingrained in your model for success are these forces?
- Is your organization's success and/or profitability masking an element of destruction?

Advice for the Innovation Leader

Find ways to engage key people in a conversation about looking for the elements of destruction present at creation. Use the examples in this book to help generate ideas.

In summary, to deal with destructive forces, you should:

- Accept that they are there.
- Understand them.
- Assess which ones are head winds and which are tail winds.
- Develop a list of the strongest opposing forces.
- Break them down to the next level:
  - *Identify which ones are genetic:* part of the DNA of your organization.
  - *Identify which ones are transient:* based on the desires of individuals currently in leadership positions.
- Develop strategies and related tactics to negate these forces.
- Leverage the forces that can create tail winds.

The ideas of genetic and transient forces are vital for analysis and implementation. Genetic forces are much harder to overcome than transient forces. If the elements come from your organization's DNA, it will be ingrained in everything. This makes correction very difficult. If the elements of destruction are transient and based on the desires of certain individuals, there are ways around them, no matter how high on the chain the "element spreaders" are.

As emphasized earlier, you need to understand the guiding principles of your organization and their origins. If you don't understand their origins, you might fall into the trap of having policies that people don't understand but follow anyway (much like the monkeys did). Trouble often ensues when people follow methods and actions without regard to their underlying principles.

Remember

When operating under the status quo leads to minimal progress, it's time to stop doing things "the way they've always been done." It's time to set your "Charles Ketterings" free.

Part I

Chapter Four

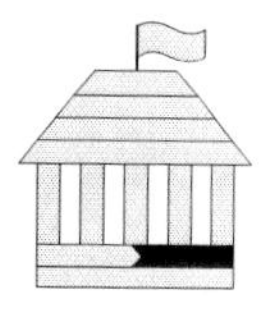

Soft Values Drive the Organization

Three girls, aged 11, 11, and 12, broke into a private residence in New Smyrna Beach, Florida, and vandalized the mansion, causing about $30,000 in damages. Rather than referring the matter to the police and courts, the owner met with the three girls and their mothers. He told *The Daytona Beach News-Journal*, "I tried to be lenient with them, but I wanted to punish them." He also commented that he "wanted to show them there was a better way than the way they were going."

The owner devised a punishment that included four conditions. Specifically, each girl had to:

1. Write, "I will not vandalize other people's property," 1,000 times.
2. Abstain from watching television and playing video games for six months.
3. Read a "good book" for three hours a day.
4. Submit weekly written book reports to him for the next 13 weeks.[1]

In retrospect, the homeowner could have easily allowed the courts to deal with the girls, but that is not how S. Truett Cathy prefers to treat people. Cathy, the founder of Chick-fil-A (a quick **service** restaurant chain in the United States specializing in chicken), carries this same attitude about people into his business world. In an article written by John Miller, one paragraph sums up Cathy's view of his employees:[2]

> "Companies that are open seven days a week may try to rotate days off so that everybody gets one day off every week," says Cathy. "But if the business is open, you're going to be thinking about it, even if it's your day off. That takes away from your relaxation." Moreover, Cathy believes that shutting down on Sundays attracts employees who are oriented toward faith and family. He wants his employees to devote themselves to Chick-fil-A, but not at the expense of something greater.

> "It's sad when people neglect their families," he says. "You can gain the whole world and lose what's most precious." This is hardly conventional corporate philanthropy, but it is nevertheless a gift to the people who work for Cathy.

Is it any wonder Chick-fil-A's turnover rates are very low (averaging 5% to 6% among restaurant operators versus a fast-food industry average of 35 percent, and an hourly employee turnover rate of about 50 percent versus an industry where 140 to 300 percent is more the norm)?[3]

In today's world, we have done a great job of defining, measuring, and improving **hard values**. Hard values are the tangible evaluations that organizations typically use to measure success. Often, they involve measures of finance, productivity, and time. Lean Six Sigma (quality and productivity optimization) was born out of hard values. Other examples of hard values include profitability, number of new products launched, targets for reducing operating expenses and increasing sales, and so forth. Hard values show results; however, they generally do not provide sustained inspiration for people.

As far as organizations have come in recognizing an emphasis on hard values, there is still incredible room for growth in how they analyze and treat soft values. The final part of the foundation of the Innovation House is the soft values that cause people to be motivated and engaged. Hard values are how you measure business success. Soft values are how you achieve that success.

Performance driven by hard values alone will be less than optimal. However, mix a solid business model with the appropriate soft values and watch your business grow. Soft values are easy to talk about but difficult to sustain. When people are motivated, they will be inspired to perform beyond their job description. They will innovate because they want to, not because they are told to.

In your business, do people do their work because they are internally motivated or for the sole purpose of collecting a paycheck? While we will discuss motivation in greater detail in Chapter 21: Reward and Recognition, it is important to understand that, as you move from evolutionary to revolutionary innovation, the degree of intrinsic (internal) motivation must also increase.

Evolutionary innovation can be successfully accomplished with either **extrinsic** or **intrinsic motivation**. Revolutionary innovation, by its very nature, is almost always accomplished via intrinsic motivation coupled with the appropriate extrinsic support systems. As such, understanding and utilizing the human principles of innovation are desirable for evolutionary innovation but are critical for sustained revolutionary innovation.

A great example of intrinsic motivation is the story of the Wright Brothers. They pressed on, even through many failures, to reach their goal of flight. Many organizations see examples of non-internalized extrinsic motivation every day in people who dislike their jobs but still go to work every day to support their family. If new jobs came along, they'd be out the door. There is some overlap between this type of motivation and intrinsic motivation. No one functions entirely on purely intrinsic motivation but, the more intrinsic motivation a person has or an organization helps spur on, the better the innovation results will be.

In keeping with ideas behind the Innovation Continuum, when looking for revolutionary innovation, you must engage people whose primary motivation is at the intrinsic end of the continuum. You need these people because revolutionary innovations take time and effort – and people who are motivated to work beyond a normal 8 to 5 workday often solve the problems associated with them. Intrinsically motivated people will be thinking, tinkering, and scribbling notes on potential solutions at 3:00 a.m.

If your company is only interested in evolutionary ideas, it can probably get by without a strong focus on the human element. Granted, your organization is likely to be a poor place to work, but it can still be financially successful. Yet, after you hit a certain point on the Innovation Continuum, if you don't focus on the human element, the probability that your organization will be able to generate the desired type of innovation will significantly decrease. The importance of the pillars and elements of the Innovation House are dramatically amplified as an organization strives for revolutionary innovation.

The question then becomes, what are the goals of your organization and how will you achieve them?

Psychological Contract

Why all this talk about soft values? Because the **psychological contract** between employee and organization has been broken in many companies. The psychological contract outlines the commitment of an organization to its people and of its people to the organization. On the positive side, what do you think the psychological contract is like between Cathy and his Chick-fil-A employees? On the negative side, what do you think the contract is like in an organization that cuts 30% of its workforce or forces its employees to take significant salary reductions, while simultaneously giving senior management millions of dollars in bonuses?

When we enter into a relationship with another person or entity, we each promise certain sets of behavior. If one decides to unilaterally change the contract without informing the other, the psychological bond is broken. We may not know it right away, but we learn quickly through observing behaviors that the trust has been damaged.

If the psychological contract is broken by the organization (e.g., with a significant staff reduction), employee loyalty and focus quickly moves toward individual needs rather than the needs of the organization. The focus becomes one of self-preservation, with associated actions and behaviors becoming centered on what is best for the person. In physiological terms, people drop down in **Maslow's hierarchy** of needs (as applied to an organization) into a mode of self-preservation.[4]

As the psychological contract erodes, people become more reluctant to take risks and are less inclined to jump on board any type of high-risk innovation. If the psychological contract is broken, then a fear of individual failure may result in protectionism – which will ultimately destroy the possibility for revolutionary innovation. When companies break the psychological contract, employees begin to ask, "What is the point in trying? What do I win if I win? If I'm successful, so what?"

We have seen organizations get very frustrated with their employees. They ask, "Why won't my people just do what they are supposed to do? Why can't they just do their jobs and be done with it?" The answer lies in the level of motivation the employees have. We are all people, not programmable robots. As such, we can't demand performance. We can invite it, but we can't demand it.

One way of looking at this is by understanding that we all have a certain amount of time and energy to devote to the different arenas of our lives (work, self, family, and friends). The **innovation manager** can demand a certain amount of this energy be expended as a prerequisite to maintaining employment. The **innovation leader**, however, is able to motivate people to go beyond the minimum to both maintain employment and tap into energy from the other arenas to help the organization excel.

Looking again at the Innovation Continuum and, particularly, at the evolutionary end, an organization can get by with a minimal level of energy and commitment from its employees. In contrast, at the revolutionary end, it will need employees who will go above and beyond the call of duty. Due to the nature of the higher risk and greater obstacles to be overcome, the organization will need employees to be motivated and committed to making the new innovation successful. This motivation must be driven by the soft values reflected in the behaviors demonstrated by management in the organization and, in particular, the innovation leader.

This concept has evolved over the last 30 years. We have been so focused on hard values and evolutionary innovation that the impact of soft values has been either minimized or forgotten.

The world has now changed from a manual world of work (we will tell you what to do) to a knowledge world of work (help us get to where we need to go). Organizations need more people who are "critical thinkers" and truly engaged in their work. They need people who are improving, optimizing, and creating new things.

It is true that some of the psychological contract is anchored in the hard values of the organization (e.g., salary, benefits, etc.). Yet, the real core of the psychological contract is anchored in the soft values exhibited within the organization. These values are behind the scenes; they are generally invisible. They either motivate or demotivate. One way to look at soft values is to look at them as if they were part of an iceberg (Figure 4.1).

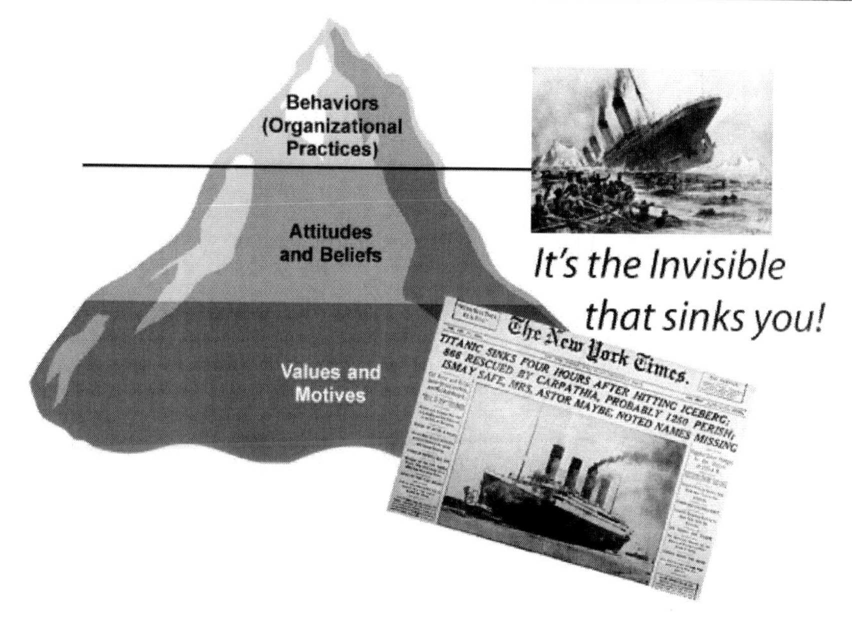

Figure 4.1
Soft values are the invisible drivers that play a significant role in the motivation or demotivation of the employees in an organization.

Behaviors and practices in a company are observable and visible. However, most of an iceberg is below the water line. Similarly, attitudes, beliefs, values, and motives are the things that normally can't be seen. They are inferential and, for the most part, invisible. Yet, when a boat approaches an iceberg, what destroys the boat and rips the bottom apart are things below the water line, not above it. This is also true of organizations – the things that cannot be seen and that no one talks about truly impact the organization and its performance.

Building on this analogy, it is important to know how icebergs break up. According to Dr. Stephen E. Bruneau, "Simply put, icebergs melt. In the process, they often calve[5] and fracture into many pieces, which can create trails, or halos of smaller floating pieces. Usually icebergs melt the fastest at the water line by the action of waves. The water line 'notch' that forms induces calving of overhanging and submerged blocks."[6]

You can physically see an iceberg melt at the water line, but the fissures and cracks are really created below the water. The water line is the gap between the visible and invisible. If your business has unseen erosion in attitudes, beliefs, values, and motives, it will fragment and break apart. When that happens, your organization will have numerous, smaller fiefdoms all floating and drifting on their own. You may not have seen this coming, because culture changes were well below the water line.

When it comes to recruiting new people, what kind of people will your organization attract? If you're not conveying the right messages, you're going to attract the wrong people. Experts know and interact with each other. They go to conferences or meet virtually. This means word of mouth concerning your soft values plays a huge part in who you bring in.

Think about a company with a reputation on the street of being "dog-eat-dog." People who work there get tremendous experience but are burned out and discarded. What kind of talent will such a company attract? How committed will its employees be to success? How easy will it be to build and sustain an innovation effort within? How easy will it be for the company to change this perception? Soft values impact hiring, turnover, and retention.

For the most part, the hiring process for top talent often comes down to values. Hard values are easy to compare and include beliefs about salary, benefits, location, etc. So, unless the hard values are far superior from one organization to the next, what closes the deal? Answer: The soft values – or how they think it will be to go to work every day, how much freedom they think they will have to innovate, and how much support they think they will receive for exploring new ideas. In these three statements, the key phrase is "they think."

As we said earlier in this book, what you value gives you the energy to put a principle into action, which can then lead to results. If your organizational belief system is made up of only hard values, eventually you will run into an iceberg. Therefore, it is vital to understand whether you are putting energy toward soft values or just using buzzwords and slogans. Are the things lying under the water line (attitudes, beliefs, values, and motives) perceived as real or just fluff?

In many organizations, beliefs and values are verbalized in formal mission statements, vision proclamations, or value declarations. These words are plastered on websites, appear on signs hung throughout the workplace, and/or molded into trinkets placed on office desks. However, as the saying goes, "Actions speak louder than words." Beliefs, values, and motives are lived and felt in your heart and demonstrated in your way of life. In an organization, they may be represented by either formal or informal norms. And if they are not lived (or demonstrated via actions), then they don't really exist.

In 2009, Fortune magazine named NetApp the best company to work for in America. An interview with the outgoing CEO Daniel Warmenhoven provided a glimpse of why NetApp was chosen for this honor.[7] He pointed out that the company's primary focus is on customer relations. He explained, "You must have a holistic system, where the customers and business partners all feel good about the company. You can't be the best place to work unless the customers love you and the employees get positive reinforcement from the customer community." In building their organization, employees of NetApp used a team-oriented approach (as opposed to a hierarchical one). They believe that the executive team is charged with helping to establish the organization's objectives based on recommendations that come from within the organization. Having employees know that their voices are being heard and valued allows them to feel like they have a "piece of the action."

And Warmenhoven took this idea very seriously during his tenure at NetApp. A recent blog from a ten-year employee of NetApp reinforced that Warmenhoven truly demonstrated the behaviors he talked about. "His office was a cube, just like everyone else's. In fact, the entire executive team sat in identical cubes. His email was open to everyone within NetApp."[8] Through his actions (and not just his words), employees at NetApp knew they could believe the CEO's words. Warmenhoven lived the soft values that he tried to instill within the organization.

With regard to innovation, our experience has shown us that soft values can serve as either tail winds or head winds (as described earlier in Chapter 3). As such, they are visible through positive and negative elements. Some of these elements are included in Figure 4.2 and are defined in the glossary appearing in Appendix I.

Positive Elements	Not Evident				Very Evident
Purity of Motive	1	2	3	4	5
Spirit	1	2	3	4	5
Open-mindedness	1	2	3	4	5
Camaraderie	1	2	3	4	5
Humility	1	2	3	4	5
Patience	1	2	3	4	5
Service	1	2	3	4	5
Negative Elements					
Discord	5	4	3	2	1
Stubbornness	5	4	3	2	1
Pride	5	4	3	2	1
Discounting	5	4	3	2	1
Passive Advocacy	5	4	3	2	1
Indiscriminant Criticism	5	4	3	2	1
Dominance	5	4	3	2	1

Write Total Score For Each	
Respected Innovation Leader	◊
Ineffective Innovation Leader	Δ
Yourself	□

57 or higher:	Excellent
43 – 56:	High Average
29 – 42:	Low Average
28 or lower:	Serious need of improvement

Figure 4.2
Soft values assessment chart for examining the tail winds (positive values) and head winds (negative values) within your organization

Think about what is important in your organization. What soft values do you want to encourage and reward? Which ones do you want to discourage? Create your own list of the positive and negative elements.[9] Then, for each element, using a scale of 1 – 5 (with 5 being Evident and 1 being Not Evident), rate:

- A respected innovation leader in your company = ◊
- A leader in your company you think is ineffective = Δ
- Yourself = □

Total the scores for each individual. What does this information tell you?

Repeat the assessment for your organization as a whole. Using a scale of 1 – 5:

- Where is your organization today? = T
- How should the chart look for your desired organization? = D

Upon completing this assessment, what are the critical gaps (if any) that you have identified? Record your observations from the assessment.

Leading people by soft values guides them in such a way that they can feel good about accomplishments, possibly without knowing they've been led. The ancient Chinese philosopher Lao-Tsu showed that soft values are timeless. In 565 BC, he said, "The leader is best when people are hardly aware of his existence, not so good when people praise his government, less good when people stand in fear, worst, when people are contemptuous. Fail to honor people, and they will fail to honor you. But of a good leader who speaks little when his work is done, his aim fulfilled, the people say, 'We did it ourselves.'"[10]

How Do You Drive Soft Values?

Now is the time to discuss ways to keep things solid beneath your water line. **The key to driving soft values is leadership.** Following this principle will lead to success: "Let deeds, not words, be your adorning."[11] If leaders don't walk the talk, it doesn't matter. People need to see the soft values behaviorally.

Once the leadership is on board, then the leaders have to **hold the people who report to them (their direct reports) accountable** for supporting the soft values. Leaders can't assume their direct reports will behave a certain way, just because they've been told to do so. Instead, leaders must coach and mentor them along the way – direct reports also need to be held accountable for their deeds, not words.

Once the soft values are cascaded by top leaders and their direct reports, then top leaders need to be held accountable for their direct reports until these values are internalized throughout the organization. When soft values are prevalent within, then employees should be recognized for demonstrating them. If leaders don't positively recognize appropriate actions by employees, the soft values become just words without meaning.

Knowingly or unknowingly, leadership gives others permission to act. A great example of this is the way people dress. At a company where there is no dress code, if a senior VP begins to wear a coat and tie every day, how long will it take before their direct reports start wearing a coat and tie every day? Direct reports of the direct reports will then follow suit. Even though there is not a dress code and the VP says they don't have to wear a coat and tie, employees will emulate what they think is required to be successful. Again: If leadership starts walking the talk and demonstrating the soft values they are looking to cascade, then people will mirror their behaviors. And if they don't, people will emulate that, too.

To drive soft values, start a snowball effect that runs from the top down.

Change Partners™

Another way to drive soft values is by forming **Change Partners**. Change Partners are trusted influencers who can help to shape soft values. **They become the educators to the rest of the company.** Their work is especially important when an existing culture that has worked very well in the past doesn't work anymore. When the change that is needed is massively different from the present state, leaders must call upon the rest of the organization in order to facilitate it. However, this typically makes leaders uncomfortable. Or, if your organization has a limited trust foundation, change will also be very difficult. Everything that comes from the top will then be viewed through a highly skeptical lens. Therefore, when it is time for a major change, start with the leadership and incorporate Change Partners.

Change Partners have both head and heart trust with other employees and they are aligned with the leadership team. They are typically partners and stewards who have a strong sense of ownership and commitment to success of the business. They understand the vision and goals and, in many cases, they have invested in that vision. They want the organization to become more successful. They know change is necessary and can see the benefits of supporting it.

Change Partners must be early adopters. They are people who quickly see and adopt change. And they do not need to be individuals who are high-ranking managers. An administrative assistant, as well as a senior manager, could serve as a successful Change Partner™, depending upon the circumstances.

Change Partners should be provided with very specific training (in our case, four days of formal classroom time teamed with ongoing **coaching** and mentoring). They need to be developed so that they understand what they must do. As such, it is vital that you choose the right Change Partners. There may be many early adopters, but only those who also are trusted and influential are good candidates for being Change Partners.

Similarly, there are people who are trusted and influential; however, they are slower to accept change. Therefore, while valuable to the overall process, they are not good candidates for Change Partners. Many organizations make political appointments when assigning Change Partners. We've seen private companies choose family members and large, public firms choose "yes-people" as Change Partners. But the wrong Change Partner can stop or significantly impede the process. Once again, honesty and communication are critical here. The crucial question to ask becomes, "Who are your trusted influence peddlers?"

Completing a network analysis or sociogram is a somewhat formal way to generate a short list of the key influential individuals in your company. An informal way is to observe who people go to after a major meeting or announcement to discuss its implications. Another way is to identify individuals who always seem to have people around them trying to find out what is going on and why. These people tend to be the ones to whom others in the organization listen to – and they will be asked their opinions on any cultural change that an innovation leader might implement. So ask yourself, "Do you want these people on your side from the beginning?" At a minimum, innovation leaders need to know where they stand, since others will listen to them when deciding whether or not they will accept and support change.

Depending upon the size of your business, once potential Change Partners have been identified, you should refine the list in order to select a smaller, key group of Change Partners. Important criteria for selecting the final Change Partners include locality and distribution (across organization levels, discipline, current assignments, etc.). The goal is to create a very diverse team that will have the broadest possible impact. Once selected, this group will become a key resource for the innovation leader, who must then consult with the group on a regular basis in order to gauge progress. This core group will tell the truth about what is working and what is not working. They become another set of eyes and ears for the innovation leader to assess the impact of what is happening because of the necessary changes.

However, under no circumstance should these individuals be used as "organizational spies." They must be valued and respected by innovation leaders for who they are: individuals who are listened to and trusted by other employees. Violating this puts Change Partners at risk of losing their trust among peers and can turn them from being enablers of tail winds to being generators of significant head winds.

Advice for the Innovation Leader

- Find ways to engage key people in a conversation about soft values. Have them rate your organization, using the same form you filled out here. Then look at their input to determine the current state of affairs.
- Ask these individuals to identify where you need to be in the future.
- Identify the critical gaps between the organization's current and desired states.
- Develop strategies and tactics to close critical gaps, with an emphasis on rewarding desired behaviors.
- Reassess the organizational climate every six to nine months to ensure progress is being made and then modify strategies and tactics as required.
- When dealing with organizational shifts, think about the Change Partner process.

Remember

Soft values motivate and inspire. They drive people to go above and beyond their job descriptions. They cause revolutionary ideas to become realities.

Part I

Chapter Five

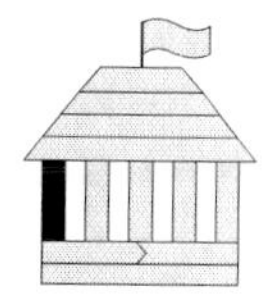

Leveraging Differences

In 1934, Walt Disney assembled all of his artists in an empty sound stage and acted out his vision for a full-length animated film. This became the script for the film that his brother, Roy, and his wife, Lillian, tried to talk him out of doing. Most of the entertainment world referred to his production as "Disney's Folly." But in December 1937, *Snow White and the Seven Dwarfs* was released.[1,2,3]

Much has been written about the technical and business issues related to the production of *Snow White*. The film used new technologies, including rotoscope, to provide more realistic human animation and the multiplane camera to add depth. Walt initially estimated that the film could be produced for $250,000, or about 10 times the budget for producing a typical short film at that time. Actual production costs exceeded $1.7 million. Walt was betting the future of Disney Studios, and even his own house, on the success of the film. Over Walt's objections, his brother Roy showed a partially completed portion of the film to Bank of America. After viewing the film, a call was made by the banker: "Give Mr. Disney the money." The initial release of the film brought in about $4.2 million in revenue.

One arena that received far less publicity was the blending of unique talents utilized to create *Snow White*. While Walt provided the creative genius and Roy provided the business acumen, it also took hundreds of artists, sound people, photographers, etc., to turn the creative idea into a breakthrough innovation. Walt hired the best artists he could find from around the world. He allowed them to pursue their own passion. While they could have drawn most anything, Walt encouraged them to focus on what they were most passionate about: faces, people, animals, etc. His only requirement was that they do it extremely well.

What Walt Disney demonstrated was an understanding that people have unique skills and passions. He allowed people to pursue them in an environment that treated people as individuals rather than interchangeable parts. He allowed the potential for greatness to emerge.

Almost 70 years later, Hong and Page demonstrated mathematically that a diverse group of intelligent problem solvers will outperform a non-diverse group of the best problem solvers, thus supporting Disney's approach.[4] Embedded in this notion is the understanding that looking at how a person thinks and valuing **diversity** of thought processes is more important than merely measuring a person's IQ or examining educational credentials.

We have observed this being demonstrated in organization after organization. One company in particular that we've worked with was hoping to provide ongoing breakthrough innovation. Leadership was consistently disappointed that the ideas being brought forward were almost exclusively in the evolutionary to expansionary arena. They were perplexed that a group of literally world-class engineers and scientists could not generate a greater number of breakthrough ideas. Only after examining the invisible characteristics of individual employees did the issue become visible. Their organization as a whole, while comprised of extremely intelligent and qualified people, had very little diversity in thought process. The lesson learned from Disney and many of our clients is:

Only by understanding and leveraging individual differences, coupled with fostering a trusting environment and appropriate soft values, can innovative potential ever be truly maximized.

Leveraging differences is vital for success today. In a lot of respects, the world is becoming flat.[5] But when looking at individual differences, the world is anything but flat. According to management guru Peter Drucker, "The most important contribution management needs to make in the 21st century is creating a fifty-fold increase in the productivity of knowledge work and the **knowledge worker**."[6,7]

Our experience has shown us that many managers struggle with leveraging the knowledge worker. They do not recognize there is a difference between the manual worker and the knowledge worker. Knowledge workers think, act, and behave differently. Their wants and needs are also different. All of these differences dictate the need to create specific environments, systems, and processes so knowledge workers can be most productive.

How do you leverage differences? By matching people to the appropriate task, problem, or job.

As the leader of an airline, you would not assign a chief mechanic to be a pilot today and a mechanic next week. Nor would you have your pilots working as mechanics. Each has specific skills that need to be applied appropriately to make the airline function. Individuals are not interchangeable components; they each have unique skills and capabilities. Understanding these is critical to having them in the most effective roles.

It doesn't make sense to have process-driven Six Sigma experts trying to create out-of-the-box revolutionary concepts. It also doesn't make sense to assign an individual with a predisposition towards revolutionary innovation the task to streamline an existing process. Yet, we continually see managers trying to cut-and-paste people into roles for which they are not a natural fit. If you use the wrong people for the wrong thing, you're going to get the wrong results.

To leverage individual differences, you need to analyze and understand each employee's visible attributes and skills, as well as their invisible predispositions. As depicted in Figure 5.1, individual attributes fall along a spectrum ranging from the visible to invisible. That is, there are attributes which can be identified from a photograph and are very visible. At the other end, there are psychological attributes which are largely invisible to most of us.

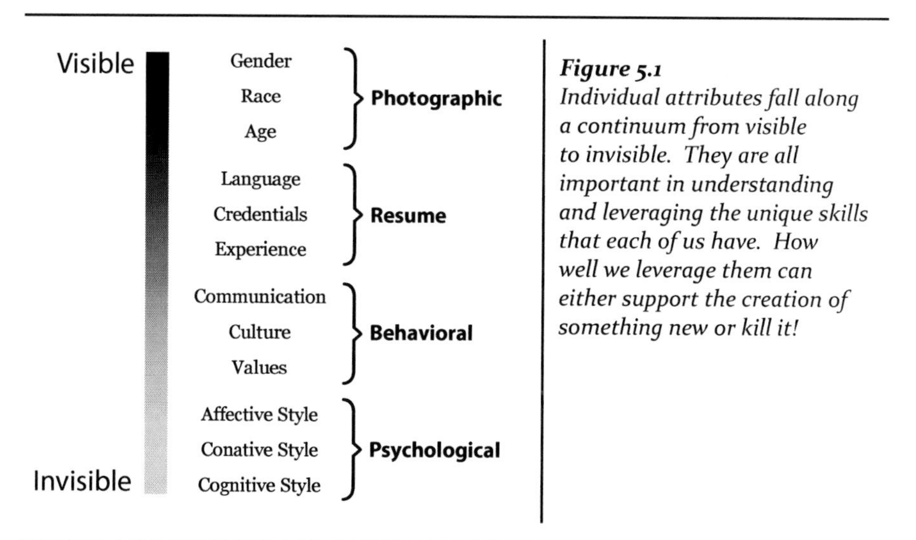

Figure 5.1
Individual attributes fall along a continuum from visible to invisible. They are all important in understanding and leveraging the unique skills that each of us have. How well we leverage them can either support the creation of something new or kill it!

When teams are selected today, most of the attention is given to the visible (or upper) end of the scale: Who has the right technical skills or experience, who is available, do we have the correct racial or ethnic mix, etc.? Very little attention is devoted to the lower (or invisible) end of the spectrum: Do we have the right values mix or the most appropriate psychological mix? Do we have people most comfortable with evolutionary innovation focusing on Six Sigma? Do we have those individuals most skilled at revolutionary innovation working on breakthrough ideas? Only by considering attributes at the invisible end of the spectrum can we select the best team members.

Successful innovation requires understanding and incorporating important attributes of:

1. Individual practitioners
2. Key decision makers
3. The organization

To begin understanding the individual practitioners and key decision makers, we need to have a basic understanding of their psychological makeup, as presented via three axes utilized in psychology:[8]

- **Affect** – *To feel:* It is associated with a person's emotional state.
- **Conation** – *To act:* It is an aspect of a person's mental processes or behaviors directed toward action or change, including impulse, desire, volition, and striving.
- **Cognition** – *To know:* It is how people take in and process information, and how they put that information to work to make decisions and solve problems.

Being aware of these differences will help people:

- Understand themselves and their behaviors.
- Appreciate others and thereby make constructive use of individual differences.
- Understand that approaching problems in different ways can be productive.

We are often asked, "How do I make visible the way people think, feel, and act? How do I figure out the best way to utilize someone's unique talents?"

Tools and Instruments

There are numerous tools or instruments that may be used to differentiate between people. In our work, we have used many – such as the Myers-Briggs Type Indicator (MBTI), Kirton Adaption-Innovation Inventory (KAI), Fundamental Interpersonal Relations Orientation-Behavior (FIRO-B), Strength Development Inventory (SDI), Intercultural Development Inventory, and the Kolbe System, among others. While these are excellent tools to help address specific questions, until the ISPI® was developed, there was not an effective way to integrate the information from the individual tools into a composite picture. Without this integrated view, leveraging the information was difficult for the innovation leader.

As we talk about tools, it is imperative to understand that they must be looked at holistically. They are subject to a variety of influences (even the ones with very highly repeatable results). Therefore, it is critical for the innovation leader to:

- *Not* over-interpret the results.
- Avoid stereotyping based on scores.
- Realize that the scores are not a measure of intelligence or mental health.

Note: Scores provide information to help the innovation manager better understand individual attributes. They play an important (but not all-defining) role in identifying key strengths to leverage and mitigate potential blind spots.

The Innovation Strengths Preference Indicator® (ISPI)

We have utilized all of the previously listed tools with success. However, they were not developed with the innovator in mind. Therefore, we decided to create a tool for the innovation leader and individual innovators using similar principles but in different applications. The Innovation Strengths Preference Indicator (ISPI) is a tool that combines the three different psychological axes into a single indicator. It highlights an individual's predispositions toward a certain type of innovation, as well as how they prefer to interact with others. The results of the ISPI cover 12 different orientations. They are:

Innovation Orientation (iO™) – how you prefer to innovate

1. Overall ISPI (your total for Ideation, Risk, and Process)
2. Ideation (your approach for generating new ideas)
3. Risk (your approach for taking risks)
4. Process (your approach for establishing and following processes)

Innovation Orientation Modifiers (iOM™) – how you prefer to innovate with other people

5. Control (your approach for taking charge or allowing others to do so)
6. Relationship (your approach for establishing personal relationships)
7. Networking (your approach for establishing and being part of networks)
8. Input (your approach for seeking information: concrete/visionary)

9. Flow (your approach to pursuing divergence or convergence)
10. Passion (your approach for taking action)
11. Output (your approach toward making decisions)
12. Energy (your approach for seeking energy to solve problems)

Malcolm De Leo, an innovation leader who has used the ISPI extensively inside an organization describes the ISPI as showing people how they create, interact, learn, and execute.

The results of the ISPI can be used for individual awareness, team development and analysis, as well as for creation and analysis of organizational innovation systems.

We can't cover the ISPI in its entirety in this chapter but, to start, we will go into detail on the cognitive aspect (innovation Orientation – the **Builder** to **Pioneer** model of Ideation, Risk and Process) because we use many related concepts and definitions in the remainder of this book. We do not mean to imply that other aspects are less critical, only that we need to define some of the key elements and models so that we can use them for exploring other principles and applications.

Recall that cognition means "to know." It is used to refer to the human capacity for processing information, applying knowledge, and dealing with change. It's how people take in information, make meaning of information, and also how they put that information to work to make decisions and, ultimately, solve problems.

People generally possess the skills to be creative, generate novel thought, solve problems, and interact with each other synergistically. It is true that we each have a unique cognitive orientation, but very few of us know how to capitalize on this orientation or understand and leverage differences between individual orientations. The key is to understand and leverage the unique capabilities in each of us.

Six Legends

As an example of different people (by perceived ISPI) excelling in a similar field, we are going to tell you about six legends in the field of science and innovation:

- Friedrich Wilhelm Herschel
- Marie Curie
- George Washington Carver
- Thomas Edison

- Benjamin Franklin
- Leonardo da Vinci

Friedrich Wilhelm Herschel (1738-1822) was an astronomer who used a forty-foot telescope to methodically map double stars and moons. He discovered Uranus and two of its moons, as well as the 6th and 7th moons of Saturn. He also designed and manufactured telescopes.[9,10] In his field of scientific pursuit, Herschel went very narrow and deep.

Marie Curie (1867-1934) was a pioneer in the field of radioactivity and the first person to receive two Nobel Prizes.[11, 12] Her field of interest was radioactivity (a term she coined). Included in her many accomplishments were the discovery of polonium and radium. She and her husband refrained from patenting the process for isolating radium so that the scientific community could use the process.

Throughout her life, Marie Curie promoted the use of radium to reduce suffering from illness and injury. She had to break through the gender barriers associated with being a woman, working in a man's field, to have her work accepted. At one point, she ensured that the world knew she was responsible for theorizing that two uranium materials (pitchblende and torbernite) must contain other elements to account for their levels of activity. Curie's work and interests were broader than that of Herschel; however, it was still somewhat focused.

George Washington Carver (1864-1943) was an agricultural scientist who revolutionized the economy of the southern United States. He invented over 300 products from peanuts, ranging from peanut butter to extractions of peanut oil. He also invented over 100 products from sweet potatoes. He created the concept of crop rotation and soil conservation. And he was the first African American faculty member at Iowa State University.[13,14] Carver was a scientific observer. He did not patent many of his discoveries and was quoted as saying, "God gave them to me. How can I sell them to someone else?" Carver was a little broader than Curie; however, he focused in one general area and was very methodical in his approach.

Thomas Edison (1847-1931) was an inventor with 1,093 patents to his name. His areas of invention include the phonograph, electricity, the light bulb, film projectors, motion pictures, kinetophone, and kinetoscope. Edison's expertise was in testing and refinement.[15] His goal was to make things people could use. "Never waste time inventing things people do not want to buy." Edison used a think tank philosophy, recruiting many ambitious inventors who became known as being part of Thomas Edison's Muckers. Edison was much broader than Herschel, Carver, or Curie. He pursued many different innovations;

however, all had the common thread of practicality and all were developed through extensive refinement and experimentation.

Benjamin Franklin (1706-1790) was known for many things. As an entrepreneur, he was one of America's earliest innovators. He saw the value of the "Double Bottom Line" (which refers to creation of wealth and social capital). Franklin was also known as a printer, inventor, scientist, economist, philosopher, statesmen, and musician. His efforts contributed to establishing fire protection, libraries, and sanitation services. Some of Franklin's innovations included swim fins, the stove, bifocals, and the harmonica. He was also known as a peacemaker and revolutionary. [16,17] Franklin's actions are summarized well by his quote, "If you would not be forgotten, as soon as you are dead and rotten, either write things worth reading, or do things worth the writing." Unlike the previous four legends, Franklin's interests were much broader. He moved easily from one pursuit to another, incorporating both scientific and social innovations.

Leonardo da Vinci (1452-1519) was a "Renaissance Man."[18,19] As an unrepentant left-hander who sometimes wrote backwards, he spent a lot of time pondering universal truths. Da Vinci's work is known throughout the fields of art, architecture, mechanics, and medicine (for his understanding of the human body). For example, his work led to discoveries in the organs and artery system of a woman and an embryo in the uterus. He tinkered with the giant catapult, cannon, flying machine, and a tank-like vehicle. Da Vinci also brought to the world his paintings, such as *The Last Supper*, *Mona Lisa*, and *Virgin and Child with St. Anne*. Even with all of these accomplishments, da Vinci failed to finish much of what he started because his interests were too broad. Da Vinci's interests were the broadest of the six legends, so broad that he would be easily distracted from completing many of them to pursue a different one that interested him more at the time.

So what can we learn from the stories of these legends? We see that there is no ideal cognitive orientation. People differ in the manner in which they solve problems, because they each possess a stable preference that fits somewhere on a continuum anchored by what we refer to as either a "Building" (Herschel) or "Pioneering" (da Vinci) approach toward innovation.

These six legends were all scientists, but you can identify legendary experts in any other field and find the same range of innovation preferences. All are experts in some regard, but they do so using different orientations or approaches to innovation or problem solving. Within your organization, depending on what you are trying to do, you would tap each expert for different types of innovation.

In today's world, here are some tasks you might assign to these legends:

- Friedrich Wilhelm Herschel – Leading Lean Six Sigma programs.
- Marie Curie – Developing a new process (versus optimizing an existing one).
- George Washington Carver – Expanding existing product lines to meet broader market needs.
- Thomas Edison – Leading the development of new products for a near-term market.
- Benjamin Franklin – Leading a new venture program.
- Leonardo da Vinci – Generating ideas for a revolutionary breakthrough.

The Innovation Relay Race

In an ideal innovation world, you could start by gathering your da Vincis and letting them "play" by generating new ideas. At the same time, you would not want this group leading the implementation charge.

The Relay Race would start with your da Vincis who would then pass the ideas to your Franklins, and they would pass to your Edisons and so forth. At the end, your Herschels would be optimizing the idea.

The Innovation Relay Race allows for paradigm-changing ideas to be played with and expanded upon, and then eventually grounded and brought into executable reality. If your da Vincis played and the next step was to bring their work to a Herschel-like decision maker, the ideas would more than likely be killed – not because the ideas are bad but because of the ISPI interactions that would take place. The communication breakdowns would be immense between these two groups.

As an example of the importance of invisible interactions, here is a quote from *The Wharton School*: "**An innovative idea doesn't necessarily depend on its strength or weakness, but on who is pitching the idea.** One study finds that strongly performing subsidiaries of multinational corporations are more likely to offer – and seek – intellectual resources than underachievers. A company's success, ultimately, is less about the availability of innovative ideas and more about the human beings who need to share them."[20]

Paradigm Builders and Paradigm Pioneers

Our research and experience has taught us that people prefer to solve problems in ways that span across a continuum, from those who view the problem statement as concrete, to those who view it as merely a suggestion. We call this a Personal Paradigm Continuum™: At one end, you have a **Paradigm Pioneer**; on the other end, you have a **Paradigm Builder**.

A pioneer challenges things, focusing on possibilities and doing things differently.

A builder accepts, focusing on reality and doing things better.

By overlaying the Personal Paradigm Continuum with the Innovation Continuum, the innovation manager can begin to determine which people to assign to different tasks (Figure 5.2).

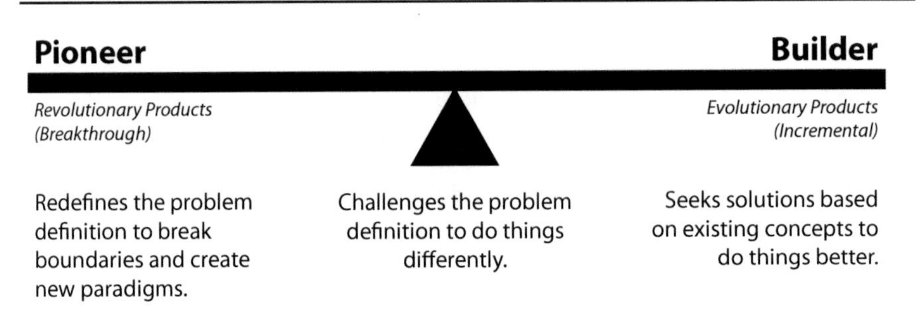

Figure 5.2
Personal Paradigm Continuum vs. the Innovation Continuum. Matching an individual's preferences to the appropriate innovation task helps to ensure greater efficiency and success.

Remember, it is imperative to understand that one group is not better than the other. All types of people are needed to sustain innovation. This continuum shows how their strengths are different, but not their capacities.

Generally speaking, for revolutionary innovation, paradigm pioneers are most likely to be successful. However, for evolutionary innovation, paradigm builders are most successful. Since we will refer to these terms throughout the rest of the book, understanding the difference between a builder and pioneer is critical.

Builders are seen as disciplined, precise, reliable, efficient, sound, methodical, prudent, conforming, dependable, and organized. They seek solutions using tried and true methodologies. They tend to be an authority within a given structure. Builders are able to maintain high accuracy during long spells of detailed work.

In contrast, pioneers are seen as spontaneous, energetic, ingenious, and unconventional. They are catalysts, creators of dissonance, independent, and capricious risk takers. Pioneers approach tasks from unexpected angles and tend to cut across current paradigms. They often take control in unstructured situations. Pioneers are capable of doing detailed work, but only for short bursts of time.

Builders generate insights that fit within current paradigms. They associate existing elements to optimize current systems and produce new thought (Figure 5.3).[21]

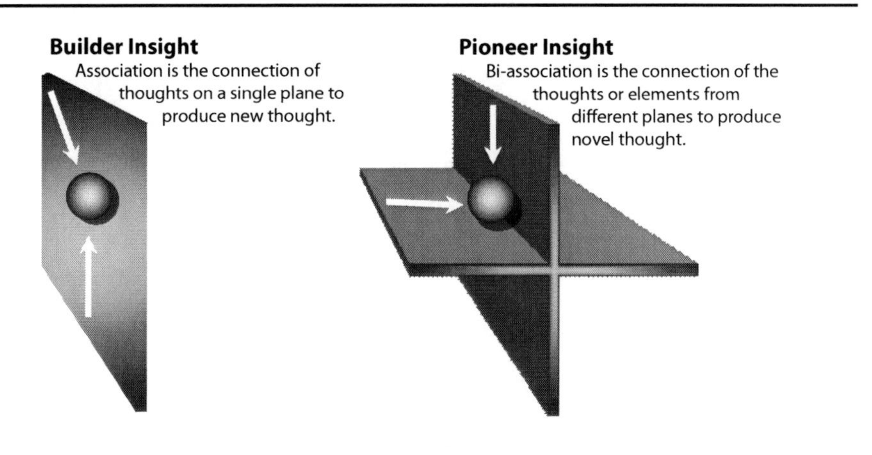

Koestler, A. (1964) The Act of Creation. New York: The Macmillan Co.

Figure 5.3
Builders tend to generate insights that fit within current paradigms, whereas pioneers tend to generate ideas that associate elements from different domains to develop breakthrough ideas.

Pioneers generate insights that may not fit into current paradigms. They tend to **bi-associate** elements derived from multiple sources, to develop new ways of looking at things and to produce novel thought (Figure 5.3).

In terms of Ideation and Risk, builders offer a sufficient number of ideas and will self-censor ideas they deem to be irrelevant. Once they solve a problem, they move on to the next one. They seek to build and maintain group consensus. They demonstrate respect and appreciation for rules and norms. Builders generally like checklists or detailed instructions on how to do something.

In terms of Ideation and Risk, pioneers generate large numbers of ideas and easily interject ideas that may or may not be relevant. Even when they solve a problem, they will continue to come up with new ideas and potential solutions. They prefer to rock the boat and are irreverent with regard to norms and rules.

In solving problems, builders tend to follow a linear, **incremental** pathway. We call this **pongging™**. Pioneers tend to follow a non-linear path and often appear to be going off on a tangent that has little or nothing to do with the problem being addressed. We call this **pinging™**. These processes are depicted in Figure 5.4. Builders follow a process of creating evolutionary solutions through steady, incremental innovations. In contrast, pioneers develop more unique solutions through a non-linear, often erratic, process.

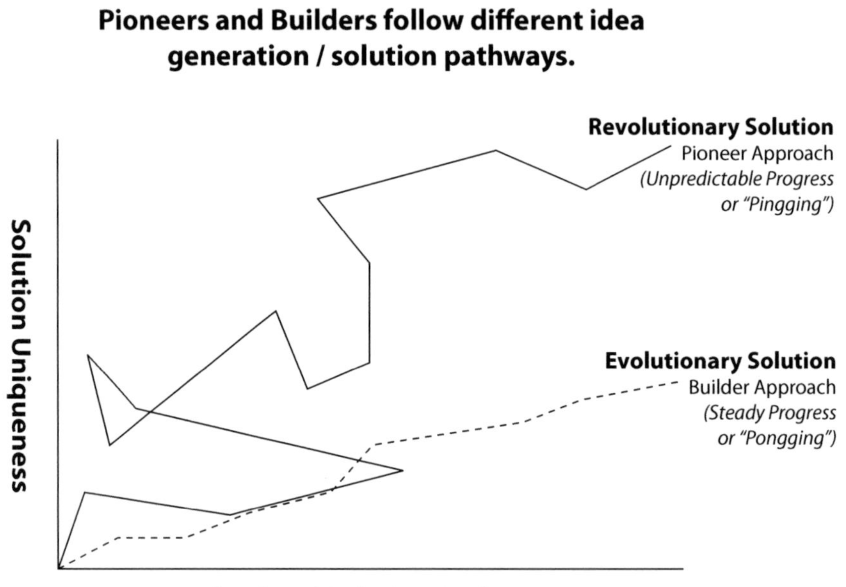

Figure 5.4
Builders follow a linear, incremental approach to solving problems (pongging). Pioneers follow a non-linear approach that we define as pinging.

In terms of Process, a builder creates systems external to themselves. A builder's desk will often be neat, with their file drawer organized so that anyone can find a particular file. By comparison, pioneers create systems that are internal to themselves and generally invisible to others. Their office will often have stacks of papers and appear totally disorganized. Go into a pioneer's office alone and you will find chaos. But go with the pioneer and you will probably find what you are looking for. Typically, the pioneer will know which stack of paper contains a certain item, and how far down in the stack the particular item is.

A strong builder would be Friedrich Wilhelm Herschel. Recent examples include W. Edwards Deming (for quality and productivity improvements) and Bill Smith at Motorola (for Six Sigma).

Leonardo da Vinci was a strong pioneer. In today's world, examples include Steve Jobs (Apple Computer), Dr. Michael DeBakey (inventor of the artificial heart), and Charles Kettering (See Kettering story, page 3).

We all have preferred orientations. Take a moment to think about people who stand out to you as builders and pioneers within your organization. By recognizing their strengths and leveraging them, you can have more effective and efficient teams. By recognizing their differences, you will be able to understand why some people can't hear the ideas that others express. You will also recognize why some people can't express ideas in ways that others can hear them. Notice how each orientation has distinct personality traits in how they think, act, and solve problems, as well as what things cause them stress and the behaviors they use to cope with that stress.

Characteristics of a Revolutionary Innovator

If you think about a product's life cycle, the beginning can be traced back to some form of a revolutionary idea. Unfortunately, many times the **originator** of the revolutionary idea is not recognized or rewarded. Some of the reasons for this include:

- The idea originator does not develop it into a recognized quantifiable gain.
- A different organization winds up driving innovation and, ultimately, gets the recognition.
- The idea originated when nobody in the organization saw it as solving a significant problem.

Whatever the reason that they are not recognized, most of the revolutionary ideas are formulated by the people in the organization with a predisposition toward thinking and contributing at the pioneering end of the continuum. These are the individuals who are generally the least understood. Here are their general iO characteristics:

> Strong pioneers do not see boundaries as obstacles, generate lots of different thoughts, see models and patterns as compared to details, are more intuitive, are not concerned about time, are in love with concepts, are more eclectic in background, do not fit in socially, are obsessed, and are mentally multi-processing. They are non-linear thinkers, not influenced by social norms, highly passionate about what they are looking for, and good at start-up but not at follow-through. Finally, they are generally very hard individuals to manage.

This is where organizations struggle. The "classic" manager sees strong pioneers as hassles, not as assets. We see them as spirited horses. You don't want to put bits in their mouths. Rather, you want to let them run and then do your best to guide them. These people are hard to harness but, once you figure out how, great results often follow.

Do you know someone inside your organization that you would consider a strong pioneer, a potential revolutionary innovator? How are they treated? Do they still work for your company? Have they been allowed to develop into a "Kettering"?

iOM™ – Innovation Orientation Modifiers

The iO (innovation Orientation: Builder to Pioneer) is just the first piece of the ISPI. To bring the ISPI together, we will scratch the surface of the iOM (innovation Orientation Modifiers). At a high level, the iO is someone's preferred way to innovate. The iOM is the way a person prefers to innovate and interact with others.

The following table, Figure 5.5, is called the ISPI Totem, which is a one-page snapshot of someone's ISPI Feedback. Since we have already covered the iO piece, we will briefly discuss how the iOM fits into the puzzle.

ISPI™ Totem

iO™

	Builder	Mid-Range	Pioneer
Total			
Ideation			
Risk			
Process			

iOM™

	No	Flex	Yes
Control I Initiate			
Others Initiate			
Relationship I Initiate			
Others Initiate			
Networking I Initiate			
Others Initiate			

Input	**Concrete**	**Flex**	**Visionary**
Flow	**Converge**	**Flex**	**Diverge**
Passion	**Prudent**	**Depends**	**Action**
Output	**Heart**	**Flex**	**Head**
Energy	**Self**	**Flex**	**People**

Figure 5.5
ISPI Totem that summarizes an individual's results for their iO. It addresses preferred innovation orientation and the iOM, which focuses more on how an individual innovates and interacts with others.

Flex: Before we walk you through the ISPI Totem, we need to explain Flex. If you are in a Flex zone, how you interact will depend on the situation. If you score outside of Flex, your preference will be very strong in that particular area and it will be difficult for you to shift to the opposite zone.

Control helps you to determine your preference for taking charge and allowing others to take charge. I Initiate: This answers whether or not you prefer to be in control of the situation and others, or if it depends (Flex). Others Initiate: This answers whether or not you are comfortable allowing others or the situation to control you, or if it depends (Flex).

Why does this matter? Because your preference to be in control can lead to clashes with others. We can't go through all of the scenarios, but if you are a Yes/No (Yes, I want to be in control and No, I don't want anybody to control me) and you're working closely with other people who are Yes/No's, the potential for clashing exists. If you are an Innovation Leader, Yes/No's may be harder for you to manage, but they may also be able to drive innovation efforts on their own in ways that others can't.

Relationship deals with depth of relationships. The first piece deals with whether or not you prefer to initiate relationships and get to know people intimately, or if it depends (Flex). The second piece deals with your preference for either having people approach you and establishing meaningful relationships or leaving it up to the situation (i.e., it depends – Flex).

If you are a Relationship Yes/Yes and you work with a lot of No/No's, you may feel as if people don't like you. That could very well be the case, but it is more likely that the No/No's just want to work and not go into depth about their lives (or yours).

Networking deals with breadth and number of interactions you have with people. Networking tends to involve interacting with less depth than relationships.

First, think about your preference for initiating networking-type interactions. Do you enjoy it? Do you dread it? Or does it depend on the situation?

Second, how do you feel about people approaching you in networking environments? Do you want people to approach you? Do you want to be left alone? Or does it depend?

If you are a No/No, you will probably not want a job that is heavily dependent on finding people to help you with innovative ideas. That will be difficult work for you. You can do it, but it will be stressful.

Note that some people may prefer networking but not building deep relationships, and vice versa.

Input explains how you prefer to seek and receive information.

Do you prefer to get the big picture first (Visionary)? Do you prefer to initially get all of the real world facts, **data**, and details (Concrete)? Or, do you Flex here depending on the situation?

Input impacts the type of projects and tasks that you enjoy working on. It also has an impact when you are presenting ideas to people. The Input of a potential decision maker will greatly influence what they "hear" as well as what they "don't hear."

Flow addresses how you prefer to come up with solutions.

Would you rather play with a lot of different options (Diverge)? Or would you rather focus on honing in on a specific solution (Converge)? Or does it depend (Flex)?

A team can sing in harmony when their Flow is aligned. On the other hand, when a team is mixed and a task calls for playing with ideas, the divergers will thrive and the convergers will cringe. At the same time, when it is time to implement a potential solution, divergers will want to continue "playing" with potential ideas, while convergers will have been ready to "do something" for a long time.

Passion examines how you prefer to take action.

Do you want to do it right away (Action)? Do you want to weigh it (Depends)? Or do you try to de-risk it as much as possible (Prudent)?

The Passion orientation can be a reason why some people who are action-oriented get frustrated with those who are more prudent. "All we do is talk, weigh, and analyze. Why can't we just do something?" This could be seen as "analysis paralysis." On the other hand, someone who is action-oriented may move quickly in certain situations and, in doing so, hurt the individual or team's chances of success.

Output highlights how you make decisions.

Do facts drive you (Head)? Do your values drive you (Heart)? Or does it depend (Flex)?

Someone who works at a job because it has a great impact on people's lives is probably more heart-driven. Alternatively, someone who crunches numbers and puts data ahead of people's opinions is probably more head-driven.

Energy shows where your problem-solving energy comes from.

Do you prefer to work with other people for long stretches of time (People)? Or do you want to get marching orders and then go to work by yourself (Self)? When it's time to recharge your batteries, do you want to find a group of people to chat and interact with (People)? Or do you want to hole up and be alone (Self)? Or does it depend (Flex)?

When we run ideation sessions, we try to provide time and space for the "self-people" to process. Usually, this comes after about 60 to 90 minutes of group work. We say, "Let's take 30 minutes to process."

The self-people happily scurry out of the room and find a quiet place. Those in the people group either stay where they are and continue talking or move out into the hall and continue the conversation. It is important to know that self-people can bring the same number of ideas to an ideation session. They just need quiet time to process information. If they get their alone time periodically, then they will be back in sync with the group. If they are forced to ideate for eight hours straight, then they may be present physically, but they will be stressed.

It is important to recognize that many facilitators are people-oriented by nature. They may say, "Break? Why do we need a break? Let's keep the discussion going." For ideal ideation and brainstorming, you need to match the facilitator to the goals and to the people participating.

ISPI Summary

There is no right or wrong answer for any information relative to the ISPI. No one type is better or worse than another. Yet, there are people who are better suited to be working on certain tasks than others. It doesn't mean that others can't make themselves perform all tasks, but we feel it makes sense to match people to their work. While it is true that you can dig a hole with a spoon, you can also decide to set the spoon aside for more detailed work and use a shovel to do the major excavation.

The people you use for certain tasks should depend on the project and the goals of your organization.

As an innovation leader, it is important to do what you can to leverage the natural (and invisible) strengths of people. It will improve the output of the individual, the team, and the innovation of your organization in the long run.

Go back to the ISPI Totem and try to calibrate the ISPI for yourself. Go through each piece and think about who you are. Then think about those close to you – your spouse, significant other, children, parents, siblings, boss, and co-workers. Where might they fall relative to the ISPI? As you begin to observe the various elements of the ISPI, you will become better able to leverage differences. This means you will take advantage of your strengths, as well as the strengths of others.

Organizational Personality

We have covered a lot of ground regarding the predispositions of individuals, but the personality of your organization also plays a major role in innovation. Your organization may have a prevalent risk orientation, be able to create certain types of products (but not others), and attract certain types of people (but not others). The personality of an organization impacts business success. If the innovation leader doesn't understand and isn't able to leverage differences, they will not be able to retain the people required for innovating along the entire innovation continuum. You will end up with clones acting, thinking, and behaving the same way. What you get is the expression, "The nail that stands up gets hammered down." Also, if your only tool is a hammer, everything you have is a nail. If you're only dealing with nails, you'll be in great shape. But in the world of innovation, we deal with people, not nails.

As innovation leaders start to understand and leverage individual differences, they will start to understand the personalities of their organizations. Only then can they truly evaluate and sort potential innovative ideas into those that are aligned with their organizations and those that are not.

In most cases, innovations leaning toward the evolutionary end of the spectrum will naturally be aligned with the organization. Gaining organizational support for these programs is relatively straightforward. Innovation toward the revolutionary end, however, is often not aligned with the current organization. The high-risk nature of these programs requires the innovation leader to understand personalities of both the organization and the key decision makers. This is required when it comes to being able to develop the most appropriate influence strategy to maximize the probability of getting support behind a program.

Advice for the Innovation Leader

Innovation leaders must be comfortable with understanding and identifying differences between people. You must be "bilingual" in your ability to communicate, listen to, and be heard by builders, pioneers, and differing iOMs. You must appreciate and positively recognize the strengths of all people and realize that they are not interchangeable.

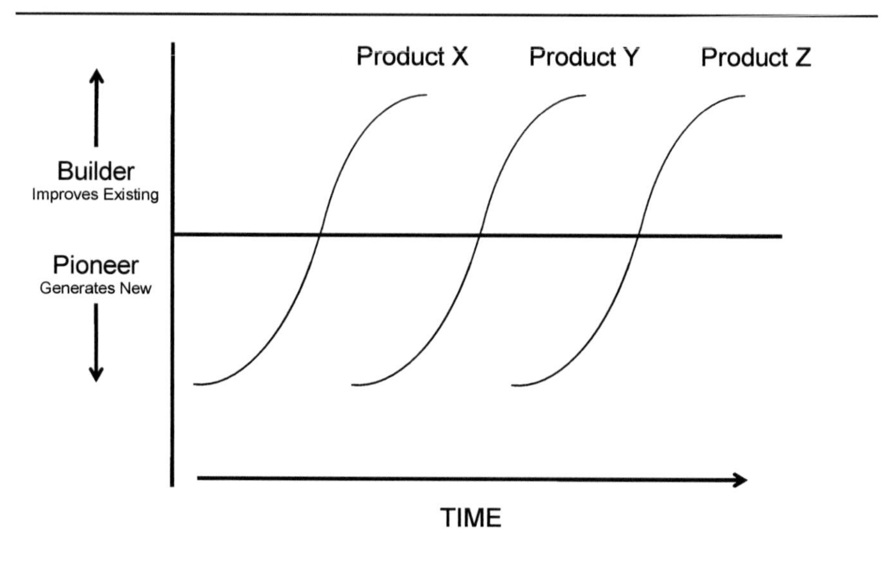

Figure 5.6
As a product goes through its life cycle, the ratio of pioneers to builders shifts. At the beginning of the cycle, the mix is weighted toward the pioneers. As the product matures, the mix shifts to a combination of pioneers and builders and then to mostly builders. As this shift occurs, the pioneers begin development of the next new product to ensure organizational sustainability.

The following model (Figure 5.6) shows a basic way for builders and pioneers to be used in relation to the timeline of a new product or process.[22] It is comparable to a relay race. At the start, you want to go heavy on the pioneers. As the product matures, more mid-range pioneers and mid-range builders should be integrated. At the end, the builders are accountable for optimization, and the pioneers are working on developing a new S-curve. Note that an S-curve for a product or service can last 20 years, 20 months, or 20 weeks.

You can have ideal business practices, technological aids, and creativity tools, but if you have the wrong people, it will be difficult to meet your innovation goals. For innovation to flourish, you need the right people with the right skills, innovation orientation (iO), and innovation orientation modifiers (iOM) – as well as the right tools for working on the right tasks at the right times.

As an innovation leader, you need to:

- Make it a practice to note the iO and iOM of the people you work with. Over time, your eyes and ears will help you identify personality orientations.
- Use iO and iOM as one of the variables in putting together your project teams.
- Use your knowledge of iO and iOM to guide your approach when you try to present to, influence, or manage others.
- Help others understand their invisible differences and how to leverage them.

As the leader, you link the human pieces of the innovation puzzle with the appropriate business and technical pieces. In addition, your job is to help others understand their differences and why the differences within the team are a benefit. The degree to which you value differences will determine the degree to which others will value them.

Remember

Differences are a gift! Look for the gifts and leverage them!

Take the ISPI

As a reader of this book, you are eligible to take a free ISPI. Please send an email to *bookISPI@innovating.com* and an ISPI link and instructions will be sent to you.

Part I
Chapter Six

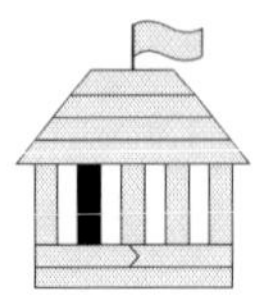

Co-Locate For Effective Exchange

In his bestselling book, *The World Is Flat,* Thomas Friedman presents the argument that in today's world of instant communication, the Internet, open source software development, outsourcing, and so on, the world has become a level playing field.[1] Companies can now develop new products 24/7 and create new software in an open software world (Linux,[2] Apache[3]). More and more people are working out of their homes. When we call to get software help, make reservations, talk to customer service representatives, etc., often we are talking to somebody in a different country – in a totally different part of the world. So, given the age of a "flat world," why are we talking about the need for co-location?

The answer lies in understanding the nature of the innovation being pursued. There are organizations that have been very successful in developing products using teams distributed around the world. Similar to open source software development, these complex systems could be partitioned into reasonably well-defined activities so that each team could perform independently. The innovation that these teams developed, however, has generally been more toward the evolutionary to the expansionary end of the continuum.[4,5] Other than coordination and integration, the level of personal interaction required between team members has been minimal. Similarly, the level of intellectual trust needed to be high; however, the need for emotional trust was minimal. And there was no overriding need for Creativity Partners between the groups.

On the other hand, revolutionary innovation, by its very nature, does not lend itself to clear definitions up front or the necessary separation to allow groups to operate independently. The need for ongoing, frequent interaction is required for maximizing the probability of success. The need for both intellectual and emotional trust is very high here – and teams need to have the open and trusting communication demonstrated by Creativity Partners.

For Creativity Partners to be successful, trust is essential. Trust encourages imagination, allows them to take risks, and spurs on the passion that makes difficult problems solvable. Development of trust between people is enhanced when all human senses are involved in the development of relationships. It helps to be able to examine facial expressions, body movements, and tone of voice.

One way to involve all of the human senses is through co-location. We use the term co-location to mean physical proximity to people. The best way for innovation to occur is for Creativity Partners to be in a face-to-face environment. This means co-location goes beyond conference calls and e-mails. Having people interacting with each other develops trust, understanding, and provides the opportunity to leverage differences.

Building trust and relationships through co-location is especially vital during the early days of developing a new innovation. Co-location is critical during the creation, generation, and brainstorming stages. Human nature causes us to enter into new situations with preconceived notions and to keep our guard up, thus hindering our innovation potential. To quickly and efficiently expand and enhance a new idea, maximizing its potential to turn into a significant innovation, we need a high level of trust among team members. This trust is what allows us to move beyond the internal issues associated with, "Who can I share ideas with? What is their agenda? Will someone steal my idea? And who can I believe?"

As team members get more comfortable with each other, the face-to-face meeting frequency can be reduced, but not eliminated. There will always be a need for periodic reinforcement, face-to-face. The timing will be different for each group, but once trust is established and processes are put in place, then the team can take advantage of technology options – like video and teleconferences and e-mail. However, while team members may use technology for transmitting information, they cannot use it for creating trust.

There is an interesting case study by Adva Dinur from Long Island University that details the acquisition of a Japanese pharmaceutical company by a larger international company.[6] As part of the acquisition, the new company had to learn how to share knowledge with the other research groups. To accomplish this, the following actions were taken:

- An experienced manager was sent to Japan to become the new manager for the first few months.
- There were regular short-term visits by employees to and from the Japanese unit.
- There were long-term exchanges of employees for a period of up to one year.

Despite the above activities, communication issues emerged. Upon analyses, it was determined that "the use of video- and teleconferences could not facilitate mutual understandings, as [could] face-to-face discussions." As a result, the decision was made that major meetings would only be held when all of the key people could be located in the same room. Only later on did more distant communication approaches, via the use of technology, become successful. The bottom line was that, until trust and mutual understanding of the different cultures was established, people needed to meet in person.

The need for co-location varies, based on the goals of the project. When a project is risky, co-location is a necessity – not a "nice to have." In this case, we increase our focus on emotional (heart) trust as opposed to focusing solely on intellectual (head) trust. The less risky the project, the less critical co-location becomes, and the more emphasis there will be on intellectual trust. This is not meant to imply that emotional trust isn't important; however, if the project is of minimal risk, it doesn't need to be a primary concern for the innovation leader.

Another way to look at co-location is to place it on a continuum displaying the innovation goals (Figure 6.1 - next page). At this point ask, "Are the organization's goals evolutionary, expansionary, or revolutionary?" If they are evolutionary, co-location is "nice to have." If they are revolutionary, co-location is a "must have." Co-location provides the opportunity for the team to develop the head and heart trust required to undertake risky innovation programs.

To build trust, the innovation leader should provide the time and opportunity for people to get to know each other beyond the work environment. When people have discussions about things other than work, it lets them relax and lowers inhibitions and internal defenses, allowing them to comfortably take greater risks. This leads to the ultimate goal of disclosure, which builds deeper trust.

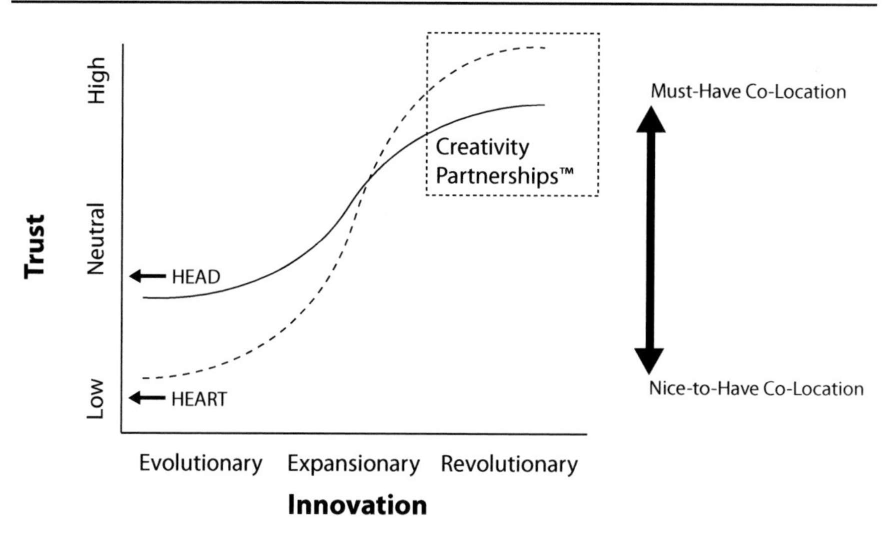

Figure 6.1
Evolutionary innovation can be successfully accomplished with minimal heart or emotional trust so that co-location is not mandatory. In contrast, revolutionary innovation by its very nature is high risk and, therefore, requires a very high level of both head (intellectual) and heart (emotional) trust. Achieving this high level of trust requires that people get to know each other on a face-to-face basis.

There are numerous team-building programs available (including Mosaic Partnerships), but the key here is to provide opportunities for people to get together and interact in ways that facilitate a maximum connection. In the U.S., our culture encourages us to connect one-on-one, whereas other cultures encourage connection in groups. The innovation leader must understand the organization's culture and utilize the approaches best suited for them.

The goal is to allow for appropriate interaction between team members so that trust will be created and enhanced. It doesn't matter how that is accomplished. What is important is that trust builds. As an example, consider the scenario where a group member offers the use of their home for conducting a team activity. When we visit someone's home, we get to know them in a way we don't get to at work. We see the way they live and some of the things most important to them. It provides a sense of open communication that leads to enhanced understanding and trust.

Through co-location, we have seen huge improvements in dysfunctional groups. These groups start off closed but, once they engage in discussions and share personal information, powerful relationships are forged. These types of relationships are obviously productive in the work arena, but they can last well beyond the life of the project or group. The key is taking people out of the work setting and allowing them to get to know each other as people, as opposed to engineers and scientists, business managers and accountants, etc.

Heart (emotional) trust developed in this way tends to create a long-term bond. As discussed in Chapter 2, once trust has been built and people are relating to each other, they don't have to continually communicate. And once the trust is there, it can be rekindled quickly when needed. Time exists in a different dimension with trust.

Advice for the Innovation Leader

In co-locating a team within the same building, make provisions so that people who are working together on an idea can be in close proximity. Arrange offices in ways that encourage dialogue and interaction, which will create trust and the generative communication (Figure 2.1, page 17) required for innovation. We realize there are many reasons for how and why people are assigned offices, but having co-location for innovation as one of them is important. And it might mean avoiding individual offices or breaking away from traditional (often hierarchical) floor plans.

One tip we'd like to offer is that, if possible, locate key Creativity Partners on the same floor and as close together as is practical. Studies have shown that people will walk down a long hall to meet face-to-face more often than walking a flight of stairs. The stairs act as an unknown barrier.

If space is at a premium or the organization's floor plan is set in stone, make meeting rooms readily available. In that way, when a new idea or breakthrough occurs and it needs to be discussed, individuals and groups can meet sooner rather than later. And providing common areas for people to gather and talk informally are major boosts toward innovation. This common area used to be the "water cooler," but it has now evolved. Many companies have break or "creativity" rooms with a relaxed atmosphere that encourages informal interaction and, consequently, allows one to break free from doing and to flow into thinking.

If co-location is not feasible, the innovation leader must create ways to have people interact personally, even for a short period of time. To maximize these short bursts, we recommend using the Mosaic Partnerships Model discussed in Chapter 2. While the Mosaic Partnerships process can't be rushed, it can significantly accelerate the trust-building process (as compared to letting relationships build ad hoc). As was noted earlier, the speed of progression of trust development is different for each individual, and respect for each person's privacy must be maintained. However, the need for progress is required for trust to continue to grow.

In cases where organizations are spread out geographically, it can be more difficult to co-locate. However, there are numerous ways to tackle this issue. One example comes from one of our clients where the team was located all over the world and meeting face-to-face was impractical. The solution was for the innovation leader to fly to each team member and meet with them individually. Because of the one-on-one relationships she built, when the group held conference calls, members had acquired a trust for each other because they trusted their leader. In Chapter 2, we referred to this notion as "transferral of trust" in relation to networking. The same principles apply here, only within the team.

Regardless of whether employee offices are in the same building, or the innovation leader is the trust transfer catalyst, or periodic face-to-face meetings are conducted, the common thread is that for trust to be developed and enhanced, you must find way for people to be "physically" present and interact with each other. This will build the level of trust needed for innovation to occur (especially for building heart trust and working on revolutionary innovations).

Remember

For high levels of trust to develop, people must get to know each other as individuals. The more revolutionary your innovation goals, the more co-location is needed.

Part I

Chapter Seven

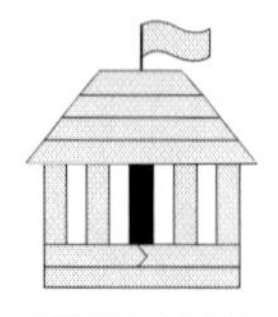

Passion Is the Fuel and Pain Is the Hidden Ingredient

The center pillar of the Innovation House is Passion and Pain. The reason for this is that innovation is a complicated road with many bumps, forks, wrong turns, and potholes. The process of creating something new does not happen overnight. Passion is what transforms people's energy and actions into profits, yet it never shows up on a balance sheet. Passion is the fuel that keeps people moving forward on the innovation road.

In some cases, it can take multiple years to turn an idea into an innovation. In 1968, Dr. Spencer Silver, a researcher at 3M, created what became Post-it® Notes.[1,2] At that time, 3M's focus was on adhesives that "worked," not ones that didn't stick. Dr. Silver spent five years sharing his invention internally, but to no avail. Post-it® Notes did not fit the 3M model.

In 1974, Art Fry, an employee of 3M who had been introduced to Post-it® Notes, decided to use the notes to mark pages in his hymnal book. Over the next six years, Fry **championed** Post-it® Notes (both internally and externally), eventually leading to large-scale success in 1980.

Because of the internal dynamics of 3M and the marketplace, it took 12 years for Post-it® Notes to go from idea to successful innovation. At any time along the way, Silver or Fry could have given up their push. But they didn't – and it was their passion that propelled Post-it® Notes to a must-have on desks around the world.

The passion required for innovation is directly proportional to the degree of risk being undertaken. Referring back to the Innovation Continuum, revolutionary innovation requires a greater amount of individual and organizational risk and, therefore, carries a far greater need for passion than evolutionary innovation (Figure 7.1). As an example, consider that the amount of passion it takes for a person to walk up five flights of stairs is much different than the passion it takes for that same person to climb Mount Everest.

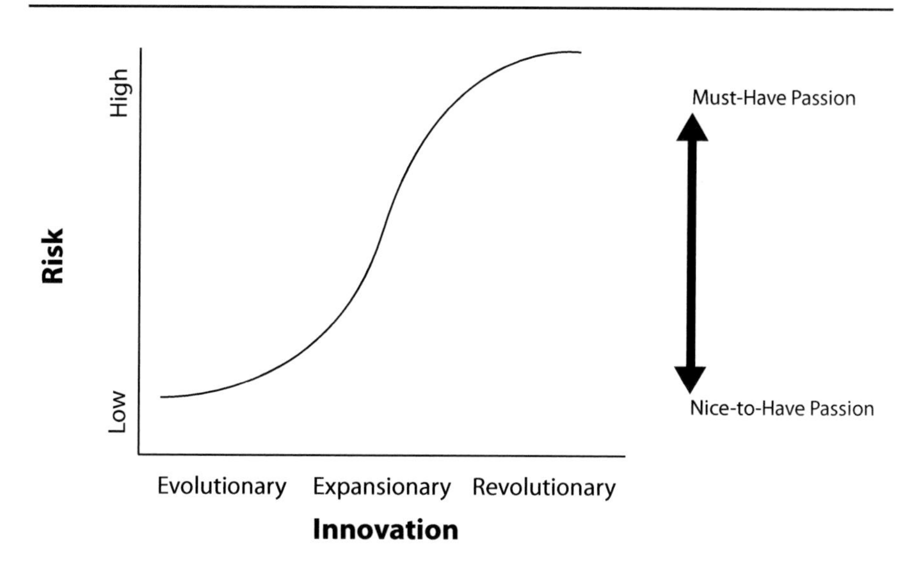

Figure 7.1
Evolutionary innovation can be successfully accomplished without significant levels of passion. Revolutionary innovation needs passionate people, due to the high level of risk and associated obstacles that must be overcome. Passion is the fuel that allows people to accept the risks and overcome the obstacles.

To understand passion, we need to start at the individual level. In any field, there are people with similar abilities and opportunities. Yet, we continuously see examples where individuals are able to move from average to extraordinary and accomplish more than their peers. In sports, there are countless examples of people with lesser natural abilities being able to outperform their peers and of significant underdogs beating individuals or teams with potentially greater talent. What powers them to do so? What powered Bill Gates and Paul Allen to drop out of college and lead Microsoft to superiority? What fueled Martin Luther King and Mahatma Gandhi to create change in their countries?

Two of the key fators are:

- Passion and drive
- The ability to overcome obstacles (or pain)

Are there people you know or have heard about who have achieved greatness without being passionate about what they do? Our guess is probably not.

Now think of two or three people in your company who are (or were) passionate. What distinguishes them from everyone else? Does your organization truly trust passionate people? If they have left the organization, why? If they have stayed, why?

In our work, finding passionate people is not the problem; it is protecting and nurturing them so they produce results.

"The man with a new idea is a crank until the idea succeeds."
Mark Twain[3]

Mark Twain's comment rings true, because new ideas are inherently risky and different. Just ask Dr. Silver or Art Fry.

And don't forget the story of Charles Kettering. He created a solution at General Motors that reduced the amount of time for paint to dry on a car from 17 days to one hour. Yet, from idea creation to idea implementation, Kettering's new way of doing things was met with resistance and obstacles. He was told, "It's not our standard."

There are many times in Kettering's story where organizational close-mindedness or bureaucratic roadblocks could have derailed his idea. He could have said, "Oh well, the timing just isn't right." If his energy level was sapped, he might have said, "I just don't care anymore." He could have given up or shelved the idea and said, "I'll come back to this."

In innovation, there will be many times when it might be easier to give up rather than to push on. That is why passion is so important. Without passionate people, ideas and results will be lost. People lacking passion often give in to thinking, "There will be a better time for new ideas."

But Kettering's innovation became a reality because of his passion. If he wasn't passionate about his job at General Motors, Kettering could have given up. He could have done what we've seen other passionate people do: shut down, remain silent and never share their ideas, try and derail other people's ideas, become passive-aggressive, quit, or become a clock puncher (i.e., someone who has quit mentally, yet still shows up every day to collect a paycheck).

Passion Is Misunderstood

Passionate people, especially Extreme Pioneers and Pioneers, are misunderstood. We have seen time and time again where they are ostracized because they "rock the boat" or create havoc and tension. They are looked at as people to be avoided or gotten rid of. We have seen regime changes and downsizing cause a disproportionate number of pioneers to be let go because they are outliers from the normal culture.

People like Silver, Fry, and Kettering need to be nurtured. This is not always easy, because passionate people are different and typically don't fit in. Passionate people are hard to predict and hard to control. They make most leaders nervous. When we have people who are unpredictable and hard to control, we don't utilize them. We shun them or try to fit them into a box so, if they do get out of control, their potential harm will be minimal. But there is a catch here: The people predisposed to create and implement revolutionary ideas are exactly the people who shut down when controlled or put into a box.

The dichotomy is this: Organizations want new, revolutionary ideas and innovations, but they don't work well with the people who best produce them.

Take a moment to think about how passionate people are viewed in your organization. Are they seen as irritants who need to be expelled? Are their sometimes erratic and unpredictable behaviors continuously met with disapproval? Are their failures viewed as too numerous for their own good? Do they cause pain?

Alternatively, are they seen as people who (if supported, tolerated, and nurtured) could produce extraordinary results – results no one else could achieve?

The more you can fit passionate people into your organization and innovation systems, the more they will positively impact both top-line and bottom-line results.

You might be asking, "What distinguishes people of passion?" First, they are oblivious to normal reward and punishment. Acceptance and approval are not very important to them. Time and social commitments are secondary. The thrill of discovery is what really matters. As such, they inherently cause pain.

However, this pain is the hidden ingredient. It is an indicator of their emotional attachment to their idea, job, and organization. The pain of passionate people can be both internal and external. It might cause anguish and frustration, long days and sleepless nights, rejection and ridicule by peers, missed appointments, ignored deadlines, anger from others, or (at the extreme) sabotage. And the pain can extend to family, co-workers, and management.[4]

Without a doubt, we know that you can't buy passion, but you sure can destroy it. Passion can be killed easily, but it cannot be grown instantly.

How do you foster passion? First, you must acknowledge that you can't force someone to be passionate. However, you can foster passion by nurturing trust and soft values, by choosing the right innovation system, by putting people in assignments that build on their passions, as well as by placing and managing passionate people differently.

Passion Has a Fuel Cell

"Every production of genius must be the production of enthusiasm."
Benjamin Disraeli[5]
English Writer and Politician

We've already said that revolutionary innovation is not easy. During the implementation of almost every new idea, there will be junctures where people can give up, wait for a better time, or press onward. Passion, energy, drive, and determination are what spur ideas forward. Organizations must function as enablers, not deterrents, for passionate people so that they can generate positive results.

All people have fuel cells. Innovation results are dependent on how much fuel gets devoted to innovative activities. No matter how much passion someone has for something, if there is roadblock upon roadblock, then the passion will disappear. If your company is made up of a close-minded bureaucracy, passionate people will be hindered. If people feel trusted and encouraged, they can focus on innovation.

The secret is in analyzing the roadblocks to ensure that you are not settling for "good enough" when you might achieve greatness. If the path is too easy, an innovation can falls short of its true potential. If the path is too burdensome, however, the innovation may not come to fruition. Much like successful coaches who know how to get the most out of their players, the innovation leader needs to push the passionate innovators, but do so without directing all of their passion toward fighting unnecessary obstacles.

The Innovation Leader

Innovation leaders play a vital role in passion and pain. They must identify the people they want on their team. It is important to know that there are two fundamentally different types of passionate people. The first are people with the passion but not the skills for innovation. The second are people who are both passionate and skilled – they are the **Paradigm Creators™**.[6] They are people like Benjamin Franklin, Marie Curie, Bill Gates, George Washington, Mother Teresa, Martin Luther King, Albert Einstein, Mahatma Gandhi, Confucius, Susan B. Anthony, Steve Jobs, Muhammad Yunus, and others all around the world. They are individuals with the passion and skill to overcome the pain associated with breaking free from existing paradigms. They are people who have changed the world. Likewise, they can be a phenomenal asset to an organization when nurtured and leveraged appropriately.

It is critical for an innovation leader to assess whether a person is a Paradigm Creator™ or simply someone with a misguided passion who is creating undesirable dissidence. It would be nice if there were a simple psychological instrument that would allow the innovation leader to distinguish between the two. Unfortunately, there isn't.

Even though the "misguided to genius" instrument is not readily available, think about sitting down with a successful Paradigm Creator in the early stages of their creation of a new idea. What type of discussion could a successful innovation leader have here? Why did Einstein move away from Newtonian Physics? Because Newtonian Physics was not adequate to represent observable phenomenon; so Einstein thought there must be something else. New paradigms are created when the existing ones are no longer adequate to represent current realities. So, it is imperative to examine the rationale for why the current paradigms may be inadequate and to determine if the proposed new ones will meet current needs. At this point, it becomes a judgment call on the part of the innovation leader as to whether or not the Paradigm Creator possesses the requisite skill set.

In Chapter 5, we discussed the ISPI and the continuum of an individual's predisposition for solving problems (from builder to pioneer). In the context of Passion and Pain, Paradigm Creators do not always have to be pioneers. Similarly, not every pioneer has the capability to become a Paradigm Creator. Paradigm Creators possess both passion and drive for overcoming obstacles (and the related pain) associated with creating new paradigms. They may lean more toward being builders, taking a pioneering idea and making it a reality. In fact, many extreme pioneers do not have the focus or people skills to be able to create new paradigms.

Successful innovation leaders have the ability to pair potential Paradigm Creators with the appropriate idea generators in order to create a desirable mix of breakthrough ideas. In so doing, they will introduce people with enough passion and drive to successfully turn such ideas into revolutionary innovations. We advise organizations not to put bureaucrats in charge of projects that require passion or a significant level of revolutionary innovation, as they will end up being more of a liability than an asset to these projects. When an innovation leader is supportive, protective, and nurturing, passion fuel will be released. If the innovation leader does not have these skills, passion fuel will be diverted toward trying to convince others in the organization that the innovation is necessary, or toward overcoming bureaucracy.

In every innovation group, there is a quantum level of passion. Innovation leaders must determine how they want that passion used: fighting to get things done within the system, or running with ideas and pulling out all the stops to turn them into quantifiable gains.

Advice for the Innovation Leader

Manage the passion (and the pain), not the person. Doing so will require a trusting relationship between the innovation leader and the person with passion.

- Remember that passion is not available on command.[7]
- Protect the person with passion.
- Gently focus that person's attention and energy.
- Provide encouragement.
- Find (or create) a place in the organization that person can fit into.

Remember:

Do not be afraid of passionate people. They provide the fuel to make innovation happen. If your organization supports and nurtures them, when the going gets tough, they will keep going.

Part I
Chapter Eight

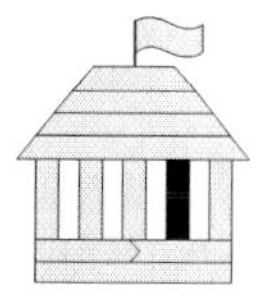

Innovation Starts When Problems Are Converted Into Ideas

In 1851, Elias Howe received a patent for an "Automatic, Continuous Clothing Closure."[1] This was the earliest disclosure of a device that we now take for granted. It is believed that Howe did not pursue this invention because: (1) he was more interested in the sewing machine, and (2) he did not see a significant need for the closure device at that time.

In the 1890s, Whitcomb Judson had a friend who had a bad back. He was unable to bend over and lace up his shoes. Judson, who loved machines and gadgets, developed a slide fastener that could be opened or closed with one hand – similar to what Howe had developed 40 years earlier. Judson eventually invented the "clasp lock" and patented it in 1893.[2]

A Swedish-born scientist named Gideon Sunback refined Judson's original idea. Sunback continued to improve on the device and patented his "separable fastener" in 1917. The U.S. Army in World War I adopted this redesign, which made the fastener more streamlined and reliable.

Only after the B.F. Goodrich Company began to incorporate the device into galoshes in 1925 did the device known as the "clasp lock" become trademarked as the "zipper."

What started as an idea without a real problem became a solution (70 years later) for a real problem – for a friend who could not lace up his shoes.

We all generate countless ideas every day, the majority of which end up being forgotten almost immediately. Only those ideas that have the potential to solve problems that are important to us have the potential to be nurtured and developed into innovations. Sometimes ideas are generated where we need to find the problem that the idea solves, like George de Mestral's invention of Velcro.[3] In his case, he discovered the idea of Velcro (combination of the words velour and crochet) on a walk with his dog. At the time, he was not trying to solve any identified problem. Other times, ideas are generated specifically to solve a problem we have already identified (such as Judson developing a zipper to help his friend). However, whether the idea or problem comes first, ideas are still required for the innovation process.

For effective ideation, innovation leaders must consider the three elements depicted in Figure 8.1.

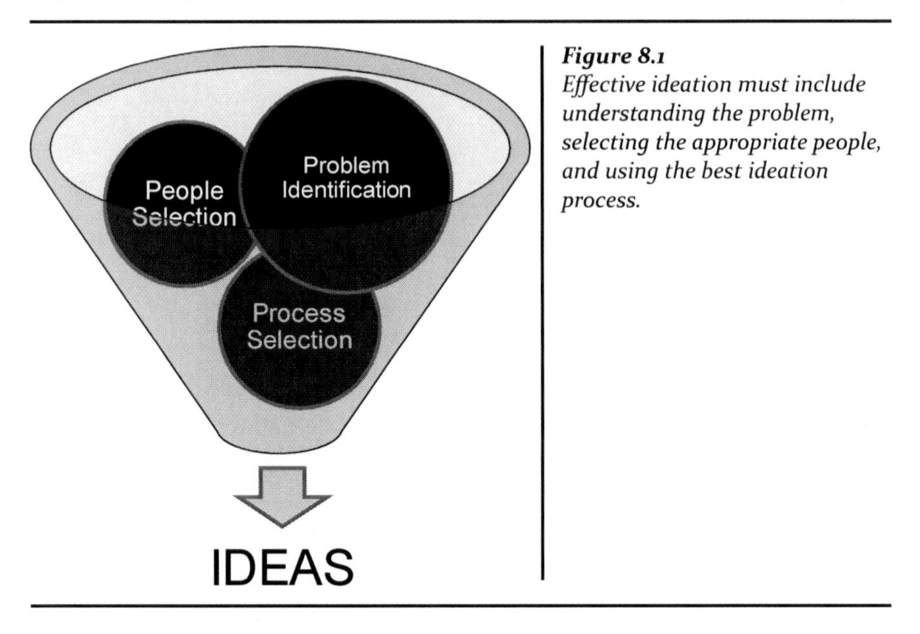

Figure 8.1
Effective ideation must include understanding the problem, selecting the appropriate people, and using the best ideation process.

Only by fully understanding the problem can an innovation leader define the types of ideas to be sought. Through this understanding, the best mix of people and processes can be selected to maximize potential for generating relevant ideas.

Many believe that the more ideas you generate, the more innovation you will have. This is simply not the case. **Ideas by themselves do not create innovation.** Only ideas that can be used to solve real problems have the ability to turn into innovations.

A **problem** is an issue or anything that challenges you. For example, take a moment to look at the objects in your current surroundings. Whatever you see is likely something that has been modified or is the result of someone having an idea. The pen you use to take notes with, the paper this book is printed on, the light that allows you to read, the heat or air conditioning that allows you to be comfortable, and the laptop you browse the Internet with are all examples of someone converting a problem into an idea and, ultimately, an executable solution.

An **idea** is a mental concept or image. Ideas originate from people. Some of these people are great; some are ordinary. But all have at least one thing in common: They are able to identify ideas that allow problems to be solved.

Ideas come from three types of stimuli: external, internal, and group. In Rosenfeld's book, he showed an example of **external stimuli** with the story of Georges de Mestra (1907-1990) and his discovery of Velcro. His discovery was based on examining cockle burrs on his coat after taking a walk in the woods with his dog. Friedrich Kekule's (1829-1896) insight that the carbon chain of the organic compound benzene was ring-shaped was based on a dream that he had about snakes.[4] This is an example of **internal stimuli**. And the story of Kodak linking two ideas, one from a security guard and one from a chemical engineer, which solved a new security problem,[5] is an example of **group stimuli**.

All three forms of stimuli are important to innovation and have shown success throughout history. Since group stimulus is more aligned with how the innovation leader can directly influence the bringing together of people and ideas, this chapter is primarily focused on the use of groups to generate ideas to solve existing, predefined, or previously unidentified problems.

Knowing where ideas come from is one thing; knowing how they develop is another. Graham Wallas defined a timeless model of idea development that was explained in Rosenfeld's book; therefore, we will only summarize it here.[6,7]

Preparation involves investigating a problem resulting in a comprehensive problem statement. The importance of this activity is often overlooked. People jump into seeking solutions too quickly. The more the problem can be clearly stated (and, therefore, understood), the better the solutions will be.

Incubation is a time when one takes a break from the problem. Many people maintain that this is the time when the unconscious mind takes over to work on the problem.

Illumination leads to a flash of insight where things that were not connected suddenly come together – sometimes referred to as the "Aha!" moment.

Validation is when this flash of insight is tested in ways that can be verified.

Again, the first step in effective idea generation is problem identification. Through understanding the true nature of the problem, the innovation leader can identify the types of ideas required. Mapping the problem onto the Innovation Continuum (see page xiv) will help in further defining the types of ideas wanted.

One way to do so is to examine where your organization is relative to the Product Life Cycle Continuum (or PLCC), as displayed in Figure 8.2. Where you are on the PLCC determines where you are on the Innovation Continuum – and determines the types of ideas needed and, subsequently, the types of people needed to generate those ideas.

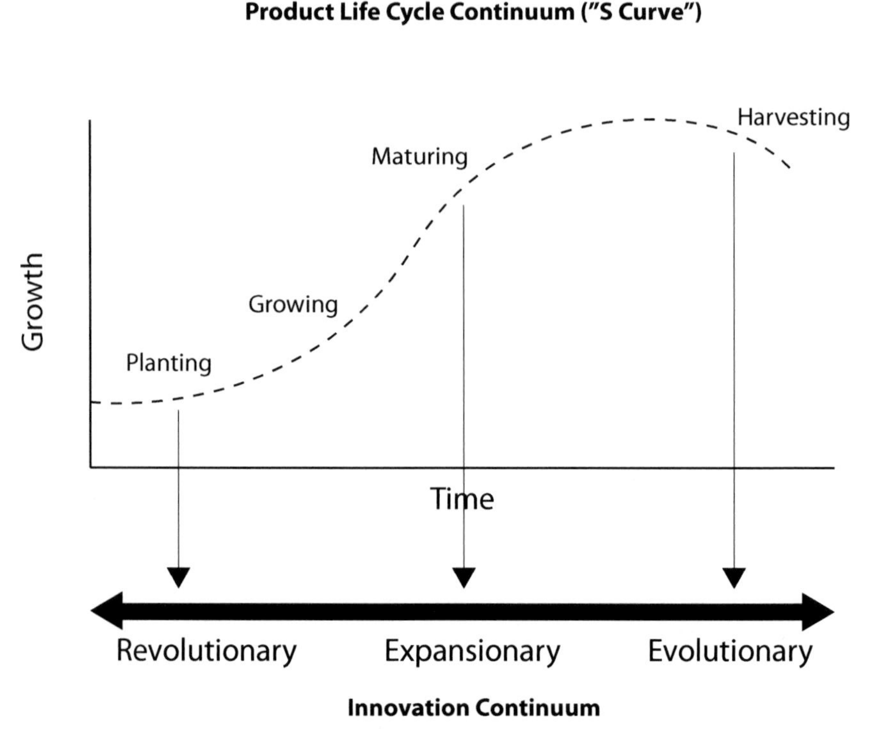

Figure 8.2
Product Life Cycle Continuum (PLCC) or "S Curve." Knowing where a problem focus is on the PLCC allows an innovation leader to identify the types of ideas required.

Look at the PLCC as if you were a farmer. In the winter, you would decide what you want to grow, what seeds you want to use, and what tools you will need for planting in the springtime. This starts a new S curve. Once the seeds are **planted**, they need to be nurtured and allowed to **grow** and mature. At the end of the cycle, the crop is **harvested**. Once the harvest is over, the life cycle of that crop has ended. All products go through a similar life cycle. At the end of a product's life cycle, we squeeze out as much revenue as we can.

By considering the PLCC in relation to the Innovation Continuum, an innovation leader can gauge what types of ideas are desired. If your organization is maintaining its product line (harvesting), you'd generally want to encourage more evolutionary ideas. If you are looking for brand new products and ideas (planting), however, you'd want to seek out more revolutionary ideas.

Once a problem is identified, there must also be alignment between the types of ideas required and the people generating them. Remember, as discussed in Chapter 5, people have a predisposition for idea generation based on their ISPI scores.

If your organization is addressing Lean Six Sigma problems, you want people who are more in the evolutionary or expansionary range on the Innovation Continuum. You also want a process that is structured. Generally, people who have a predisposition toward the builder or mid-range builder fit well here.

If you are looking for revolutionary ideas, though, you want significantly different people. The process required for revolutionary ideas would drive a Six Sigma person crazy! People who have a predisposition toward extreme pioneering or pioneering fit better into the domain of generating revolutionary ideas.

When you examine people in your organization, realize that their (internal) attitudes will lead to their (external) behaviors. If they are generally optimistic, they will be good at building on ideas. If they are accepting of new things, then they will give early support to ideas. If they enjoy connecting with people, they will help set up win-win relationships. If they are open and available, others will not fear being punished for bringing new ideas to them. If they assume something will work, they will spur on positive cooperation. (The ISPI is an excellent tool for helping you analyze people's preferences.)

If you don't have access to the ISPI when thinking about your people, assess their preferred ideation orientation using our Ideation Competency Assessment Tool (Figure 8.3 – next page). Note that a high score is not better or worse than a low score; rather, it is all dependent on goals for ideation. Consequently, it is very important to accurately identify the problem.

Once you have your people in place, **you will need to place them in the appropriate environment to effectively generate ideas**. In the next chapter, we will explain in more detail how innovation needs a system. For now, it is important to note that an office environment is generally not conducive to generating revolutionary ideas. Disney World may not be

ATTRIBUTE	Not Evident			Very Evident	
Drives own ideas	1	2	3	4	5
Intrinsically motivated	1	2	3	4	5
Tolerance of ambiguity	1	2	3	4	5
Pursues novelty	1	2	3	4	5
Considers others' viewpoints	1	2	3	4	5
Openness to experience	1	2	3	4	5
Associated expertise	1	2	3	4	5
Broad life experiences	1	2	3	4	5
Creative synthesis	1	2	3	4	5

Total of the scores: ____

SCORE	
8 - 16	Very structured ideation process (e.g., mind mapping)
16 - 32	Fairly structured idea generation processes (e.g., brainstorming)
32 - 40	Open / minimal structure (e.g., excursionary, dream interpretation)

Figure 8.3
Look at your potential idea generators. Rate each person on a scale of 1 - 5 (with 1 meaning they don't possess an attribute, and 5 meaning they possess it strongly). What does this tell you? What does it tell you about the type of facilitator you need?

the ideal location to develop evolutionary ideas, either. The key is that the environment must be aligned with both the people and the process. It must be conducive to allowing the participants to feel comfortable, safe, and willing to share their thoughts and ideas.

Most organizations have two main types of ideation (or idea generation): Planned and Unplanned.

Planned ideation (similar to **Targeted Innovation** in Chapter 9) is directed from the top down. It is part of normal management strategies. Many of these ideas are in response to specific problems or challenges. Planned ideation generally produces incremental to expansionary ideas. If you have the proper mix of Pioneers and Extreme Pioneers, it can also produce revolutionary ideas. Planned ideation is based on the notion of having predefined problems for groups to address.

In contrast, **unplanned ideation** (similar to **Originator Assisted** in Chapter 9) rises from the **bottom up** and tends to be untidy, erratic, and unpredictable. Results often come serendipitously, meaning we seek one idea and find another. Unplanned ideation generally produces more breakthrough ideas and is often generated concurrently with the problem definition.[8]

Whether planned or unplanned, ideation requires the innovation leader to understand the three steps of turning problems into ideas: Problem Identification, People Selection, and Process Selection. These steps are interrelated and must work synergistically. They will lead to maximized potential for the organization and provide the ideas required to drive your innovation systems. (We will be discussing Innovation Systems in the next chapter.)

In most cases, without a champion to promote them, ideas that are generated often go into a "**black hole.**" They fill up notebooks (or databases) that sit on shelves collecting dust. Effective use of ideas requires that they be moved forward quickly, either to further development or to being consciously shelved. Ideas that have been generated and go unaddressed are actually worse than not having them at all. If your organization is not going to actively do something with these ideas, why spend valuable time and energy to generate them?

Unfortunately, too many businesses spend the time to generate ideas, but not the time to screen them and develop the good ones into innovation concepts. This not only wastes resources, but (more critically) the employees witness the related behaviors and follow suit – i.e., they stop generating ideas. If nothing happens with ideas, how excited will employees be to generate them? What message does this send about how their ideas are valued?

Advice for the Innovation Leader

You must have a flow of ideas to drive your overall innovation system, and they need to be aligned with the goals and objectives of your organization. To accomplish this, you need to consider the following 10 steps:

Define the problem:

1. Determine what the focus is, using the Product Life Cycle Continuum
2. Identify the problem and the types of ideas needed.
   - Evolutionary
   - Expansionary
   - Revolutionary

Define the ideation process:

3. Determine the approach to be used.
4. Based on numbers 1, 2, and 3, identify and select the proper participants, including facilitators and content expert(s)
    - We use the ISPI to help us do this. It allows us to have **domain experts** who collaborate and communicate effectively. (See Chapter 5).
5. Identify the appropriate environment.
6. Conduct the session.
7. Transform the output into final concepts to be addressed.

Sell the ideas:

8. Identify key champions for the concepts.
9. Move concepts forward quickly.
10. Communicate concepts appropriately.

When considering these steps, ask yourself the following questions:

- Do you and your innovation leaders have a burning passion to find and develop new ideas?
- Do you have a system for finding new ideas?
- Does your system for finding new ideas allow everyone in your organization to contribute where appropriate?
- Does your entire infrastructure support finding and developing new ideas?
- If so, why? If not, why not?

Remember

All innovations start with problems being converted into ideas. Generating ideas requires good problem definitions, along with engaging the right people and processes

---

Part I

Chapter Nine

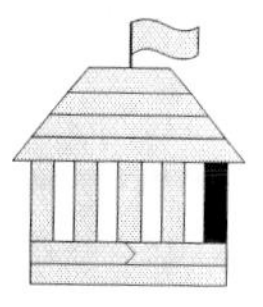

Innovation Needs a System

The B-17, or "Flying Fortress," was instrumental in winning World War II in Europe. In total, 12,700 planes were produced.[1] Surprisingly, the B-17 was almost never built. In July 1935, the Boeing Model 299 (which ultimately became the B-17) was in an evaluation flight against the Douglas and Martin entries.[2] In all of the previous tests, the Boeing entry significantly outperformed the two rival entries. Indeed, the assumption was that the final evaluation flights were merely formalities. From Wright Field in Dayton, Ohio, the plane began a smooth takeoff and climb – only to stall and crash. The Boeing Model 299 not only lost the competition but also nearly ceased to exist.

The investigation into the crash revealed pilot error. The pilot neglected to release the elevator lock pin prior to takeoff, which ultimately caused the crash. Even though the Army Air Corps gave the contract to Douglas for the Douglas DB-1, several key members of the Air Corps decided to allow Boeing to keep the Model 299 alive and ordered 13 experimental airplanes for further testing. Boeing and the Air Corps both realized that if there were any further accidents, the program would be stopped. The key issue was that the plane was viewed as too complex for a pilot to fly.

The pilots got together and came up with an innovation that is still a part of aviation today. They devised the first set of aviation checklists that outlined what a pilot needed to do before takeoff, during flight, before landing, and after landing. They took what was "too much airplane for any one man to fly" and turned it into a phenomenal success story. Today, aviation checklists are an integral part of professional life for both military and civilian pilots around the world. This relatively simple innovation was crucial for allowing B-17 pilots to successfully navigate through the complexities of flying this state-of-the-art, multi-engine bomber. Similarly, without a checklist, navigating through the complexities of innovation in large organizations can be just as daunting as trying to fly a B-17.

Clearly defined systems are a must for innovation so that people can readily understand or have "checklists" to help them. This does not mean that there must be a rigid innovation process. The processes themselves can be quite flexible and easily adapted to the type of innovation being pursued. However, they need to be visible to the innovators. Otherwise, the innovators are flying by the "seat of their pants" with the end result being that good, innovative ideas are often lost or, worse yet, become innovation vampires: programs that never move forward or die, but simply suck the lifeblood out of a company and discredit overall innovation efforts.

Another way to look at this is to think about what would happen if you tried to drive around any major city in the world in the absence of street signs. Unless you had a GPS[3] device, you would probably get lost. The same is true for people and organizations. Since there are no innovation GPS devices, people need to know how to navigate the system(s) in order to turn innovative ideas into innovations.

Innovation systems provide an infrastructure that helps release the creative potential of employees. The GPS doesn't dictate the desired destination – it only supplies directions on how to get there. Likewise, an innovation system is not there to tell the innovators what they should be doing. Instead, it is there to facilitate converting their ideas into successful innovations.

Innovation systems are there to serve the innovators, not the other way around.

Understanding Innovation Systems

Just as there is not a generic model for all businesses, there is not a universal innovation system. Different types of innovation require different types of systems. Sadly, too many organizations develop a single system and try to force all innovation through it.

This situation occurs when innovation leaders become too attached to what has historically worked for organizations. They try to force fit what they have become comfortable with into all situations, not realizing that they have just created major roadblocks for innovators. As we discussed in Chapter 3, the adherence to a "This is how we've always done it" approach creates a significant element of destruction. It would be like a professional golfer trying to use a driver for all of their golf shots, or an innovation leader trying to use Lean Six Sigma for all innovation needs within an organization.

In Rosenfeld's earlier book, five generic types of Innovation Systems were identified and described in detail. Therefore, we will only reference them here and provide a brief definition for each one.[4]

- **Originator Assisted** – Helps employees transform their own ideas into business opportunities (bottom up innovation). Creating, installing and maintaining an **Office of Innovation** requires the selection of an Innovation Champion and **Innovation Advocates**. The training and mentoring for the staff is extensive and ongoing. Results will span the entire Innovation Continuum from revolutionary to evolutionary. True game changers can be derived from an Originator Assisted system.

- **Targeted Innovation** – Develops solutions to meet a specific need (top-down driven innovation). It requires identifying the problem, determining the ideal people to participate, setting up the proper ideation process, and then communicating the ideas. When you need to innovate, Targeted Innovation can provide immediate impact. Results typically range from evolutionary to slightly beyond expansionary, but may extend towards more revolutionary with the right people and process.

- **Internal Venturing** – Helps launch new businesses that don't fit the company's current lines of business.

- **Continuous Improvement** – Provides incremental improvements that lead to cost savings or increased quality (e.g., Six Sigma).

- **Strategic Transfer** – Shifts technology or knowledge from one point to another for the purpose of leveraging capabilities.

As shown in Figure 9.1 (next page), the five different types of systems tend to focus on different parts of the Innovation Continuum.

What we have found is that all successful innovation programs include one or more of these systems. The key is to understand what type of system (or

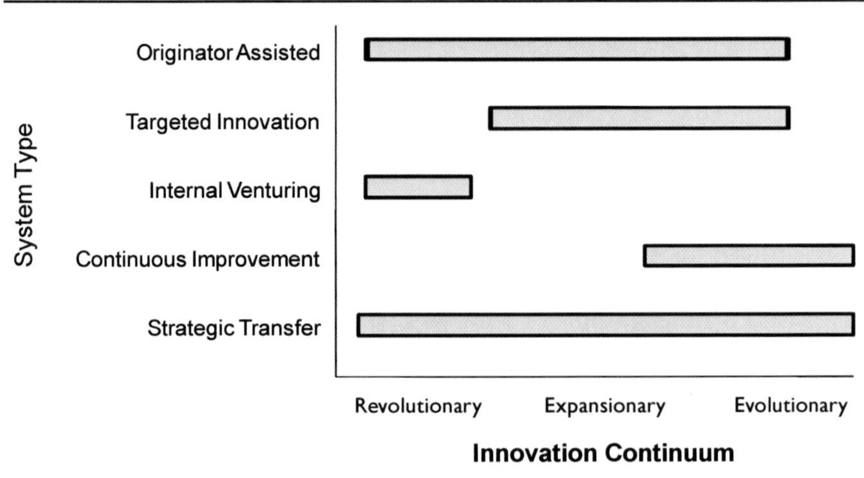

Figure 9.1
Different types of systems are generally required to support innovation targeting different areas of the Innovation Continuum.

hybrid) is most appropriate for the desired innovation focus and to make the system visible enough to allow the innovators to leverage it effectively. This requires understanding the:

- organization's innovation priorities
- types of problems being addressed
- ISPI (or like indicator) of innovators
- stage of development relative to the product life cycle continuum
- needs of innovators and key stakeholders

Innovation leaders can optimize the systems for addressing evolutionary, expansionary, or revolutionary ideas; depending upon what they are facing, all of the five systems (or a hybrid of them) may be necessary.

Current System

Every business currently has systems in place. They may be formal and visible, or informal and invisible. The system for processing new ideas within a company of three may be decision-making sessions over coffee. In contrast, a company of 30,000 will have many more steps in its decision-making process. The bigger the organization (and associated bureaucracy), the more important it is to provide people with innovation street signs (or a GPS system).

In large bureaucracies that do not have the street signs or GPS systems, successful innovators learn to develop informal systems to get their work accepted. We refer to this process as the "informal grid." These ad hoc, generally invisible, systems are the connections and steps people use to get things done that circumvent a broken or confusing system. While these systems can be successful, not all innovators will be able to navigate through the informal grid. And because they are informal, it is harder to analyze and track the strengths and weaknesses of these innovation systems. In addition, which energy is more desirable: energy expended on moving the innovation forward, or that which is expended to overcome unnecessary bureaucracy?

If your innovation programs aren't working out as planned, stop and take a breath, reserve judgment, and follow the informal grid to answer these questions:

- How do things really get done?
- If you really want to do something, how can you make it happen?

At the same time, realize that bureaucracy in and of itself is not a bad thing. The human body is like a bureaucracy. It runs the same way every day and, when it doesn't, we get sick or die. If an organization's innovation system is understood, streamlined, and supportive of what people are trying to do – and they see it as an asset – then they will use it. If not, they will develop an informal grid to get around it.

Innovation Portfolio

Now that you know why having a system is vital to the success of innovation, the next step is to understand the type of system(s) needed. As such, you must first understand your company's current and desired innovation portfolio. The idea of an innovation portfolio was introduced in Chapter 1, Figure 1.3 (page 12). However, we are going to expand this analysis to help you: (1) look more closely at your organization's current state with regard to innovation, and (2) examine where you need to be to meet growth objectives.

The road map to developing an innovation portfolio begins with two basic questions:

- Where is your growth coming from now?

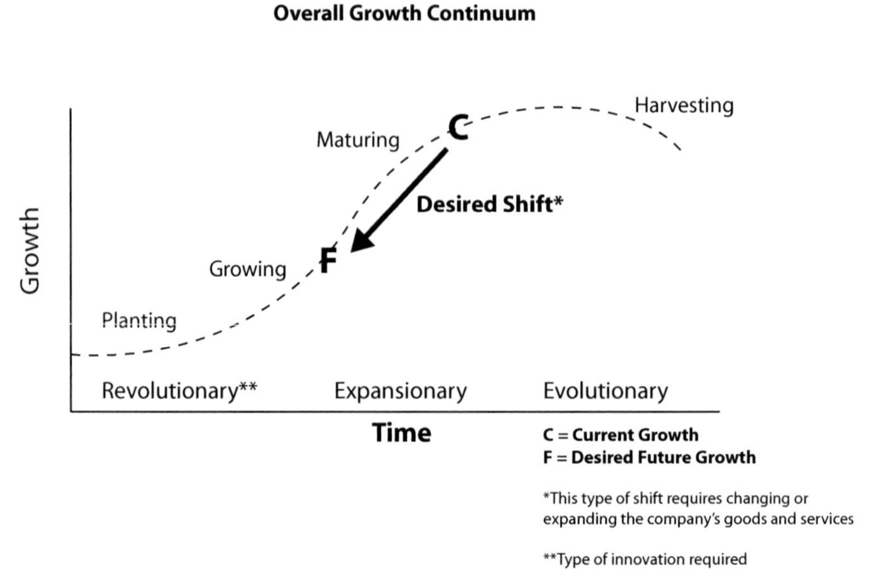

Figure 9.2
Analysis of the current versus the desired future growth mechanism. This is the first step toward beginning to define the types of systems your organization will need to support its desired innovation activities.

- Where do you want your growth to be coming from in five years?

One way to uncover the answers to these questions is to look at them on a Growth Continuum S Curve (Figure 9.2).

As an example, in Figure 9.2, we have plotted the current growth (C) toward the top of the "maturing" section of the S curve. This implies that there is still room for potential growth without making a significant shift. However, the cost of getting this growth (due to cannibalization[5] and actual development costs and complexities) may result in failing to achieve desired growth. Assuming this is the case, in our example we plotted desired future growth as being more of a balance, resulting in a shift backward toward the upper end of the growing section (F). To achieve this type of shift, a company must expand its portfolio of goods and services.

Figure 9.3
Matrix of an organization's growth based on the current mix of existing and new markets and products/ technologies. This matrix allows the innovation leader to analyze and determine how to rebalance the organization's innovation portfolio.

Once you have a general visualization of the current and desired future growth mechanisms, the next step is to translate this into the Growth Portfolio Matrix (Figure 9.3 - next page).

The data for this matrix is generated by looking at the following four questions:

1. What percentage of growth will come from existing Products/ Technologies for existing Markets (Quadrant I)?
2. What percentage of growth will come from new Products/ Technologies for existing Markets (Quadrant II)?
3. What percentage of growth will come from existing Products/ Technologies for new Markets (Quadrant III)?
4. What percentage of growth will come from new Products/ Technologies for new Markets (Quadrant IV)?

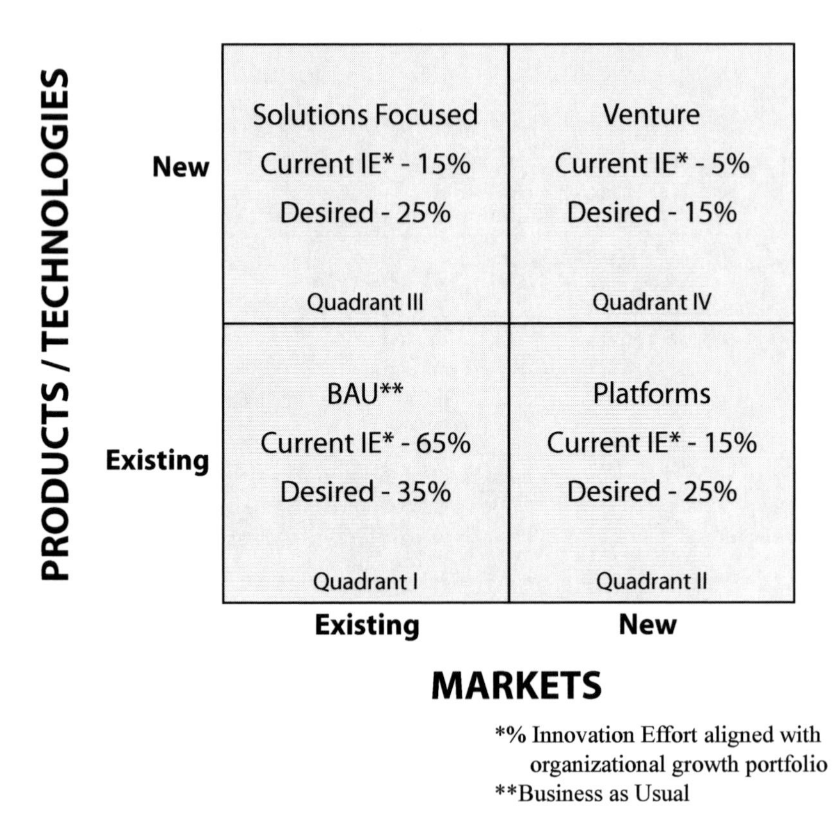

Figure 9.4
Rebalanced innovation portfolio based on the desired organization growth rebalancing in Figure 9.3

These questions are first answered for current growth and then, later on, for desired future growth. In our example, the current and desired percentages align with the desired shift in the growth mechanism from Figure 9.2 and reflect a desire to rebalance the growth to include new markets, as well as new products/technologies.

The innovation leader can now translate the desired rebalancing of growth into a rebalancing of the total innovation portfolio. This involves not only looking at the growth matrix, but also at the risk/probability of success associated with each area of the innovation portfolio. Innovation in the "existing/existing" quadrant (I) has a high probability of success, whereas innovation in the "new/new" quadrant (IV) has a very low probability of success. Therefore, achieving a 5% desired growth in the new/new quadrant requires a disproportionate level of effort (as compared to a 5% growth in the other quadrants). Keeping this in mind, we present a rebalancing of the innovation effort for our organizational example (Figure 9.4 - previous page).

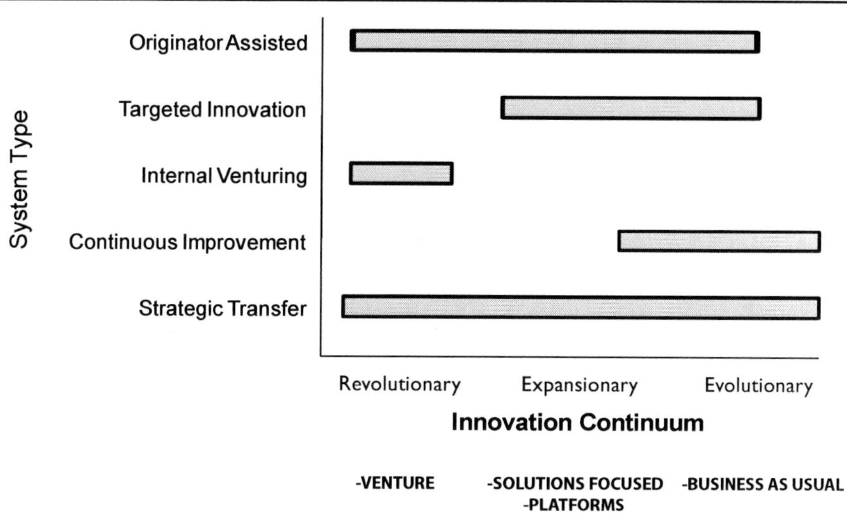

Figure 9.5
Matching basic innovation systems with the desired innovation portfolio

One of the dilemmas facing the innovation leader is understanding the implications of rebalancing and determining the most appropriate innovation systems to support the needed efforts. As shown in Figure 9.5, the different quadrants of the innovation portfolio matrix also align with different parts of the Innovation Continuum.

If your organization's innovation portfolio requires a focus on new Products/Technologies and new Markets, then some combination of Originator Assisted/Targeted Innovation systems would be most appropriate for generating revolutionary-expansionary innovation. An innovation leader needs to remember that revolutionary innovation is risky because only a small percentage of the ideas in this area are implemented or generate a quantifiable gain. To successfully implement a system that will generate revolutionary-expansionary innovation, the foundation of the Innovation House must be solid. Only if an organization has a solid foundation of trust will employees believe in the system and be willing to tackle almost any risk.

Another generality indicated via this chart is that if targeted growth is located primarily within the "Existing/Existing" boxes, the most logical system will be one of Continuous Improvement. There is much less risk here, which means that the foundation of the Innovation House is not as critical. The types of innovation generated via this system will be very evolutionary in nature.

Based on our example organization, the innovation leader needs to consider implementing an innovation system that will be a hybrid of an Originator Assisted/Targeted Innovation system focused on new growth. Current continuous improvement activities need to be maintained; however, they would most likely be scaled back to help fund/staff the desired growth agenda. Finally, if a form of strategic transfer is not already in place, the innovation leader needs to include one geared toward improving overall effectiveness of the innovation engine.

No matter what system your organization requires, always remember:

Systems do not create innovations; people do.

Advice for the Innovation Leader

Determine your innovation goals and the types of systems needed.

- Identify the real Innovation Supporters in your organization and engage them.
- Identify and understand key stakeholders, both supportive and restrictive.[6]

- Understand current organizational culture and the implications for innovation systems.
- Design a system (based on one or more of the five systems) that will meet the needs of stakeholders and employees within your organization.[7]
- Work with your team of Innovation Supporters to implement your new innovation system.
- Communicate and publicize early successes. However, ensure they are not publicized prematurely.
- Continuously re-evaluate and adjust the systems utilized to meet ongoing needs of the organization and the innovators within.

Remember

Innovation systems that are people-based help provide an infrastructure for turning ideas into innovations.

Part I
Chapter Ten

Summary of Part One

In the Introduction, we described the Innovation House model (Figure I.2, page xx) that is used throughout this book. Part 1 has focused on the bottom of the house, which included the three principles of an innovation environment (the foundation) and the five principles which make up what we refer to as the essence of innovation (the pillars). Together, the eight principles form the invisible foundation for an innovative organization.

The foundation of the Innovation House and pillars are highly interdependent. If you get cracks in your foundation or lose a pillar(s), the entire house is weakened. It is the same way in your business. If you ignore one of these principles, you will have trouble creating and sustaining innovation.

Thus far, one of the constants in each chapter has been the role of the Innovation Continuum. Some of the human principles become more critical at the revolutionary end, while others are critical across the board. The greater the risk, the higher the levels of trust, passion, and co-location that are needed. Leveraging differences, creating the appropriate innovation systems, turning problems into ideas, understanding the elements of destruction, and having soft values are necessary across the entire Innovation Continuum.

Client Requests

There are three common themes we hear from clients. The first is their hope for a quick, easy fix. Granted, a speedy solution can happen but, more times than not, it takes time and effort. These clients say, "Just fix it. Of the five innovation systems, an originator assisted system seems like the best. Please put it in place and make it work." Yet, while doing our preliminary research, we typically find an environment that is oppressive and doesn't accept bottom-up ideas.

Other clients say to us, "Tell me what the right value set is and we'll make sure everybody in the organization understands that they are the values we want." They end up listing values on plastic posters that adorn the hallways and conference rooms. But the attitudes and actions of the leaders do not change. Everything that occurs in the eight principles must be lived. It's not just thought about or put on posters. As we discussed in Chapter 1, principles and values result in actions, not slogans.

Further, other clients ask, "We see the eight principles. We understand they are important, but can't we just implement a subset?" The answer is yes, you can implement a subset, but not if you want sustained top- and bottom-line growth. Again, the principles are interdependent.

Closing

As the eight human principles are interdependent with one another, the bottom of the Innovation House is interconnected with the top. Now it is time to put your knowledge of the bottom of the Innovation House into action. In the remaining chapters, we will climb the House by focusing on more visible activities and results.

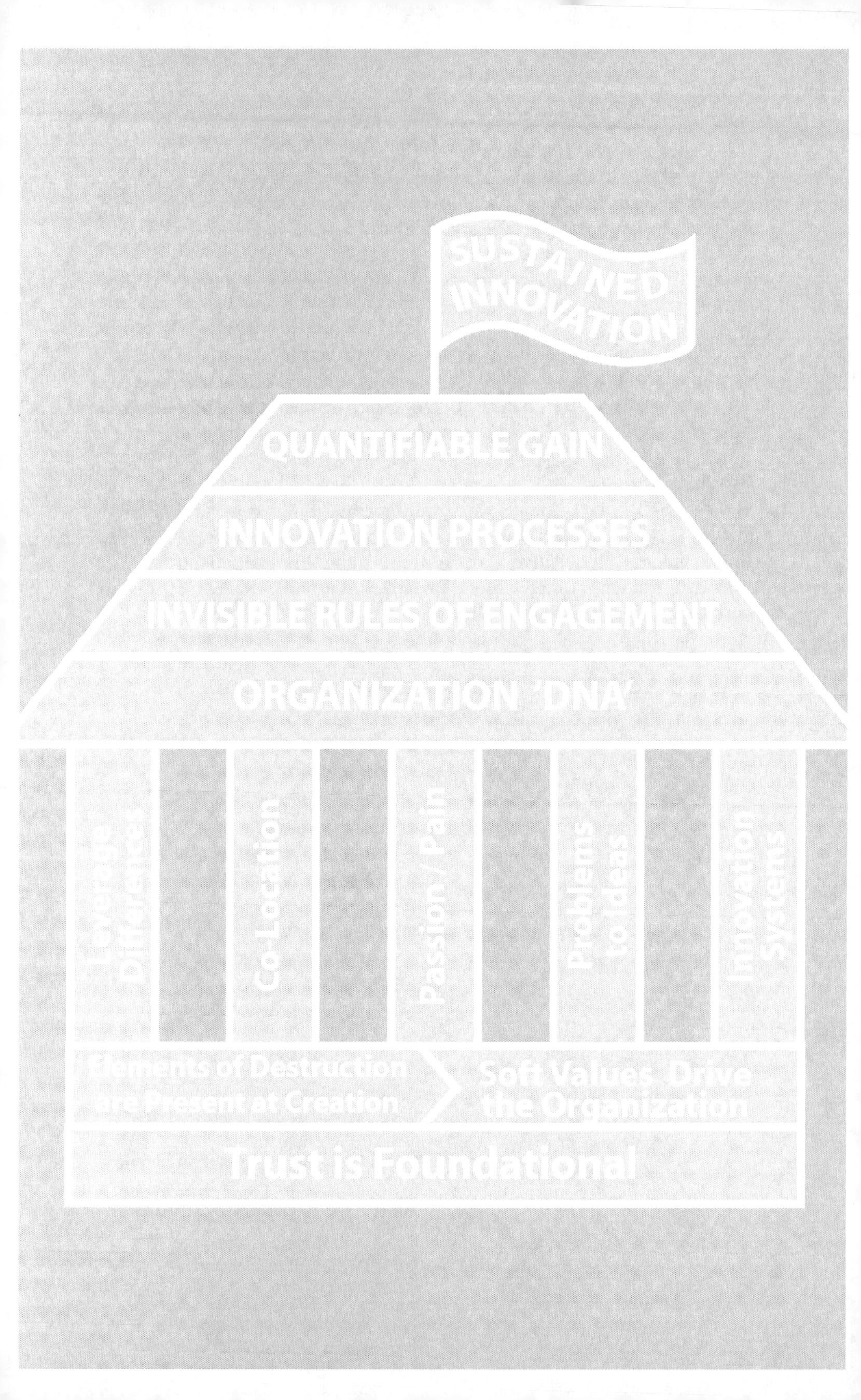
SUSTAINED INNOVATION
QUANTIFIABLE GAIN
INNOVATION PROCESSES
INVISIBLE RULES OF ENGAGEMENT
ORGANIZATION 'DNA'
Leverage Differences
Co-Location
Passion / Pain
Problems to Ideas
Innovation Systems
Elements of Destruction are Present at Creation
Soft Values Drive the Organization
Trust is Foundational

Part Two

Putting the Principles Into Action

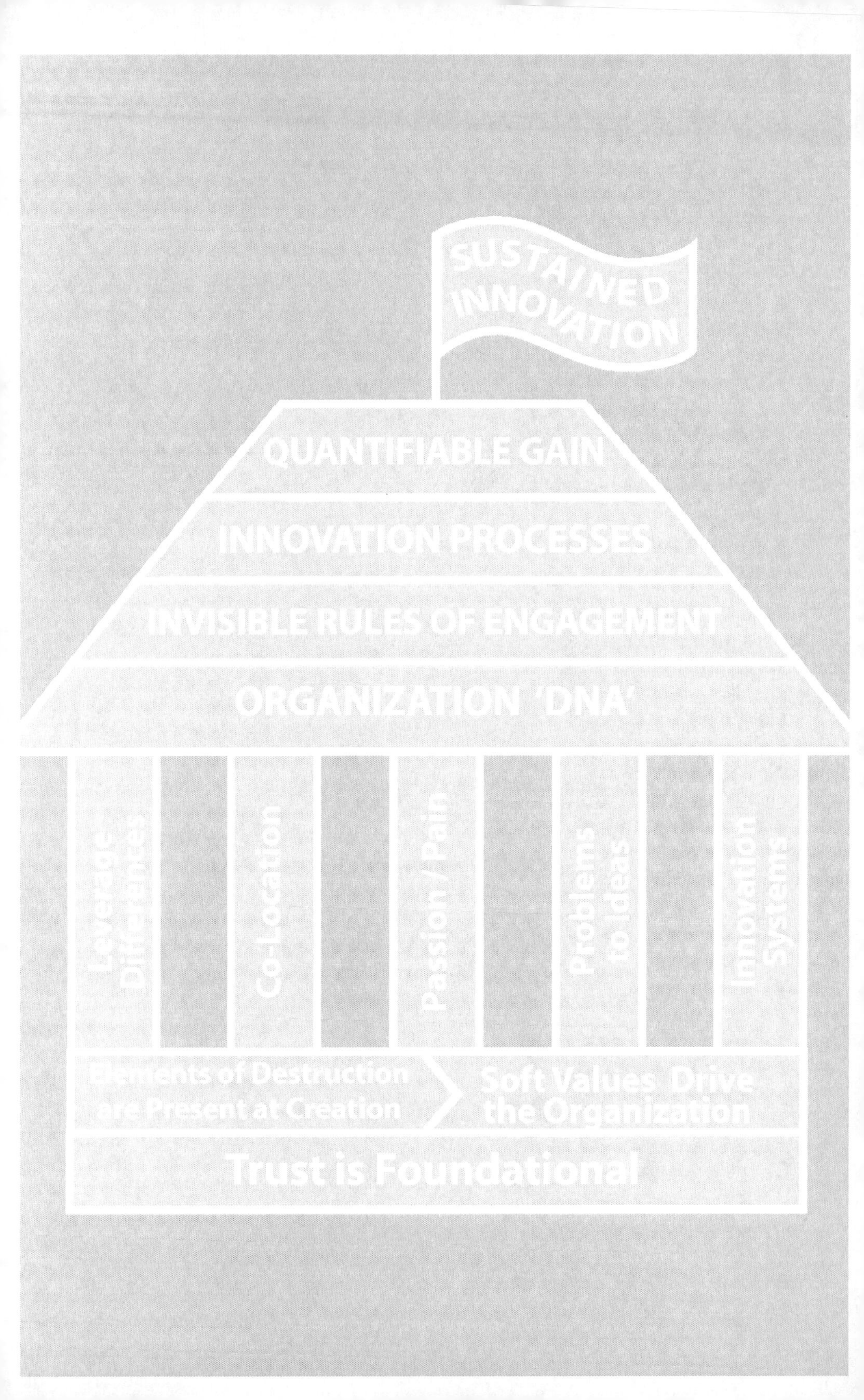
SUSTAINED INNOVATION
QUANTIFIABLE GAIN
INNOVATION PROCESSES
INVISIBLE RULES OF ENGAGEMENT
ORGANIZATION 'DNA'
Leverage Differences
Co-Location
Passion / Pain
Problems to Ideas
Innovation Systems
Elements of Destruction are Present at Creation
Soft Values Drive the Organization
Trust is Foundational

Part II

Chapter Eleven

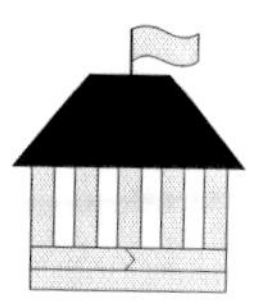

Introduction to Part Two

The first part of this book examined the eight human principles required for sustaining innovation with regard to individual interaction and partnering. Part Two takes the eight principles and expands them to a macro-organizational level. It discusses how the innovation leader can apply the principles to create a sustainable culture of innovation.

Before moving into the macro discussion, it is critical that the innovation leader understand where the organization wants to go. One way of accomplishing this is to incorporate ideas from *The World Is Flat*.[1] In his book, Friedman does an excellent job of describing the 10 events that he believes have helped to create a level or "flat" playing field. This "flattening" has allowed engineers and scientists to work from offices in their native countries rather than moving to work in a foreign country. This has allowed companies to move not only production but also many support services and design and development activities to other countries – a move that has led to significant productivity and efficiency gains. Today, companies are innovating all around the world. They are developing new products 24/7. The innovation leader of today cannot proceed in a "business as usual" mode.

In looking at this evolution, we see the evolutionary end of the innovation continuum as competing based on productivity, which allows for competition in this flat world. But the revolutionary end is about competing based on uniqueness, and this allows you to establish your own rules. It sets you apart from your competition. In other words:

Evolutionary innovation helps to flatten the world, but:
Revolutionary innovation helps make the world round.

The question is, what type of world do you want to compete in? A two-dimensional, flat playing field where people around the world can compete equally, or a three-dimensional, spherical world, where you can gain an advantage over your competition?

The Invisible Elements

When analyzing an innovation process, managers tend to focus only on what they can see. These "visible" elements are their technology, their business processes and metrics, and their people. Some examples of the technical side are patents, regulatory activity, research/development/commercialization/productivity (R/D/C/P) mix, time horizons, and current practices. Some examples of the business side are return on investment (ROI), profitability, line extensions, new enterprises, and formal decision processes. On the human side, this means analyses of structure, hierarchy, turnover rate, education or skills mix, retention, and age distribution.

But remember: It's the "invisible" characteristics of an organization that are too often overlooked. It is rare for people to talk about culture, trust, or risk tolerance. And if people do talk about any of these characteristics, they have a hard time defining what each one means.

Part Two of this book demonstrates how to apply the eight principles from Part One so that you can understand your past, present, and future organization. Once you do this, you can set goals and define where your organization needs to go. As part of this process, the innovation leader must observe behaviors of the organization today and describe and characterize them in easily definable terms, thereby identifying a common vocabulary that is communicated widely. Members of the organization can then look at past and current internal trends to understand the general direction in which the organization is moving.

Based on this understanding, the innovation leader can create a vision for the future. To most effectively move the organization towards this vision, the leader must portray it in terms that everyone understands. This allows everyone to better understand the future vision and to get behind it and help move it forward. Once behaviors and terms are identified and defined, the work can be focused on closing gaps between present and future (desired) states. Finally, the innovation leader must provide the tools required to make necessary changes.

In this part of the book, we will take invisible characteristics that often drive the innovation process and make them visible (Figure 11.1). We will examine the upper portion of the Innovation House – the portion built upon the foundation and pillars described in Part One.

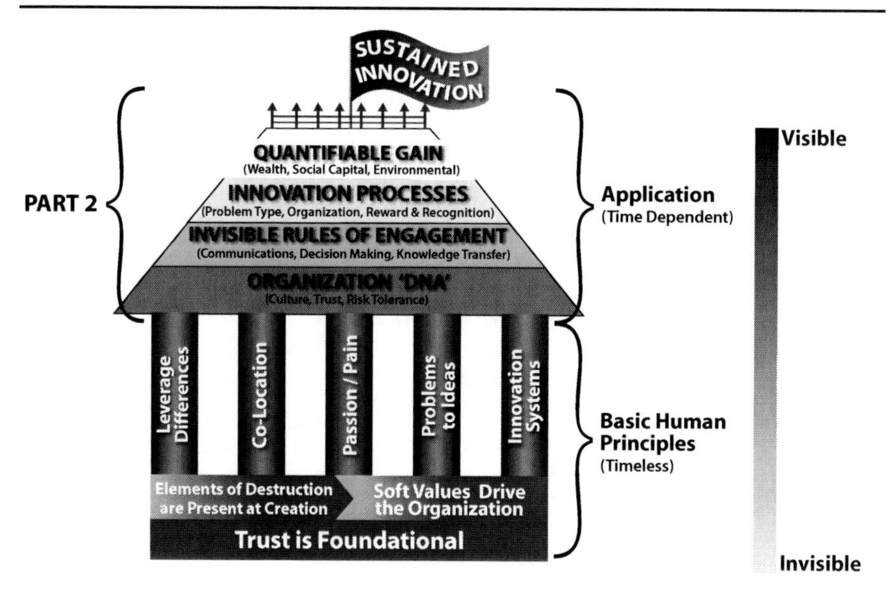

Figure 11.1
Part Two focuses on the upper portion of the house, beginning with Organization DNA and working through Quantifiable Gain.

The first three characteristics make up what we call "Organization DNA." Within this grouping, we examine:

- Culture
- Trust
- Risk Tolerance

By understanding these three organizational characteristics, you will have a clearer vision of what makes your organization unique. Then you can begin to make visible the glue that holds everything together and obtain insights into the "personality" of your organization.

Culture is defined as your organization's way of working. It is made up of demonstrated behaviors, not just words or thoughts. In an upcoming chapter, we will help you assess and diagnose the way your organization accomplishes things.

Trust involves the principles of head and heart trust applied to the broader organization. How much trust is there among members of senior leadership? How much trust is there among peers? How much do the senior leaders trust their employees? And how much do employees trust their senior leadership?

On a macro level, these questions become almost as fundamental as the notion that "Trust is Foundational." This is because we often see high levels of head trust among peers where, unfortunately, the employees (the heart and soul of an organization) do not have a high level of heart trust in senior leadership. This lack of emotional trust prompts them to operate with a fear of individual failure and risk aversion. In order to prepare you for the chapter on Organizational Trust, think about these questions: Are there surprises due to a lack of communication? Is partnering difficult? Are people resistant to sharing knowledge?

Risk Tolerance is dictated by organizational culture and trust, coupled with how key decision makers see the world. If strong pioneers predominantly lead you, your company will be more inclined to take significant risks. In contrast, if strong builders predominantly lead you, it will be very difficult for them to embrace a revolutionary idea because of the risk and uncertainty involved. Does your organization's growth predominantly come from building, balanced, or pioneering predispositions?

It is also important to determine your consumers' tolerance for risk. If you are Apple, your consumers are probably risk takers and want to have the latest gadget on the block. If you are John Deere, the livelihood of your consumers is dependent on making very reliable equipment, so they are far less likely to want to take wild risks on something new and different.

Once you understand these three elements of your organization's DNA, the next step in understanding where you are today and where you want to be in the future is to look at the Invisible Rules of Engagement. These include your organization's predominant style of communication, informal decision processes (or those that are generally always present but not documented or visible), as well as the learning and transfer of knowledge generated from previous innovation efforts.

The next level of the Innovation House builds on all of these and incorporates examining different types of innovation problems, how to structure your teams to attack these problems, and reward and recognition programs.

Finally, we will discuss what we mean by "quantifiable gain" and how important it is for your business. Once you have reached this point, you will have a complete understanding of the Innovation House. We will then discuss how to apply this knowledge to develop your sustainable culture of innovation, how to diagnose current issues, and how to attack new innovation challenges.

Part II
Chapter Twelve

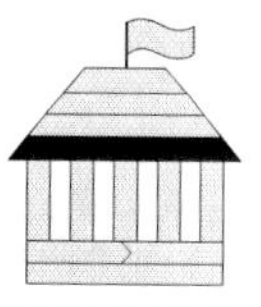

Organizational Culture

In the mid-1950s, anthropologist Kalervo Oberg[1] first used the phrase **culture shock** to describe the anxiety resulting from losing all of our familiar norms and customs that provide the bedrock for our social interactions. A friend of ours learned this the hard way after taking a new job that involved him moving to the interior of China.

Henry was part of a large United States business organization in the 1980s. They moved him from the U.S. offices to their China headquarters with the goal of spurring on their innovation capabilities. His job description was pretty broad – "help them innovate" – he was excited by the opportunity and arrived with big plans. At that point in time, China was a rather new market, and Henry's U.S. company did not provide him with much training or preparation on the human element of China.

He began his new role and worked long hours trying to get to know everyone and their way of doing things. Everyone treated him with respect and smiles but, as time went on, Henry was not seeing the productivity and results he had hoped for.

During his fourth month, he had a conversation with one of the Chinese managers that he had become friends with. Henry said to the manager, "It seems like everyone is motivated and working hard, but we just aren't getting to where I thought we would. What can I do?"

As part of his response, the manager told Henry, "The company says we are a family and that we should trust each other, but how can we trust each other? We don't know each other."

What the manager meant was that in most of China, the hiring practices were centered around family and friends. A manager or company would hire people they trusted outside of work and bring them into the organization. Henry and the U.S. company used the U.S. model of hiring – from resumes and want ads. While they had good people, they did not have the same level of internal trust that most other organizations in China did because the human culture was off.

Henry was not getting the results he wanted because he did not understand the culture he was in. He tried to copy-and-paste U.S. people practices to China. It did not work.

This story illustrates that when we think about culture, it is more about beliefs, attitudes, and actions, as opposed to words or slogans. Culture is invisible – and the only way to see your organization's culture is through its behaviors. What statements your company makes or what employees say inside may be very different from what they actually do. Trust what they do.

In looking at the lower level of the Innovation House, all elements are manifested in culture. There are six human principles that are directly associated with defining culture. They are: Trust, Elements of Destruction, Soft Values, Passion/Pain, Co-Location, and Leveraging Differences. These six principles help define what the culture is. They help determine the way you do things. The type of organizational culture you have impacts how members of your organization convert problems into ideas and how they utilize the organization's innovation systems. The six principles determine what goes in. The other two principles dictate what comes out (Figure 12.1).

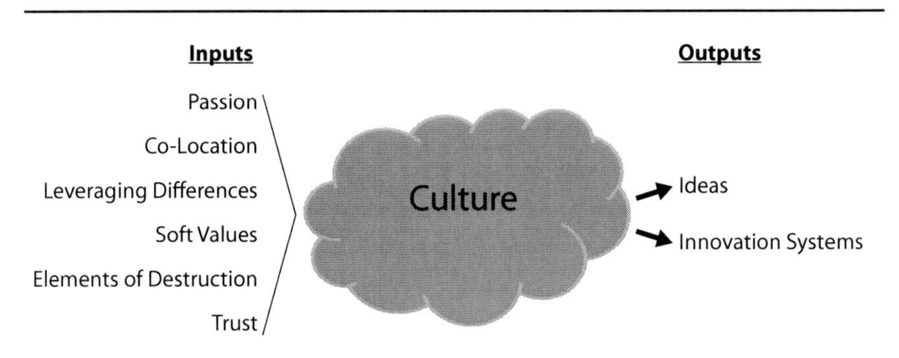

Figure 12.1
Six of the human principles help to create an organization's culture. This culture influences the types of ideas generated and innovation systems used by the organization.

What Is Culture?

Similar to innovation, the word "culture" has different meanings to different people. Therefore, it is important to have a shared understanding of what we mean by "culture."

The culture of a community or an organization resides in the minds and hearts of its people. It is the way they do things!

At its source, culture is invisible, but it can be seen through behavior. Culture is the force that shapes common behavior. It leads to high versus low **spirit**, teamwork versus individualism, and concern for others versus indifference.

Culture springs from the shared values and assumptions of people, made visible through their individual and collective behaviors. This, in turn, leads to whatever results are achieved. This is clearly seen in the nature of the institutions that a community or organization establishes.

For example, Google established many "benefits" that contributed to their overall culture such as an onsite laundry, workout facility, and dining facilities.[2]

Large companies have different departments like human resources, finance, accounting, sales, etc. The existence of these departments is an acknowledgement of the fact that they each have unique characteristics. Culturally, the way a finance department is organized and managed will probably be very different from that of the sales department. In essence, they each have different "currencies of the realm" – with different metrics that they value.

Attending to culture is important because it drives the informal decision-making processes used by individuals to make thousands of daily decisions about their lives and work. Culture can attract, retain, or drive away good people. It affects individual, group, and organization performance. In so doing, it affects the ultimate satisfaction of all stakeholders (including customers, employees, investors, and others).

One way to identify your organization's desired culture is to consider it to be the intersection between organizational needs and personal needs (Figure 12.2, see next page).

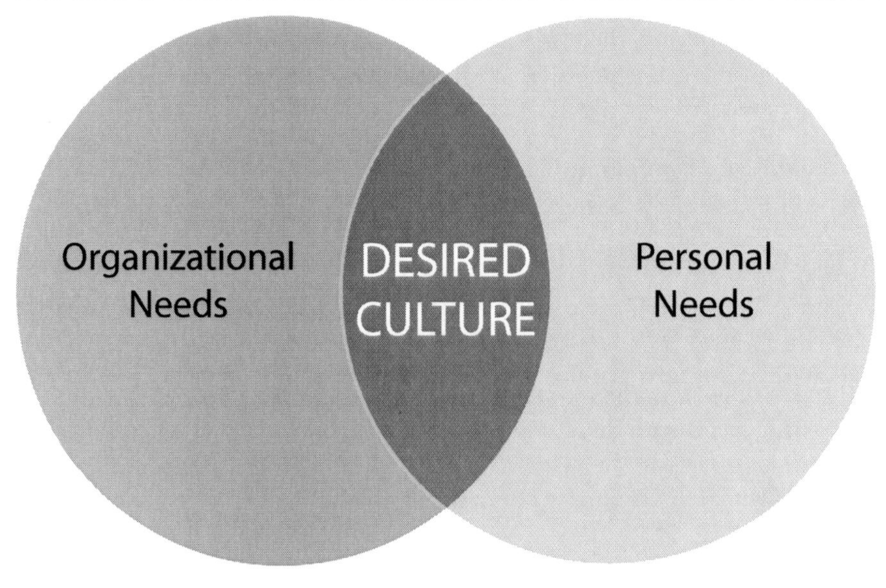

Figure 12.2
Desired culture should satisfy both the needs of an organization and the needs of the people within it.

What Is the Culture of Your Organization?

Having a clearly defined answer to this question may not be readily apparent to you at this time. By reading the rest of this chapter, you should be able to more easily recognize the culture of your organization.

There are a number of tools you can use to help examine culture. The Organizational Environmental Survey (OES)[3] provides a means to look at organizations as either large or small in comparison to behaviors and attitudes. Neither is better or worse. For example, is your organization more entrepreneurial in spirit (small), or highly structured and driven by analytics (large)? What do behaviors look like? Survey respondents are asked to examine the environment facing their organization relative to where it was five years ago, where it is today, and where they would like to see it five years from now.

The results for one Fortune 100 company are shown in Figures 12.3a and 12.3b. The first figure is the current trend, which is toward a larger organizational mindset that is highly structured. The second figure shows that employees want to move toward a more entrepreneurial (or smaller) organizational

Figure 12.3a
Organizational Environmental Survey summary results for a Fortune 100 company. Current direction is toward a larger organizational mindset.

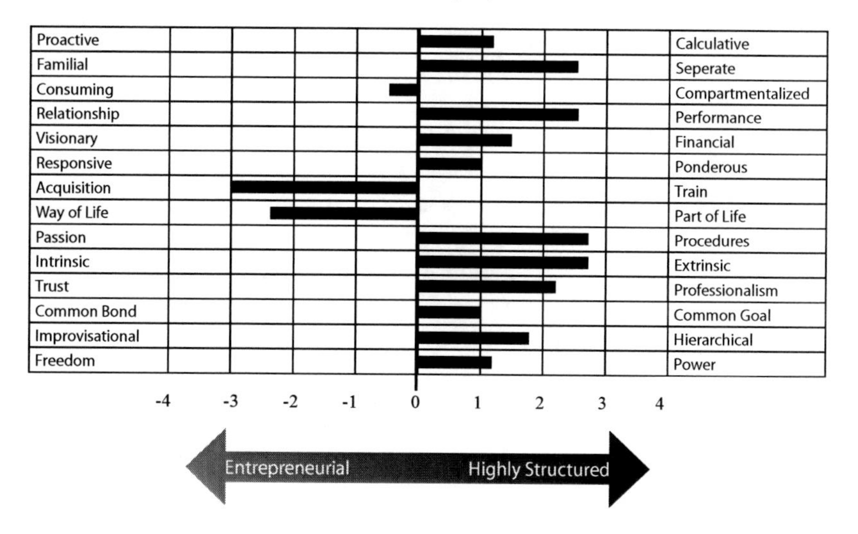

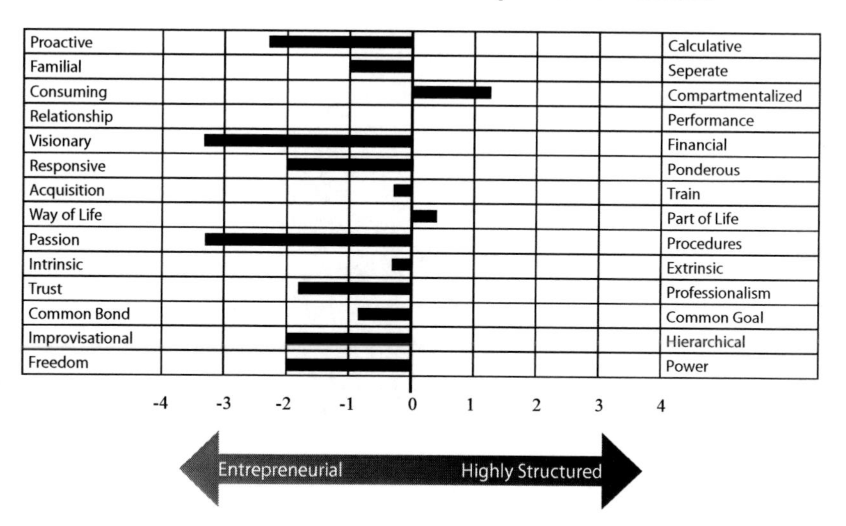

Figure 12.3b
Organizational Environmental Survey summary results for a Fortune 100 company. Desired trend is toward a smaller organizational mindset.

mindset. By looking at the relative shifts from today toward the future, senior leaders can then prioritize the areas needing immediate attention, as well as those areas which should not be allowed to shift dramatically.

Individuals can compare their specific data to the overall consensus to determine the degree of their internal alignment with the rest of the staff. Am I aligned with where the organization was, where it is currently, and the consensus direction for the future?

Another assessment-based tool is the Denison Culture Survey.[4] This survey is an externally normative, metric-based instrument used to benchmark an organization's effectiveness against high-performing ones. It is similar to a "cultural annual report." It is a way for you to get a snapshot of your organization's culture at present and how well it is doing relative to other organizations. A key advantage of the Denison Culture Survey is that the results are compared to normative groups within the Denison database. This normative comparison gives you a calibrated benchmark, as opposed to the non-normative data generated by many internal employee opinion surveys.

There are four main categories measured by the Denison Culture Survey: Adaptability, Mission, Consistency, and Involvement. Each of the four main categories has three subcategories that are measured for a total of 12 "scores" (Figure 12.4).

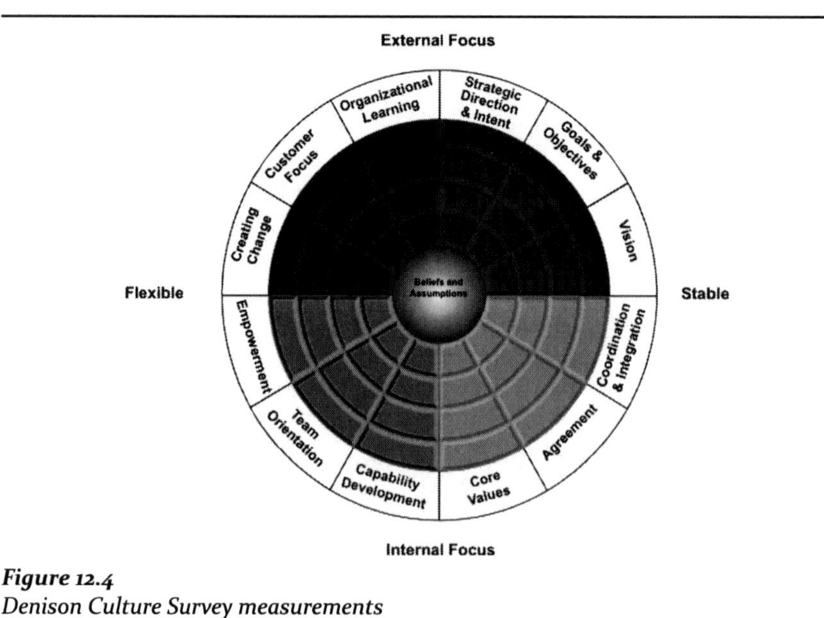

Figure 12.4
Denison Culture Survey measurements

As with an annual report, the Denison Culture Survey provides an assessment but does not necessarily lead to development of a vision for the future. To help develop this future vision, we use two different tools: 1) the previously mentioned Organizational Environmental Survey (OES), and 2) a Four culture model (adapted from the work of Goffee and Jones[5]).

Four Cultures

The other tool we use to create the vision for where an organization wants to go is called the Four Cultures. It is a diagnostic tool that defines an organization's cultural characteristics to make visible its current state and provides the framework to create a desired future state. It helps make visible to everyone in the organization what the goals are and the reasons behind them.

The Four Cultures Model is based on two dimensions: Sociability and Solidarity.

Sociability is the level of friendliness – or how well employees get along with each other. Sociability is determined by how much people:

- like one another and get along
- socialize outside of work
- do favors for each other because they like one another
- make friends without agendas
- confide in each other about personal matters
- build close long-term relationships
- know a lot about each other and their families
- are flexible and work things out as they go along
- can work around the system to get something done

Solidarity is the level of alignment on common tasks, mutual interests, and shared goals. Solidarity is determined by:

- how clearly people understand business objectives
- the extent to which people can change work procedures to get the job done
- the speed and firmness with which poor performance issues are addressed
- the degree of alignment around shared purpose
- how quickly people respond in order to capitalize on opportunities
- the clarity of reward systems
- the level of determination by teams to achieve objectives

To assess your culture we will ask you to plot an assessment. Think about where your organization is today relative to sociability using the descriptors listed above. Rate sociability on a nine-point scale, with 1 being very low and 9 being very high. Afterward, do the same thing for solidarity. Plot the ratings for the current organization on the grid in Figure 12.5 (C = Current). Do the same thing for where your organization was five years ago (P = Past). Finally, do the same thing for where you would like to see your organization five years from now (D = Desired).

Note: In Figure 12.5, we have provided an example of a current organization in quadrant I (C), the past in quadrant II (P), and the desired future organization in quadrant IV (D).

By utilizing the Four Cultures Model, you can determine your organization's degree of sociability and solidarity. There are four cultures provided in this index (as noted in Figure 12.6). We will refer to these four unique cultures throughout the rest of the book:

1. **Fragmented**
2. **Mercenary**
3. **Networked**
4. **Communal**

It is important to know that each of the four cultures has the potential to be successful. Yet, the culture must be aligned with your organization's mission and people. As an example, trying to force a university to be communal may be counterproductive. For a large organization where the currency of

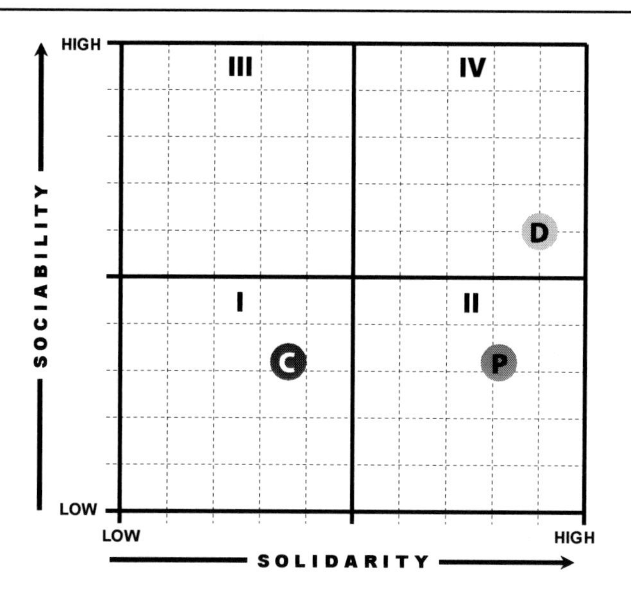

Figure 12.5
Scoring grid for the Four Cultures Model. Plot ratings for your current organization (C), your past organization (P), and your desired future organization (D).

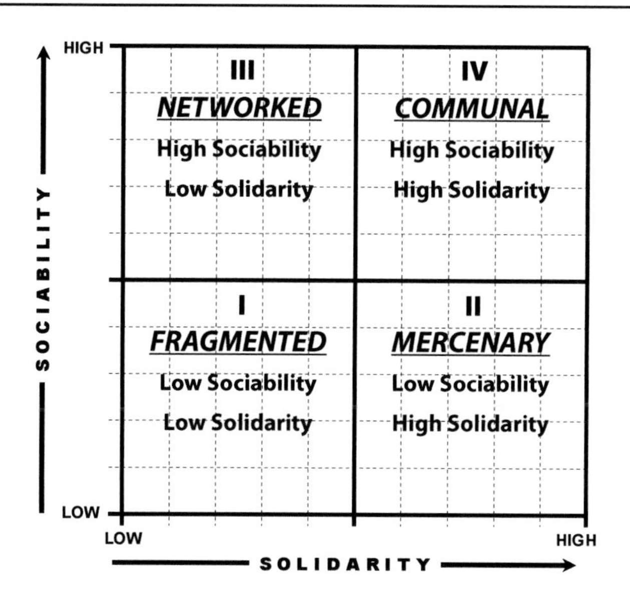

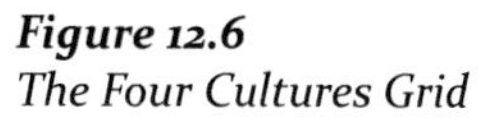
Figure 12.6
The Four Cultures Grid

the realm is primarily financial gain, it will be difficult for innovation to be sustainable without higher solidarity and sociability.

The following is a brief summary of core competencies and potential weaknesses for each of the types within the Four Cultures Model.

A **Fragmented Organization (Quadrant I)** is low on both sociability and solidarity. It will predominantly have employees who are independent professionals, tied to the organization only by the status, resources, and professional opportunities it provides.

Some of the core competencies are:

- Professionalism
- Freedom and **autonomy**
- Individual creativity
- Individual stars versus high performance teams

Some possible weaknesses of a Fragmented Organization are:

- Employees are out for themselves
- Freedom of autonomy is abused
- Employees may undermine each other
- Institutional learning is hindered, particularly when it involves tacit knowledge

A **Mercenary Organization (Quadrant II)** is lower on sociability and higher on solidarity. It will predominantly have employees with a clear understanding of the organization's goals who will readily align themselves.

Some of the core competencies are:

- Clear focus toward business objectives
- Rapid response to threats
- Quick to unify around/against threats
- Better at improving what they do versus creating something new

Some possible weaknesses of a Mercenary Organization are:

- Lack of creativity and innovation
- Competition between departments/business units for meeting targets
- Lack of employee loyalty
- Absolute adherence to "the numbers"

A **Networked Organization (Quadrant III)** is higher on sociability and lower on solidarity. It will predominantly have employees who help each other and share information without expecting reciprocity.

Some of the core competencies are:

- High level of friendship/trust among employees
- Availability of tacit knowledge
- Fast and fluid information movement
- Flexibility and agility

Some possible weaknesses of a Networked Organization are:

- Too consensus-driven, resulting in "analysis paralysis"
- Opportunities missed due to inability to rapidly adjust to changes in the external environment
- Risk avoidance
- An insidiously political and manipulative workplace

A **Communal Organization (Quadrant IV)** is high on both sociability and solidarity. It will predominantly have employees who are deeply loyal to the organization and passionately opposed to (or dismissive of) competition.

Some of the core competencies are:

- High level of friendship and openness
- Powerful sense of family
- Free flow of creativity
- Intense, close culture
- Clear focus
- Performance focus and energy
- Employees identify with values and mission
- The "credo" is lived

Some possible weaknesses of a Communal Organization are:

- Groupthink
- Lack of awareness of the external stakeholders
- Breeds disciples rather than suitable successors
- Excessive inward focus

You can be successful at different types of innovation within each of the four cultures. Note that within each culture there will be successful leadership behaviors and attributes that impact the whole culture as well as "dark side" behaviors. Your culture will also impact the type of employees you attract and their reciprocity styles.

To further break down the four cultures, think about how well people get along in your organization (sociability). This is a predominate driver of interaction. It builds on many pieces in the lower portion of the Innovation House. If your organization has very low sociability, it is difficult to have a high level of heart trust because people don't know each other. You can have head trust but not a lot of heart trust. However, if you are trying to drive revolutionary innovation, it is difficult to do without both head and heart trust.

At the same time, you can achieve revolutionary innovation without solidarity of vision, but the revolutionary innovation is going to be more difficult to sell to the broader organization. It will be difficult to obtain the necessary backing for revolutionary innovation if it is not properly aligned with the organization's vision and if there isn't a reasonable amount of solidarity. To reach the ideal "sweet spot" for long-term, sustainable, revolutionary innovation, you need reasonably high levels of both sociability and solidarity. A communal culture is best for sustained, revolutionary innovation.

We've seen many cases where high solidarity mixed with low sociability (mercenary culture) has resulted in success with regard to creating evolutionary and expansionary short-term innovations, but it doesn't make the innovation activities sustainable in the long term.

When we start overlaying culture on top of the Innovation Continuum, your organization can pursue evolutionary innovation regardless of the culture quadrant. However, once you start moving toward revolutionary innovation, your organization must start to move toward a more communal culture to make such innovation sustainable.

Within each culture, you can support some degree of revolutionary innovation – provided you understand how to work the system to get it. However, this is not the same thing as having a culture that supports sustained innovation along the entire continuum.

Advice for the Innovation Leader: Cultural Rules

While examining your culture, remember that culture changes over time. Some of these changes are planned and some are unintended consequences of key decisions or events. As culture changes, the types of employees and leaders required to make the new culture successful also change.

Many people tell us that they are fragmented and want to move toward a communal culture. To do this, focus first on improving solidarity.

To improve solidarity, leaders must establish a clear vision, and then they must share the vision with the entire organization: "This is where we are going and this is how we will get there." Furthermore, the vision must be reinforced by behaviors from the top down. Once everyone knows the vision and knows how to get there – and the leadership lives the vision – the silos or walls between different parts of the organization will break down and solidarity will improve.

As a rule, solidarity is easier to accomplish than sociability. If you start with solidarity, addressing sociability will be easier. To raise sociability, you must first understand why it is lower than desired. Is it because of a trust issue? Are the people too widely dispersed within your office complex or located in different cities? By first understanding the drivers for low sociability, specific actions can be developed to reinforce the behaviors you want in your organization.

Another rule is that if you are in a communal culture that is in a state of decay, it will either decay down to a mercenary culture and then move over to a fragmented culture, or it will move over to a networked culture and then move down to a fragmented culture. In any case, the final stage will result in a fragmented state. We have seen many examples of these types of shifts. In one example, the organization started with a communal culture in the 1980s. Due to competitive pressures, the organization shifted to a mercenary culture in the 1990s. As the competitive pressure was reduced, they shifted to a fragmented culture with a significant number of internal silos. They are currently starting the process back to a communal culture and are supporting innovation more toward the revolutionary end of the Innovation Continuum.

The key is to analyze the past and then look at the present. You should be able to see the direction in which your organization is going. At that point, you can make a conscious decision to continue in that direction or shift toward another path.

The very difficult part about culture is that **if you are in any culture other than fragmented, it takes energy to remain there**. If you lose the energy to maintain sociability or solidarity, you will decay.

If you decay, you will often keep the residual characteristics from where you came. For example, if you move from a mercenary culture into a fragmented one, you could bring the same intensity level for fighting. However, rather than fighting an external enemy, you will now be fighting each other. This decay leads to a high potential for significant infighting.

Organization DNA Table

At the end of the following three chapters, we will plot an example of an organization's DNA. We will use a fictional name for the organization, "Organization XYZ." Once the chart is filled out, it will allow you to reference appropriate characteristics of your current and desired organization for later discussion.

Organization XYZ DNA Table

	Past	Current	Desired
Cultural Type FRAGMENTED NETWORKED MERCENARY COMMUNAL	MERCENARY	FRAGMENTED	COMMUNAL
Trust			
Risk			

Figure 12.7
Chart that allows for beginning development of the organizational DNA table

On the chart (Figure 12.7 - previous page), we have recorded the past, current, and desired cultural type for Organization XYZ. We will fill out the rest of this chart in the next two chapters. Please complete the chart for your own organization type.

Appendix III contains a compilation of the characteristics for all of the DNA combinations.

Remember

The culture of your organization resides within the hearts and minds of your employees.

Part II

Chapter Thirteen

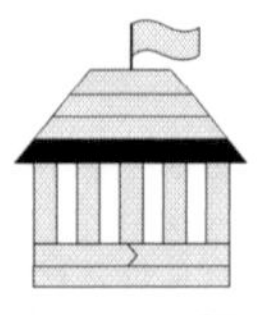

Organizational Trust

In Chapter 2, we discussed the principle of trust and how it applies to the relationship between two people. Here, we expand the discussion to look at trust in an overall organization. While trust between two individuals is a fundamental building block for organizational trust, the overall presence or absence of trust sets the stage for how successful innovation will be.

A few years ago, a major organization went through a significant and painful reduction in force (RIF). Throughout the process, there was abundant communication to the employees as to what was happening and why. This helped them deal with the uncertainty of the situation but did not eliminate the feeling of vulnerability, distrust, and fear for themselves and their families. The one theme that was repeated over and over was that if you made it through this rough time, you were part of the new organization and did not need to worry about any additional rounds of layoffs. Everybody was told that on "Black Friday" you would meet with your supervisor and find out if you were part of the RIF or what new assignment you would be starting on the following Monday.

Black Friday came and the staff was reduced by over 20%. Those remaining, while not directly celebrating, breathed a collective sigh of relief. A huge burden was lifted from their shoulders and they could move forward.

During the downsizing process, a senior vice president made the decision that about a dozen people who were on the RIF list would not be told on Black Friday. Instead, they would be told at some point during the next six months. For all of these individuals, working a few more months would allow them to qualify for early retirement rather than the standard severance package. The senior VP was trying to help them as much as he could, but he did not communicate his plan to the people or others in the organization. He felt at the time that he could not trust them or the rest of the organization with the information.

Unfortunately, when they received their termination letters, everyone took it as a major breach of trust. The negative domino effect spread throughout, starting with the downsized employees' friends. The question for those still working became, "Am I next?"

Did the senior vice president do the right thing in trying to help these individuals? Absolutely yes. Did this cause the trust level of the company and its senior leader to go into a freefall? Unfortunately, yes! People can only see behaviors. They cannot see intent. Behaviors are the most important component in determining the overall level of trust.

Because the leader didn't trust his people, he couldn't fully help them or the organization. This is the difference between leadership and acting on compassion alone. Leadership helps the people, the organization, and the leader.

Our advice in a scenario like this is as follows. Prior to Black Friday, we would have taken the people into our office, one at a time. We would have said something along these lines: "As you know, layoffs are coming. Based on your tenure with us, you only have a few months to go until you qualify for early retirement. Today, I am going to share something that puts me at risk. You are going to be let go, but not on Black Friday. I want you to reach your early retirement, and once you do, then you will be let go. I am taking a big risk in telling this to you, so I am asking you to keep this between us. I appreciate the work you have done here. I am not a fan of the layoffs, but that is what is happening. Please keep up your effort and, again, please keep this between us."

When we first started writing this book, trust was an issue in the world and in organizations, but not a dominant one. With the recent events in the financial markets around the globe coupled with illegal activities by some major entities, trust has become a more visible and critical issue. When people feel they can no longer trust representatives of their financial institutions, businesses, or governments, they tend to become overly conservative with their own resources. They stop investing and eliminate non-essential purchases. All you need to do is look at the news of market impacts reported in 2008 and 2009 to see the direct consequences of erosion of public trust.

As we have discussed throughout this book, people trust actions over words. The fundamental rule of trying to change anything in an organization, be it trust or culture or soft values or whatever, is that behaviors of senior leaders must be aligned with desired change. If they aren't, people will become suspicious and draw the conclusion that change is not something that they can believe in. They will view the desired change as simply being lip service depicted by "posters on the wall."

Organizational Trust

Organizational trust is the prevailing feeling of trust within the organization between:

- peers
- employees and their managers
- employees and the senior leaders

Many companies do not understand the real meaning of trust. Some believe that they've been successful while not worrying about trust, so why do they need to worry about it now? The simple answer is, it depends on what you are trying to accomplish. If you are content with primarily evolutionary innovation (with an occasional expansionary one), then the need for a high level of trust is reduced. However, even at this end of the innovation continuum, a lack of trust will still impact the efficiency of executing innovation programs. In addition, a low level of trust will negatively impact the quality of work life and the ability to retain your most talented employees.

If a business needs long-term top- and bottom-line growth, it needs a balanced portfolio of innovation across the entire continuum from evolutionary to revolutionary. To accomplish this on a sustained basis, a reasonably high level of both head and heart trust is required. People are not going to take the necessary risks required to successfully execute toward the revolutionary end of a balanced portfolio unless they trust the organization. Only if they feel the backing of their senior leaders will people step forward and take personal risks. Without this backing, they will make decisions based on protecting themselves first, followed by what is good for the organization.

Examining Organizational Trust

In looking at organizational trust, it is important to begin to understand some of the key drivers that can build or reduce trust.

Job Security: If we go back to the Relationship Spectrum introduced in Chapter 2 (page 28) and further depicted in Figure 13.1, the mindset of people drives the overall trust level. As people move toward being a partner, their trust goes up. As they move toward being more of a contractor, trust decreases. An unintended consequence of the downsizing that many companies went through in the early 1990s, as well as in the economic downturn of 2008, was a dramatic shift of employees to the outer rings of the chart and a corresponding reduction in trust. Many implied employment contracts were shattered, leaving employees feeling that they should look out for themselves first.

If workers have a very high level of head and heart trust in relation to key people in the company, they will be inclined to take risks and put in more effort. It will be a comfortable place, which will lead to an increase in the number of ideas shared. Trust will allow them to be more inclined to be partners or stewards, which will lead to optimal results.

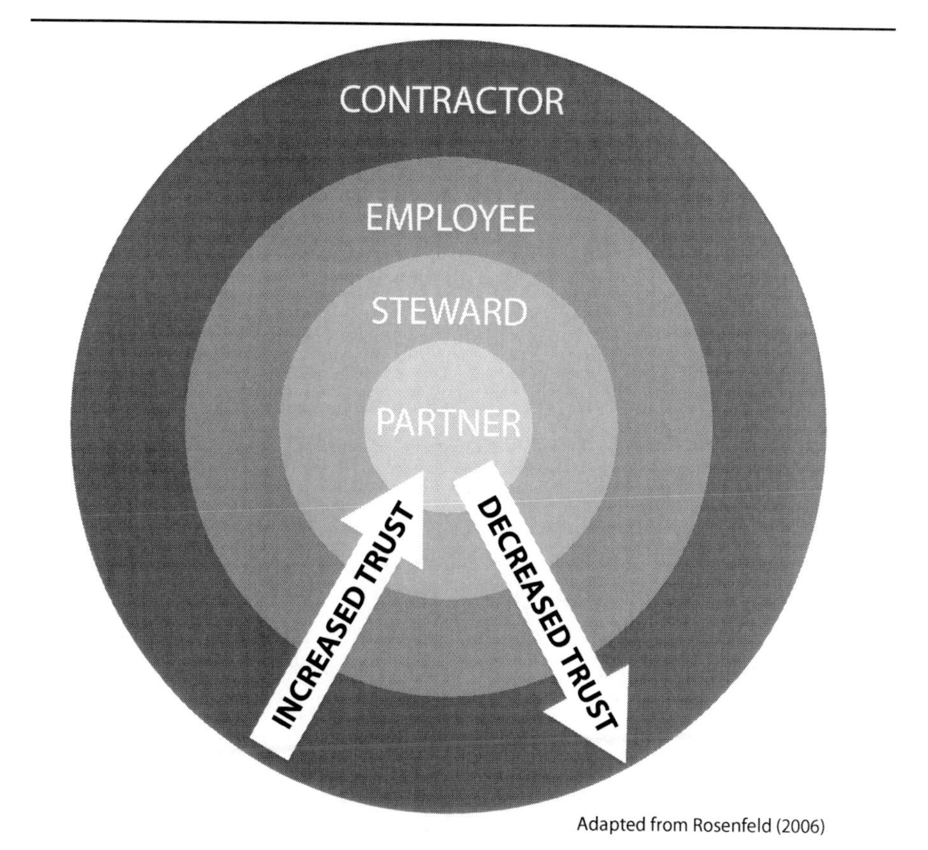

Figure 13.1
Organizational mindset and trust are directly related. As trust increases, people tend to have the mindset of stewards or partners. As trust decreases, the mindset shifts towards employees or contractors.

An organization with high levels of head and heart trust can sustain levels of innovation across the entire innovation continuum. But as that trust erodes, it becomes more and more likely that the innovation will shift to the evolutionary end of the axes, which is the safer end of the scale.

If heart trust starts going down, people may still feel comfortable on a technical or intellectual level, but will be more inclined to be guarded and filter their communications. As trust decreases, the individual will start making decisions that are based on "what's best for me," not the impact on the company. They will wonder, "If I'm wrong on this (and in innovation, wrong occurs more often than right), and because nobody is looking out for me, how will this impact me?" When trust is diminished, the "fear of individual failure" filter has a major impact on the daily decisions employees make.

This self-preservation mode (versus organizational focus) is also seen along the lines of Maslow's Hierarchy Of Needs.[1] As we feel more threatened or less comfortable because we don't feel we can trust people, we start dropping down into a self-preservation mode. Rather than looking out for the company, we look out for ourselves and our friends.

Friendships can still exist within a low-trust organization, but they will be individual relationships and they will be slower to form. Disunity and a lack of trust may also bond employees together to complain about the organization. Diminished trust generates a level of dissonance that can be completely destructive.

Yet, there are some people who like a low-trust environment because they can leverage it. They understand it allows them to accomplish individual goals. They are there to use it, not support it. The organization is viewed as a stepping-stone to help them get to where they want to be. Low trust levels will cause people to act purely as contractors. You will not find many partners and stewards staying in a place that is in a state of disunity.

Risk Capital: In each of us, we have a **zero-sum game** on the level of risk that we are willing to take. The amount of risk capital is different in each person and is called "risk homeostasis."[2] If one takes a lot of risk in one domain, they compensate by taking less risk in other domains. In an organization with high emotional distrust, one puts a lot of their risk capital into dealing with trust-related issues. If they're putting risk capital there, then they're taking it away from innovation.

Omission versus Commission: We can correlate the number of errors due to omission versus **commission** to the level of trust. These two errors are defined here:

- **Errors of Omission** come from not taking action. They may be a result of not having the required knowledge, not understanding the action needed, not realizing the importance of some aspect, etc. Not taking action was not premeditated to mislead anybody.
- **Errors of Commission** are a result of specificactions taken with the intent to mislead (or cover up something). This includes "spinning" information or withholding it for personal gain or advancing some hidden agenda.

Errors of omission are far easier to deal with than errors of commission. People are more accepting of omission errors and, because of this, omission has very little to do with overall trust. Omission occurs because we haven't discovered the solution or don't know the answer. We don't say something about what is going on because we don't know. As a consequence, we may be held to task for not knowing the information or answer, but we did not consciously withhold information.

Errors of commission are more directly associated with levels of trust. We have found that where there is low trust, there is an increase in commission. This plays out in various forms and may be found in the stereotypical top-down communication process. Or it shows up frequently on an individual basis between employees at various levels.

An error of commission is when we know something is not working and withhold that information from management who must make decisions based on our input, such as: "I don't trust my boss to help solve the problem. Therefore, I won't tell them what's going on." So what happens when people make decisions that affect the well-being of the company based on data that is heavily filtered and tells only half the story? How can there be long-term success when decisions are made based on only partial data?

One major Fortune 500 company tried to address this issue by implementing a campaign focused on more timely and complete information sharing. The goal was to allow more timely decisions to be made with the appropriate amount of input. However, as the program only involved slogans and wall posters, not behaviors, it was not surprising that it had little impact. Real change requires a change in behaviors – starting at the top.

Low trust leads to filtered and less frequent communication, a feeling of risk aversion, and a fear of individual failure. Distrust also makes it difficult to put knowledge systems in place because people don't want to share their knowledge with others and thereby put themselves at risk. If there is a high level of trust, people will err on the side of sharing data; whereas, if there is a low level of trust, people will err on the side of waiting and caution.

Assessing Trust Level

Many companies are looking for something they can do to solve the trust problem. In essence, they want a silver bullet. In reality, trust is human and emotional. Trust is built over time through our behaviors. The key to trust is actions that are aligned with the words.

Changing organizational trust is not a short-term fix. It requires a long-term, integrated effort. Trust is very difficult to achieve because much of it is based on emotion. One bad experience can break trust. Once that trust has been broken, it takes much longer to reconstruct it.

And the reconstruction phase is very people-dependent. Trust can't be mandated – it can only be invited and nurtured via the appropriate conditions. Change will take effort and commitment from both leaders and employees. There is no magic trust pill and no placard on the wall will facilitate it. Trust is all about walking the talk.

Before beginning a program to shift trust level, it is imperative to know the current level of trust (or lack thereof). Some of the tools we use to make the level of trust more visible are outlined here.

The first one is to listen and think about what people are saying – and why. For example, the following are actual quotes from employees of a Fortune 500 company:

- *"I've got several ideas, but I don't know who I can talk to about them. The last time I talked to my boss, he took the ideas and presented them as his own. That's the last time I'll do that."*
- *"Why should I take a risk? The rewards are non-existent and, if I fail, my career will be over."*

- *"How can we make this totally positive? I just want to get in and get out without controversy so we can have time to work through the issues." (comment made before a senior management review)*
- *"I know what I'm signing up for; a risky program with no payback for at least two years, so my review this year is already in the tank."*
- *"Why should I share what I know with ___? At the end of the year, I'm competing with them for my review rating."*
- *"Why is it that every time my boss's name comes up on caller ID, I immediately start wondering what I've done to get into trouble?"*

Can you relate to any of these quotes? What do you think they say about the trust within that organization? And what kind of innovation would you expect this organization to be undertaking? By comparison, what is your organization saying and what are the unstated implications?

Taking this a step further, let's explore some of the symptoms of a low level of trust (Figure 13.2).

Observation	Potential Issue
Limited partnering within the organization	Based on individual desires vs. organizational necessity
Difficulty in creating a learning organization	People are reluctant to share
Risk-taking replaced by "individual fear of failure"	Self-preservation
Decisions being made with filtered data	Potential for serious consequences
Employee/contractor mindset vs. partner/steward	Do what you are told
Suppression of individual passion	Safety in maintaining neutrality
High degree of skepticism of any "top down" changes	They are out to get me
Other?	

Figure 13.2
Examples of observations within an organization and potential underlying causes/ issues

To further understand what is happening with regard to trust, look at the behaviors of the different groups around you (peers, managers, direct reports, etc.). What are the causes for this behavior? Go back and think about the Principles to Results Model (PRM) in Figure 1.2. Based on these observable behaviors, what do they say about your values and principles? Is a high level of trust valued?

Similar to what we did in the previous chapter for culture, we will create a scale for organizational trust.[3]

Read through the Organizational Trust Characteristics in Figure 13.3. Think about these characteristics in relation to your organization.

Organizational Trust Characteristics

- There are almost no surprises in my organization due to lack of early warnings/open communications.
- I get both good and bad news without having to ask for input.
- People seek me out to help resolve issues.
- People in my organization:
  - readily take well-thought-out risks.
  - celebrate well-executed programs whether successful or not.
  - readily share information/knowledge.
  - readily seek out peers to ask advice when starting a new innovation program.
  - are evaluated based on performance and willingness to take intelligent risks...not strictly bottom line metrics.

Figure 13.3
Characteristics of a high trust organization

Next, think about these characteristics relative to your peers. Rate them from 1 – 9, where 1 means that they do not represent your interactions with peers and 9 means that they define your relationships with peers. We have filled out the following form based on our example organization.

Identify your current peer situation (Current = C), where you were five years ago (Past = P), and where your desired level would be (Desired = D). Plot these similar to the table in Figure 13.4 on the next page.

Now, do the same thing for your organization's relationship with the senior leaders. First, look at the organization's current view of the senior leadership (C). What was the view five years ago (P) and what would be the desired level (D)?

Similarly, do the same thing – only from the perspective of the senior leaders. How much do the senior leaders trust the organization? Examine their behaviors. What do they suggest about the current and past levels of trust they have for their organization? What is the desired level? Plot these on the same scale. You now have a composite picture of where you are today and where the desired organization should be.

Finally, where would you put your organization's overall past, current, and desired trust levels? We have filled out the table below for our example Organization XYZ.

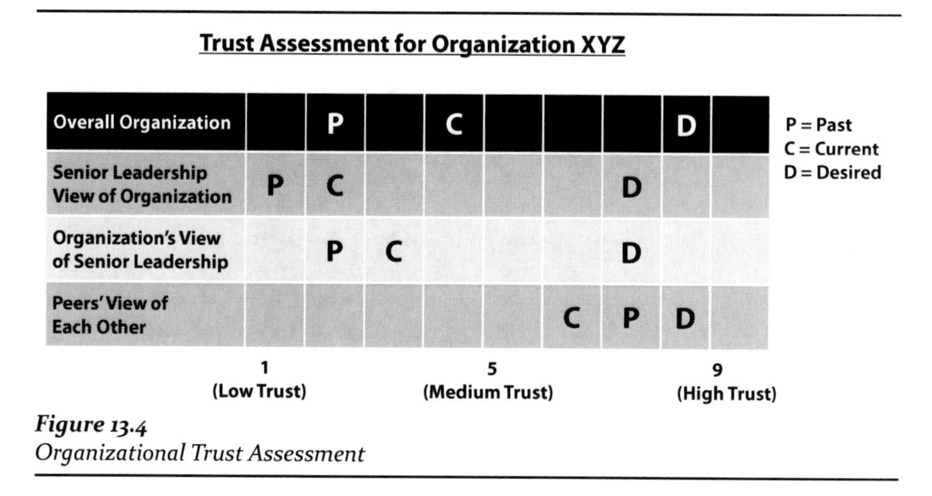

Trust Assessment for Organization XYZ

	1 (Low Trust)	2	3	4	5 (Medium Trust)	6	7	8	9 (High Trust)
Overall Organization		P		C				D	
Senior Leadership View of Organization	P	C					D		
Organization's View of Senior Leadership		P	C				D		
Peers' View of Each Other						C	P	D	

P = Past
C = Current
D = Desired

Figure 13.4
Organizational Trust Assessment

Organization XYZ (based on an actual Fortune 500 company) currently has a low-to-medium overall level of trust. Peers generally trust each other, but employees do not trust senior management, and the behaviors of senior management suggest that they do not trust the employees. This organization should be able to successfully execute evolutionary innovation but would likely struggle with expansionary or revolutionary innovation. Based on desired levels of trust, they want to shift dramatically upward. If they are successful from a trust perspective, then they should be able to sustain a balanced portfolio of innovation across the entire continuum.

Advice to the Innovation Leader: Building Organizational Trust

With our example in mind, one might ask, "We have a low level of trust in our organization – what should we do?" As noted earlier, trust is built over time by exhibiting appropriate behaviors, and the key is action – the walk being consistent with the talk. The actions of leaders demonstrate whether they uphold and enforce value systems and whether they treat employees in positive (or negative) ways.

Trust is not treating everyone the same. Nor is trust only for people we favor. Trust has to do with what is fair and just, based on the core values of the company. If the core values are inappropriate, an organization won't sustain trust, and it will be much harder to reach innovation goals.

To evolve, senior managers must truly have a desire to change the level of trust. Without this desire to change, there may be some short-term gains; however, the second there is stress, workers will revert back to behaviors which will create the earlier state of distrust.

A desire to change must be represented in values and demonstrated in actions. Creating behaviors independent of values is not sustainable. Having senior leaders behave in ways not aligned with fundamental values is like going on a crash diet without changing exercise or long-term eating habits. **Only when change is truly valued are behavioral shifts sustainable.**

If senior management desires to change the trust profile, a first step will be to get some independent (generally outside) coaches who will tell them what's really going on. Coaches must communicate the truth about what is going on in the organization and how people view it. This feedback is a prerequisite to understanding what changes are necessary.

The second piece involves leadership – they must start building bridges into the organization. They need to identify individuals who can be Change Partners (as described in Chapter 4) or the individuals who have significant influence and trust within a broad spectrum of the company. By building trusting relationships with these individuals, there can be a significant amount of transference of trust to the broader organization. If these influencers know their leaders are committed and this shift is not just a placard on the wall, other people will respond. You need this assistance from the inside; if the organization fosters distrust, as soon as people start to see a difference in the leadership's behavior, it will be met with rampant skepticism. Employees could undermine the process because they don't think it is real. People need to know the behaviors are genuine and that their leaders are not just saying, "We have changed." They need to hear your influencers say, "The leadership is changing for the better."

Building organizational trust is a long-term, integrated plan that includes:

- Determining the severity of the issue
- Having a desire for change by the senior leadership
- Getting help for them along the way via coaching
- Making sure they walk the talk
- Being consistent
- Creating individual partnerships with key Change Partners
- Listening and responding to concerns and issues raised by the key influencers
- Having the key influence champions share in being the voice of change
- Reassessing progress every few months
- Making mid-course adjustments as required

Organization DNA Table

In continuing to build the organizational DNA for Organization XYZ, we are now adding the organizational trust level to the Organization DNA Table (Figure 13.5).

Organization XYZ DNA Table

	Past	Current	Desired
Cultural Type FRAGMENTED NETWORKED MERCENARY COMMUNAL	MERCENARY	FRAGMENTED	COMMUNAL
Trust LOW TRUST MEDIUM TRUST HIGH TRUST	LOW TRUST	MEDIUM TRUST	HIGH TRUST
Risk			

Figure 13.5
Continuation of building an Organization DNA Table

Remember

Individual risk-taking is directly correlated with feelings of trust in an organization. The more trust there is in the organization, the greater the potential for revolutionary innovation.

averse. So in the TV example, the audience is very bold and wants the contestant to take extreme risks, since the audience has nothing to gain or lose except more entertainment. The contestant, on the other hand, has something to lose. Mentally, however, the money is not theirs as yet. At this point, they are really playing with "house" money rather than their own. Yet, they still have a significantly greater interest in the outcome than the audience.

Let's apply this example to your organization. The audience is similar to a lot of innovators who want their work funded, but do not want to accept any risk on their part. They often get frustrated with what they perceive as leadership's lack of risk taking. The contestant's position is similar to that of senior executives who make risk/reward trade-off decisions on whether or not to fund new innovations. They have a significant stake in the game; however, they are generally not using their own money. Except in extreme cases, they are risking, at most, some of their bonus or advancement potential, but not their family's livelihood or well-being. In smaller companies where the decision maker is often the majority or sole owner, the decisions move to a different plane altogether and become very personal. They are making decisions on how to allocate their own money. The whole difference between these groups is the level of personal accountability associated with the decision.

What is your organization's risk tolerance?

When thinking about your organization's risk tolerance, it will be helpful to revisit "Leveraging Differences" (Chapter 5) – and specifically, the notions of Builder versus Pioneer. We will apply these terms to the broader organization.

A building organization uses tried-and-true methods to achieve results and is focused on streamlining existing processes. Employees of this type of organization are focused on moving up the S curve. (See Figure 8.2, page 90) Many manufacturing organizations tend to be building organizations. They have a significant level of innovation resulting from Lean Six Sigma programs.

In contrast, a pioneering organization uses unique and sometimes unconventional methods for achieving results and is focused on creating totally new goods or services. Employees here are more interested in creating new S curves than in moving up the existing curve. As an example, many basic research labs tend to have more of a pioneering mindset and are focused on new breakthroughs, rather than optimizing existing products.

Part II
Chapter Fourteen

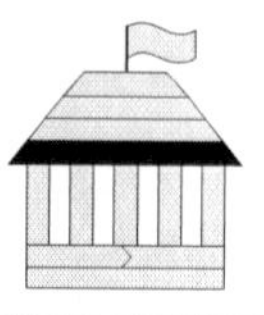

Organizational Risk Tolerance

The final piece of Organizational DNA is Risk Tolerance. Understanding the factors that contribute to your company's risk profile is critical in shaping its long-term goals. Diagnosing your risk tolerance will also help determine the most effective type of innovation programs and systems for you to achieve your long-term goals.

The TV show *Deal or No Deal* is an interesting example of how we look at risk.[1] In this program, 26 briefcases are assigned a random amount of money from one cent to one million dollars. A contestant picks one of these cases as their own. Then the contestant opens the other cases, hoping not to uncover the million-dollar case. After each stopping point, the contestant is offered an amount of money for their case. The question is then posed: "Deal or No Deal?" At this point the audience is almost always screaming, "No Deal!" while the contestant weighs the option of taking the offer and quitting, or turning it down to open additional cases and trying to win even more money. There is also the distinct possibility that they may lose what they have just won. This continues until the contestant opens the final case or accepts the offer for their case.

At times, the contestant is turning down $200,000 or more for a 25% chance that their case holds the million dollars or one of the other large sums of money ($750,000, $500,000, etc.). The interesting question is, how many people would write a check for $200,000 out of their own bank account in order to gamble on the possibility of winning $500,000 or more? The answer is, likely, not many. If you give up something that is yours, you are more risk averse than if you bet with something that isn't yours. The same is true in organizations.

Prospect Theory is used to explain this phenomenon.[2] This theory asserts that if you have to give up something of your own, you will be more risk

Is your organization focused on advancing up an S curve (building)? Or is it focused more on creating a new S curve (pioneering)? Or are you balancing going up existing S curves while developing new ones?

When you create a new S curve, you look for revolutionary innovation. This type of pioneering activity requires taking higher risks, allowing longer time for development, and incurring greater costs. Over time, as you go up the S curve, the innovation moves from revolutionary to evolutionary and into the need for more building behaviors. Building activities have lower risk, shorter development time, and lower cost. Your risk goes down as you focus on moving up the S curve.

Ideally, the right time to start looking for a new S curve is when things are going well, although this does not occur often enough. Most groups scramble for new ideas when the building part of the S curve has run its course. It takes time to create new S-Curves.

Examining Your Organization's Risk Tolerance

There are four main factors that make up the risk tolerance of a company. One of these factors is the level of trust in the organization. As we said in the previous chapter, if employees trust the organization, they will be more inclined to take risks. If they don't, they will act based upon self-preservation. For the rest of this chapter, we will make the assumption that the trust established in your organization is sufficient to support the types of risks needed. If it isn't, it won't change the risk tolerance analysis presented below. Instead, it will create a different dynamic around risk – a disconnect between the expected level of risk taking and actual behaviors. We will talk more about this situation in the next chapter (where we summarize Organizational DNA).

Organizational Risk Tolerance: The other axes of risk tolerance are determined by three main questions:

- How does your organization want to grow?
- What is the risk profile of your key decision makers?
- How far will your consumer allow you to go, relative to risk?

The starting point is to ask, "How are we currently growing?" Is your organization's growth primarily through evolutionary innovation that requires more of a builder mindset? Is it expansionary? Or is it more revolutionary with a pioneering mindset? As you move along the Innovation Continuum from evolutionary to revolutionary, the risk goes from low to high. The descriptions in Figure 14.1 will help make these growth mechanisms more visible.

We often use the following assessment tool to help people better understand their prior, current, and desired growth mechanism and, therefore, where they position themselves on the builder to pioneer continuum (Figure 14.2). To use this assessment tool, place a:

- "C" where your current organization is relative to each of the statements in the chart below,
- "P" for where it was five years ago, and
- "D" for the desired state.

Add all of the numbers associated with the "Cs" to determine where your organization is currently. Then add the numbers associated with the "Ps" and "Ds" to determine where it was five years ago and where you desire to be.

Again, we have filled out the assessment in Figure 14.2 for our example organization.

For our Organization XYZ, the growth mechanism (GRM) in the past (GRM-P), current (GRM-C), and desired (GRM-D) are:

- **Total GRM-P = 9 → Builder Organization**
- **Total GRM-C = 12 → Builder Organization**
- **Total GRM-D = 25 → Mid-Pioneering Organization**

Therefore, to meet the desired long-term growth, there needs to be a significant shift from evolutionary/builder types of innovation to growth fueled by more expansionary and some revolutionary/pioneering innovation. Note that we will use these results later in the chapter when we complete the risk assessment.

Decision Makers: The next step is to look at the individual decision makers in terms of where they are on the continuum from builders to pioneers. From their behaviors, where are they on the builder-to-pioneer continuum? Remember: Builders tend to "de-risk" the situation, while pioneers tend to take on greater risk.

Your decision makers play a huge role in establishing overall risk tolerance. If builders lead your organization, it will be difficult for them to grasp the need for revolutionary innovation and will be uncomfortable supporting it. If pioneers lead you, they will have trouble with the process work at the top of

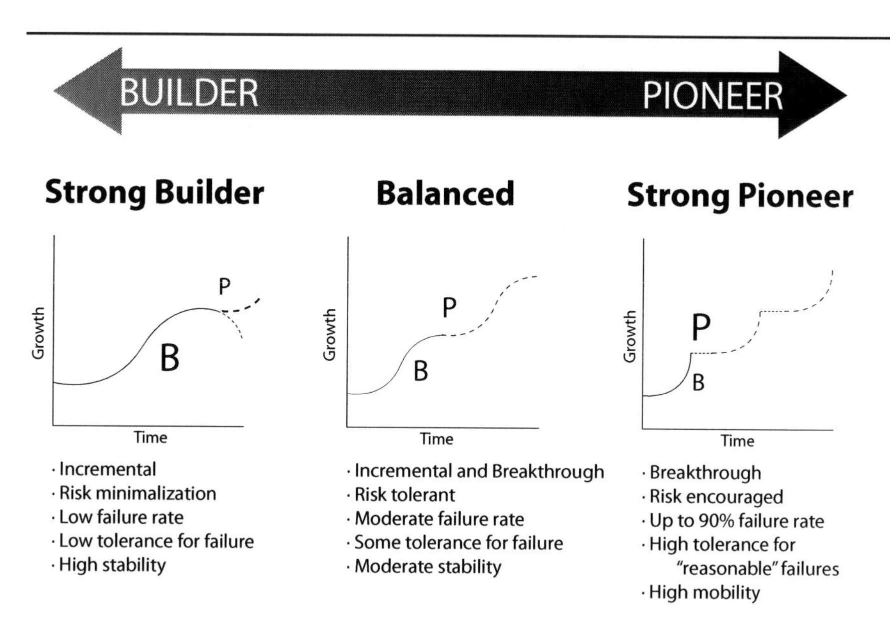

Figure 14.1
Organizational mindset determines the predominant growth mechanism.

Growth Descriptors	Strongly Disagree		Neutral		Strongly Agree
Growth is primarily from new products vs. productivity	1 P	2 C	3	4 D	5
New products are highly incremental (vs. Replacing existing business)	1 C/P	2	3	4 D	5
New products or services are outside current categories	1 C/P	2	3 D	4	5
Significant percentage (>75%) of organization is on focused long term	1 CP	2	3 D	4	5
New developmental approaches continuously being tried/examined	1 C	2 P	3 D	4	5
Organizational bureaucracy does not hinder product development/advancement	1 P	2 C	3	4 D	5
People are free to talk with anybody in the organization to solve program issues	1	2 P	3	4 C/D	5

SCORING

- **Add the scores from Growth Descriptors**

- **Builder Organization:** ≤ 14
- **Mid-Builder Organization:** 15 - 21
- **Mid-Pioneer Organization:** 22 - 28
- **Pioneering Organization:** ≥ 29

Figure 14.2
Organizational Growth Assessment Tool

the S curve. These decision makers set the tone for what happens in the rest of the company.

Think about your key decision makers. Based on what you learned in Chapter 5, where do they fall on the builder-to-pioneer continuum? If you are in doubt, look at their behaviors and talk with other people who know them well. Make a list of these decision makers and note your assessment of where they fall similar to what is shown in Figure 14.3. Average their problem-solving preferences or orientations and determine the predominant orientation for this group.

For our example, we have identified six key decision makers:

- Ron (R) – Mid-Builder
- Julie (J) – Mid-Builder
- Trish (T) – Pioneer
- Mark (M) – Builder
- Samantha (S) – Mid-Pioneer
- Ian (I) – Mid-Builder

We have plotted their problem-solving preferences in Figure 14.3 and have estimated the predominant orientation of the group.

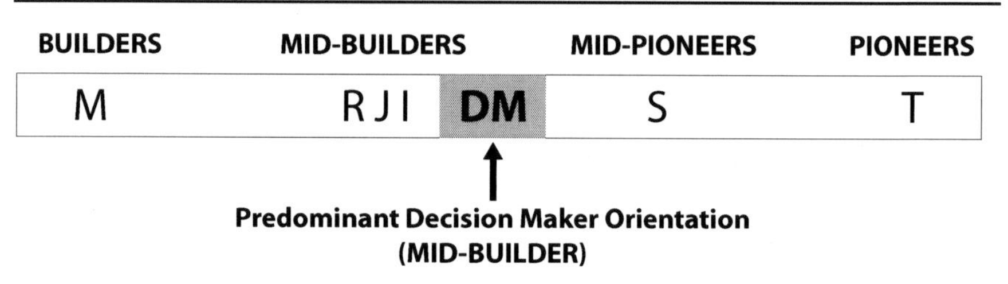

Figure 14.3
Based on the individual decision maker's preferred problem-solving orientation, you can assess the orientation of the overall group. This will allow you to begin to understand the overall risk tolerance of this group.

When mentally averaging orientations for the group, try to factor in the weight of influence of each of the decision makers. In our example, if Trish was the least influential of the group, then the average would move more toward builder. If she is the most influential, however, then the average would move more toward pioneer. Again, we will use this information in the final risk analysis later in this chapter.

Now you have two key points: the current growth profile and the analysis of your decision makers. The last element is to determine what your consumers will allow you to do in terms of risk.

Consumer Risk Tolerance: There are two ends of the customer risk spectrum. At one end is a company making tractors, where farmers' livelihoods are totally dependent on the reliability of their product. The technology may exist for a remote-controlled GPS tractor where a farmer can sit on the porch and drive a tractor remotely. But most farmers will not buy this product because it will be perceived as too risky. Yet, on the other end of the customer risk spectrum, customers camp out for days for the release of a new product like the iPhone™, Xbox™, or Wii™, sight unseen.

The consumer risk determines the types of organizational risk you can take. For our tractor company, much of their growth is going up the S curves rather than innovating totally new offerings. Their time between new S curves is usually very long. Their product doesn't change much because their consumers are not looking for the latest and greatest. Apple is almost the polar opposite of our tractor company in this regard.

In general, if a product or service is associated with an individual's livelihood or safety, consumers tend to be builders in mindset. Technology and entertainment consumers tend to be pioneering and want to be the first to own the latest and greatest new products. See Figure 14.4 for how we generally map consumer risk tolerance on the builder-to-pioneer continuum.

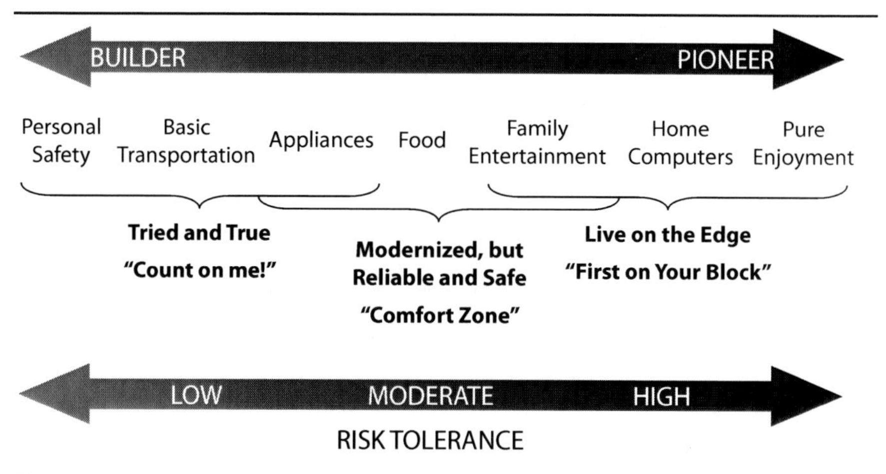

Figure 14.4
Consumers have a significant influence over the degree of risk that an organization should take when developing new goods or services.

These are general guides we have seen in working with different companies. You need to assess your own consumer base to determine where they fall. Our example company is primarily dealing with family entertainment. Therefore, consumer risk (CR) is in the moderate-to-pioneering zone for risk tolerance.

Risk Tolerance Gap: Once you identify the current state on all three levels, then you need to analyze your future state. Knowing where you are currently and where you need to go will determine your tolerance gap. Do you need to change your strategy to grow? Depending on where you are on your S curve(s), this may mean moving from a builder to pioneering mindset, or vice versa.

Your risk tolerance gap will show you how far on the Revolutionary/Pioneering or Evolutionary/Building spectrum your organization can shift. It is important to know that you just can't flip a switch from builder to pioneer, or vice versa, overnight. Risk tolerance shifts take time.

You can start to close the tolerance gap by making it visible to your organization's leaders and employees. You also need to gain an understanding as to the rate (or speed) at which you want to try and close that gap. To do so, make sure the organization is generating the types of ideas you are really looking for. By setting the stage and communicating the new goals, you can start moving in the desired direction.

It is highly unlikely that you can change decision makers or consumers overnight because they are both relatively fixed. The following diagnostic tool will also allow you to make visible some of the preferences and orientations of your decision makers. Do they need to be educated on the fact that they are going to need to take greater or lesser risks than they are currently comfortable with?

Consider: Are consumers going to let you move your organization to where you want it to go? Or are you going to have a long-term target to get your consumers to accept the kind of development your company needs to pursue?

Therefore, let's look at how to analyze your organization and determine your risk tolerance gap. In Figure 14.5, we have plotted data from our example organization's growth mechanism and the risk profile of decision makers and consumers. By comparing the desired growth mechanism (strategy) of Organization XYZ from Figure 14.2 against consumer risk tolerance (Figure 14.4), the current growth mechanism (Figure 14.2), and decision makers' profile (Figure 14.3), everyone will be able to identify risk tolerance gaps

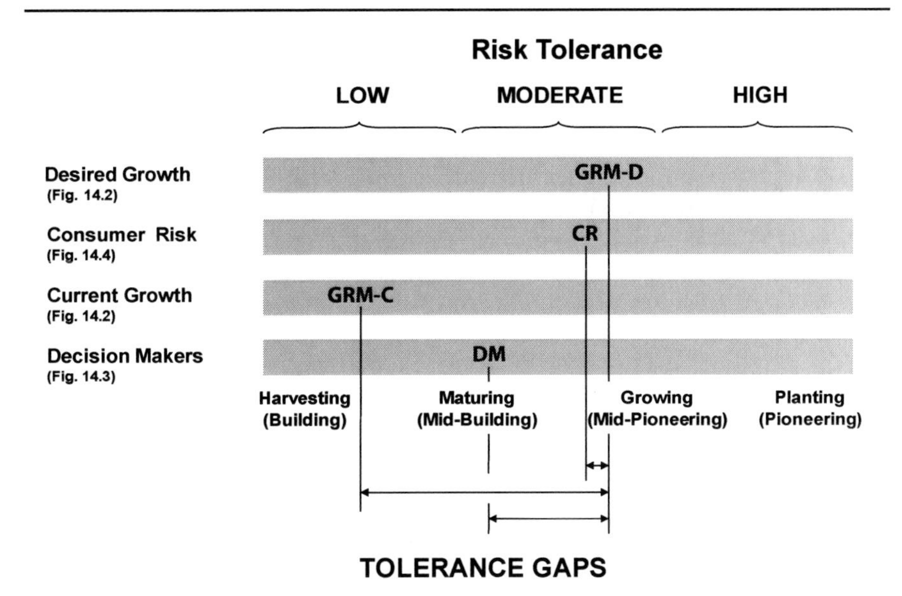

Figure 14.5
The organization in this example has a desired growth mechanism (strategy) that is aligned with the risk tolerance of their consumers. There are significant gaps between the current growth mechanism, decision makers' risk tolerance, and where the organization needs to go.

that must be addressed. By making these gaps visible, you can then begin to develop strategies and action plans to close them over time.

This analysis is a way to start making visible the drivers of risk and where the gaps are going to occur.

Advice for the Innovation Leader

Leaders need to understand that they must educate their people on risk tolerance and creative orientation, as well as communicate what the organization's orientation actually is. By doing so, employees will begin to understand the "sweet spot" for their innovations and, by making it visible, your organization will have a greater chance for success.

As an innovator, you need to know whether or not you are in the right company for your orientation of innovation. Knowing if you are in a building or pioneering organization will allow you to better navigate the innovation waters. It may allow you to flourish, even if your company is not a true fit for your individual orientation. We have seen people become very successful at pioneering new, non-product-driven ideas within a builder organization (e.g., a new quality control system, new processes, new packaging, etc.). At the same time, when they tried to pioneer a new product, their success was limited. It's knowing who you are and where you are living.

Also, understanding risk tolerance will help you position potential innovations when communicating them to key decision makers. Ideally, you would like to take a revolutionary idea to a decision maker who is more willing to take risk. But if you don't have that flexibility, you can still examine the decision maker's risk preference (and overall ISPI, iO, and iOM such as Control, Passion, Input, and Flow) to help you formulate and present your strategy for moving an idea forward.

As an innovation leader, you need to also determine your personal risk tolerance relative to the current state of your organization and where it needs to go in the future. This will help you to determine the way you should interact with your managers, employees, and peers. It will also allow you to better understand the type of innovation that you want to champion.

If you have a significant risk tolerance gap with where the organization needs to move to in the future, then develop a network (either inside or outside of your company) that can help you adapt your natural tendencies to meet the needs of your organization. If you need to take greater risks, find people who can help you minimize the uncertainties associated with taking those risks. If you are inclined to take risks greater than those needed or wanted, again find people who you trust (e.g., Creativity Partners) who can help keep you more grounded. You must realize that, as an innovation leader, you cannot allow a significant personal risk tolerance gap to continue unchecked. It will not serve you or your organization well. It is also important to know that it is difficult to change your personal risk tolerance. Attitude toward risk is part of our hard wiring! By understanding your own risk preference, however, you can seek out people you trust who are different than you and ask them to assist you in making decisions.

Organization DNA Table

While continuing to build our Organizational DNA, we will now add risk tolerance to the Organization DNA Table on the next page. Note that for this analysis, we will use the overall growth mechanisms (current and desired). In the next chapter, we will tie the Organization DNA together using the data from this table 14.6.

Organization XYZ DNA Table

	Past	Current	Desired
Cultural Type FRAGMENTED NETWORKED MERCENARY COMMUNAL	**MERCENARY**	**FRAGMENTED**	**COMMUNAL**
Trust LOW TRUST MEDIUM TRUST HIGH TRUST	**LOW TRUST**	**MEDIUM TRUST**	**HIGH TRUST**
Risk LOW TOLERANCE MODERATE TOLERANCE HIGH TOLERANCE	**LOW**	**LOW**	**MODERATE**

Figure 14.6
Completed organizational DNA analysis table for use when looking at the characteristics of your organization

Remember

Innovation requires taking risks. Are the risks associated with your growth strategy in alignment with the risk tolerance of your decision makers and consumers?

Part II
Chapter Fifteen

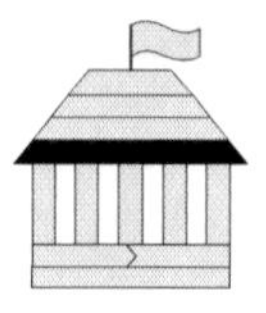

Organizational DNA

We have used the analogy of the DNA helix to illustrate interactions between the business, technical, and human elements involved with innovation (Figure 1.1, page 6). We see these as the basic building blocks required for innovation. In a similar manner, we see culture, trust, and risk tolerance as basic building blocks that, when combined, provide a model of behaviors that result from an organization's fundamental principles and values.

A secondary reason for choosing this model is related to the story of Francis Crick and James Watson, who together received the Nobel Prize for their work in discovering the structure of DNA in 1962[1]. As with most scientific breakthroughs, their work was based on that of many other scientists. Work on DNA dates back to at least 1868 to the work by Friedrich Miescher, a Swiss physician who isolated a compound he called "nuclein." Today, it is called nucleic acid, or the NA of DNA.[2] Fifty years after Crick and Watson, we now have the Human Genome Project (HGP) that has given us the genetic blueprint for a human being.[3]

While the discovery and subsequent work on DNA over the past decades has changed and will continue to change for the rest of our lives, the combination of Crick and Watson is a great example of many of the principles that go into defining an organization's DNA. Robert Wright's 1999 article for Time Magazine's 100 Most Important People of the Century provides an insight into the lives of these two men.[4] Each were from dramatically different backgrounds, with Crick starting out in physics and Watson studying ornithology. Their attraction to DNA brought them together in the same laboratory at Cambridge University. Here, in essence, they became Creativity Partners. As a colleague put it, it was, "that marvelous resonance between two minds – that high state in which 1 plus 1 does not equal 2, but more like 10." The two were passionate, had little use for authority, and did not value the opinions of others. One quote from Watson sums it all up: "One could not be a successful scientist without realizing that, in contrast to the popular conception supported by newspapers and mothers of scientists, a goodly number of scientists are not only narrow-minded and dull, but also just stupid." When faced with the question of which name would be first on their findings, they flipped a coin.

The working relationship between the two men was based on high solidarity and sociability (communal culture), being Creativity Partners (high emotional and intellectual trust), and a willingness to go against authority and other peers (high risk tolerance). They embodied the organizational DNA most suited to producing revolutionary innovations. How does your organization's DNA look?

The three previous chapters should have made the separate pieces of your DNA more visible: Culture, Trust, and Risk Tolerance. Yet, the separate pieces don't really help unless you can see how they integrate into the big picture and then see where that big picture takes you. Your DNA impacts the organization as a whole, as well as the leadership and the people. Putting it all together will point you to the preferred type of communication and invisible decision-making process.

To diagnose the entire picture, we will use our example from the previous three chapters. Refer back to Figure 14.6 (page 153) as needed.

Chapter 12 examined culture and defined the Four Cultures Model. In looking at this model, remember that there are four different quadrants. We gave the example of a fragmented organization today that needs to be communal in the future. This requires first raising the solidarity level, then working on improving sociability.

Chapter 13 examined organizational trust levels in the three categories of low, medium, and high trust which allowed you to better see the impact of each on the characteristics of the company, leadership, and individual employees.

Chapter 14 examined organizational risk tolerance. We considered the current and desired growth algorithms, the impact of decision makers, and the types of risk your consumers will accept to determine where your business is today and where it should be in the future.

This analysis allowed for the development of the overall matrix of the DNA (Figure 14.6, page 153) with the past, current, and desired future state. By going through the DNA analysis, you can start taking action toward where you want to go. Based on this analysis, in Appendix III you will find a breakdown of 36 different types of organizational DNA with individual, overall, and leadership characteristics. It is important to complete the DNA chart and read the corresponding characteristics for your organization. The list of characteristics is not meant to be all-inclusive; rather, it is intended to give you an overview of the characteristics, which will serve as a starting point. As you analyze your particular organization, you will add additional characteristics that are unique to it.

Figures 15.1, 15.2, and 15.3 are summaries of the characteristics for our example Organization XYZ. Comparing information in the three summaries will allow innovation leaders to begin looking at where significant gaps are between the current state and the desired future state relative to the past. Using this information, an overall strategy can be identified for transforming the organization and specific actions determined. Both can then be made readily visible to the entire organization.

Organization XYZ: Past

Characteristics of a "Mercenary/Low Trust/Low Risk" Organization

Overall

- Clear focus on business objectives/emphasis on probability.
- Rapid response to threats/quickly unified against an enemy.
- Slavish adherence to numbers/intolerant of ambiguity.
- Risks are taken only when there is a well defined 'safety net' in case of failure.
- Organizational surprises occur frequently due to filtered or 'spun' communication.
- Growth through enhancements/productivity improvements to existing businesses/operations.
- Predominantly focused on many near-term programs.

Leadership

- Goal-oriented/obsessive desire to complete tasks once started.
- Thrives on competitive energy/strong sense of ego.
- Minimum levels of sociability/failure to build relationships
- Execution adherence to established methodologies.
- Well established bureaucracy with policies and procedures covering most day-to-day activities.
- Strict hierarchical organizational structure (if there is an organizational structure).

Individuals

- Calculate assistance and sharing based on 'Negotiated Reciprocity'
- Hit individual targets/do only what is measured.
- Information/ideas are only readily shared with people the individual truly trusts - information/ideas guarded and/or filtered before sharing on a broader scale.
- Examining of the motivation for challenging of ideas oftentimes gets greater focus than the content of challenge itself.

Figure 15.1
Characteristics of the past state of our example organization

Organization XYZ: Current

Characteristics of a "Fragmented/Medium Trust/Low Risk" Organization

Overall

- Independent professionals/focused on outside markets.
- Individual creativity/"individual stars."
- Lack of teamwork/small 'fiefdoms.'
- Only moderate risks are taken with minimal concern for consequences of a failure, more significant risks need well defined 'safety net.'
- Organizational surprises occur due to lack of open communication or filtering of the information.
- Growth through enhancements/productivity improvements to existing businesses/operations.
- Predominantly focused on many near-term programs.

Leadership

- High autonomy/strong sense of self.
- Analytical vs. intuitive.
- Minimum levels of sociability/failure to build relationships.
- Execution adherence to established methodologies.
- Well established bureaucracy with policies and procedures covering most day-to-day activities.
- Strict hierarchical organizational structure (if there is an organizational structure).

Individuals

- Be valuable to the organization/invest in oneself.
- Focus on outputs/organization's reward system.
- Try to get help without providing 'reciprocity.'
- Individuals will generally share non-sensitive information/ideas without significant concern for negative consequences.
- Sensitive information/ideas are only shared with the people the individual truly trusts.
- Examining the motivation for challenging of ideas has equal weight as the challenge itself.

Figure 15.2
Characteristics of the current state of our example organization

Organization XYZ: Desired

Characteristics of a "Communal/High Trust/Moderate Risk" Organization

Overall

- Powerful sense of family/natural concern for co-workers.
- Inward focus/potential lack of external awareness.
- Clear focus/strong sense of urgency aligned with organization's mission.
- Risks can be taken with minimal organizational-driven 'fear of failure.'
- Organizational surprises due to lack of open communication are minimal.
- Growth through balance of enhancements/productivity improvements to existing businesses/operations and creation of new businesses.
- Focused on several near-term programs along with a few long-term new business programs.

Leadership

- Create high degree of enthusiasm for organization's vision and values.
- Building disciples/intimidating followers.
- Fosters teamwork/loyal to those who perform well.
- Execution primarily guided by established methodologies.
- Established bureaucracy with policies and procedures covering most day-to-day activities.
- General adherence to hierarchical organizational structure.

Individuals

- Freely provide assistance with no expectation of return - it's good for the company/organization.
- Trust your colleagues to know/follow the leader.
- Identify with organization/invest time with peers talking about things important to the organization.
- Individuals readily share information/ideas without significant concern for negative consequences.
- Challenging of ideas is accepted with minimal feelings of personal attacks or value judgments.

Figure 15.3
Characteristics of the desired state of our example organization.

This analysis is not set in stone. Your leadership characteristics may be different than the core organization on the trust, cultural, and/or risk axes. For example, your leadership team may be far more sociable than your employees.

You may also have a different view if you are looking at the situation of your organization as a leader (versus an individual contributor). And, in looking at larger organizations, there may be several different DNA structures operating together.

We have worked with a client at a Fortune 100 company who has found two distinctly different patterns. One describes the senior staff and their behaviors. Another pattern describes the rest of the organization. The key is to recognize that multiple DNAs may exist and to understand each one of them. Then, the innovation leader can begin to form a more comprehensive view.

If you were the innovation leader of Company XYZ and wanted to move from a fragmented culture to a communal culture, you would normally start by getting alignment on where your organization needs to go. Getting strong solidarity is faster and easier than sociability. Moving up the solidarity axis requires ensuring the organization has clear, measurable objectives. From there, everyone needs to understand the objectives and see how what they are doing is aligned with the objectives. The leadership must demonstrate that they are unified and strongly agree with the objectives. Once strong solidarity is in place, then you can focus more attention on moving up the sociability axis. This requires allowing the opportunities and time for people to get to know and trust each other. The leadership must demonstrate that they know this is important by modeling the behavior within the organization. Similarly you can develop tactics to continue moving your organization's trust level and to shift its risk tolerance.

Advice for the Innovation Leader

DNA characteristics are all based on observable behaviors. As discussed in Chapter 1, behaviors are a direct result of the principles and values of an organization, its leaders, and its staff. Using the Principles to Results Model (PRM in Figure 1.2, page 10), you can use characteristics of the current organization to make visible the values and principles driving it.

For example, some of the principles and values that drove the past state of Organization XYZ (mercenary, low trust, low risk) included:

- Winning is everything.
- My interests come first and the organization's second.
- Avoid all significant risks.
- Hide behind the numbers/process.
- Near-term success is top priority.

To understand the current direction your organization is moving toward, assess your organization's DNA using information from five years ago. Comparing behaviors and underlying values and principles from this past analysis with where you are today will provide you with a solid understanding of current movement. Then, adding in the desired future state, principles and values will allow you to understand if the future is a continuation of the current trends or a dramatic shift, either toward the past or away from it in a completely different direction.

Having this understanding is critical for gaining alignment and support for desired change. It will allow you to address issues associated with the principle we discussed in Chapter 3: Elements of Destruction Are Present at Creation. Are you trying to change systemic behaviors that date back to the beginning of your organization? Or are you trying to change behaviors that are far less deeply rooted? The tactics will be quite different, depending on which ones you are trying to change.

Regardless of the type of change you are undertaking, remember that you are trying to change behaviors. Therefore, you need to model these behaviors, train key influencers relative to your expectations, and communicate which behaviors will no longer be rewarded or encouraged.

A friend of ours compared innovation to genetic engineering and skeet shooting. "It's like going out skeet shooting, putting the gun over your shoulder the opposite way, and not knowing when the skeet was let go." In this case, hitting the target is a random event at best.

We have found the Organizational DNA model to be a more accurate form of targeted genetic engineering. We know the "effect genes"[5] of innovation, and we know how and where to insert them.

The DNA model allows you to define desired behaviors in terms that everybody can understand. As an innovation leader, you can complete the diagnosis based on the three previous chapters, then step back and say:

"OK, this is what I think is going on. Let me observe the behaviors to verify whether or not the analysis is correct."

It's a classic scientific discovery. You've got a hypothesis and need to do some experimentation to prove or disprove it. In this case, the hypothesis is what you think your organization's DNA is. Your experiment is to observe the behaviors and interactions between employees and leadership and the interface between them. Does it fit the hypothesis? If it does, then you have a pretty good model of where you are today. If not, then go back and modify the model analysis until you have a good fit for the current observable behaviors.

Having a good model of the current state is a critical step in developing the strategies and action plans for achieving the desired future state.

In Closing

Next, the organizational DNA model will be expanded to look at some of the invisible rules of engagement. These rules help define why some people seem to be able to get sponsors for their programs, while others (with equally as good or better ideas) cannot get any real momentum behind them. This will include examining some of the behaviors that you (as an innovation leader) must demonstrate to send the desired message to your employees.

Remember

An organization's culture, trust, and risk tolerance help to define it and dictate how it will operate. Understanding such traits will help you to successfully create a desirable future vision and road map for your organization.

Part II

Chapter Sixteen

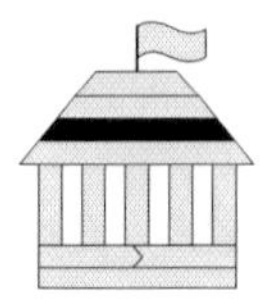

Invisible Rules of Engagement: Communications

A friend relayed the following story that happened to him at the start of his career. Jim had just graduated from Texas A&M University with a degree in Electrical Engineering and accepted a position with a major electronics firm in Dallas, Texas. He had just recently married and moved to Dallas – everything seemed to be falling into place. He was getting to know the people he worked with, he began to understand the project to which he was assigned, and he and his wife were starting to make friends.

A few weeks after he started, his boss came by to talk with him on a Monday morning. His boss said, "Jim, how was your weekend? Did you do anything special?"

Jim was elated. His boss wanted to get to know him! Jim proceeded to tell his boss about his weekend and the visit that he and his wife had with friends. But Jim was not expecting his boss's response: "That sounds like you had a lot of fun. We all missed you on Saturday in the lab. I hope that maybe you can come and join us next Saturday." And he walked off.

Jim realized after a few moments that one of the invisible rules of working at that company was that he was expected to work Saturday mornings unless he had a very good reason for being absent. From that point on, he worked every Saturday until he finally took another job.

Was the "rule" of working on Saturdays ever written down? Was it discussed when Jim was interviewing? The answer was no. However, was it part of the job expectations? Clearly, yes.

Invisible rules of engagement are not written down and they are rarely discussed. Yet, they are a major driving force for how an organization functions. Learning and understanding them is vital for innovators and innovation leaders to successfully navigate an organization's "minefields" and deliver sustained innovation.

What do we mean by the phrase, "invisible rules of engagement"? The Business Dictionary defines it as:[1]

> *Practices followed or behaviors displayed by the participants in situations of opposing interests such as negotiations. Unwritten rules of engagement determine what information is given, at what time, to whom, and in what manner; and what concession is granted and what is demanded in return.*

Every profession has its own set of invisible rules. For example, in the legal profession according to Mark Perlmutter:[2]

> *"Lawsuits proceed under what I call 'game assumptions' – unspoken rules of engagement governing the particular 'game' we are playing with the other lawyer. The game assumption will normally crystallize in response to a specific provocation and will often bring us to mutter indignantly: 'Oh, so that's the game we're gonna play!'*
>
> *The various possible game assumptions divide into two categories: competitive and cooperative. The competitive game assumption most lawyers acknowledge playing is: We shall use every means permitted by the rules to prevail over the other side.*
>
> *An example of a cooperative game assumption is: We shall exchange enough information to permit a reasonably accurate evaluation, make good faith efforts to settle, and failing that, afford each other a fair opportunity to present the merits."*

In the National Hockey League (NHL), fighting is considered part of the game. However, it is technically against the rules. Players generally receive a five-minute penalty for fighting; however, there are several unwritten rules of engagement, including:[3]

- Both players will drop their gloves at the same time to avoid the two-minute instigator rule.
- Players don't pick fights at the end of shifts if they are just coming onto the ice to start their shifts.
- Players don't pick fights with rivals just recovering from injuries.
- Players usually pick fights with others their own size.

Every person and every organization has unwritten or invisible rules of engagement (IRE). Think about you and your company. What are some of the IREs that control your actions? Your company's actions?

The next three chapters will focus on three key areas within the arena of invisible rules of engagement: 1) communication, 2) decision making, and 3) knowledge transfer (Figure 16.1). We feel that these three areas are critical in helping you understand your organization's IREs as they pertain to the human dynamics associated with innovation. They are the fundamental, behavioral building blocks that allow you to genetically modify your organization's DNA. They represent those visible actions that people look for when evaluating whether or not they believe that a change is sincere. Highly successful innovation leaders understand the IRE and are able to use them to gain alignment with regard to their innovative ideas and programs.

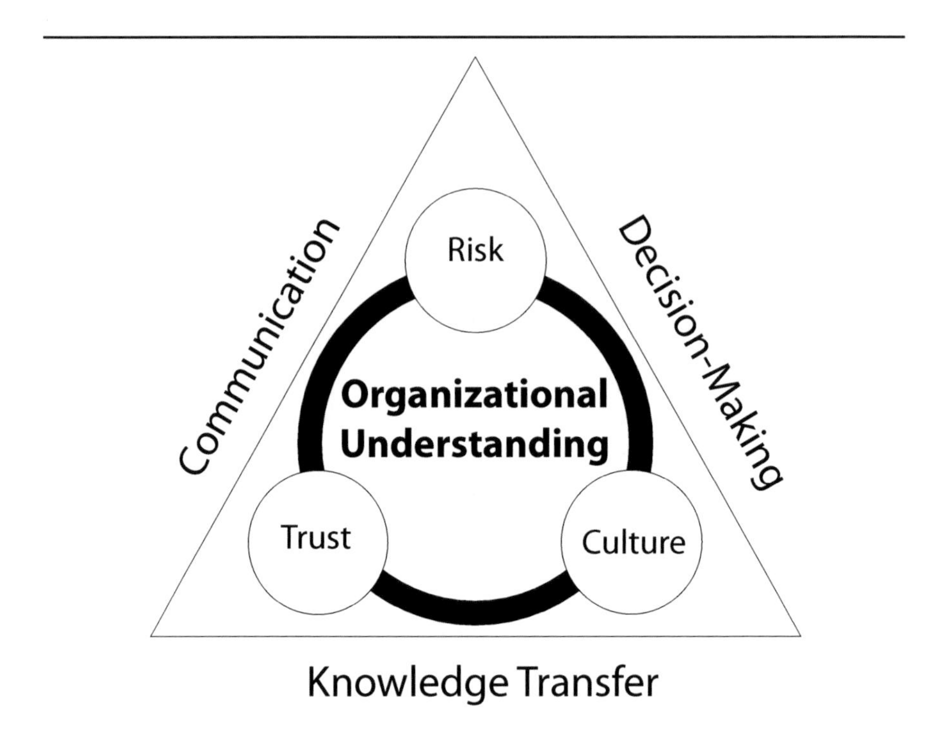

Figure 16.1
Invisible Rules of Engagement are driven by an organization's DNA.

As depicted in Figure 16.1, the IREs are driven by the DNA of the organization (culture, trust, and risk). In this chapter, we will discuss communication, which is largely a function of risk tolerance and trust. Culture influences the communications, but is not a primary driver. Similarly, decision making is driven by culture and risk tolerance with trust being an underlying influence. Knowledge transfer is controlled by trust and culture and influenced by the overall risk tolerance of the organization and individual. These three IREs make up the next level of the Innovation House.

IRE: Communication

In Chapter 2 (Figure 2.1, page 17), we discussed the idea of Generative ("above the line") and Destructive ("below the line") communication. To reiterate: "Above the line" communication is about listening to learn, understand, and create, whereas "below the line" is about win-lose and listening to respond. "Above the line" supports innovation; "below the line" impedes it. When we look at the IREs for communication, we assume that the overall organization tends to operate "above the line." Therefore, the focus will be on the type and content of the communication required to support the desired type of innovation.

As we have said before, looking at an organization's behavior is the key to understanding its core values and principles. One of the most visible behaviors is communication "content." To understand content differences, we will refer to the definitions in Figure 16.2. Examining your organization's **communication content** in this way will provide significant insight into the type of innovation being supported.

Level	Name	Definition
1	**Physicality**	Physical description of an item *(color, taste, shape, etc.)*
2	**Analytical**	Analytical analysis of a physical item *(economics, production capacity, market/sales potential, etc.)*
3	**Evolutionary**	Potential enhancements without changing basic form *(size, color, shape, etc.)*
4	**Expansionary**	Slight changes to basic form *(SUV vs Sedan)*
5	**Revolutionary**	Significant changes to basic form *(plane vs car)*

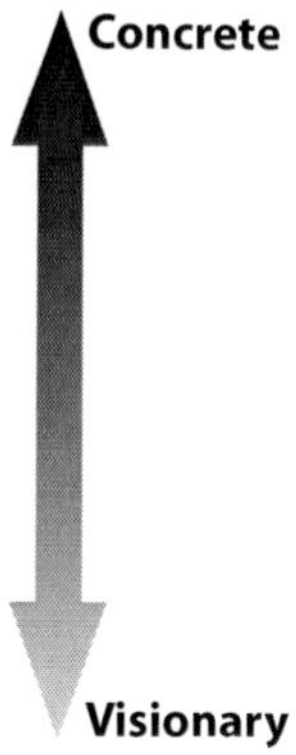

Concrete ↕ **Visionary**

Figure 16.2
Communication Content Definitions

Organization XYZ from Chapter 15 showed the current DNA of a fragmented, medium trust, and low risk company. Being fragmented, little communication energy was devoted to how a proposed idea might take advantage of the overall capability of the organization. The moderate trust limited the extent to which the innovation leader felt safe discussing the more revolutionary end of the Innovation Continuum. The internal "fear of failure" filter by employees would become dominant. And being a low risk company would force discussions toward the evolutionary end of the continuum. The internal perception was that higher risk programs had little chance of being sponsored. Therefore, innovation leaders would not even bring them up.

In this scenario, we would expect that communication would be largely centered around levels 1 and 2 (See Figure 16.2) and, potentially, level 3 discussions around the physical description and analytical analyses. Very little time would be spent in looking at the potential for the innovation to create something towards the revolutionary end.

For one successful business, we looked at annual strategic plans for three consecutive years. Roughly 60% of these plans addressed the description of slight improvements or changes to existing products and the analytical analysis to support these changes. About 10% were transition-focused, while the remaining 30% targeted potential product enhancements. The company was focused on moving up S curves via evolutionary innovation with no focus on creating totally new products. Where is your company focused today?

Advice for the Innovation Leader

Going back to Company XYZ in the last chapter, the desired future DNA included being a communal, high trust, and moderate risk organization. As an innovation leader, to demonstrate that you believe in the validity of direction in which you need to move, you must model the communication behaviors consistent with this change. To move to a more communal organization requires starting to look at what is best for the whole organization, not just your portion. It requires showing concern and trust for all of the employees. Questions and discussions must be above the line. They are about understanding and expanding ideas.

Creating a higher level of trust requires that you first take a risk and trust the organization. You must be willing to move beyond your own internal fear of failure and discuss ideas much further along the Innovation Continuum. If you want employees to bring revolutionary ideas to you, they must see that you are receptive to them. They need to see that you are willing to pitch them to the broader organization. Coupled with this notion is a shift in the discussion from levels 1 and 2 toward more of a balance including levels 3, 4, and 5 (Figure 16.2). This is not to imply that levels 1 and 2 are any less important, but there needs to be a balance. Your myopic focus on the lower levels (at the expense of the higher levels) tells potential innovators that you are not interested in fostering anything but evolutionary innovation.

The communication content from a low to high trust and low to high risk tolerance is shown in Figure 16.3 (next page). A "low-low" communication will be all about the description of the idea and the analytical analysis. Shifting to a higher risk tolerance without changing the trust will bring a limited discussion around expansionary innovation. Shifting toward "high-high" communication will allow the communication content to have a balance between all five levels. Where is your organization today? Where does it need to be in the future?

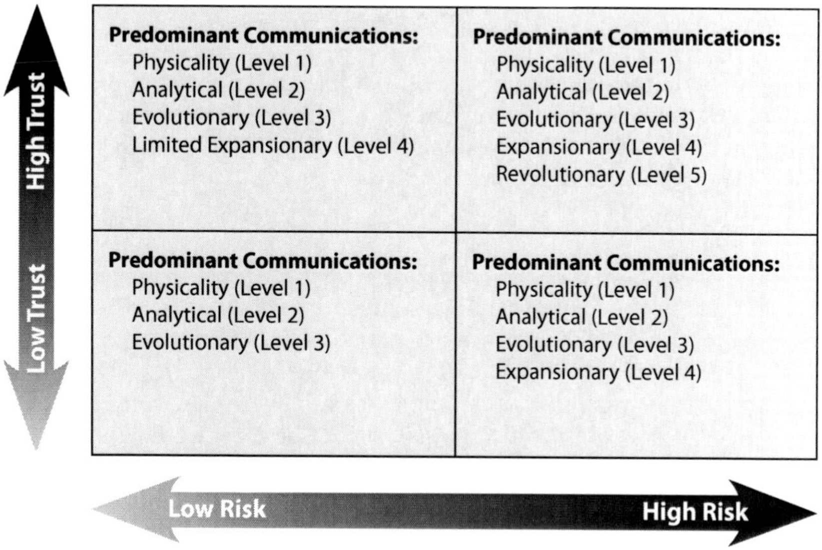

Figure 16.3
Predominant communication content based on an organization's DNA analysis

How would you characterize your communications? Are you in a predominantly level 1 and 2 world, or a balanced one that includes all of the levels? If you don't know the answer to this beyond a reasonable doubt, have a trusted peer analyze some of your typical conversations with innovators in your group, with other innovation leaders, and with innovation sponsors. Examine the distribution of communication and determine which quadrant you reside in.

Based on this analysis, are you aligned with your organization's current DNA? If the desired organizational DNA requires a significant shift, can you make the shift? Have someone you trust and who attends most of your meetings randomly assess the content of your communication, relative to the five levels. This insight will provide the feedback necessary for you to ensure that you are really making the required shift. If the shift isn't occurring as you would like, engage a coach to work with you. Do whatever you need to make the transformation. As a leader, people are looking at your behaviors to determine whether or not they believe your desire to change is real. They will take your lead in establishing their own communication content and style.

Note that if you are a very senior leader, having someone internally help you may not work well. Often senior leaders, for various reasons, are unable to rely on an internal resource or are uncomfortable using one. In these cases, finding an external coach is the best approach for helping you make required changes.

Remember that making a fundamental shift in your behavior (and related communication) is a long-term process. In times of stress, be acutely aware of how you communicate. Stress generally makes us revert back to our old habits until the new ones have become permanent.

In Closing

When you walk into meetings, are people saying, "That is a really cool idea. What else can we do with that?" Such a response is more risk tolerant, encouraging, and will help move things toward the revolutionary end of the innovation continuum. On the other hand, are people saying, "The ROI for this project is very good. The probability of success is high, since it is a minor change to what we are already doing. It should be completed by the end of the next quarter." This response is characteristic of a lower risk organization focused on evolutionary innovation. Where is your organization? Does it have the appropriate balance of communication aligned with the desired innovation portfolio?

As an innovation leader, if you are trying to encourage moving toward generating an increased number of revolutionary ideas, you must change both communication and behaviors. These become very tangible pieces of the change process.

If you are trying to lead a change in your organization, you need to be able to say, "Andrew, this looks like a great opportunity. I know it will be high risk, but I will protect you. This is going to be my decision. It's my risk. I'll give you the **air cover** and the resources." Here, you've just given that person or team permission to focus on making the idea successful.

We have seen many ideas shot down because leaders expect nothing but numbers (levels 1 and 2). They don't ask questions that need to be asked. "I know you've got the numbers, but let's talk about where this can go. Why do I want to do it? Is it a viable platform in the future?" By asking and listening, you will start to change the way you think, as well as the thoughts and behaviors of your employees.

A desired change in DNA may start at the very top, but it is truly influenced by the innovation leaders. If you are in an organization that is at the distrust and risk adverse end of the spectrum, people will aim toward protecting themselves. This means they will not be as likely to share new and innovative ideas. Therefore, as a leader, you must try to eliminate as much risk as possible which will then squelch the "fear of individual failure."

We have seen innovation leaders falter because of failure aversion. An idea would come in, and the manager would give the person 40 reasons why what they wanted to do was ridiculous and would never work. Yet, at the end, the leader would say, "But you seem really committed to this, so go ahead and do it." Here, innovators would walk away planning to take action, but also knowing they will be hung out to dry if failure occurs. The leader protected themself to either take credit for the success or shed the blame for failure. Innovators knew they had no backing or safety net. They were taking the fear of individual failure on themselves.

What you cannot do as an innovation leader is transfer your fear of failure to the people working for you. If you are in a distrusting organization that is making decisions based on the "fear of failure filter," someone has got to take on the job of ownership and responsibility. If nobody will, a revolutionary innovation will never get off the ground. Your organization must have a champion who's going to free up employees to focus on how to succeed, not what happens if they fail.

Summary

Your organization's IREs are a product of your Organizational DNA – Culture, Trust, and Risk. Your IREs are made up of:

- Communication
- Decision Making
- Knowledge Transfer

Your communication style as an organization and as a leader will impact your innovation results. To make innovation happen, especially on the revolutionary side, initial communication on ideas should be more visionary in nature. Behaviors trump words, so be aware of your communication content. (See Figure 16.2, page 165) Depending on your goals, you may need to work on your communication style.

The next two chapters will discuss the IREs associated with decision making and knowledge transfer. Understanding how decisions are really made is critical to being able to get programs accepted. Similarly, knowing how to effectively transfer knowledge and create a learning environment is crucial to meeting the ever-increasing demands for faster and better innovation.

Remember

Communication content is a window into your innovation focus.

Part II

Chapter Seventeen

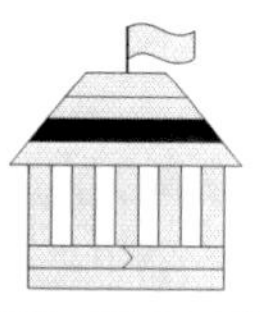

Invisible Rules of Engagement: Decision Making

Have you ever had this happen to you? You and your team prepare for a major presentation. The whole focus is on getting approval for the next phase of your program. The meeting goes better than you could have hoped for. Everything came together and the stakeholders all agreed that you should proceed. You left the meeting ready to celebrate. The next morning, your boss calls to inform you that your program isn't going to be approved after all. In the informal meeting of the stakeholders that occurred after you left, the decision was reversed without you or your team having any input.

Or on a different day, you walked into a meeting to review and discuss a new idea. You thought everybody was there to share their points of view and reach a group consensus. Unfortunately, you discovered that others had met informally prior to the meeting and had already reached an agreement.

We'd like to think these scenarios don't happen. However, they happen all the time. We've seen this in virtually every organization we work with and have experienced it ourselves on more than one occasion. In this chapter, we will go into detail on the informal decision-making process.

In thinking back to a story we related in Chapter 1, Kettering was finally able to move forward to use the new paint and primer only after he convinced the plant general manager to send the paint manager fishing for six weeks. Was this part of their formal decision-making process? We don't think so.

You won't find wall posters proclaiming:

- Decisions reached in formal meetings are only temporary until the informal meetings afterward have concluded.
- Meetings to discuss new ideas are only necessary to inform the outsiders of decisions made before the meeting.
- Unenlightened managers need to be sent fishing for six weeks to get them out of the way.

Potentially, one of the most well-known forms of informal decision making is the use of "back channel communications." President John F. Kennedy's brother, Robert, used secret back channel negotiations to avert a military showdown during the Cuban Missile Crisis.[1] In his book, *Kissinger,* Walter Isaacson writes about President Nixon and Henry Kissinger using back channels to go around the State Department.[2] According to Isaacson, Kissinger conceded that he actually encouraged using it. "Like the overwhelming majority of high officials, I had strong views and did not reject the opportunities to have them prevail."

At a seminar in 1968, the year before Kissinger joined the government, he talked about the need to keep the bureaucracy "working away in ignorance" while key decisions were made. He explained:

> "One reason for keeping decisions to small groups is that when bureaucracies are so unwieldy and when their internal morale becomes a serious problem, an unpopular decision may be fought by brutal means, such as leaks to the press or to Congressional committees. Thus, the only way secrecy can be kept is to exclude from the making of decisions all those who are theoretically charged with carrying them out."

We are neither advocating nor refuting the use of back channels or invisible decision processes. We are only pointing out the existence of myriad invisible or informal decision-making processes. Understanding them and how to effectively utilize them (without damaging trust) is a crucial skill for the innovation leader.

One element that almost all invisible decision-making processes have in common is that they rely heavily on the innovation leader's ability to influence. In this chapter, we will briefly discuss a basic process for influencing other people. In addition, we will look at the impact that the Organizational DNA model has on these processes. We will then discuss some ideas about how an innovation leader can successfully navigate through these waters.

IRE: Decision Making

Most organizations have a very visible decision-making process. These include stage gates, check lists, routing systems, and required analyses. Innovation leaders understand these processes. The really successful ones also understand that there are invisible processes that are equally as important as the visible ones.

Organizational Influence Strategy

There are many books written about influence.[3] Therefore, we will only summarize a process that relies heavily on the principles outlined in prior chapters of this book.

This process focuses on answering four key questions:

1. How aligned is the new idea with the current organization's goals and objectives?
2. What is the degree of business risk?
3. What are the implications for stakeholders?
4. What is the communication strategy?

The process of developing an influence strategy begins with the innovation leader assessing both the degree of organizational risk and the degree of stakeholder or **sponsor** risk. These two analyses, coupled with analyzing communication requirements, provide the basic information needed to formulate an influence strategy.

Risk Assessment

When assessing the organization's risk associated with a proposed new program, the innovation leader needs to examine the degree of business alignment relative to the business unit's vision, mission, and DNA. The fit with the mission determines first whether an idea must be viewed as a new venture or if it fits within the current scope. If it is a new venture, then it must be considered a high risk, revolutionary idea (for your organization).

If it fits within the current scope, then the innovation leader must determine where the idea falls on the Innovation Continuum, be it evolutionary, expansionary, or revolutionary. This determination will help define the degree of risk that must be assumed by the organization in order to proceed. Doing the risk assessment provides an overall understanding of the business risk for the new program, which is required to begin putting the influence strategy together. In Chapter 23, we expand this analysis to examine the program, marketplace, and internal organizational risk separately.

Having completed this detailed risk assessment innovation leaders can further refine and focus their influence strategy.

Stakeholder Analysis

The other fundamental analysis the innovation leader needs to complete is to identify the key stakeholders or sponsors for the proposed innovation program and the people who can influence them. To develop this list, begin by asking the following questions:

- Who has or would be supportive of the idea?
- Who has been supportive of other related ideas?
- Who has expressed skepticism about the idea?
- If successful, who stands to benefit?
- Who might perceive that they are losing if the idea succeeds?
- If the idea/program doesn't succeed, who would lose the most (besides you)?

Once this list has been developed, the innovation leader needs to:

- Categorize this list into groups of people who will most likely be supporters, neutral, or opponents to the proposed program.
- Select the subgroup of key stakeholders whose support is necessary to gain broad organizational support and sponsorship.
- Assess the level of overall risk that each stakeholder will assume in order to support the idea, oppose it, or remain neutral.

Through understanding these risks, the innovation leader can develop strategies to help mitigate them and thereby significantly improve the probability of getting sponsorship for the innovation program.

The innovation leader has now answered the key questions associated with assessing the business and individual stakeholder risks. In addition, they now have a list of key people who could have an impact on the approval of the new program. The next step is to understand how to most effectively communicate with each of these people. How can the innovation leader encourage an "above the line" discussion with them to ensure that they understand the program?

In general, we suggest trying to have these discussions one-on-one or in small group settings. You want each of your key people to understand that their input is being heard and valued. They will need to see that they had a hand in shaping the final program.

Stakeholder/Sponsor Communication Strategy

Creating a communication strategy includes thinking about the ISPI orientations for each of the individuals (Chapter 5) and integrating it with the organization's DNA. For example, should the leader start with the big picture and work into the details (Visionary), or vice versa (Concrete)? Should the discussion focus primarily on levels 1 and 2 details (Chapter 16), should it be balanced, or should it be more about the possibilities (levels 4 and 5)? Should the focus be on the welfare of the entire organization or destruction of the competition?

The communication strategy is primarily about identifying how to talk about the overall program. How will this particular innovation help grow the organization and help make it more successful in the long term? Second, communication needs to address the different aspects of the program that must be emphasized to meet the needs of the individual stakeholders (without changing the basic message).

The ISPI will help you understand the preference of communication for each of the stakeholders. By going through each of the 12 different orientations, you can quickly put together an idea of how best to communicate with each of them. For example, if they are on the pioneering end of the spectrum, emphasize the novelty of the idea. If they are on the builder end, emphasize how the idea leverages existing ideas or concepts. If they tend to be visionary, then start with the big picture. If they are more concrete, start with the details and build up to the vision. In a similar fashion, go through the full ISPI Totem (both iO and iOM) to build an overall orientation preference for each of them.

Using the Organization DNA components will help you determine the potential content of your conversations. The following looks at each of the components (Culture, Trust, and Risk) to help you understand the content needs and what to emphasize.

Organizational Culture: Culture is one of the major drivers of both visible and invisible decision-making processes. With regard to visible decision making, culture will influence whether decisions are consensus-driven or based on a hierarchical chain of command. Culture provides the backdrop for evaluating the merits of an idea. Does the idea help "win the war"? Does the idea help move the organization forward as a whole? Understanding the overall culture will help you understand the history behind the visible decision-making process.

There are also invisible components of decision making that arise from the culture that affects the process as well as the attitude of key individuals on your list.

Recall that the cultural portion of the DNA was divided into four different types: 1) fragmented, 2) networked, 3) mercenary, and 4) communal (Chapter 12). Each of these types has a predominant influence on decision making as outlined in Figure 17.1.

NETWORKED (high employee interdependence)	**COMMUNAL** (organizational loyalty/clear focus)
Decisions often based on: • Consensus • "There's enough to go around" • Usually very slow decision-making process	**Decisions often based on:** • What does the organization need? • May be hierarchical...But more likely some form of consensus
FRAGMENTED (independent professionals)	**MERCENARY** (goal driven)
Decisions often based on: • Focus of independent "fiefdoms" • Significant evaluation/analysis • Often based on "political" capital of the "champion"	**Decisions often based on:** • It's all about the numbers • How does it "defeat the enemy" • Usually hierarchical • Significant analysis until decision must be made

SOCIABILITY (Degree of Personal Interaction)

SOLIDARITY (Unity of Vision)

Figure 17.1
The dominant culture of the organization will have a significant impact on both visible and invisible decision-making processes.

You won't see many of these rules printed in the company manual or posted on a wall. However, understanding them and being able to put them into context for your particular innovation program is vital. They will help you figure out how to position your idea.

For example, if you have a strong mercenary culture, presenting a new idea and explaining that there is enough market share to go around won't work. Instead, you will get further by explaining that your idea is needed in order to address a burning platform, or that the top and bottom line will grow by taking X% market share from competitor A and Y% from competitor B. The culture will dictate how aggressive you should be when promoting the program, the expected level of analysis and re-analysis that will be required, and the time that must be allotted for decision making.

While the discussion here should help you understand how to present the idea and associated program, it won't help you determine the level of detail you must provide when you present to each individual. After all, individuals will make the decision – not the organization. You must look at the individuals (and their ISPI) against the backdrop of the overall business team. We are not suggesting that you modify the general positioning for each individual, but only determine what information should get more or less emphasis when talking with the different people on your list. Some examples of information you might want to emphasize for each of the quadrants follows:

- **Fragmented:** What's in it for them? How will they be rewarded for supporting your idea? How will their individual risk be mitigated?
- **Networked:** Who else is supporting the idea? How will it help the people in the organization? And how does everyone win together?
- **Mercenary:** What competitors should be targeted? How much of their business can we capture? Are we being too aggressive – or should we be more aggressive?
- **Communal:** How will this idea and associated program promote growth of the organization? How are you putting the company's interests ahead of our own? Ask the stakeholder to help you understand if this is what the organization needs.

In addition to the previous summary of what information to emphasize to particular individuals on your priority list, there are specific thoughts you should keep in mind based on the culture defined in your DNA analysis.

For example:

- *Fragmented*
    - Wear a "bulletproof vest" and don't let others shoot down your ideas.
    - Make sure your ideas are aligned with the organization's focus.
    - Be willing to live within a "quid pro quo" system of reciprocity.

- *Networked*
    - Know the key influencers and their confidants. Acquaint yourself with as many as you can.
    - Make sure you are at the meetings before and after the formal meeting.
    - Be patient. Don't expect immediate results. You're running a marathon, not a sprint.

- *Mercenary*
    - Focus on the analysis. Let the numbers speak.
    - Communicate that you are a winner and will continue to defeat the enemy.
    - Move fast – the enemy isn't waiting.

- *Communal*
    - Demonstrate that you are part of the family. You live to see the organization succeed.
    - Talk about how your ideas will help the entire organization, even at your personal expense.
    - Educate the leaders, but remember that they are always right in the end.

Organizational Trust: The organizational trust factor comes into the process more on an individual basis. How do the stakeholders view and trust the innovation leader? Does the leader have a proven track record of successfully delivering new innovations? Has this leader been successful in the past with this type of innovation? How committed is this leader to the program? These are all critical aspects of the decision process, which are semi-visible. Unfortunately, the innovation leader cannot control or influence this portion of the decision-making process. Only by emphasizing a proven track record can you increase stakeholder trust.

If you are new to the organization or do not have an established track record, one way of overcoming this is to find a champion(s) who will help move your idea forward. The champion is a person(s) who is trusted by leaders of the business unit and who people will listen to. By leveraging their support in presenting the idea, you will obtain a transferral of trust. Stakeholders will be far more likely to want to listen to the merits of the idea if a trusted champion is telling them that it is worth their time to do so.

To find and recruit a champion, begin by looking at well-respected innovators. Go to them with your idea. Ask them for their input as well as for suggestions on how to improve on the idea. Seek their advice and counsel on not only the idea, but also on how to get it approved. Finally, ask them to help you. If the idea is really worthwhile, you will find one or more champions willing to endorse it. If you can't find a champion, then go back and re-evaluate the idea. Is it really good, or does it need to be modified? Perhaps you should shelve it for consideration at a later date?

Assuming that you are ready to take your idea forward either on your own or with a champion(s), the next step is to think about the people on your stakeholder priority list. Do they trust the organization? What is their mental commitment (partner, steward, employee or contractor, as presented by the Relationship Spectrum, page 28)?

If people have the mindset of contractors with limited trust in the organization, you must make sure to minimize their personal risk. There must be significant personal gain for them to be a sponsor for your idea. On the other hand, workers with a partner mindset and a high trust level should be targeted for discussion on how your idea will benefit the overall company – you need to convince them.

While this may seem obvious, it is important to understand that there is a process for gaining stakeholder support. When asking somebody to take a risk to support your idea, you must understand their mindset in order to position the idea appropriately. This does not mean you should withhold or embellish key information. Rather, it is about identifying and understanding what each of these stakeholders will require to allow them to be comfortable supporting the new idea.

Organizational Risk Tolerance: The risk tolerance of the organization also plays an important role in both visible and invisible decision-making processes (Figure 17.2). Understanding this fact will allow you to leverage the degrees of freedom available to you to help get your program approved.

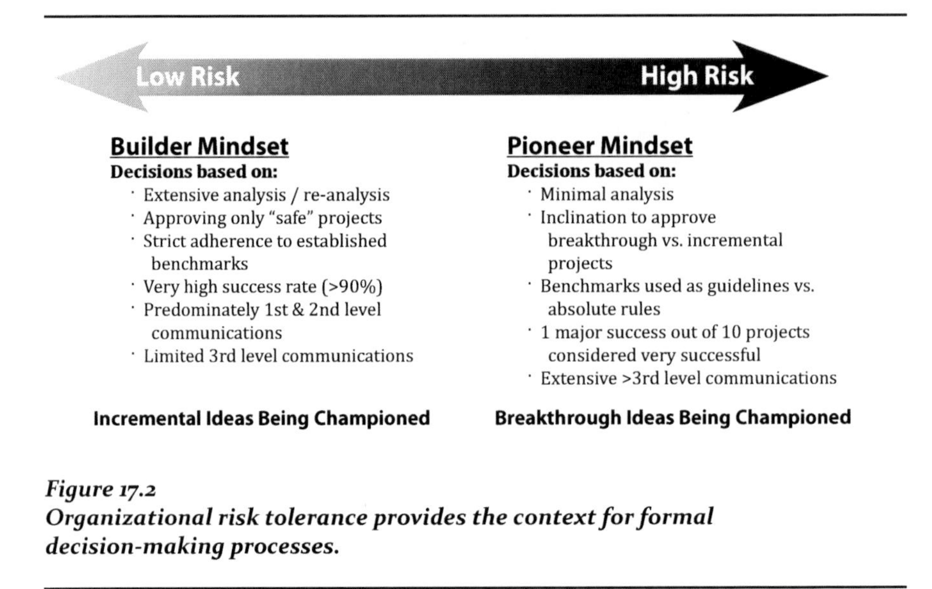

Figure 17.2
Organizational risk tolerance provides the context for formal decision-making processes.

On the visible side, the risk tolerance will dictate the type of innovation that will generally be sponsored, as well as the level of analysis and type of communication. This will help you understand where your idea fits within the context of the organization's "sweet spot." It helps to further define how the overall idea needs to be positioned.

Similar to the discussion about how to identify individuals on your stakeholder priority list, you will also need to think about their specific risk tolerances. (Think about their ISPI Risk and Action orientations.) Your idea may fit within the organization's "sweet spot," but it may be completely outside of the comfort zone of a key stakeholder(s). Again, it is not about changing the overall positioning but is about emphasizing different aspects of the idea based on the individuals to whom you are speaking. If they tend to be risk averse, emphasize the analysis that demonstrates the expected returns and how risks should be minimized (not eliminated, just minimized). For those who tend to take greater risks, emphasize the potential follow-ons to your program. Talk about the long-term potential.

Advice for the Innovation Leader

Decisions drive the organization. Understanding the invisible elements behind these decisions is what will often make the difference between either getting the result you want or abandoning your idea. Why are there meetings after the meetings in which the actual decisions are made? Why are there pre-meetings held to make decisions rather than waiting for the formal meeting? Why do people use back channels? There are many answers to these questions. But they all come down to the fact that decisions are made by specific individuals who have specific needs above and beyond what is documented as the formal decision-making process. It might be the need for secrecy and power (such as with Kissinger). It may be the need to avoid public confrontation (such as with the meetings before the meeting). It might be due to a lack of sufficient information to make a final decision in the formal meeting (resulting in the meetings after the meeting). Whatever the reason(s), these processes exist and can make the difference between success and failure.

Informal decision-making processes provide a significant opportunity for the innovation leader to either build trust or destroy it. In an ideal world, every decision would be made using a visible, pre-defined process. Unfortunately, in the world that we all live in, this is not the case. There will be informal decision-making processes, whether acknowledged or not, that will occur behind the scenes which will impact the formal ones. Our advice to you is to acknowledge the existence of these processes with your team. Have your team be a part of these processes whenever possible. When not feasible, keep them apprised of what is going on and reiterate how they can help you.

Getting your programs sponsored is arguably one of the most difficult, but critical, activities for an innovation leader. Without sponsorship, innovation does not happen. Unless you are in a position to make the final decision (e.g., you own the company), you need to identify the invisible drivers behind both formal and informal decision making. Ultimately, you will need to use the information discussed in this chapter to influence the key stakeholders. If your idea is low risk and fits within the normal business activities ("business as usual"), the process can be quite simple. However, if your idea is outside of the normal business focus, the process becomes more complex as well as more critical to getting the stakeholders' support.

Remember

You can rely on the formal process and hope to get sponsorship. Or you can understand that there is an invisible process and be proactive in leveraging it.

Part II

Chapter Eighteen

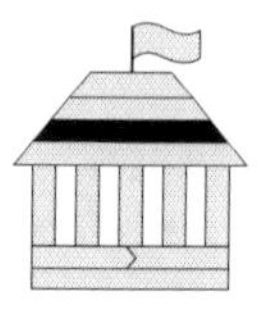

Invisible Rules of Engagement: Knowledge Transfer

Sir Francis Bacon was the first to state, "Knowledge is power."[1] In today's age, Peter Drucker modified this quote to be, "Knowledge has power."[2] Unfortunately, knowledge not shared is knowledge that becomes lost and must be relearned. For businesses today, there must be a sharing of knowledge in order to realize its true value. In the world of innovation, withholding, not capturing, or not passing along knowledge forces people to repeatedly relearn and reinvent the wheel. It leads to the reality that,

Innovation forgotten is innovation repeated.

The IRE of knowledge transfer takes advantage of the experience base and knowledge of the organization. Without a knowledge transfer process, your organization will not learn from previous innovation wins and losses. Knowledge transfer allows innovation to happen faster and makes it easier to have sustainable innovation results. This chapter will help you characterize your organization's learning environment, understand the PAR Process (Peer Assist, Action Review, Retrospect), and offers how-to points for forming successful knowledge transfer systems.

Innovative organizations generate new knowledge on an ongoing basis. This knowledge may be applicable in a variety of areas, including product or efficiency improvements, improved methods for selling or marketing, better accounting or administrative procedures, and/or even new and different products and technologies. One of the differences between an average and a great innovative company lies in what the company does with this knowledge. Is the knowledge easy to find and apply for those who need it, or is it hidden?

Knowledge transfer is part of the invisible rules of engagement because most groups rely on informal or ad hoc methods for transferring knowledge. This inhibits critical knowledge from being made available to the overall organization. By leveraging what we collectively know today, we might be able to develop new solutions faster and more economically.

Before we get into discussing the transfer of knowledge, it is important to have some common definitions.

- **Wisdom:** The accumulation of knowledge and the ability to use that knowledge across different domains.
- **Knowledge:** The critical combination of information and collective experience that enables people to make decisions, create solutions, or change positions.[3]
- **Information:** The interpretation of data to create understanding.
- **Data:** Raw measurements, observations, or test results.

Directly related to knowledge transfer is whether or not your organization has an environment that is conducive to learning. Does your organization's culture and trust level support people wanting to learn and share what they have learned? For example, organizations that tend to be fragmented with a low level of trust do not provide this learning and sharing. They will not support long-term sustained innovation across the Innovation Continuum.

Transferral of knowledge in a non-learning environment is similar to trying to teach a group of students who have no interest in learning. They may retain enough to pass the test, but no real learning will occur. They will forget what the teacher said the minute the class and the test end. They have been given the knowledge, but they have chosen to take it in merely as information. Only those individuals really interested in the subject will take in the information, interpret it and develop knowledge, and utilize it to take an action or develop new insight. Are your employees disinterested students or are they active learners?

Many leaders tell us they want sustainability, but their behaviors trump their words. They discount the importance of their organization's learning environment because of the invisible return on investment (ROI) as well as the time and effort it takes to disseminate knowledge. Many leaders focus on their next quarter, board meeting, or annual report, rather than the long term. To achieve a sustainability goal, you need knowledge coupled with a learning environment to help your people innovate more effectively and efficiently.

Assessing Your Learning Environment

In thinking about knowledge transfer and the eight principles, trust is imperative. Without trust, people will be much less willing to share their expertise. Addressing the elements of destruction is also very important. Knowing the past and how the past is impacting what is going on now is vital for expedient and sustainable innovation. Soft values will help determine how strongly your people will want to learn and pass on their experiences. By leveraging differences, you will be looking at diversity of knowledge and points of view coming together.

To make visible where you are relative to knowledge transfer and having a learning environment, rate your organization on the following 14 characteristics:

My organization can be characterized as having...	Strongly Disagree	Disagree	Neutral	Agree	Strongly Agree
	1	2	3	4	5
High turnover					
A moderate to low commitment to long-term growth					
A lack of trust within the organization					
Frequent cases of repeated mistakes					
A high number of pending retirements					
A reliance on usage of e-mails asking if anybody remembers					
Retired employees called in to help due to their unique knowledge					
Programs generally skewed towards evolutionary to expansionary innovation.					
High loyalty to organizational growth					
Programs taking longer due to not leveraging prior results					
Significant storage of reports/presentations/memos without a summary of key knowledge content					
Key knowledge/results not always being well documented					
A skewed employee age/experience distribution					
To rely on 'word-of-mouth' to transfer knowledge					

Figure 18.1
Tool for assessing your organization's risk relative to knowledge transfer and having a learning environment

Once you have filled out this assessment, add the numbers to get an overall score for your organization. The chart in Figure 18.2 (next page) provides an overall assessment of your organization's risk, relative to knowledge transfer.

Where do you rate your organization? What do you need to do now? What needs to be put in place for the future?

Knowledge Transfer Risk Assessment

Low Risk (14-32)	Medium Risk (33-51)	High Risk (52-70)
Best case – maintain status quo Worst case – become less effective over time	Best case – maintain status quo Worst case – decay into High Risk category	Continued erosion of knowledge base
Potential to shift to a higher risk category without knowing it	Missing significant opportunities for greater organizational effectiveness	Loss of competitive edge
Missing potential opportunities for greater leverage	Compromised ability to keep up with future demands	Inability to keep up with future demands
Not taking advantage of time available for gradual, controlled change	Missing time horizon for making phased changes	Longer training times for new employees

Figure 18.2
Risk assessment for your organization relative to knowledge transfer and existence/ effectiveness of the learning environment

Accessing Knowledge

Many companies believe in storing huge amounts of information and data. They also include systems to access it but, unless the end user knows the specific report that contains the information pertinent to what they are working on, they are not likely to take the time required to determine which reports are meaningful and which are not. In some cases, it is easier and cheaper just to run a new test. By creating a way to capture, manage, and transfer knowledge, this scenario could completely change.

Organizations have a combination of explicit and tacit knowledge:

- **Explicit knowledge** is documented in reports, papers, patent disclosures, etc.
- **Tacit knowledge** is what is contained in someone's head and is not documented anywhere.

In many organizations, 10% of knowledge is explicit. That means 90% of the knowledge is tacit/stored in the minds of the people.[4]

Some of our clients try to force their people to write things down. We've seen that you can't mandate knowledge transfer, because there is little incentive for people to document their past experiences. With the advent of PowerPoint and e-mail along with internal staff reductions, having a library of good technical reports is becoming a thing of the past. Also, most people will not read a report unless they know that it contains the information that they need. There is very little driving people to spend the time to write or search for information. When someone completes a program, they want to go and do something new. They don't want to spend the time thoroughly documenting the prior program. The information/knowledge generated in that program resides in the individual's mind, not someplace where others can readily access it. **The whole idea between explicit and tacit knowledge is that you must tap into your employee's minds.**

Organizations generally do not do a good job sharing tacit knowledge – instead, they rely on a variety of different approaches, including:

- **Reinventing the Wheel**
  "Didn't we do this 10 years ago? I wonder if anybody is still around who remembers anything about it?"
- **Accessing Informal Networks**
  "I need some prototypes to test consumer reaction to our new product idea. Who should I talk to about making them?"
- **Losing Knowledge Forever – Resignations**
  "Did Dick leave any paper trail behind before he left for that new job? I need to understand, between our vendor and us, who owns what and why."
- **Continuing to Make the Same Mistakes**
  "How many times do we need to make the same mistakes before we learn?"
- **Relying on a Historian**
  Question: "Does anybody remember Fugles? We are looking at redeveloping it."
  Answer: "Which Fugles? The '85, '91, or '96 version? I doubt anybody has any recollection about the '85 version other than Mike."
- **Accessing Retirees**
  "Let's see if Mary is willing to work as a contractor to remake this product. I know she's retired, but she is the only one who knows how to make it correctly."
- **Archiving Data, but not Knowledge**
  "We have thousands of studies in the file, but I have no idea how to find the ones I need!"

- **Relying on "Good Intentions" after Reorganization**
  "Don't worry. I'm not going anywhere. I'll be here to answer any questions that arise."

Do any of these scenarios sound familiar? We guess that you could add several additional ones. Some add value in the quest to be able to learn from and reapply knowledge from the past, while others simply demonstrate where an organization is relying on a wing and a prayer.

So what is the answer? In today's world of instant everything, we can no longer afford to continue with business as usual. We must learn how to improve the quality of goods and services that we provide, while reducing time and costs spent on ongoing development activities. To do this, we must understand how to transform our businesses into learning organizations. In order to improve future outcomes, we need to take advantage of prior knowledge, knowledge that can be learned and leveraged as we go along, and knowledge gained from newly completed projects.

This is even more important today. As we mentioned earlier, the RIFs in the 1990s destroyed implied employment contracts, and (as a result) workforce dynamics changed. In addition to the impact on organizational trust and commitment, there has also been a dramatic impact on how long people will stay with the same company. People no longer stay as long, which causes even greater information gaps and loss of knowledge. This situation impacts new hires, newly promoted managers, and overall innovation efforts. Think about the tacit knowledge of all the baby boomers who are now beginning to retire. What are we doing to ensure that all of that knowledge doesn't walk out the door with them?

We have seen many changes where the people assigned to a new position have little or no knowledge transfer. Their only course of action is "on-the-job," so they only learn as they go. This often results in a significant drop in productivity and momentum until the new manager has had time to "come up-to-speed." The same holds for moving people between projects. How well do your new project leaders understand what has worked in the past and what to avoid?

Creating a learning environment is only the first step in the process of facilitating effective knowledge transfer. You still need to look at the individuals who have the knowledge and those who need it. Does your organization encourage and reward the sharing of knowledge? Does it support employees seeking out others for input? What do your behaviors say about how much you value sharing knowledge?

The Learning Organization

To foster effective knowledge transfer, an environment that supports learning must be fostered. An excellent way to begin creating this environment is to implement a Peer Assist / Action Review / Retrospect (PAR) Process.[5] A model of the PAR Process is shown in Figure 18.3.

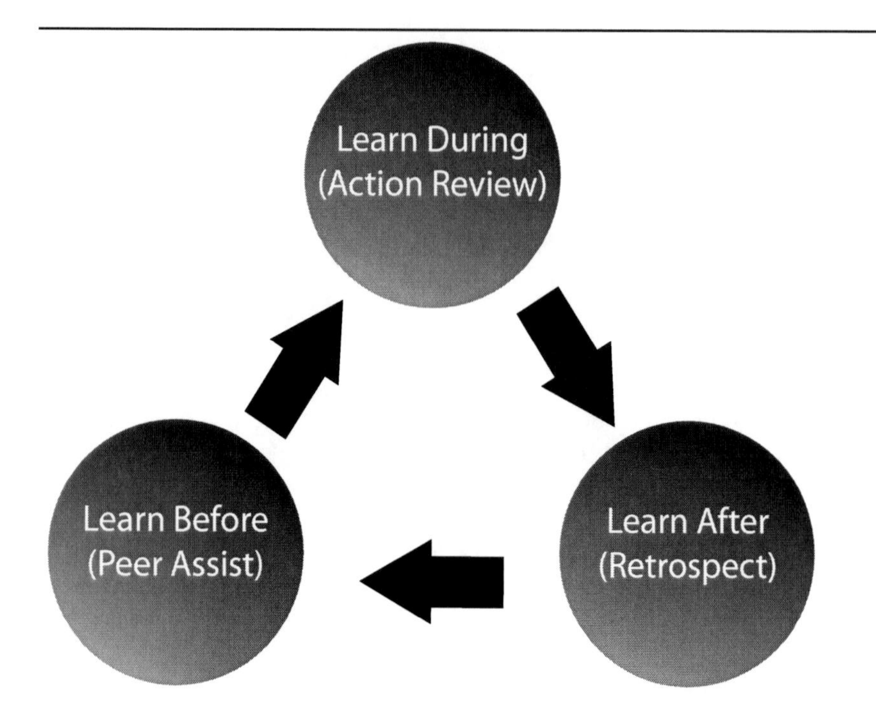

Peer Assist: Applying prior knowledge to help in a new context.

Action Review: Making improvements after every identifiable team event.

Retrospect: Identifying valuable lessons and enhancing collaboration after project completion.

Adapted from:
Collison & Parcell; LEARNING TO FLY

Figure 18.3
Peer Assist/Action Review/Retrospect (PAR Process) used as the foundation for creating a learning environment

The PAR Process begins with conducting a **peer assist** prior to initiating a new program or project. This involves getting people with prior knowledge relevant to the upcoming project together to review the new work and share their specific insights. The idea is, if we can leverage our prior knowledge, then we can start out much higher on the learning curve and produce better results, faster. Through the use of peer assists, we can minimize the issues and lost productivity associated with continually reinventing the wheel and making the same costly mistakes over and over.

This became painfully clear to one of our former co-workers. Steve walked into the office one Monday morning and complained about his continuous household ordeal of fixing underground sprinkler systems. He had cut through one of the main lines, which caused a small gusher in front of his house. To stop the gusher, he had to turn off the water to the whole house. His wife was understanding, but an immediate fix was required.

After some analysis, he realized that there was no way he could dig up enough of the pipes to ever put a coupling between the two ends. Suddenly, an episode from the TV show *This Old House* flashed in his head. It was about making a "slip coupling" for this very application. After spending the entire afternoon unsuccessfully trying to make the coupling and keep it from leaking, Steve finally gave up and capped the line off until he could get a sprinkler expert to come to his house and fix the pipes.

The next day, I said to him, "Steve, if only you had called me, I had the same thing happen a couple of years ago. You can get a slip coupling to fix the pipe at almost any builder's supply store or large landscape company."

By not using the knowledge readily available to him through a simple phone call, Steve ended up (unsuccessfully) trying to reinvent the wheel. It cost him time, effort, and significantly more money, since he ended up calling somebody to fix the break. If he had called a knowledgeable friend, he could have fixed it himself with minimal effort and expense.

While this is a simplistic story illustrating the value of peer assists, how many times do we do the same thing at work? How often do we begin development of a new product or process without doing a patent search or looking for prior art in the literature? There is a friend of ours who is a marketing consultant who has been asked to do the same study three times in the past ten years. The last time, she simply referred them to the person who requested and paid for the last one. By not finding out what is already known and applying that knowledge, we waste significant time and resources.

As illustrated in Figure 18.4[6] (see next page), by sharing knowledge before starting a new program, we can begin higher on the learning curve.[7] This shortens the overall program time and, therefore, saves resources and dollars.

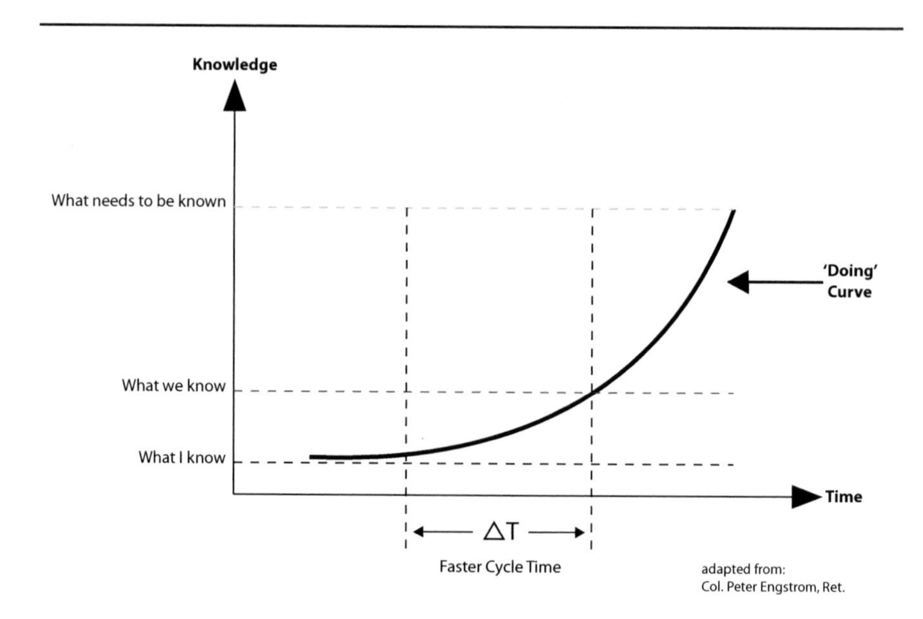

Figure 18.4
By sharing our collective knowledge before beginning a new project, we can begin higher on the learning curve and reduce the overall program time and related costs.

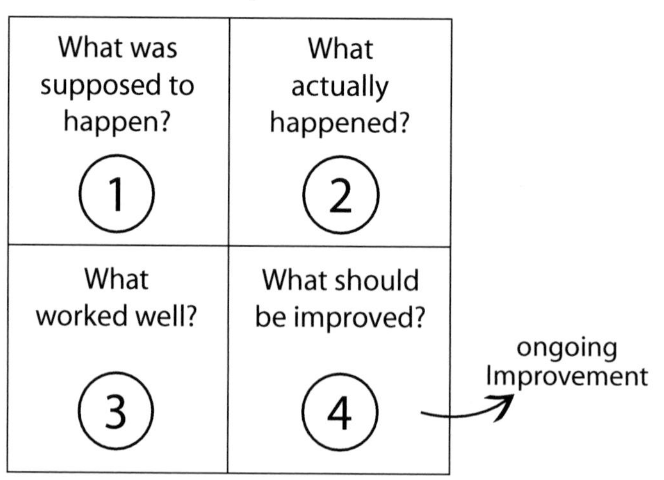

Figure 18.5
Action reviews allow teams to continuously improve during the development program.

The second part of the PAR Process, the **action review**,[8] is a quick way to capture what the group has learned and allows for continuous improvements at every step along the way. The action review looks at four questions outlined in Figure 18.5 (opposite page). Note that you need to ask these questions in the order given in the figure.

This quick (five- to ten-minute) exercise at the end of each meeting or key activity allows the group to identify what is working and should be maintained, as well as what could be done differently the next time. By documenting the answers and learning as you go, the "Learning While Doing" Curve shown in Figure 18.6 can actually change shape and dramatically improve both the efficiency and quality of the ongoing activity as depicted below.

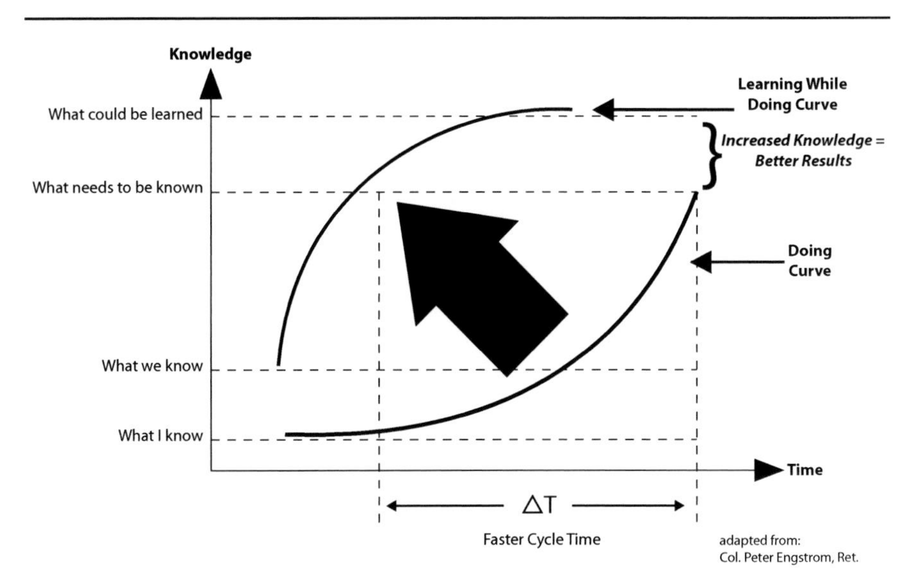

Figure 18.6
Coupling action reviews with peer reviews can actually change the shape of the "Learning While Doing" curve. This will save time, reduce costs, and improve the quality of final results.

The third step in the PAR Process, **Retrospect**, is to capture key knowledge gained from a major program just completed and then make this knowledge available for use on future programs. Whether having just completed a Six Sigma project or a revolutionary innovation, getting the team together immediately to ask four key questions, document the answers, and make the output of this meeting available to others is a vital step toward creating a learning environment.

The following four questions are similar to an action review; however, there is a greater focus on why things happened:

1. What was the objective of the program?
2. What was achieved?
3. What were their successes? Why? How can success be repeated?
4. What were the disappointments? Why? How can they be avoided in the future?

The goal is to understand how to repeat the positives and avoid the negatives. The four questions should be discussed in the specific order given. Primarily, getting the successes on the table first allows the team to focus on the positives and ensures that these are captured before examining areas for improvement. If the team focuses on areas for improvement first, there is a much greater probability of the team members feeling defensive. This can result in missed opportunities for capture and transfer of key knowledge – both positive aspects and areas for improvement.

Knowledge Sharing

There are two complementary sides to knowledge sharing: teaching and learning. The goal for knowledge transfer is to effectively connect the two sides. This requires meeting the needs for both simultaneously. For the 10% of knowledge that has been written down (explicit), this process can be fairly straightforward and highly visible. The real key is how we leverage the tacit knowledge – the knowledge that we have spent considerable effort to create that has not and, most likely, will never be documented.

Successful learning environments are comprised of networks where knowledge is passed from person to person and where employees readily understand the networks and how to tap into them.

To capture tacit knowledge, you first need to have the appropriate culture, level of trust, and rewards system. If your organization's culture has low sociability, the free sharing of knowledge will be more difficult. Sharing here will be based on reciprocity – in other words, employees will ponder, "If I share my knowledge, what will I get in return?" High sociability will make the process of knowledge sharing easier, since people are more likely to do this when there is a desire to help each other. If people don't trust the organization, it is going be very difficult for knowledge sharing to occur because they will think it's either going to be used against them or not to their advantage. If your organization has a performance appraisal system where people are ranked against one another, what is their incentive for sharing knowledge openly? The perception of employees here will be that they are being asked to share what they think is their competitive advantage relative to their peers.

Second, to reapply prior knowledge, the process must allow for the domain expert (who is the repository of the knowledge) to be able to share this knowledge without spending the time and laborious effort associated with writing detailed reports. In today's world, people are not looking for reports to read. They are looking for short "sound bites." They are only interested in getting into the details once they know that it is directly applicable to what they need today. Therefore, the knowledge process or system must allow for the easy capture of "**knowledge nuggets**" (short sound bites that describe a key learning) and enable the user to quickly assess applicability of the knowledge.

In their book, *Learning to Fly*,[9] Collison and Parcell discuss the idea of capturing "knowledge nuggets" from domain experts. These nuggets are then made available to the rest of the organization to use as trigger points for people to go and find the source of knowledge. A quote from *Learning to Fly* sums up their approach: "You don't want to create an encyclopedia of information; you want to create a system that keeps track of (the domain experts) who know the recipes."

Successful knowledge transfer systems include the following characteristics. They:

- Allow domain experts to share their knowledge easily, with minimal time and effort.
- Provide a safe environment for domain experts to reduce the potential issues associated with a lack of trust.
- Establish incentives for rewarding domain experts that will encourage them to share their knowledge.
- Create knowledge nuggets so that the user can quickly assess the value of this knowledge for addressing a particular problem.
- Ensure that the knowledge nuggets are **vetted**[10] so that the user has a higher level of trust in the content.
- Allow the user to establish a level of trust with the domain expert.

Knowledge Transfer Process

One way that Science Applications International Corporation (SAIC)[11] and many other organizations have been successful with knowledge transfer is by creating a series of videos and audio sound bites. This not only keeps the domain expert from writing and editing, it creates an immediate level of trust for the end users. Videos are difficult to alter, so conducting video interviews in an informal setting (as opposed to a studio) will allow the user to get a feel for who the experts are, what they have to say, whether or not they are approachable, and whether or not employees will want to speak with them.

A series of detailed knowledge nuggets broken into short sound bites and placed on a searchable website will allow for easier searching of information and sorting for relevance and merit. It will then allow end users to go to domain experts to obtain the knowledge that they are seeking, which will allow understanding to be transferred without bureaucracy.

Knowledge nuggets from domain experts help people understand what they need to know, who to go to for certain insights, and how to interface with the right people. They provide the context that creates action. They generate a learning environment that helps make your invisible knowledge transfer process visible to the entire organization.

The following is an overview of the steps we generally use in creating the knowledge transfer process:

- **Define the "domains of interest"** as the basis for developing the overall system architecture. Examples include estimating project costs and schedules, working with outside experts or sub-contractors, conducting specialized tests, etc.
- **Identify** up to three or four domain experts.
- **Conduct initial interviews with each of the domain experts.** The interviews should be in the form of informal conversations around the areas of interest, as well as on the background of the experts. Conversations should be videotaped to allow sound bites (knowledge nuggets) to be created for future use in the knowledge system. (Note that as part of the video process, a commitment should be made to allow the expert to review and approve all sound bites from the video prior to releasing them in the system.)
- **Create the overall knowledge system architecture based on these interviews.** Generally speaking, the architecture should be sequential, hierarchical, topical, or some combination of the three. This architecture will help to define the internal structure to be included in the final system.
- **Develop a detailed list of topics** to be included in each of the major areas and identify domain experts for each area.
- **Interview each expert.** This includes going back to the original ones for a second interview, as well as conducting first

interviews with newly identified experts. All of these interviews must be videotaped following the format outlined above. Background information on each of the experts must also be included, which will allow users to better understand their background and assess the usefulness of their input.

- **Edit the videos to create knowledge nuggets**, generally less than one minute in duration, for inclusion in the final system.
- **Compile all of the knowledge nuggets** and videos into the web pages of the knowledge system. Publish the final system as part of a searchable, internally networked system or as individual stand-alone systems.
- **Identify the individual(s) accountable for maintaining and updating the knowledge system.** These people do not have to be domain experts; however, they must be committed to ensuring that the knowledge system is an asset that is accurate, timely, and readily available.

In Closing

Many companies continue to feel the excruciating impact of not knowing how to manage and retain their tacit knowledge. When people leave, so do their connections, experiences, and knowledge. By creating a learning environment, you will foster the transfer of knowledge between employees within your organization. This will increase the speed and efficiency of your innovation processes and practices because employees will learn from past and the present experiences. Your organization will move away from "lightning bolt" innovation and closer to sustainability.

"The idea is not to create an encyclopedia of everything that everybody knows, but to keep track of people who 'know the recipe,' and nurture the culture and the technology that will get them talking."
Arian Ward, *Learning to Fly*[12]

It is not about technology or software systems – it's about people and how to leverage their collective know-how/why/what/who/where/when. The key is to create the culture and systems to facilitate knowledge sharing over and over and to continuously expand and improve it.

Remember:

Innovation forgotten is innovation repeated.

Part II
Chapter Nineteen

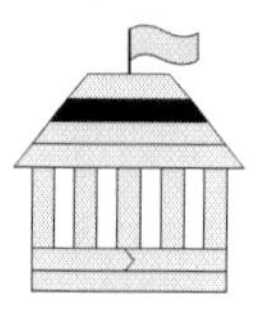

Problem Characterization

In the previous three chapters, we discussed some of the most important invisible rules of engagement: 1) communication, 2) decision making, and 3) knowledge transfer. We are now ready to move upward to the next level of the Innovation House. This level is comprised of three aspects associated with creating appropriate innovation processes, which include:

1. **Understanding the type of problems you are facing (Chapter 19).**

   The starting point for creating your innovation process is understanding the types of problems facing your organization and the implications that go along with them. Where does your primary focus lie on the Innovation Continuum? Do your problems have definitive answers, or is the final solution based on, "It's good enough"?

2. **Creating the appropriate organizational structure to try and solve the problem, including the roles and responsibilities for key individuals (Chapter 20).**

   Only through understanding the issues associated with the types of problems being undertaken can you develop an appropriate organizational structure. Organizations must be designed around what needs to be accomplished, rather than around specific individuals. This is true whether you are part of a small start-up company or a large multi-national corporation, or whether a group is internal to a company or a virtual one that leverages outside resources.

3. **Implementing a reward and recognition system to reinforce desired behaviors (Chapter 21).**

    Finally, once the problems are understood and a structure defined, there must be an appropriate reward and recognition system. If you don't reward the behaviors you need for success, then it won't matter how well you've executed the first two steps. Remember the principle that has been reiterated several times: Organizations Don't Innovate, People Do.

Types of Problems

In Chapter 8, we stated that innovation starts when problems are converted into ideas. Taking this a step further, you need to understand the types of problems facing your group. In innovation, these problems form a continuum from those easily solved to those virtually impossible to solve. Using the terms first defined by Rittle and Webber, this continuum is made up of problems from **Tame** to **Wicked.**[1]

Most of us are familiar with defining and tackling tame problems. They are the problems with the answer in the back of the book that we all liked in school. They have a specific goal or resolution in mind and they have a right or wrong answer. Some examples of tame problems are:

- Putting together a puzzle
- Balancing your checkbook
- $(((2 + 2) \times 6 - 8) \times 4 - 9) \times 0 + 1 =$___

Tame problems can be solved in a linear fashion by defining the problem, gathering and analyzing data, formulating possible solutions, and then implementing the desired solution. Six Sigma, stage gates, and other structured programs often deal with solving problems toward the tame end of the spectrum. Tame problems are usually more evolutionary on the Innovation Continuum.

Tame problems have solutions that allow you to prove your answers. As we will discuss in the next chapter, this becomes a driver toward defining the role of the key stakeholders. In dealing with tame problems, stakeholders do not have to be heavily involved during the innovation development process. Once a solution has been identified, it can be demonstrated as to why it is correct.

Wicked problems are a different animal because there is no book to refer to in dealing with them. **Wicked problems don't have a concrete answer. They have a "best choice" or "it's good enough" answer.**

Wicked problems have incomplete, contradictory, and changing requirements. In thinking about the Innovation Continuum, they are more revolutionary in nature. Rittel and Webber stated, "While attempting to solve a wicked problem, the solution of one of its aspects may reveal or create other, even more complex problems."[2] This is what makes wicked problems so complicated. A solution may be agreed upon and implemented, but the solution may set off a chain reaction of new problems or unintended consequences that need to be resolved.

Wicked problems require a different mindset because they are "solved" via a **non-linear system** whose behavior is not simply the sum of its parts or their multiples. They are often difficult (or impossible) to model and their behavior, with respect to a given variable, is extremely difficult to predict.

Some examples of wicked problems include:

- Terrorism
- World Hunger
- Unity – "I have a dream that one day this nation will rise up and live out of the true meaning of its creed: 'We hold these truths to be self evident, that all men are created equal.'" (Martin Luther King, Jr., August 1963)[3]

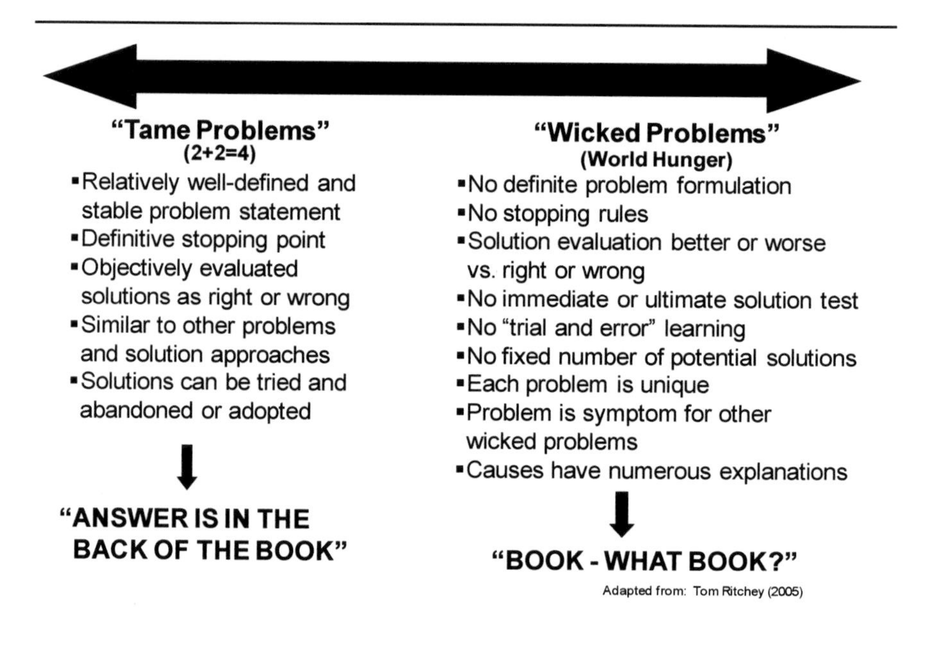

Figure 19.1
Problems form a continuum from tame to wicked and require different skills and approaches to solve them.

You say you have a solution to world hunger? Inevitably, there will be someone who can show you at least five reasons why the solution won't work. The same thing occurs with innovation. You may have a great idea that solves one problem, but someone else (be it a peer or supervisor) may come up with reasons why the idea wouldn't work for them, their constituents or, subsequently, why it may create additional unforeseen problems. Therefore, because it is difficult or impossible to prove that a proposed solution will be the correct one, it is essential to actively involve key stakeholders during the development process. We will discuss this in greater detail in the next chapter.

To solve a problem, you first have to determine if it is tame or wicked. On the tame to wicked continuum in Figure 19.1, the end points may be thought of as 2+2 for the tame end and world hunger for the wicked end.[4]

Where do the majority of the problems that your organization faces fall? Where will they fall in your desired innovation portfolio? Can you think of an example of revolutionary innovation that was not plagued by a wicked problem?

Here is an example that shows how a tame problem can become a wicked one:

- **Problem:** Choosing where you want to go out to eat.
- **Tame:** Going out to eat alone.
- **Wicked:** Having 12 other people going out to eat with you.

Why does the scenario above present a wicked problem? First of all, there is no absolute right or wrong answer. In a large city, there are countless restaurants that fulfill the need to get something to eat. It becomes a matter of personal choice. When you're alone, the problem leans toward the tame end of the spectrum. All you have to do is please yourself.

However, when others are going out to eat with you, the scenario changes dramatically. Most people really do have a preference, but out of politeness, most will say that they don't care. Someone may suggest a potential restaurant, then opinions are offered: "Well it's okay with me, even though I really don't like that place. But if the rest of you want to go there, then I'm fine with it." The group moves back to ground zero and tries to reach a consensus on where to go out to eat. This can go on indefinitely until someone takes charge and basically says, "We're going to eat at this place."

There are just too many variables to consider: type of food, taste, cost, portion size, health, previous experiences at a restaurant, location, dress code, etc.

Whether it is going out to dinner or solving a problem within an organization, **every time you add another key individual or variable to the mix, you potentially add a multiplier on the degree of wickedness.**

Think about your company. Where have you experienced wicked problems? This hypothetical example may paint the picture more clearly.

- **Context:** You are a leader in a company that produces and sells crackers. The crackers are rectangular in shape.
- **Problem:** The Food Safety Organization has requested that rectangular crackers be made safer by eliminating the sharp points.
- **Solution:** Engineering will modify the cutter to produce rounded corners.
- **Action:** Cutter modified. Crackers now have rounded corners.

Tame problem solved. Or is it? There are more groups involved than just Food Safety and Engineering. Let's look at how this one change potentially impacts other departments:

- **Legal:** What about the lawsuit in Georgia by a woman who claims that her child's throat was injured by the sharp points on the crackers?
- **Engineering:** How round is round enough? What is success?
- **Sales:** All of our photos and graphics must now be redone. Who is going to pay for this? We can't pass this cost on to our customers.
- **Packaging:** The packaging will have to be resized.
- **Purchasing:** What about all of the obsolete packaging?
- **Manufacturing:** Who is going to develop new standards?
- **Marketing:** Consumers won't like the new shape.

This example shows how one simple modification can send a ripple effect throughout the organization. What started out as a simple engineering change turned into a major organizational issue that will take months to resolve.

We will get into different problem-solving roles in the next chapter but, to integrate the ISPI with problem characterization, builders are more attracted to tame problems and pioneers are drawn to wicked problems.

Solutions to tame problems are evolutionary in nature and tend to follow a linear process that can translate into a waterfall type of diagram as shown in Figure 19.2.[5]

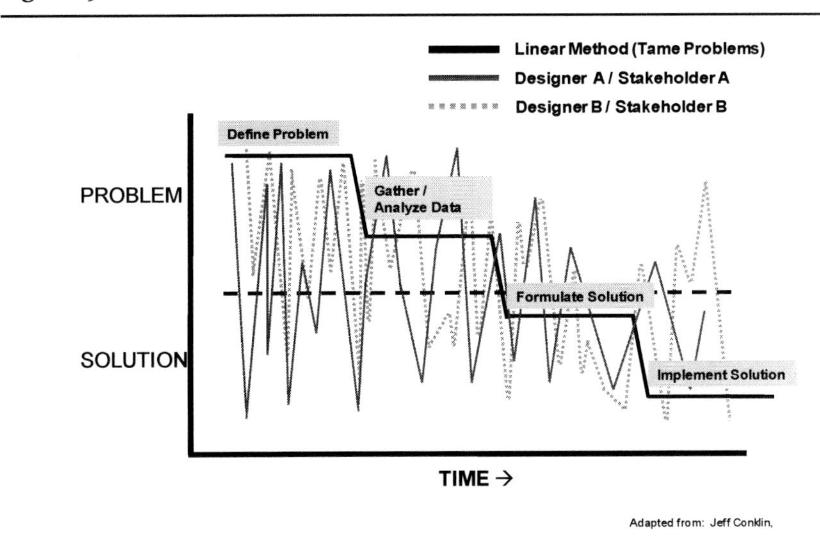

Figure 19.2
Tame problems tend to follow a linear or waterfall process. Wicked problems do not. As more people become involved, the degree of non-linearity increases.

Stage **gate** processes tend to work very well for problems positioned toward the tame end of the spectrum. Solving wicked problems, however, involves a non-linear process. Wicked problems are revolutionary in nature and do not lend themselves to classical program management/stage gate processes. Instead, they tend to be more of an iterative process and jump back and forth between all activities. It involves first understanding the problem, then moving to a potential solution, only to further refine or change the problem definition. As with the previous examples, adding more people to the team as practitioners, leaders, or stakeholders tends to increase the level of non-linearity and degree of wickedness.

Degree of Wickedness: Complexity

When trying to assess the degree of wickedness, you need to examine three major forces that are part of the definition of innovation:

1. **Business Complexity**
2. **Technical Complexity**
3. **Human Complexity**

In tame problems, these forces overlap, which makes solutions easier to identify and implement. In wicked problems, the forces diverge, which makes it harder to gauge how one will impact the other (see Figure 19.3). And in wicked problems, each one will impact the other. Because of business, technical, and human complexity, you may bounce back and forth from problem to solution to problem again – and then redefine the problem and look for new solutions. These new solutions may unearth pieces of the problem that you've never thought about. And the bouncing will continue.

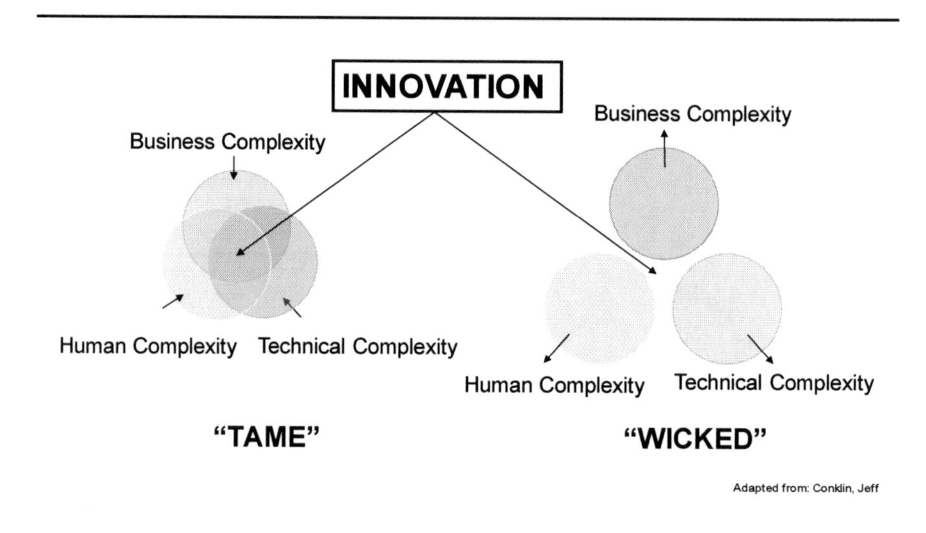

Figure 19.3
For tame problems, the business, technical, and human forces tend to converge to the "right" answer. In wicked problems, however, these forces often diverge. The degree of divergence will be related to the degree of wickedness of the problem.

To take it even further, adding more key people to the mix will cause the bouncing to become even more out of sync. Remember, the more people you add (and in many cases, it is vital to add them), the more mixed the ideas and thoughts become (Figure 19.2).

The business complexity of problems includes specific factors such as budget constraints, competition, marketing, price points, and consumer uncertainty, among others. An example of a complex business problem where these elements overlap is a city government putting in a new highway loop. The human element is rather tame because the voting is done and the project is approved. The technological know-how to create the loop is well understood. However, the question becomes, where do we put the loop? If it is too far out, is it going to satisfy the needs of the community? If it is in too close, does it allow for future expansion? Until it is built, it is impossible to prove the actual impact of its location.

The technical complexity of problems refers to the specialized and intersecting factors required to create a solution. An example of a technical problem was the United States' push to be the first country to safely land a man on the moon. The problem by itself was wicked on all three levels, but President John F. Kennedy helped tame the business and human complexity by lending his vision and influence, stating, "I believe that this nation should commit itself to achieving the goal, before this decade is out, of landing a man on the moon and returning him safely to the Earth." (President Kennedy, May 25, 1961)[6]

Here, the real issue wasn't gaining support from the top or lack of resources. Rather, it was technology. Questions included, "How do we conduct experiments and know they represent what happens in space? How do we build a spacecraft? How do we test a lunar landing module on earth? How do we get our people ready to go into space? How do we prove the best solution?"

It is vital to recognize that one single person operating in a vacuum will not solve wicked problems. Wicked problems are most successfully addressed by teams that collaborate effectively. That being said, the final source of wickedness is the human element. Part 1 of this book focused on the human element that we believe will usually become the most wicked of the three sources. You can come up with somewhat concrete solutions for business issues. You can determine if you are making progress technologically. Yet, human complexity is driven by trust, emotion, and ego. The entire Innovation House is an integral part of effectively attacking a wicked problem.

The issue of human complexity is so prevalent in wicked problems because there are no concrete solutions. This situation causes stress and then the stress causes trust to be broken. A lack of trust causes fear of individual failure. As trust erodes, the degree of wickedness goes up. **People then apply a self-protection filter to their decision-making processes.**

It is unavoidable that wicked problems will cause things not to go as planned. When that happens, the **blame game** goes into effect. According to Conklin:[7]

> "In times of stress the natural human tendency is to find fault with someone else. We tend to take the problem personally, at an organizational level, and assume that the chaos we see is a result of incompetence or, worse, insincere leadership. Since our education and experience have prepared us to see and solve tame problems, wicked

> problems sneak up on us and create chaos. Without understanding the cause, there is finger pointing instead of learning."

People get frustrated with wicked problems because they don't understand what they are dealing with and they look to blame others, stating, "It's their fault." That is human nature. Many times, employees (i.e., the practitioners) in the process of trying to solve the problem will point their fingers at management, thinking, "If our management had a clue about what we were trying to do with this, we could solve it. But they change their minds every other day."

Similarly, management can point fingers in the other direction, thinking, "What in the world are our people doing? Why is this problem not solved yet? And how can we get them focused?"

Example: Kettering Paint Story

Let's briefly analyze the Kettering paint story that we used in Chapter 1. (See page 3) Was this a wicked problem? Why or why not?

- **Business Complexity**

  Was there a clear business need for reducing the painting time? Yes. So, from a business complexity perspective, the problem was closer to the tame end.

- **Technical Complexity**

  Was there a clear right or wrong technical answer? Was the technical development a linear process? Was the final solution the "perfect" paint? No, no, and no. The development followed an iterative process of improvements that revealed additional issues. This iterative process continued until all of the key technical components could be developed. Kettering went from having a solution to expanding the problem (needing a new primer, so the new paint wouldn't fall off). From a technical perspective, the development of a new painting system made this a wicked type of problem.

- **Human Complexity**

  Did Kettering face significant resistance from the different human constituencies? Yes! From the paint conference in which the "experts" tried to convince Kettering that what he wanted to accomplish was impossible, to the paint manager who wouldn't look at a different primer – at every step along the way, people tried

> to tell him that he couldn't do what he wanted to for one reason or another. So, from the human perspective, this was definitely a wicked problem. And sending a manager on a fishing trip to get him out of the way was a fairly innovative, although extreme, way to solve a degree of wickedness.

Thus, the development of a new paint system was an example of a wicked problem driven by technical and human complexities. Think about the problems you are facing. Where would you put them on the tame-to-wicked problem continuum relative to business, technical, and human complexities? Are you trying to solve them based on a linear, stage gate process?

Advice for the Innovation Leader

When starting a new innovation, think about the three drivers of innovation complexity (business, technical, human) and determine if you are dealing with a problem toward the tame or wicked end of the problem continuum. Many evolutionary innovations tend to be positioned toward the tame end. The problems may be difficult, but there is generally a pretty clear answer as to whether or not the innovation was successful. The business and human complexities are usually manageable due to lower risk and faster timelines associated with these types of programs. This is why stage gate processes work well for these programs.

Most new product development tends to fall toward the wicked end. The solutions are not based on what is right or wrong. With "good enough" solutions, there will always be some people in the organization who will support the solution and some who will not. The business case is often based on assumptions that cannot be verified prior to product launch. The technological complexity can be a wild card that drives the innovation to be more wicked or helps tame it to some degree.

The following is a summary of how to deal with wicked problems:

1. **Admit or recognize that you have a wicked problem.**
    - Accept the reality that the classical linear approach will not work.
    - Define the context of the problem.
    - Identify potential alternatives, competing interests, priorities, and constraints.
    - Identify "degrees of freedom" available for leverage in developing potential solutions.

2. **See if the problem can be tamed – dramatically reduce the social complexity.**
   - Reduce number of stakeholders (ideally to one who is at a very high level).
   - Develop a clear problem statement.
   - Minimize the number of people involved with development of the solution.
3. **If the problem cannot be adequately tamed, accept that it is wicked.**
   - For problems solved through discussions and iterations, you must accept change as a normal part of the process.
   - Focus on relationships between discrete vs. incremental alternatives.[8]
   - Concentrate on possibility rather than probability.
   - Force incremental action, dialogue, and feedback.
4. **Prepare for the Blame Game.**
   - Wicked problems are not solved easily or in a timely manner.
   - This causes stress, which results in finger pointing.

Remember

Tame problems can be solved through linear processes and have right answers. Wicked problems are solved through non-linear processes and yield "good enough" solutions.

Part II

Chapter Twenty

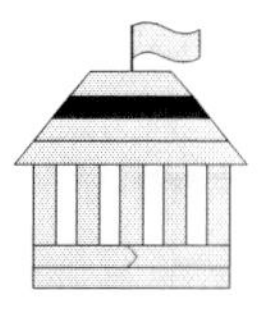

Attacking Wicked Problems

Once you know the type of problem you are facing, you need to set up the organizational method to try and solve it. An example of attempting to solve a wicked problem occurred in 1787 when 55 delegates met in Philadelphia, Pennsylvania. They met to revise the Articles of Confederation and try to save a new nation – the United States of America. At the start of the convention, the new country was failing: The Articles of Confederation weren't working, the states were bitterly divided, the Continental Dollar was worthless, New England was threatening to secede, and both England and Spain were waiting to snatch up the states once the Confederation failed.[1] Rather than "fix" the Articles of Confederation, the delegates created the Constitution of the United States. While the results of the convention are well known, it is useful to look at some of its infrastructure.

The delegates themselves formed an interesting mix of both highly educated and self-educated individuals who ranged from being rich to living on borrowed funds during the convention, as well as from wanting a strong government to wanting almost no government. While George Washington was elected president of the convention, almost all of the work was done by the "Committee of the Whole," wherein all of the delegates discussed, debated, and persuaded each other until a consensus was reached. Only then did delegates vote as a formal committee. All of these discussions were held in private to allow the delegates to make concessions, change their opinions, and move toward an agreement without the risk of public embarrassment. The goal was not to reach a compromise but to continue the discussions until consensus (and a resulting agreement) could be reached.

In the end, only three key issues ended up being settled by compromise: slavery, proportional representation, and regulation of commerce. This goes back to what we said in Chapter 19: Wicked problems don't always have a concrete answer. The founders of the United States compromised, but it came back to haunt the country later in the form of a Civil War. They did what made sense at the time, only to face additional problems that were created afterward. This is often the case with wicked problems.

What started out as a convention to fix the Articles of Confederation ended up being an opportunity to create the Constitution of the United States. Some fundamental keys to success of the Constitutional Convention included:

- A broad spectrum of delegates with varied backgrounds (diversity).
- The mutual respect that allowed them to understand differing perspectives and to reach a consensus on almost all of the issues (listening and communication skills).
- The ability to discuss issues outside the hierarchical pathways of the formal convention structure (a safe space).
- A passion among the delegates to make the convention (and, therefore, the United States) successful (commitment and loyalty).
- The wisdom among leaders to allow the process to move forward without feeling the need to overly control it or predict the outcome (consultative, non-micromanagers).

While this example happened more than 200 years ago, it provides interesting insights about dealing with wicked problems.

When thinking about organizations, we ordinarily think about the formal methods of aligning people for optimal management of talent and, consequently, the reporting structure that needs to be in place. There are many ways to establish a structure on paper. Almost all of them can be made to work and support innovation along the entire continuum.

The key lies in the semi-visible way in which organizations actually function. How do various groups interact? Are the communication pathways hierarchical or networked-based? How involved are the senior leaders? Are they micro or macro managers? How are the project leaders selected?

In this chapter, we will discuss some of the characteristics an organization must have to support sustained innovation. Our focus will center on attacking problems toward the wicked end of the tame-to-wicked continuum. If you can effectively deal with wicked problems, you can easily solve tame ones. Unfortunately, the converse is generally not true. Finally, we will look at innovation from expansionary to revolutionary, which normally falls into the wicked domain.

Information up to this point has been provided to help you understand the key elements required for creating and sustaining an innovative culture. Now it is time to examine how to attack wicked problems. We will help you see how all pieces of the Innovation House integrate together.

While you may decide not to go through every step in putting the pieces together, it is important for you to consider them and decide whether or not they fit your particular situation. What is important is that you decide how your team should function based on your assessment of the problem(s) needing to be solved. This includes understanding:

- Overall team structure and communication pathways
- Who should be on the team
- The role of each team member
- Problem ownership
- The team's "DNA" and Invisible Rules of Engagement

Communication Pathways

To attack a wicked problem, first you need to analyze your communication structure. Most large companies are structured either hierarchically or as a matrix in which there are parallel reporting structures. The flow of communication follows these predefined pathways, as opposed to crossing over via independent paths. This flow allows managers to stay "in the loop" and filter what goes outside their sphere of control. Tame problems can be effectively managed this way. However, wicked problems require a more networked approach. Information needs to flow along both the predefined management pathways and across paths to different groups (Figure 20.1 - next page).

As an example, let's look at how a research and development (R&D) division might interact with the Operations division. In a hierarchical type of network, information typically starts with the engineers or scientists in R&D, and then goes upward through their management before it crosses over

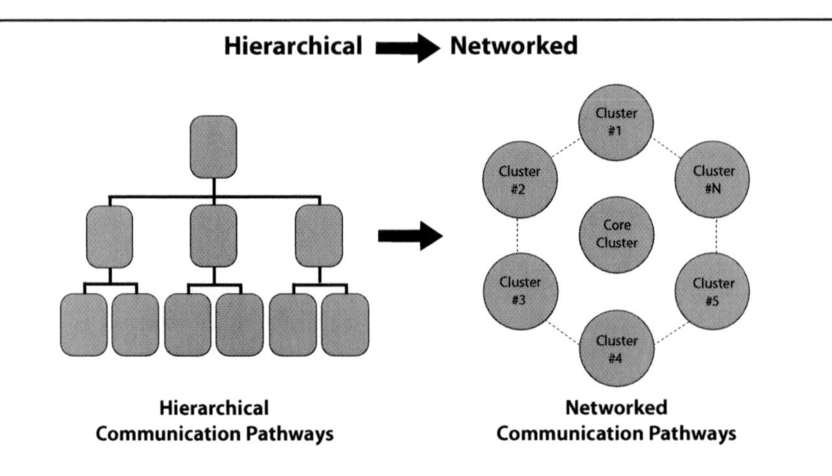

Figure 20.1
To attack wicked problems, communication within the organization needs to be networked and more horizontal, as opposed to strictly hierarchical.

and back down the chain of command within Operations. In a networked environment, the key innovators in R&D talk directly with their counterparts in Operations, typically at a low level in the hierarchy. Rather than the R&D group manager interacting with the Operation's plant manager, the R&D innovator talks directly with the processing line manager. Both of these individuals keep their respective managers informed but do not have to rely on them as the conduit for flow of communication.

Unfortunately, many managers struggle with this concept. The reason is that classical management styles rely on control and prediction of outcomes. This approach can be very effective when dealing with linear, tame problems. A different approach is required to deal with non-linear, wicked problems, where outcomes are not easily controlled or predictable. They are solved through networks of people working together who bring different points of view, contribute unique skills and experiences, and learn together. When subordinates are not trusted to talk to other groups without their managers being in the loop, the organization will struggle to solve wicked problems.

Based on the premise that wicked problems are solved through networks of people, you need to answer: "What can I do to facilitate these networks

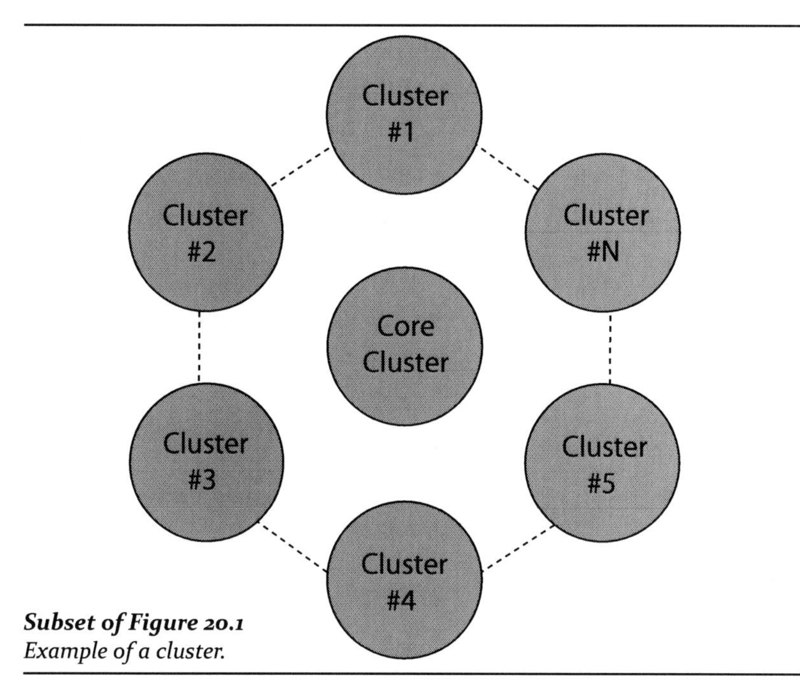

Subset of Figure 20.1
Example of a cluster.

within my organization? How do I ensure that the right people are encouraged to talk directly with each other?"

Wicked Clusters

To knock down hierarchical boundaries and facilitate flow of information, look at the problem itself and ask if it can be broken down into logical domains or subsets. Once these subsets are identified, you can create clusters or small teams to attack them. In the end, you may have a whole network of clusters with each one assigned to one or more aspects of a problem. (See subset of Figure 20.1 above.)

Within the network of clusters, there are specific roles that need to be understood and appropriate individuals selected to fill them.

- **Wicked Sponsor** – owns the problem.
- **Wicked Advocate** – sells the solution to the organization.
- **Wicked Leader** – creates the environment within an **individual cluster** to solve the problem.
- **Wicked Practitioner** – innovates within a cluster as an individual team member.

If we examine Kettering's role in developing the new painting system, he fulfilled all of these roles at one point or another. He definitely owned the problem. Without his ownership, the idea of reducing the paint time from 17 days to an hour would have died at the initial paint conference when the experts said it was impossible. He sold the new process to the divisions (and even sent the paint manager fishing to do so). Kettering led the effort and was instrumental in identifying the solution.

In larger organizations, different individuals generally fill these roles. In smaller ones, a single person may fill several roles. However, whether filled by a single person or several people, activities must be performed successfully to resolve a wicked problem. Let's look closer at these roles to understand the responsibilities of each.

Wicked Sponsor: The wicked sponsor is generally a single person who is key to the entire process. This role is the most difficult to fill. The wicked sponsor defines the problem and provides the vision for the clusters and also communicates that vision to the organization as a whole. Wicked sponsors provide the air cover and resources to work on the problem. They become the spokesperson or face of the problem. President Kennedy, Martin Luther King, Jr. and Charles Kettering were sponsors of their wicked problems.

The role of the sponsor is not to make micro decisions, but to set the vision and then make high level, macro decisions. The major responsibilities of the sponsor are to review progress and to facilitate communications between the clusters, including the sharing of new knowledge. Sponsors exist to provide the necessary resources and to buffer these resources from the rest of the company. Sponsors must also be active participants along the way and be part of the communication network. They need to be aware of key lower level decisions as they are being made, even if they are not actually involved in making these decisions. As part of the ongoing dialogue, they need to present their point of view on these decisions, but empower teams to proceed to make micro decisions independently.

Without the right sponsor, there will be a high probability of a disconnect between the sponsor's vision and the wicked team's focus. We have seen sponsors who do not become involved until the "eleventh hour" and then jump in challenging decisions that were made earlier. They derail the program, causing teams to virtually start over. We have also seen sponsors micromanaging the effort and making directional changes every week. This leaves the group wondering where they are going and whether or not anybody really knows. Both approaches lead to the "blame game" scenario that we discussed in the last chapter. The successful sponsor needs to be actively involved, but balance their role between being an advisor and mentor, versus a decision maker.

To be successful, sponsors need to be partners or stewards relative to the problem and team. They need to be committed to solving the problem and they must have the passion to help overcome significant obstacles that will always be part of solving highly wicked problems. If they act like employees or contractors, they will not be successful in leading the clusters to overcome these obstacles.

To feel like partners or stewards, sponsors must trust the broader organization. Serving as the face of the problem, if they don't feel a high level of trust, then their decision process becomes clouded by fear of failure: "If this doesn't work, I'll be hung out to dry and my career will suffer." As we said earlier, when trust erodes, the degree of wickedness goes up.

Wicked Advocate: The wicked advocate provides the interface between the idea generators, clusters, and the organization as a whole. They are part of the **core cluster** and report to the sponsor. The advocate becomes the spokesperson for the wicked team (all of the clusters put together) to the broader organization. There are usually one or two advocates per wicked team (not one advocate per individual cluster). They help sell the chosen solution.

The sponsor sometimes also handles this role but, in many instances, different people are involved. Advocates are needed when the sponsor does not have the skills or time to assume the related responsibilities. Advocates need to be highly networked and understand the informal decision-making processes.

Wicked Leader: Each individual cluster will have a wicked leader who will drive the solution for that particular cluster. The leader will provide guidance for the cluster and interact with the advocate and sponsor on high level decision-making.

The key skills for a wicked leader include being well networked, being able to deal with the uncertainty of not knowing exactly where their cluster is going, and being able to learn along the way. Because of the heavy networking focus, wicked leaders need to be chosen based on their networks outside of their particular domains. This means wicked leaders may not be managers on the hierarchical organization chart. We have seen managers who are extremely good at managing people in their department, but are not as good at interfacing with people outside of this group. They are not ideal wicked leaders. When choosing a wicked leader, you should consider:

- Who has the right technical skills and brings the right technical network to tap into?
- Who has the right people skills and understands how to leverage the invisible strengths and differences in others (ISPI)?
- Who can design a strategy or put together a team to design a strategy?
- Who has the right influence skills and is well connected outside of the cluster's particular area?

Wicked Practitioners: The final key role is that of the wicked practitioner. These people are the creators and the doers. Ideally, the practitioners act as partners or stewards to the problem's solution; however, this is not a requirement. Individually, they need to interact as Creativity Partners within the cluster. Head and heart trust are vital within the cluster to leverage the group's differences and tap into their spectrum of cognitive, technical, and experiential backgrounds. The goal is to facilitate diversified networks and diversified thoughts.

When selecting wicked practitioners, you will want to try and have six to ten per cluster. You need to consider the following individual perspectives:

- **Sociological:** How people view the world. What lenses do they look through? What filters are in place that limit or color their views? Filters include items such as work and non-work experiences, education, professional and non-professional networks, and personal interests. You may derive some of this data from resumes, sociograms showing technical and personal networks, and conversations with them.
- **Psychological:** How people take in information, what they do with it and how they interact with others. This data is derived from instruments such as the ISPI, which include cognitive, conative, and affect characteristics.
- **Intellectual:** Capacity of individuals to grasp new ideas and integrate them with the problem at hand. While there are tests to help with making this determination, we suggest looking at prior results. Have people demonstrated the ability to quickly see patterns and transform information into usable knowledge?

Or do they struggle with new concepts? When considering intellectual capacity, acknowledging that we are all different individuals with different strengths and opportunities is critical. One way of looking at this is via Howard Gardner's seven distinct intelligences as outlined below:[2,3]

1. *Visual-Spatial* – Thinking in terms of physical space (architects, sailors, pilots)
2. *Bodily-Kinesthetic* – Using the body effectively (dancers, surgeons, athletes)
3. *Musical* – Showing sensitivity to rhythm and sound (musicians)
4. *Interpersonal* – Understanding and interacting with others (sales people, managers)
5. *Intrapersonal* – Understanding oneself (independent thinkers)
6. *Linguistic* – Using words effectively (writers, speakers)
7. *Logical-Mathematical* – Using reasoning, calculations (engineers, scientists)

What sets of intellectual skills do you need on your team? Remember that in attacking wicked problems, you want to come at them from different perspectives, which requires having a wide variety of intellectual skills.

We will talk more about defining characteristics for who should be on your team as wicked practitioners when we discuss individual clusters later in this chapter.

Cluster Characteristics

As we discussed earlier, to effectively facilitate communications, networking, and interactions within the group, we recommend that you look at your team in terms of clusters (Figure 20.1). We are not talking about your overall organizational structure, only how you might look at structuring your team. It is more about defining communication pathways and individual effectiveness. Let's look at the characteristics of the core cluster.

Core Cluster

The overall team leadership is found in the core cluster. Membership in this group includes the wicked sponsor and any other key stakeholders who need to be involved on an ongoing basis. The team also includes the wicked leaders from the individual clusters and the wicked advocate(s). Ideally, this group should be less than 15 people to allow each member to effectively interact and contribute. The responsibilities of the core cluster are to:

- Review what is taking place on a frequent basis, including current results, next steps, and any resource requirements.
- Share the collective knowledge from prior programs and current activities and integrate this knowledge to help define where the overall program needs to go.
- Share the sponsor's vision and what has been learned inside each of the clusters, as well as assist in broadening the team's array of networks.
- Facilitate securing the required resources, protecting them, and communicating between the individual clusters and the rest of the company.

Within the core cluster, there are several key attributes required for success. These include:

- Leadership
- Ownership/Commitment
- Organization DNA
- Rules of Engagement

Leadership: Due to the non-linear nature of wicked problems, wicked leaders cannot predict or truly control development activity. They must be comfortable in the role of being a complex (wicked) leader.[4] They must:

- Encourage largely undirected interactions among individual clusters and groups of clusters to create an uncontrollable and unpredictable future.
- Focus on control of macro interactions versus micro events.
- Focus on facilitating interactions between people and groups rather than on issuing directives.
- Enable clusters to innovate the unexpected.

In the words of Marion and Uhl-Bien:[5] "Complex (wicked) leaders need to be comfortable existing on the edge of chaos, just shy of anarchy, risking catastrophe to enable creativity." As an innovation leader dealing with wicked problems, you must develop the internal skills to operate within a world of uncertainty. This will be easier to do for those more pioneering in nature. Builders can also be effective wicked leaders, but they will need to cope with working in the unknown.

Ownership/Commitment: Having the wicked sponsor be mentally tied to the problem as a partner or steward is almost always a prerequisite for success. Having the rest of the core cluster also behaving as (at least) stewards is highly desirable. The more the leadership group demonstrates a commitment to doing whatever is required to resolve the problem, the more the individual clusters will follow their lead.

When people are being asked to take a significant risk, they want to know who is "in the boat" with them, especially if they are more on the builder side. If the sponsor is the only one truly committed to finding a solution, there is a risk of having too many "**we be's**" on the team, i.e., the people that behave like (and say): "We will be here before you and we will be here after you." They know that there is a high probability that as soon as the sponsor is gone, the program will be cancelled. They become organizational antibodies, waiting for the opportunity to attack and kill the invading program, because they never really believed in it in the first place.

What would have happened to the development of a new painting system if Kettering had not been there throughout the whole program? The more the leadership of the core cluster believes in the program, the less dependent the program is on the activities of a single individual. As with any complex system, single-point failures lead to disasters. Having more people than just the sponsor behaving as partners or stewards will help to provide the redundancy necessary to overcome the loss of a single person.

We worked with a government official who was assigned the task of leading an interdepartmental task force to work on a White House directive. As part of the directive, the sponsor in the White House held a conference of renowned experts in this particular field. They came up with hundreds of ideas that were added to the directive. The individual we worked with was assigned the task of meeting with representatives of several different agencies to work through the list of ideas and implement the ones that had the most merit. Unfortunately:

- The White House sponsor was done with the problem at this point.
- The different agencies knew that implementation of any of the ideas would require putting their resources behind them and giving up some power.

- None of the ideas had ownership rooted within the agencies.
- The person put in charge had no authority to get anything done. They had to rely solely on their ability to influence the others to get anything accomplished.
- The agencies knew they could not ignore the directive, so they had to show support for it.
- The agencies also knew that by the time they would actually have to commit to doing anything, there would most likely be a new administration in place and the directive would be forgotten.

The net result was that meetings were held in which all of the agencies participated, but nothing happened. As soon as the next election was held, even the meetings were no longer required. Thus, the "we be's" prevailed. Within your organization, have you seen similar types of behaviors?

Organization DNA: The core cluster group must have a strong solidarity of vision relative to the wicked problem. That is not to say that they cannot debate the vision or that it cannot be modified over time. But the overall group must be aligned with where they are trying to go, and the alignment of individuals must be visible to the rest of the group. The culture within the core cluster must be on either the mercenary or communal side of the Four Cultures Model because both are highly aligned around the goal.

Due to the greater risks involved in dealing with wicked problems, leaders must trust the organization and feel that the organization trusts them. Solving these types of problems cannot be done behind a cloud of "fear of individual failure." In addition, within the core cluster there must be, at a minimum, a high level of intellectual trust. High intellectual trust allows individuals to have an immediate trust in what the others are saying. This drives communication to be above the line where learning and understanding take place. If the trust isn't there, communications are below the line where individual defense mechanisms are activated and listening is no longer for the purpose of learning or understanding.

Since wicked problems involve taking risks to solve them, the core cluster must have a fairly high risk tolerance (mid-range pioneering to pioneering in risk is helpful). Individuals selected to be part of this group must be comfortable with the notion that they are joining a higher risk activity. If they are not comfortable with taking these risks, they should not be part of the core cluster. The ideal DNA for the core cluster and individual clusters are summarized in Figure 20.2 below. You can read about the characteristics for this type of DNA in Appendix III.

Organization DNA Table

	Core Cluster	Individual Cluster
Cultural Type FRAGMENTED NETWORKED MERCENARY COMMUNAL	**MERCENARY to COMMUNAL**	**COMMUNAL**
Trust LOW TRUST MEDIUM TRUST HIGH TRUST	**HIGH TRUST**	**HIGH TRUST**
Risk LOW TOLERANCE MODERATE TOLERANCE HIGH TOLERANCE	**MODERATE to HIGH**	**HIGH**

Figure 20.2
Organizational DNA comparison between the core cluster and an individual cluster

Rules of Engagement: Within the core cluster, visible and invisible rules of engagement must be defined and made obvious to the entire team. Since the visible rules of engagement can be defined and implemented by the team, we will only deal with the invisible ones here: communication content, decision making, and knowledge transfer.

As wicked problems require looking at many potential solutions in parallel, the communication content for the core cluster must contain a balance of the five levels (Chapter 16, page 162165). Members need to devote as much time looking at the possibilities and "what ifs" as in looking at the economics and near-term possibilities. By the core cluster encouraging higher level discussions, the individual clusters become empowered to take greater risks and consider a broader range of solutions.

The invisible decision making must be made more visible to the whole team. More importantly, members of the core cluster must force themselves to examine their individual biases relative to decision making. If they are predisposed to making decisions primarily on extensive analyses and probability of success, they need to adapt to a world of looking at decisions based more on the potential of an idea. In addition, the core cluster must identify which decisions are within the authority of the individual clusters and which ones need to be brought to the core team.

Knowledge transfer and learning as you go are fundamental to solving wicked problems. The core cluster must demonstrate that they value knowledge transfer by modeling the PAR Process (See page 188) or something similar to it. They need to:

- Share what each one already knows about the problem.
- Conduct action reviews to collect and disseminate new understandings.
- Conduct team retrospect meetings after major milestones and events to improve the overall process.

These activities allow the team to start at a higher level of understanding and provide an avenue for individual team members to make their networks available to other members. They also facilitate the sharing of new information and help to integrate new understanding into greater clarity for the program's vision and direction.

Core Cluster Summary: Independent of how you draw it on a chart or what you call it, there will be a key individual or team providing the overall leadership for solving your wicked problem. The core cluster is made up of a leadership team consisting of:

- The wicked sponsor
- Any key stakeholders (They may not be a part of the wicked team)
- Wicked advocates
- Wicked leaders

To maximize the probability of success, this core cluster leadership group must exhibit a series of key behaviors that include being:

- Comfortable leading in the complex world of non-linearity.
- Committed to solving the problem.
- Unified in their vision.

- Trusting of the organization and each other.
- Willing to take moderate to high risks.
- Able to communicate above the line and look at possibilities – not just analyses.
- Capable of making decisions based on potential rather than certainty.
- Supportive of team members learning and sharing knowledge as they go.

Core clusters provide "leadership," not "managership."

Individual Cluster
The individual clusters focus on the key aspect(s) of the wicked problem. Each individual cluster includes a wicked leader and, ideally, six to ten individual wicked practitioners. Since trust between the team members is critical, they should be co-located in a single area. If this is not feasible, they need sufficient time together to develop the level of trust needed to effectively interact from remote sites.

As we said earlier, when selecting wicked practitioners, there must be diversity in how they see the world (sociological diversity), how they interact with others and take in and process data (psychological diversity), and their capacity to integrate new ideas (intellectual diversity). It is important to map out what an ideal mix of these traits would be, given the wicked problem. Some of the questions or criteria that should go into assembling the ideal team might include:

- **Sociological**
  - What educational mix do you want (e.g., engineers vs. scientists vs. marketers, etc., educational level: high school diploma / bachelor's degree / master's degree / Ph.D., mix of schools attended, etc.)?
  - What experience base (e.g., number of years, types of industries, theoretical vs. hands-on, field vs. headquarters, patents, publications, etc.)?
  - Other interests (e.g., hobbies, academic networks, geographic experiences, etc.)?

- **Psychological (ISPI)**
  - What should be the ratio of pioneers to builders? Of concrete to visionary thinkers? Of people wanting to converge vs. diverge?

- What should the balance be of those wanting to take control vs. those wanting to be controlled? How important is the desire to build relationships and network with others?
- What should be the ratio of people with a passion for taking action vs. those who prefer being cautious? Of people making decisions based on their head vs. heart? Of getting energy from others vs. being alone?

- **Intellectual**
  - What should be the ratio between people who are grounded in reality vs. those always looking at the patterns differently?
  - What should be the ratio of "sprinters" vs. "marathoners"?
  - What should be the balance between "teachers" vs. "students"?

In very large companies, it is possible to create databases to help create an initial list of potential team members (example: ISPI Software). Similar to the Mission Impossible movies,[6] this is like putting together a team from a database of potential team members. Special forces teams also look at combinations of individuals who have both similar and dissimilar skills to give the team its highest probability of success in carrying out the mission.

In smaller organizations, the process is far more restrictive. But in moving through this process and matching the ideal versus the actual team, it will help identify strengths and potential blind spots.

The key attributes of a successful individual cluster are similar to the core cluster, with the exception of the required commitment level, culture, and risk tolerance. The commitment level for wicked practitioners does not have to be as high. Ideally, they would also be stewards or partners with the problem, but this is not a prerequisite for them to be effective team members. As shown in Figure 20.2, the culture of the individual cluster needs to be more communal. Due to the nature of highly wicked problems, the team needs to function largely as Creativity Partners. This requires a high degree of both intellectual and emotional trust – which comes with a high degree of sociability.

Finally, the group needs to have an overall high risk tolerance. Members need to pull the team further out in looking for breakthrough solutions. The core cluster is always there to help pull them back if they stray too far. But if they are never being reigned in, they are not pushing the boundaries far enough.

The most significant difference between the core and individual clusters is in how they take action. The core cluster operates primarily in an advisory/ support role. In contrast, individual clusters have the accountability for day-to-day development. As a result, individual clusters must adopt an action-oriented approach that forces action rather than continued analysis. This group of a wicked leader and six to ten wicked practitioners needs to be communal in nature with high trust between them and a willingness to work on high risk problems. They must also integrate the PAR Process (See page 188) into their ongoing activities. Being able to learn as you go and to share these learnings is a vital element for successfully attacking wicked problems.

Advice for the Innovation Leader

In dealing with a wicked problem, create an organization of clusters (teams) that facilitates direct communication, not following predefined hierarchical pathways. Team members must be encouraged to talk directly with each other. The team sponsor needs to be committed to the program and provide the resources, air cover, and support that the team will require. The sponsor needs to be involved in the program without micromanaging it.

Finally, divide the tasks so that each individual group or cluster has no more than six to ten members who are co-located. This supports the development of the trust required to tackle the problem. These groups need to focus on keeping multiple pathways open, driving action and learning, and communicating with the other individual clusters as well as the core cluster.

In Closing

Revolutionary innovation typically comes from solving wicked problems. Wicked problems are complicated because they don't have a concrete answer. They only have a best choice answer. Because they are non-linear, wicked problems require collaboration, learning, passion, and tenacity. They require having the appropriate:

- **Wicked sponsors**
- **Wicked advocates**
- **Wicked leaders**
- **Wicked practitioners**

Finally, as we will discuss in the next chapter, there should be an appropriate reward and recognition system in place to motivate the team, reinforce desired behaviors, and show the team members that they can trust the organization.

Remember

Wicked problems are not solved by people in a cave; they are solved through highly effective networks of diverse people.

Part II

Chapter Twenty-One

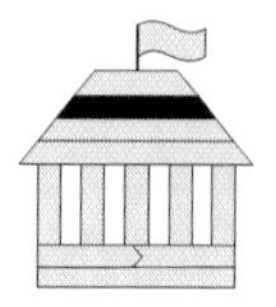

Reward and Recognition

In Chapter 1, we explained the Principle to Results Model (PRM), which states:

- Principles are fundamental truths.
- What you value determines which principles you and/or your organization will utilize.
- Methods and actions dictate how the principles are applied.
- Behaviors leading to results are the visible outcomes from the methods and actions.

Organizations apply this model to their reward and recognition programs based on the following:

- **Principle:** Businesses Don't Innovate, People Do.
- **Value:** Motivation influences performance.
- **Activities:** The reward and recognition programs that are developed and implemented guide the selection of activities.
- **Desired Result:** You have highly motivated employees working on innovation programs.

To be able to design an appropriate reward and recognition program, the innovation leader must understand both individual and team motivation.

Motivation has been defined in the psychological world as an internal state or condition (sometimes described as a need, desire, or want) that serves to activate or energize behavior and give it direction.[1] When looking at an individual's motivation, there is a continuum from purely **intrinsic** ("I feel good because I did it.") to purely **extrinsic** ("I feel good because I have prospered from my work."). Where we fall on the continuum is a function of who we are, what is going on around us at the time, and the task being undertaken.

As an example, take something trivial like mowing the lawn. There are some who are motivated because they feel good when mowing the lawn and like how nice the yard will look once it is cut and trimmed (i.e., they lean toward the intrinsic end). Others are motivated simply by the fact that if they don't mow the lawn, it will be harder to do later, or the neighbors will complain or, worse yet, the city will come in, mow it and charge for doing it (i.e., they lean toward the extrinsic end). Given a different task, however, these two individuals may very easily flip positions on the motivation continuum.

Let's look at two of the prolific inventors introduced in Chapter 5 and their quotes about their inventions:

- George Washington Carver: "God gave them to me, how can I sell them to someone else?"[2]
- Thomas Edison: "Never waste time inventing things people do not want to buy."[3]

What do these quotes reveal about where the two inventors fell on the motivation continuum? If they worked for you, would you try to motivate them the same way? In most of our organizations, we have a combination of Carvers and Edisons and everyone in between. When we begin to think about motivating people through our reward and recognition activities, it is critical to appreciate that everyone is unique. What is highly motivating for one person in a particular situation might be viewed with indifference or even negatively by someone else.

In this chapter, we will explore some of the invisible drivers of individual and team motivation, as well as how your reward and recognition programs can help drive or hinder your innovation efforts. We will not discuss specific types of reward and recognition that you might use. Instead, we will look at some of the things that need to be taken into consideration when designing these programs.

Motivational Analysis

Think about what has happened in virtually every industry providing goods and services for people. They generally start with a limited variety of offerings, similar to Henry Ford with the Model T: "Would you like it in black or in black?" Look at the variety of cars available now, from the Peoples' Car in India to the most luxurious Bentleys or Lamborghinis. People want choices. Similarly, they want reward and recognition that is aligned with who they are and what they want for performing a particular task. We need to move from the world of the Model T into the twenty-first century and look at the individual when thinking about reward and recognition.

Unlike the situation with cars, we cannot easily run focus groups or conduct consumer surveys to determine how we should reward or recognize an individual's accomplishments. True, focus groups and surveys can provide information about what is generally wanted. Yet, to motivate an individual, we must look at the individual, not at what the survey says. Understanding individual motivation requires examining what drives them to perform a particular task and then creating a reward and recognition program that accommodates their individual differences.

One of the issues with understanding an individual's motivation is that it is not static; motivation changes over time. This makes the innovation leader's task of keeping members of their team motivated over an extended period of time a challenging one. The leader must be able to understand the motivation of each team member, then increase/reinforce it to maximize the team's performance. As a way to help the leader with this task, we are going to adapt the work of Ryan and Deci on Self-Determination Theory (SDT).[4]

As shown in Figure 21.1, motivation forms a continuum from **amotivated** (disengaged) to extrinsically motivated to intrinsically motivated. The biggest

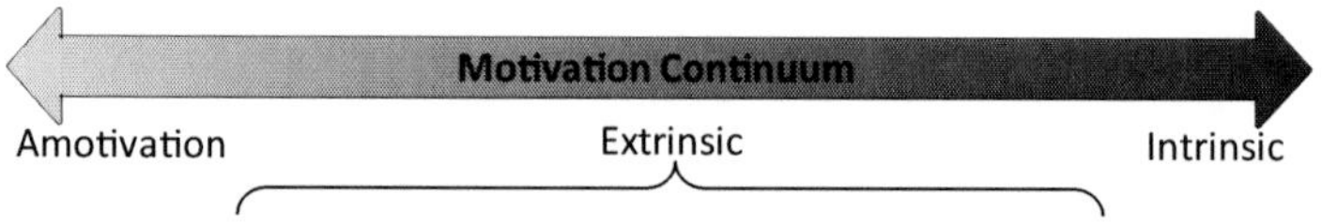

Personal Attachment	Disengaged	Non-Internalized	Slightly Internalized	Somewhat Internalized	Internalized	Self Driven
Description	•Not valuing the activity •Not competent •Does not expect it to be successful	•Activity performed to meet external demands •No ownership of activity	•Wants activity to be successful but not emotionally attached. •Very limited ownership	•Emotionally tied to success of activity. •Moderate to high level of ownership in the outcome	•Emotionally tied to success of activity. •Acts as an owner of the activity	•Emotionally owns the activity independent of the sponsor or they may be the sponsor
Trust of Activity Sponsors	Not Applicable ... Doesn't make a difference	Limited or low trust level	Moderate level of intellectual and emotional trust	Medium to high level of intellectual and emotional trust	High level of intellectual and emotional trust	High level of intellectual and emotional trust highly desirable
Action	Limited or no intent to act ... going through the motions	Do what is ordered	Do only what is required and provide input if asked	Do what is required and provide input without being asked	Actively participate in whatever is required to be successful	Owns the activity regardless of what it takes to be successful
Mindset	"Prisoner"	Contractor	Employee / Contractor	Steward / Employee	Partner / Steward	Partner

Adapted from the SDI work of Ryan &Deci

Figure 21.1
An individual's motivation is directly related to the degree of internalization held for the particular activity being undertaken.

factor determining where an individual is on the continuum is the degree to which they internalize the particular activity. If people are simply going through the motions and doing only the minimum of what they are told to do, there is virtually no internalization of activities and little or no motivation to do the work. On the other hand, if people feel total ownership and are emotionally tied to results, they are generally highly motivated (whether intrinsically or extrinsically).

To put this into action, you must first determine the level of motivation required for the innovation program. Going back to the Innovation Continuum as shown in Figure 21.2, a revolutionary type of innovation requires a very high level of motivation. Evolutionary innovation can definitely benefit from a high level of motivation, but can still be successful at much lower levels. The one area that must be avoided or dealt with immediately is when you have somebody on your team who is amotivated. These individuals are often referred to as "having retired in place."

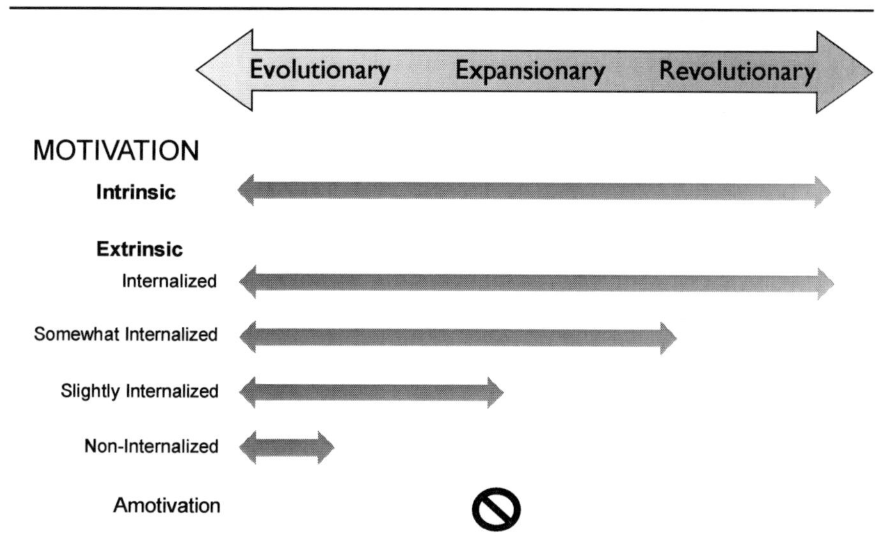

Figure 21.2
Different types of innovation require a different minimum level of motivation.

In assessing where an individual is on the continuum, using a tool like the ISPI is a good starting point for determining some generalities in what would motivate or de-motivate that individual. Unfortunately, motivation is extremely situational; solely using a person's general preference is not sufficient for understanding the current motivation. You must also understand their behaviors in the context of a particular activity. To what extent has the individual internalized it? To help in assessing the degree of internalization, think about the observable behaviors listed in Figure 21.3.

INDIVIDUAL BEHAVIOR (Degree that an individual ...)	NEVER	USUALLY	ALWAYS
1. Offers suggestions or ideas on how to improve the activity that is being performed.			
2. Engages others in discussing the current results or next steps.			
3. Asks questions to verify how their assignments will help move the overall program forward.			
4. Helps on tasks outside of those assigned to them without being asked.			
5. Seeks you or others out to discuss new results and their implications for the overall program.			
6. "Seeks forgiveness rather than permission"... doing what they think needs to be done without getting approval ahead of time.			
7. Demonstrates that they care about good or bad news concerning the program.			
8. Thinks about the program on their own time.			
9. Demonstrates that they trust you and are willing to follow your lead without necessarily knowing all of program details.			
10. Demonstrates that they've "got your back" and will not let you get blindsided or go down a wrong pathway.			

•An individual who never demonstrates these behaviors is generally either disengaged or has not internalized that particular program.

•An individual who always demonstrates these traits is generally highly motivated or has internalized that particular program.

Figure 21.3
Observable behaviors can help the innovation leader assess an individual's motivation with regard to a particular activity.

By assessing your team members individually and then collectively relative to where they have been working on the program, where they are currently, and where they need to be for the program to be successful, you have obtained the information required for a **gap analysis** that will aid you in designing your reward and recognition program. Does the program:

- Need to increase the overall team motivation?
- Need to reinforce the current level of motivation?
- Need to continue the current motivational direction on the continuum?
- Need to dramatically shift the current motivational direction?
- Need to be a hybrid to help increase the motivation of some, while maintaining the motivation of others?

When designing the specifics of your reward and recognition system, consideration must be given to the fundamental needs of individuals to allow them to more easily internalize the program.

Motivational Needs

We have heard many different motivational speakers over the years. Most have had different phrases that we were supposed to take with us to help motivate not only ourselves but also our teams. We leave the lecture feeling good and ready to take on the world. Unfortunately, within a few days we have forgotten the wonderful motivational phrases. Within a few weeks or months, we have forgotten everything except that we went and listened to so-and-so.

Are some motivational speakers merely good actors and/or entertainers? Or do they really have something that we can use? The short answer to both is "generally yes." The problem is similar to what we see in many organizations. People try to replicate motivational phrases and programs without understanding the basic principles behind them.

To understand an individual's particular motivation, we must be able to go behind the scenes and understand their needs and how they are being met, to allow them to internalize what they were doing. This creates highly motivated individuals who are equipped to be successful.

Think about somebody in your life who you view as a great motivator of teams. What makes them successful in motivating people? Is it their words that inspire or their actions?

Self-Determination Theory has identified three fundamental needs that are required for an individual to potentially internalize a problem (Figure 21.4, see next page).

The combination of **competency**, **autonomy**, and **relatedness/belonging** provides the innovation leader with fundamental principles for an effective reward and recognition program. It is not about money, gifts, or other superficial enticements. Motivation is about addressing fundamental human needs. In fact, many of the enticements used in today's reward and recognition programs end up, in the long term, being destructive to motivation.[5]

For example, think about some of your teachers. How did you respond to those who allowed you a degree of autonomy in how you did things versus those who were extremely controlling? Teachers who support autonomy also support a greater amount of intrinsic motivation.[6] The same is true of parents, coaches, and innovation leaders. In the short term, these programs

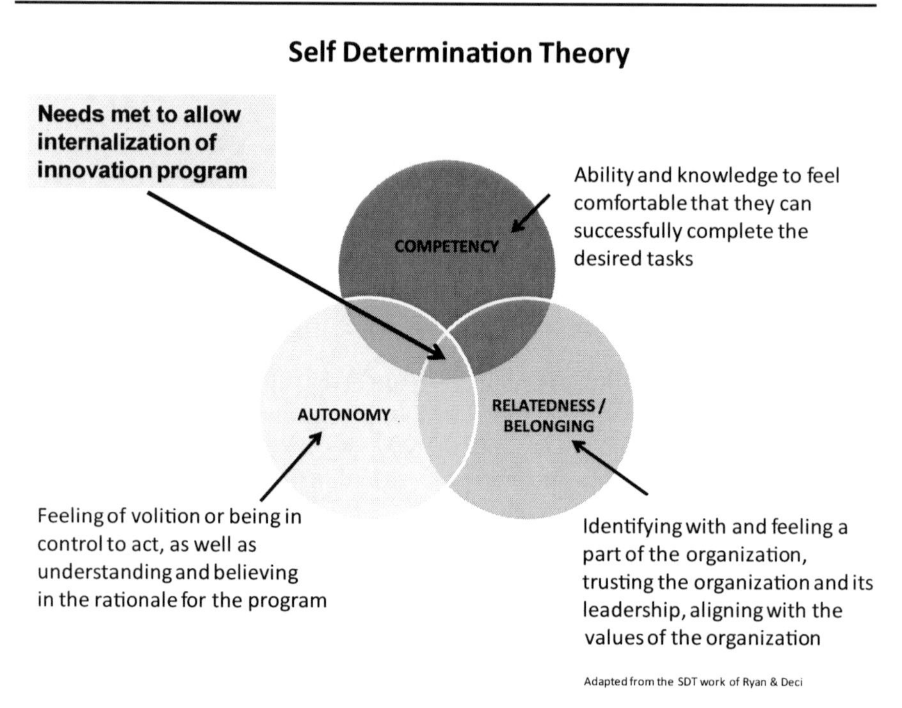

Figure 21.4
Competency, autonomy, and the feeling of relatedness/belonging are the three fundamental needs associated with an employee being able to internalize an innovation program – needs that allow for a high level of motivation.

can improve motivation, but the question is whether or not you are interested in short-term or long-term impact.

The issue for the innovation leader is to be able to understand the three needs and the implications of each. For example, if it is uncertain whether or not the individual or team feels competent to undertake a program, the innovation leader can help by having the individual or team receive special training by hiring outside consultants or coaches, and/or by acknowledging that this is an issue for the whole team, as in the case of a basic research program.

The innovation leader needs to continue to ask whether or not the individuals or team are allowed as much autonomy as possible. One of the easiest ways to stifle motivation is to project the appearance of micromanaging. Micromanaging can stem from a control issue or when the manager does not trust the people doing the job. At the same time, if the team has not been selected properly, the manager will ask, "Should the team be trusted?" The innovation leader needs to maintain balance by making sure to stay involved while, at the same time, refraining from making all decisions. Without feeling some autonomy, the team will default to not making any decisions and, thus, not owning the program.

Finally, the individuals and team need to feel that they are part of something (relatedness/belonging). This incorporates most of the principles in the lower portion of the Innovation House. First of all, they need to trust the innovation leader and feel that the leader trusts them. For most people, feeling isolated or living in a world based on distrust is a sure way to destroy motivation. As discussed previously, distrust introduces the filter of self-preservation. This filter shifts the motivation away from the program and onto the individual's need to survive. A lack of trust also moves people to the mindset of employees or contractors. This makes internalization of the program very difficult for them.

The principles associated with soft values, elements of destruction, leveraging differences, and co-location also play key roles in whether or not somebody feels a sense of belonging. If individuals can identify with and be aligned with the demonstrated values of the organization, they are more likely to feel a sense of belonging. The degree to which it is being impacted by prior history will be a significant factor in whether or not new employees feel like they belong. If employees do not perceive the organization as embracing differences (both visible and invisible), they may feel they have to adapt to survive. Survival as a motivational driver is not sufficient enough for someone to internalize a program. In a similar manner, without frequent interaction, the individual may feel isolated and not really part of the team.

Of the three motivational needs, the sense of belonging or relatedness is the most difficult for the innovation leader to positively change and is the easiest to negatively impact. It is highly individualistic and not readily visible. It requires **emotional intelligence** as well as true understanding and aptitude for applying the principles that make up the foundation and pillars of the Innovation House. Regarding any potential reward or recognition program, the innovation leader needs to ask, "Will this help or hinder the employee, relative to the feeling of belonging?"

In addition to the three basic needs, the innovation leader needs to remember that reward and recognition have a direct impact on behaviors. If rewards are all based on achieving next quarter's results, then the focus will be on the next quarter rather than on the long term.

There was a group inside one of our client's companies whose focus was on long-term innovation. This was a good thing for the organization but not necessarily for the individuals. At one of the early team meetings, people acknowledged that their reviews for that year were already predestined to be average at best, since they would not have any new products in the marketplace. They were motivated to work in the group for intrinsic and non-monetary extrinsic reasons. The innovation leader must ensure that the reward and recognition are aligned with the time expectations and risks associated with the overall program. If the focus is lower-risk evolutionary innovation, then reward and recognition may be focused more on the short term. However, if the innovation is of higher risk and more revolutionary, their focus needs to be more long term.

Advice for the Innovation Leader

After first understanding the minimum level of motivation required for the innovation program to be successful, you must assess yourself as the innovation leader. Does your motivation meet or exceed the level required for the program? If not, you need to understand why not and address that before you look at your team. They will know whether or not you are really motivated through your actions and words.

Unless you are a top executive, you will likely have more influence on intrinsic motivators than extrinsic ones. The extrinsic are typically defined by policy and hard values. With intrinsic motivation, you can get creative and use soft values to boost an individual's motivation. If you are a top executive, you may also be able to influence or develop key extrinsic motivators that will support innovation.

In looking at the motivational level of your team, start with the individuals first. How would you assess their prior and current levels of motivation? Where do they need to be? Are they on the right trajectory or do they need a mid-course correction? Once you have an understanding of the individuals, then you can put them together as a team. In this case, we are defining your team as those individuals who report directly to you. It is the responsibility of your direct reports to provide the reward and recognition required to motivate their teams.

Based on the above breakdown, you can put together a gap analysis for the overall team and each individual. This analysis makes visible for you what needs to be done, both collectively and individually. You are now in a position to put together specific reward and recognition programs that address the needs of your people and in turn, motivate them.

In Closing

The title of this chapter is Reward and Recognition. It could have just as easily been titled motivation, since it is the desired result of reward and recognition programs. We hear people talk about somebody who is considered a great motivator, but we hear very little about what that really means or what makes them successful.

In this chapter, we have outlined three of the basic needs for personal motivation: 1) competency, 2) authority, and 3) belonging or relatedness. The **synergy** between the three directly impacts the ability of an individual to internalize a particular innovation program and, thus, their level of ownership and motivation. By understanding an individual's motivation with respect to a particular program, we can focus reward and recognition efforts to address these specific needs. The more targeted the program, the more effective and efficient team members become. In today's world, one size does not fit all.

Remember

Reward and Recognition deals with motivating individuals.

Part II

Chapter Twenty-Two

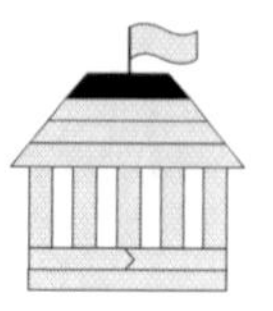

Quantifiable Gain

We have defined innovation as the creative act or solution that results in a quantifiable gain. Furthermore, we have discussed that a quantifiable gain is determined by your currency of the realm (what matters to the organization). Examples of currency of the realm include financial returns, quality improvements, new products, number of students graduating, number of publications, pollution levels, or number of people moving into a community. In this chapter, we will examine the importance of quantifiable gain in helping you to:

- Create the vision for your organization
- Measure the success of your organization's innovation program

There are countless books and workshops on goal setting. Whether you want to develop BHAGs (Big Harry Audacious Goals) as suggested by Porras and Collins,[1] **Figures of Merit** as suggested by Quinn,[2] or any number of other approaches, the key is that, for a goal to be effective, it must be specific and quantifiable. As Lewis Carroll said, "If you don't know where you are going, any road will get you there."[3] Without specific quantifiable goals, any innovation will suffice.

There is an amusing story (most likely an urban legend[4]) about Albert Einstein traveling by train and losing his ticket (author unknown):[5]

> Einstein was once traveling from Princeton on a train when the conductor came down the aisle, punching the tickets of every passenger. When he came to Einstein, Einstein reached in his vest pocket. He couldn't find his ticket, so he reached in his trouser pockets. It wasn't there, so he looked in his briefcase but couldn't find it. Then he looked in the seat beside him. He still couldn't find it.

> The conductor said, "Dr. Einstein, I know who you are. We all know who you are. I'm sure you bought a ticket. Don't worry about it."
>
> Einstein nodded appreciatively. The conductor continued down the aisle punching tickets. As he was ready to move to the next car, he turned around and saw the great physicist down on his hands and knees looking under his seat for his ticket.
>
> The conductor rushed back and said, "Dr. Einstein, Dr. Einstein, don't worry, I know who you are. No problem. You don't need a ticket. I'm sure you bought one."
>
> Einstein looked at him and said, "Young man, I too, know who I am. What I don't know is where I'm going."

Does your company know where it is going? Is the direction for it defined in measurable terms? Do employees know which "train" to take and where to get off?

To have sustainable, long-term top- and bottom-line growth, goals must be established that incorporate the organization's needs as well as individual human needs. There must be a balance between short-term and long-term objectives. Too much of a focus on the evolutionary end results in an organization "running out of runway" at some point and desperately needing revolutionary innovations to continue to grow. As an example, consider how the extreme focus on Six Sigma derailed 3M's long-term innovation engine.[6] In addition, focusing on only the revolutionary end will result in never reaping the gains from your innovation. For example, Xerox developed the technology for the personal computer, Apple commercialized it, and IBM and Microsoft captured most of the market, with Apple now making a strong comeback. So who has really reaped the benefits of Xerox's innovation?

Triple Bottom Line

Many companies around the world look at some form of the triple bottom line to assess their overall success. They examine the performance of financial capital in conjunction with social or human capital and the impact on environmental capital.[7] When we talk about financial performance, we refer to the currency of the realm. When we talk about social capital, we look at the people-related business practices internal to a company and those that impact the community. And as the name implies, when we mention environmental capital, we refer to the impact that a company and its products have on our planet.

Some examples of triple bottom line companies include:[8,9]

- Panasonic Corp.
- Unilever
- Nokia Corp.
- FedEx Kinko's
- Tata
- Whole Foods Market
- Wegmans (regional supermarket chain)
- Dell
- Patagonia

The concept of the triple bottom line is important to understanding and establishing an organization's desired quantifiable gain. First, the three components are intertwined to create the desired growth. Second, they promote creation of the required organizational and community cultures (largely driven by internal and external social and environmental influences) that will attract and retain the right people to make the innovation happen.

The components of the triple bottom line mesh in a way that is similar to the gears depicted in Figure 22.1 (next page).

For the system to work, people must identify problems that a company wants to solve. These problems are then converted into ideas, which fuel the innovation engine. The innovation engine drives the creation of financial capital, which allows the organization to successfully reach its goals and generate a profit. The profits drive the creation of the internal social and environmental capital. These help to define the organization's DNA, rules of engagement, and soft values. Together, they help to define the quality of work life that is critical to attracting and retaining the right people required for success. Internal social capital is also a driver for the development of the internal networks required for sustained innovation.

All of these elements interact to create an innovation engine that will run smoothly, provided that trust is present to keep the machine lubricated. Using your car as an example, without lubrication, the motor quickly seizes up and stops, which makes it very difficult to get it running again.

The creation of financial capital and associated profits also drives the development of the external social and environmental systems in the communities where your employees live, play, and raise their families. Having

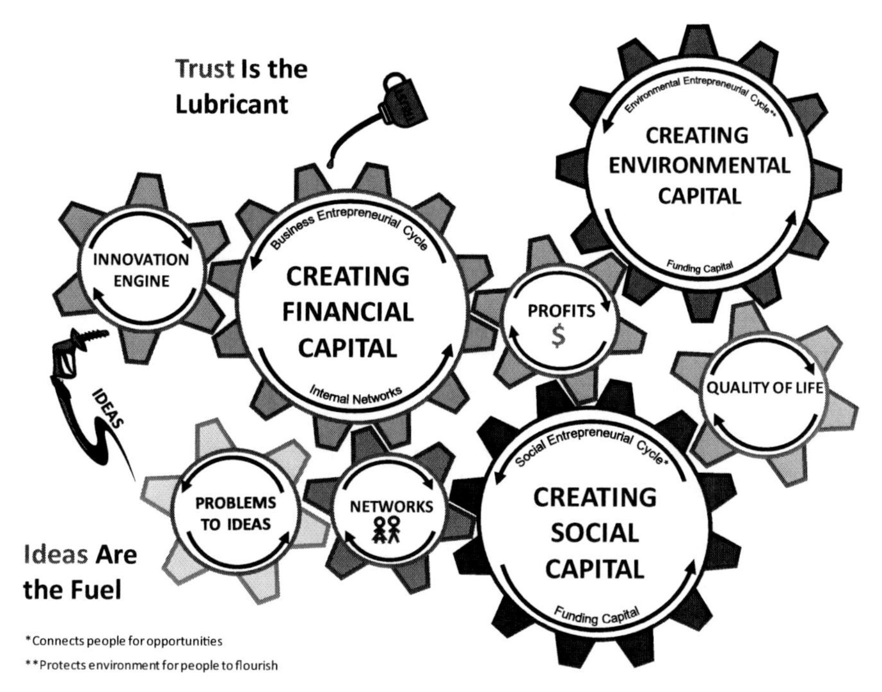

Figure 22.1
Successful integration of the activities for creating financial, social, and environmental capital is a prerequisite for achieving the desired and sustained innovation. Ideas fuel the engine while trust provides the lubricant. Both are required for sustained performance.

a highly desirable non-work quality of life for your employees and their families is arguably even more important than the internal quality of work life. As an innovation leader, how can you develop a culture of sustained innovation unless your employees are happy and enjoy where they live? Ensuring that your company is an active member in caring for the social and environmental concerns of the local community is more than a "feel good" activity. It is a prerequisite for achieving your long-term goals.

Metrics

A business leader we worked with once said, "If it is really important, we measure it. If it isn't measured, don't worry about it." We have been taught from early childhood about the importance of measurable success. Tests are given to determine how much we have learned (or remember) about a subject, and then grades are given for our individual performance. Grades are then averaged to provide an overall assessment of performance. Class rankings are determined by averaging the individual grades. Points and wins and losses govern sports. Books are rated on the quantity sold and number of stars that readers give them. Movies are given a grade by critics and often a different grade by consumers who go to see them. TV programs are rated based on the number of viewers.

Successful companies have a goal of sustained top- and bottom-line growth. In most cases, the bottom line is written in business and technical terms rather than in human terms. Think about the terms "social capital" and "environmental capital." The whole idea of using the word "capital "indicates the desire to mirror the business community by showing something tangible. Most businesses focus on hard values (like financials) because they are the most visible and measurable. Goals measured by these indicators may help to set the vision but do not address how to attain it.

Typically, having a sustained culture of innovation is not included in a company's quantifiable goals. Yet, we subscribe to the theory that, without a culture of innovation, it will be difficult for people to accomplish the goal of a sustained quantifiable gain. Improvement of the triple bottom line with regard to financial, social, and environmental capital is a successful by-product of a culture of innovation. It is a win-win for all involved. Goals are met and people feel connected to their jobs, organization, and community.

Specific metrics for creating financial capital are generally easy to develop. They can be made readily visible in a quantifiable way. Developing understandable and measurable metrics for creating internal social and environmental capital is far more difficult, however. Quantifying the soft values of your organization as a whole, as well as focusing on people within the organization, requires tapping into and measuring the way people feel.

For example, how do you measure the ability of someone to quantify differences between acquaintances and close friends? One approach comes out of our Mosaic Partnerships work, which focuses on race relations within a city or community.[10] We individually ask people 15 questions on a relativistic scale about their four closest friends. A sample question is, "To what degree will you share the problems you are facing in life and work?" We then ask the same questions about somebody they have either just met or who is merely an acquaintance. Finally, we ask them the same questions about a person they are working with closely in their organization. From there, we measure the answers for the four friends against both the acquaintance and the person with whom they work closely. This allows each person to calibrate an individual "relationship" scale. The resulting analysis identifies potential "relationship gaps" with the person at work and provides potential areas to focus on to build a higher level of trust.

We are now quantifying relationships by using soft values. This is similar to what different disciplines have been doing for years. Psychological testing quantifies such feelings as introversion versus extroversion, sensing versus feeling, wanting to be in control versus wanting others to be in control, etc. All of these tests have converted feelings into measurable scales. Other examples include the pain scale used by many doctors or measurements used in consumer research. Creating metrics for social and environmental capital follows the same thought processes used in these examples.

However, creating both soft and hard metrics is not enough. The next step is making those metrics real and visible to your employees in a way that they will understand so as to create common ground for everyone.

The question is, how do you deal with quantifiable gain and personalize it? If you want an organization of partners and stewards, you must:

1. Develop quantifiable gains that are measurable in all three areas (financial, social, and environmental).
2. Educate your people so the quantifiable gains are understood and visible.

Advice for the Innovation Leader

Go back and look at Figure 22.1 again. Do you have quantifiable goals for each of the smaller gears? Are you measuring the output of your organization to ensure that you are making the desired progress toward your goals?

To have a sustainable culture of innovation, your organization as a whole must function as a well-oiled machine. You must understand each of the gears in your machine and how they function together (which is critical). Employees must also understand the goals and metrics for each of the smaller gears, that is:

1. How is profit defined (in the currency of the realm) and what are the organization's goals? How will you measure progress toward these goals?
2. What kind of internal networking do you need and how will the level and type of networking be developed and measured?

3. How many and what kind of ideas are needed to support your innovation engine? How will the quantity and quality of these ideas be measured? How will you ensure that you are getting ideas along the entire Innovation Continuum?
4. What are the metrics and goals for your innovation engine? Are you able to assess what your innovation portfolio looks like? Do you know if it will meet the overall, required, quantifiable gains?
5. What are the critical elements that need to be present to ensure the quality of work life for your employees? How will you develop and measure progress toward them?
6. What are the critical elements necessary to have the desired quality of community life? How will you help to develop, support, and measure this?
7. What type of community networking is required to support the success of both the company and the community? How will success be attained and measured?

Your success at reaching these goals will dictate the number of cogs on the smaller gears. The greater the success, the greater the number of cogs, and the faster your organization and community will grow and prosper.

In Closing

We have now reached the top of the Innovation House. This is where you establish your vision and goals. This is also where you will ultimately measure success or failure. As we have pointed out in this chapter, your quantifiable gain incorporates much more than simply looking at top- and bottom-line performance. While these are critical, the social and environmental impact that your organization has on its employees and the community as a whole is also critical for achieving the goal of having a sustainable culture of innovation.

Remember

Without specific quantifiable goals, any innovation will get you there.

Part II
Chapter Twenty-Three

Summary

Sustained growth will not happen without sustained innovation. It is simply not possible for an organization to grow indefinitely without innovation fueling that growth. To maximize the potential for long-term growth, there must be a balance of the right business, technical, and human models:

- **Business Model** - How will we realize a quantifiable gain from new innovations?
- **Technical Model** - How will we develop and produce new innovations?
- **Human Model** - Do we have the right culture, people, and systems to successfully transform ideas into innovations?

The primary focus of this book has been devoted to the human model and understanding the role that people play in the innovation process. The reason for this focus is that, in our experience, the human model is the least understood of the three. Yet, the human model is often the primary obstacle limiting an organization's ability to have sustained top- and bottom-line growth.

We also believe that to successfully create a sustainable culture of innovation, there must be an understanding of the core principles that are its foundation. Only through understanding and valuing these core principles can we truly develop the methods and actions that will enable the organization to foster desired human behaviors and generate quantifiable gains. The understanding and valuing of the core principles are what allow us to adjust our methods and actions over time to meet the ever-changing dynamics of the worldwide marketplace while, at the same time, maintaining a culture of innovation.

In Part One of this book, we went through the eight core principles for sustaining innovation. These principles form the foundation of our

Innovation House and illustrate how the principles ultimately create a culture of innovation. In Part Two, we discussed how these principles help to define an organization's DNA, invisible rules of engagement, innovation processes and, finally, the quantifiable gain resulting from successful innovation.

When creating a culture of innovation, launching a new business or forming a division/team that is focused on revolutionary results, the innovation leader begins at the bottom of the Innovation House and works upward, just as if you were actually building a house. Conversely, when analyzing how to generate desired quantifiable gains (as defined by you or your organization), doing strategic planning or looking back on previous ROI, profitability, or productivity, you must begin at the top of the house and work down. (See Figure 23.1.)

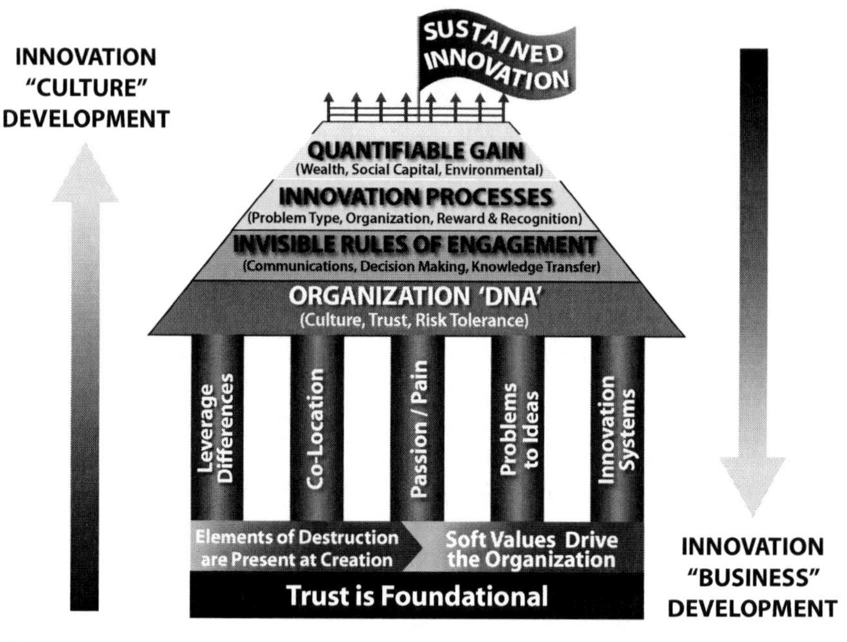

Figure 23.1
To apply the Innovation House, work from the bottom up to create your innovative organization and work from the top down to solve innovation problems.

In Chapter 1, we introduced the concept of looking at your current and desired innovation portfolios (see page 1112). This serves to make visible where your organization is currently placed relative to its innovation activities and how it needs to evolve in the future. In applying the principles of the Innovation House, we need to expand this initial model to incorporate the potential **internal and external disruptions**[1] associated with innovation at different points along the Innovation Continuum. Being able to assess the degree of external (marketplace) and internal (organizational) disruption is critical for understanding the impact the program will have on the business, technical, and human models.

As shown in Figure 23.2, every innovation program creates a corresponding level of external and internal disruption. For example, you might have an innovation program that leans toward the evolutionary end of the spectrum. Consequently, the internal disruption from this program will generally be minimal. However, the program might spawn a medium to high level of external disruption (e.g., when applying an existing technology to meet a currently unmet market need).

In this case, you may have found an ideal "sweet spot" for your innovation portfolio – a significant marketplace win with minimal internal risk and minimal internal impact. This is, unfortunately, an infrequent occurrence

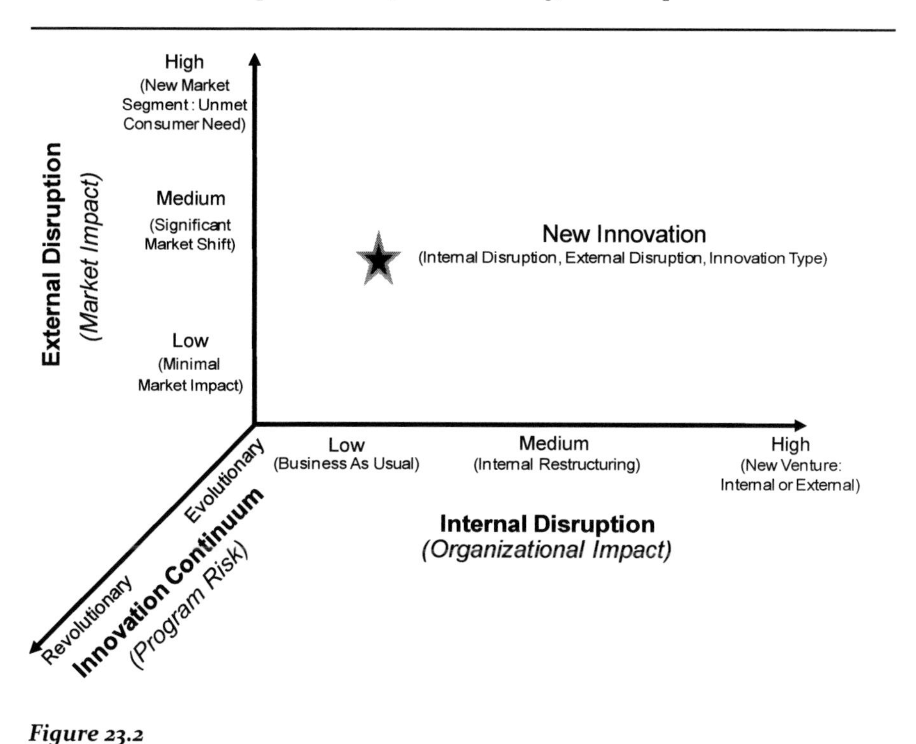

Figure 23.2
For the innovation leader to have a more complete understanding of each of the innovation programs, it is necessary to look at the type of innovation, the impact of the program on the internal organization, and its potential impact on the market.

and cannot be relied on for sustained growth. As the market matures and competition catches up, these types of successes become fewer and fewer and dictate the need to look elsewhere for continued growth.

We can combine the elements shown in Figure 23.2 to begin to create a decision matrix that the innovation leader can use when assessing an innovation program's merits, as well as its level of organizational impact. (See Figure 23.3).

Internal Disruption: Low

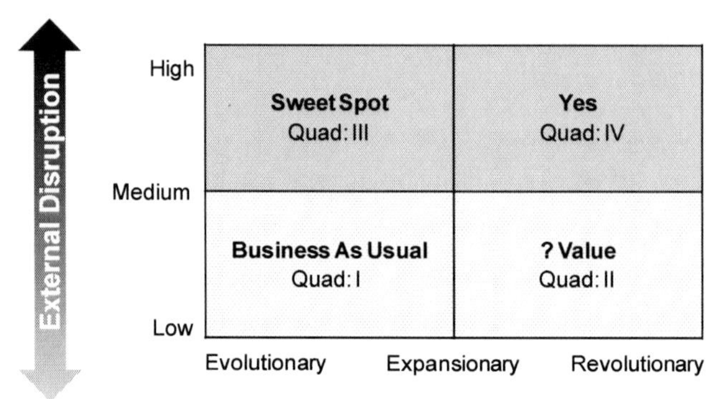

Type of Innovation

Quad I: Moderate innovation risk / moderate market impact: Business as usual
Quad II: High risk / moderate market impact: ? Value (only if potential return is significant)
Quad III: Moderate innovation risk / high market impact: Sweet Spot
Quad IV: High risk / high market impact: Yes (balanced risk/reward)

Figure 23.3
Looking at innovation programs relative to potential internal and external disruptions allows the innovation leader to make decisions on the merits of a potential program and to prioritize them.

Figure 23.4 on the next page is an integration of the three axes that will help you prioritize the programs in your organization's portfolio. It will help provide clarity of the internal impact of the program and better create appropriate and desired quantifiable gains.

To begin using this decision support matrix, you should go back to your desired innovation portfolio (Chapter 9) and look at the individual programs being considered for inclusion. Each program needs to be integrated within the desired portfolio matrix to provide you with an initial assessment of where each one falls on the Innovation Continuum and the degree of risk

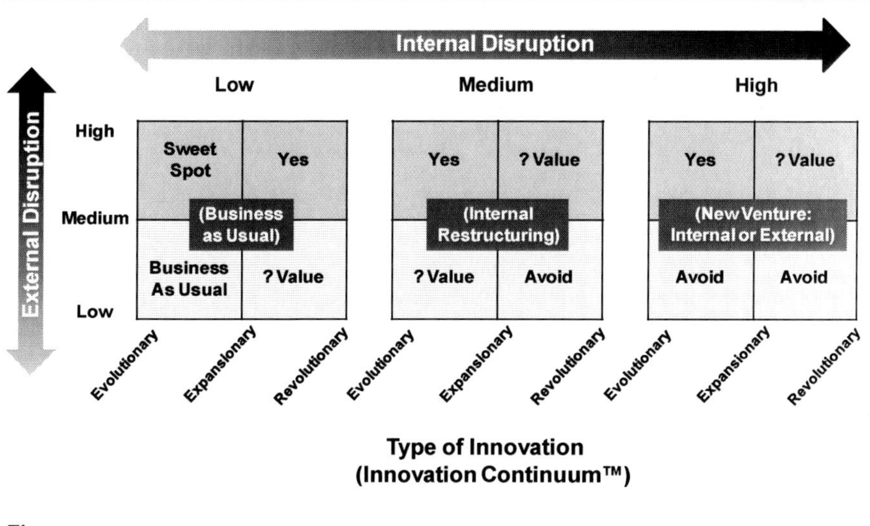

Figure 23.4
Integrated decision matrices for use by the innovation leader

involved. The next step is to ask two additional key questions for each program:

1. What is the level of external (marketplace) disruption that will result if the innovation is successful?
2. What is the level of internal organizational disruption required to maximize the organization's potential for success?

From analyses of the portfolio, external disruption, and internal disruption, you can make visible both the benefits of the program and the level of internal impact to be expected.

Most organizations will want to maximize external marketplace disruptions, minimize internal disruptions, and maximize the probability of success (evolutionary type of innovation). In reality, having sustainable innovation requires taking risks and accepting that the risk will result in internal disruptions. That means having a balance of activities in all of the quadrants in the first matrix (low internal disruption) and in the upper quadrants of the other two matrices.

The goal is to clearly understand the potential quantifiable gain for each program, the probability of success, and the impact it will have on the internal and external environments. This understanding is critical for potential program sponsors to become partners or stewards.

In Closing

Creating a sustainable culture of innovation is not a simple or straightforward process. It is a wicked problem in itself. This book is meant to provide you with key principles and potential applications to help you in your innovation journey. To reiterate just a few of the most critical points here:

- **Make the invisible visible™.** Only by making what you are trying to do, why you are doing it, and what you want to accomplish visible to everyone can your employees help you accomplish it. Moving forward without the support of your employees is not a recipe for long-term success.
- **Principles and values result in actions, not slogans.** People believe what they see, not what they read on signs hanging on a wall. You must model the behaviors you want, not just talk about them.
- **Innovate or Die.** Innovation is the engine that powers the organization and allows it to meet its long-term goals of creating financial, social, and environmental capital.
- **Organizations Don't Innovate, People Do.** Remember that people will make the difference between having short-term and long-term success. You must balance the needs of the organization with the needs of the people.
- **Individual differences are a gift! Leverage them!** Look at your people as having unique skills and qualities, not as interchangeable parts of a big machine. Be able to identify these differences and leverage them when creating your innovation teams. The ISPI can help here.
- **People must get to know each other as individuals.** In today's world of electronic communication, do not overlook the need for people to get to know each other as individuals, not only as e-mail addresses. Trust is built by seeing and knowing each other.
- **Making the past and present visible provides a foundation for creating the future.** Understanding where the organization has been and where it currently is provides the foundation and vocabulary needed to make visible where you want it to go in the future. This provides the grounding your employees will need to internalize the future vision and become partners in helping you achieve it.

Evolutionary innovation tends to flatten the world, whereas revolutionary innovation tends to make it round again. Evolutionary innovation is based on slight changes or productivity programs that contribute to leveling the playing field for you and your competition. In contrast, revolutionary innovation changes the game, creates new marketplace disruptions, and makes life more difficult for your competition – this tilts the playing field in favor of revolutionary, innovative organizations.

"Do you want to compete in a flat world or in a round one?"

Epilogue

Rosenfeld[1] used the analogy of a fruit seed and the new plant it produces to talk about how the eight human principles for sustaining innovation are intertwined. As shown in the figure below, the fruit has two major components – the seed and the surroundings, or the "pericarp." The seed contains the genetic code for creating a new plant, while the pericarp has all of the nourishment needed to sustain the seed until it can grow into a new plant. This book has expanded on the idea of growing a single plant into developing and sustaining a grove of fruit trees.

Pericarp: the external part of a fruit.

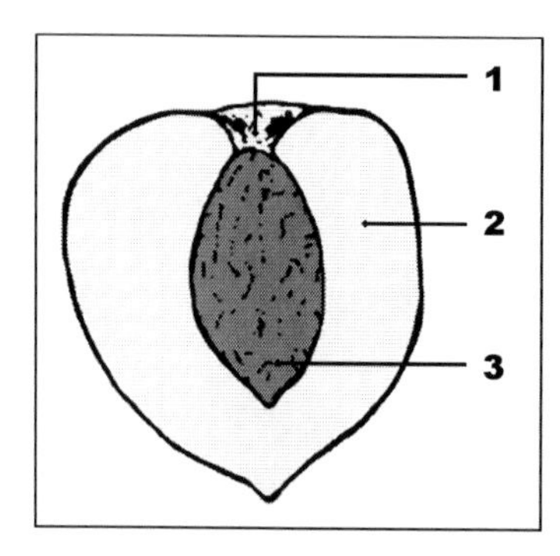

1. **Exocarp:** the outer covering, or "skin"→ **Sr. Leadership / Interface to External World**
2. **Mericarp:** the middle covering or "flesh"→ **Innovative Organization (Principles 1-3)**
3. **Endocarp:** the inner covering, in many cases the stiffened part known as the "stone"→ **Innovation Leader (Principles 4-6, 8)**

Seed: The seed is enclosed inside the endocarp → **Innovative Idea (Principle 7)**

Figure E.1
An innovative idea is like a seed enclosed in the organization's "endocarp" that consists of innovation leaders and practitioners. The endocarp provides the environment that gives the seed the best chance to survive and flourish. Just as a seed planted in the wrong soil will not flourish, an innovative idea planted within the wrong organizational environment will not flourish.

If any of the necessary conditions for the innovation (i.e., the fruit) are lacking, the new idea or project will be seriously hampered or unable to grow at all. Even the best innovative ideas (i.e., seeds) need to have favorable conditions to reach their potential and flourish. In other words, when creating a sustainable grove of fruit trees, the appropriate conditions must be present for all of the seeds, not just one or two.

As the grove matures, the owner must care for the mature trees while continuing to plant new ones to replace trees that will die. Careful planning must go into the selection of new seeds. Care must be taken to nurture them and allow them to grow and contribute to the overall success of the grove. Do the new seeds represent "what we've always planted" or have they been selected to take advantage of new developments and technologies? Will the new trees produce fruit that is preferred by consumers? Will they be more tolerant of disease and fluctuations in temperature? Will they provide a greater yield?

Creating a sustainable organization is no different. There must be a balance between sustaining and caring for the current businesses, while developing and nurturing new ones that add to the portfolio, or replacing those businesses that are no longer sustainable. This book has described the eight underlying human principles and how to apply them to create a sustainable culture of innovation. It is about creating the future. As Rosenfeld stated in *Making the Invisible Visible*, "Any fool can count the number of seeds in an apple. But who can count the number of apples in a seed?" We can all see the results of new innovation, but who can predict the future innovations that will result from that first one?

Now ask yourself this question, "Do I want my organization to be sustainable over the long term?" If the answer is yes, then how well is it doing in building its own principle-based Innovation House?

This is not the ending, but a beginning. We wrote this book to share the things we've gleaned through our lifetimes as practitioners in the innovation world. We'd like to hear from you. As an innovation leader/practitioner (you just read this book, you have now become one), we also suspect that you've gleaned some ideas along the way. If there is something you'd like to add, please write to us as we work on Book Three.

In the next book, we will delve further into the integration of the innovation portfolio relative to the external and internal disruption introduced in the last chapter. In addition, we will explore the shift from a fairly static organizational structure to one that is more dynamic and better able to respond to upsets in real time – and is, consequently, much more capable of dealing with the chronic and acute stress that occurs constantly in the business world.

Let this ending be the start of our dialogue. If you'd like assistance in achieving and sustaining your quantifiable gains, visit us at *www.innovating.com* or email us at:

Robert "Bob" Rosenfeld – *rrosenfeld@innovating.com*

Gary Wilhelmi – *gwilhelmi@innovating.com*

Happy Innovating,
Bob and Gary

Take the ISPI

As a reader of this book, you are eligible to take a free ISPI. Please send an email to *bookISPI@innovating.com* and an ISPI link and instructions will be sent to you.

Appendix

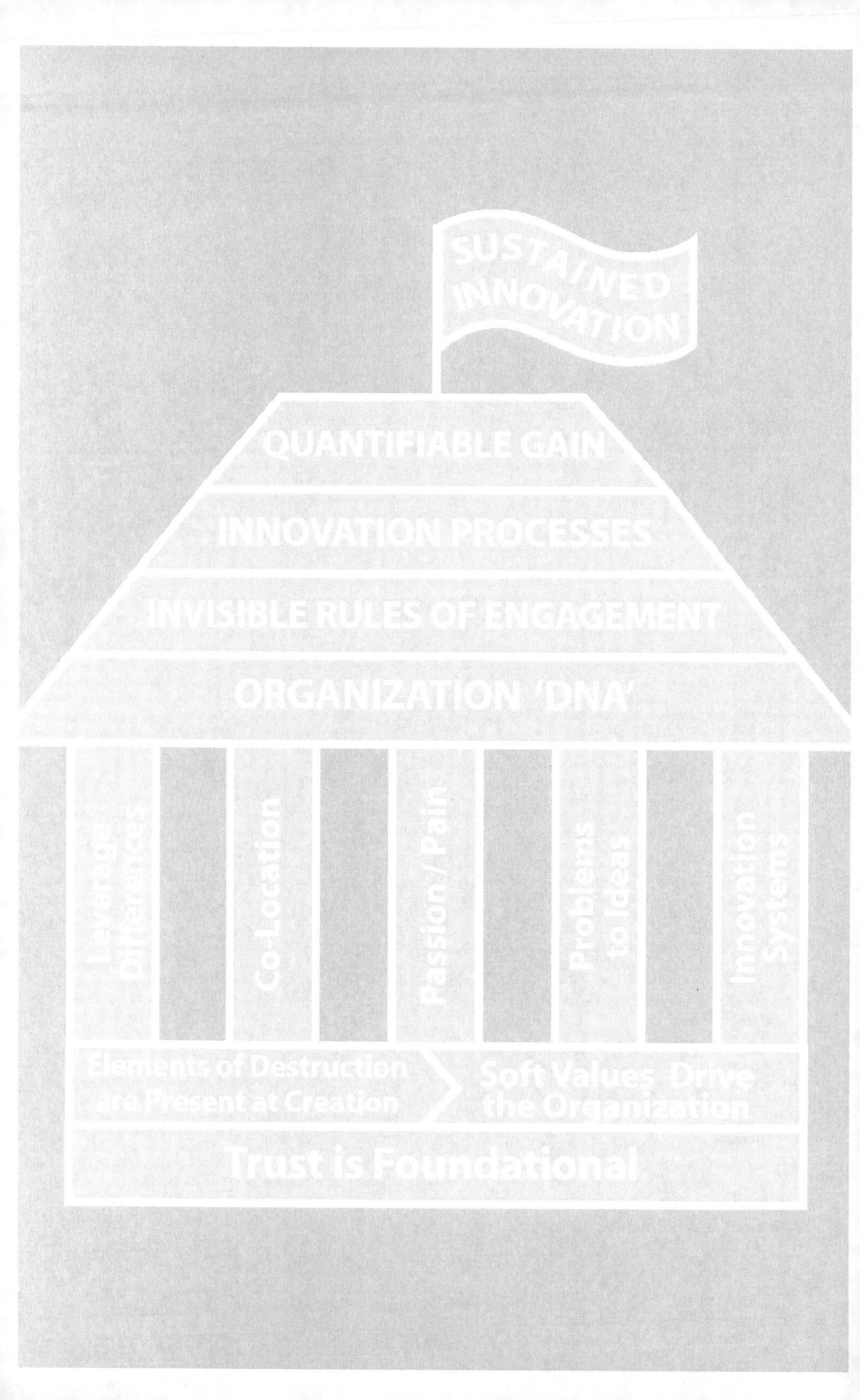
SUSTAINED INNOVATION
QUANTIFIABLE GAIN
INNOVATION PROCESSES
INVISIBLE RULES OF ENGAGEMENT
ORGANIZATION 'DNA'
Leverage Differences
Co-Location
Passion / Pain
Problems to Ideas
Innovation Systems
Elements of Destruction are Present at Creation
Soft Values Drive the Organization
Trust is Foundational

Appendix I

Glossary

(Note not all of these terms are used in this book. We have included several terms used elsewhere in looking at innovation to help you have a common understanding of them.)

A

Actions	Answer the question, "How should we do it?"
Advocate	A proponent of an idea or proposal.
Affect	Scientific term used to describe a subject's externally displayed mood.
"Air Cover"	Protecting a team from undesirable impact from the larger organization. Ensuring that they have the resources and freedom necessary to successfully attack a wicked problem.
Amotivation	Limited or no intent to act – going through the motions.
Autonomy	Feeling of volition or being in control to act.

B

Bi-associate	The connection of the thoughts or elements from different planes or domains to produce novel thought.

Black Hole Effect	Unintentional practice of reducing the submission of ideas by non-response.
Bootleg Work	Work done on projects outside the area of a person's normal billable or chargeable responsibilities.
Bottom Up	For innovation, this means ideas that come from people whose assigned area of work is different from the nature of the idea they are presenting.
Builders	Seek solutions based on existing concepts to do things better.
Buy-in	Acceptance of or commitment to an idea.

C

Camaraderie	Being eager to work with others and hearing what they have to say.
Challenge Board	A panel designed to examine an idea or solution to make sure that all angles have been addressed.
Champion	A person (sometimes a group) that is devoted to a concept and pursues it relentlessly against all odds – an individual who is willing to become a proponent of an idea at an early stage.
Change Partners™	Trusted influencers within the organization who can help influence others to help implement a desired organizational change.
Coaching	The leadership skill that enables others to develop the ability to solve their own problems and make their own decisions, thereby helping them grow in confidence, ability, self-esteem and overall value to the organization.
Cognitive Diversity	Differences in how people perceive or act upon their environment; differences in styles people use to acquire and apply knowledge.

Commission — Usually involves a conscious decision to withhold or provide incomplete information.

Communal Culture — An organization characterized as having both high sociability and solidarity.

Communication Content

- *Physicality (Level 1)* — Physical description of an item (color, taste, shape, etc.).
- *Analytical (Level 2)* — Analytical analysis of a physical item (economics, production capacity, market/sales potential, etc.).
- *Evolutionary (Level 3)* — Potential enhancements without changing basic form (size, color, shape, etc.).
- *Innovative (Level 4)* — Slight changes to basic form (SUV vs. sedan).
- *Revolutionary (Level 5)* — Significant changes to basic form (plane vs. car).

Competency — Fundamental characteristic causally related to sufficient or superior performance in a job or role.

Conation (Conative) — Aspect of mental processes or behavior directed toward action or change and including impulse, desire, volition, and striving.

Contentiousness — Inability to allow for creative disagreement or active engagement without being possessive of ideas, taking (or making) the disagreement personal, or being disagreeable.

Continuous Improvement — Process for incremental improvements that lead to cost savings or increased quality.

Core Cluster — Small number of people who take on the responsibility for direction and stewardship of an organization. They perform as a 'real team' whose members are committed to the common purpose and goals of the organization – they will hold each other accountable.

Covenant — Relationship between two or more people in which each accepts definable (written or oral) responsibility for the mental, emotional, physical, spiritual, and financial well-being of one another.

Creativity — Generation of novel ideas or new way of thinking.

Creativity Partner™ — Individual who has a high level of both Head and Heart trust used to develop or refine an idea in its early stages; trusted confidant.

Culture — Attitudes, norms, values, and beliefs that exist within an organization.

Culture Shock — Feeling an individual gets when they enter a strange culture where all of their familiar cues are removed.

Currency of the Realm — Value of an item expressed in the language and behaviors meaningful to those concerned.

D

Data — Raw observations without interpretation.

Destructive Communication — Communication to respond ("below the line") which is based on a win-lose or protectionary mentality and is a major obstacle for innovation to occur.

Discord — Negative attitudes within an organization which can tear apart the fabric of its culture.

Discounting — Belittling the contributions of others or putting down their ideas.

Discrete Solutions — Solutions that focus on novel or different approaches versus those that are slight improvements.

Disruptive (Disruption) Upsetting the status quo either internal to an organization, external (marketplace), or both.

Diversity Differences that occur in any population – both visible and invisible.

Domain Expert Person recognized within an organization as being an expert in a particular field.

Dominating Attitude (Dominance) Feeling that people you supervise "work for you" or "under you" vs. feeling that you are responsible for them.

E

Emotional Intelligence Ability to be aware of our emotions, manages the negative ones, and harnesses the positive ones to build passion and energy for individual and team goals.

Enhancement Process whereby an innovation advocate works with the idea originator to refine, develop and describe ideas so the ideas will receive serious attention when presented internally.

Entrepreneur Individual who takes on the risk of creating a business to commercialize an idea – their own or somebody else's.

Erroneous Data Input considered unreliable and discarded.

Errors of Commission Are a result of specific actions taken with the intent to mislead (or cover up something).

Errors of Omission Come from not taking action, but not taking action was not premeditated to mislead anybody.

Evolutionary Innovation Seeks solutions based on existing concepts to do things better (e.g., Six Sigma).

Expansionary Innovation Challenges the problem to do things differently (e.g., line extensions).

Explicit Knowledge — Knowledge that is written down in reports, papers, patent disclosures, etc.

Extrinsic Motivation — Motivation that comes from outside an individual such as money, recognition, or grades.

F

Figures of Merit — Define a priori when the outcome is "good enough."

Filter (Communication) — To restrict the use or sharing of information based on internal trust / motivation.

Fragmented Culture — Organization characterized by low sociability and low solidarity.

G

Gap Analysis — Technique for determining the steps or actions required to move from a current state to a desired future state.

Gate (Stage) — Passage from one stage to another in the development process.

Generative Communication — "Above the line" communications to learn/ understand which facilitates open communications and innovation to occur.

Genetic Elements of Destruction — Elements date back more than 10 years or to the beginning of the company. They are ingrained in everything and are the most difficult to overcome.

GPS — Global Positioning System for navigation.

H

Hard Values — Tangible objectives (e.g., percent profitability, share).

"Head Case" — An individual whose passion is not aligned with the core principles and values of the organization. Their passion is strictly to further their own personal agendas.

Head Trust (Intellectual Trust) — Trust of the intellectual capabilities / inputs of another individual or organization.

Heart Trust (Emotional Trust) — Trust of another person or organization that they have your best interests at heart – are not predisposed to injure you in some way.

Humility — Understanding your place in the scheme of things and being able to use your talents and abilities, without self-aggrandizement, for the benefit of the whole.

I

Idea — Mental concept or image.

Ideator — Person who generates many ideas, but may have little interest in developing them.

Incremental solutions — Solutions focusing on slight changes to the existing system or process versus a significant change.

Indiscriminate Criticism — Criticism of the organization, its policies and fellow employees, which undermines trust, threatens organizational viability, and discourages innovation.

Individual Cluster — Specific executional team (e.g., Wicked Leaders & Wicked Practitioners).

Information — Interpretation of data to create understanding.

Innovation Advocate — Person who assists originators in taking ideas through the agonizing, organizational maze. This includes helping originators:

- Refine and develop ideas to get most

favorable hearings.

- Locating resources that can be used to help.
- Coaching and encouraging originators and other team members as idea advances.
- Helping originator understand the overall process and accepting the results (positive and negative).
- Encouraging submission of more ideas.

Innovation Continuum	Spectrum of innovation from evolutionary (doing things better) to revolutionary (creating a new paradigm).
Innovation Diversity	Leveraging of diversity (visible and invisible) within an organization to stimulate innovation.
Innovation Leaders	Leaders who support and drive innovation.
Innovation Systems	People-based infrastructures within an organization that facilitate innovation.
Innovator	Person who generates creative ideas and transforms them into a quantifiable gain.
Internal Consultant	People, generally within the organization, who have expertise in the area of the originator's idea.
Internal Venturing	Process for launching new businesses that do not fit within the company's current line of business.
Intrapreneur	An entrepreneur who stays within a larger organization.
Intrinsic Motivation	Refers to motivation that comes from within an individual rather than from external sources.
Inventor	Person who discovers a phenomenon or dreams up an idea and then proceeds to transform it into a tangible product. Ideas may or may not be patented.

J

K

Kaizen Teian	A Japanese philosophy focused on continuous improvement.
Key Stake holders	Those individuals who can directly affect or are accountable for establishing the direction for the organization. They are generally the key decision makers.
Knowledge	Information in context that creates action; enables making a decision / creating a solution / etc.
Knowledge Nugget	Single bit of knowledge usually contained within a knowledge transfer system.
Knowledge Worker	An individual valued for their ability to interpret information within a specific area

L

Lean Six Sigma	A continuous improvement program, which uses the DMAIC (Define, Measure, Analyze, Improve, and Control) process.

M

Marathoner

Somebody who can stay motivated to work on a new project through to its conclusion.

Maslow's Hierarchy

NEED TO:*

- *Helping others* - Connect beyond ego → help others realize their potential
- *Self-Fulfillment* - Realize one's own potential
- *Aesthetic* - Create Symmetry / Order
- *Knowledge* - Understand / Explore
- *Self Esteem* - Achieve / Gain Approval

- *Belonging* - Affiliate with other / Acceptance
- *Safety* - Remove Danger
- *Physiological* - Meet basic physical needs: Hunger/Thirst/Bodily Comforts

(Huitt, William G., Maslow's Hierarchy of Needs, February 2004, http://chiron.valdosta.edu/whuitt/col/regsys/maslow.html)

Methods — Answer the question, "What should we do?"

Mercenary Culture — Organization characterized as having low sociability and high solidarity.

Motivation — Reason for an individual to act, to share or take in thoughts.

Motive — What really drives an organization.

N

Networked Culture — Organizational culture characterized as having high sociability and low solidarity.

Non-linear System — System whose behavior is not simply the sum of its parts or their multiples – they are often difficult (or impossible) to model, and their behavior with respect to a given variable (for example, time) is extremely difficult to predict.

O

Office of Innovation — Office created by Robert Rosenfeld in 1979 for Eastman Kodak to handle new ideas.

Office of Innovation Process

Manner in which the Office of Innovation handles ideas. There are five stages:

- Idea Generation
- Idea Screening
- Group Review

- Seeking Sponsorship
- Sponsorship

Omissions	Not providing complete information due to ignorance or lack of information.
Open-mindedness	Respect for employee's opinions and encouraging them to bring issues/concerns/ideas forward.
Originator	Someone who comes up with an idea to be developed.
Originator-Assisted	Process which helps to transform their ideas into business opportunities.

P

Pain	Suffering seen as a punishment or penalty.
Paradigm	Set of rules that defines boundaries and describes what to do to be successful within those boundaries.
Paradigm Builder	Someone who solves problems by working within existing structures / paradigms.
Paradigm Creators™	Individuals who have the right combination of passion and skills to make a significant change.
Paradigm Pioneer	Someone who solves problems by pushing the limits of existing structures/paradigms or creating new ones.
Partner	Person associated with others in some activity of common interest whose identity is entwined with the activity.
Passion	In psychology and common use, emotion is the language of a person's mental state of being; strong, enthusiastic devotion to a cause, ideal, or goal and tireless diligence in its furtherance.
Passive Advocacy	Unwillingness to allow others to know what you think or feel.

Patience and Long-Suffering
: Grace under stress. There are things out of your control that cannot be rushed; there are time frames out of your control.

Personal Sensitivity
: Degree of filtering (sharing or withholding) of thoughts based on level of potential exposure.

Physio-Culture
: Differences that are readily apparent through observation and interaction (e.g., gender, race, culture, etc).

Pinging™
: Thought/communication process usually found in strong pioneers in which they follow a non-linear process, often going off on tangents when working to solve a problem.

Pioneers
: Redefine the problem definition to break boundaries and create new paradigms.

Planned Ideation
: Is directed from the top down. It is part of normal management strategies. Many of these ideas are in response to specific problems or challenges.

Poingging™
: Thought/communication process found in the majority of the population in which people will generally follow a linear, incremental process with moderate tangents to expand their solution set in working to solve a problem – the middle ground between strong Pinggers and Ponggers.

Pongging™
: Thought/communication process usually found in strong builders in which they follow a linear, incremental process when working to solve a problem.

Pride
: Holding on to your idea so tightly that different perspectives cannot be seen or considered.

Principle
: A fundamental truth used as the basis for understanding a natural or scientific phenomenon, reasoning or action, or conducting our personal lives

Problem — An issue or anything that challenges you.

Purity of Motive — Working in the best interest of the organization without a hidden agenda.

Q

Quantifiable Gain — Measurable benefit to the organization in terms of the currency of the realm.

R

Receiver — One listening to (reading) the thoughts verbalized (written) by another.

Relatedness/Belonging — Identifying with and feeling of belonging to the organization.

Relationship Spectrum — Continuum describing the depth of a relationship from a loose arrangement on one end to a covenant on the other.

Revolutionary Innovation — Redefines the problem definition to break boundaries and create new paradigms (e.g., Wright Brothers' first flight).

S

Service — Meeting the needs of others.

Sifting — Process which separates the idea with potential from those which have reached the limit of their development.

Six Sigma — A continuous improvement program to improve the capability and reduce defects in a process using a methodology known as DMAIC (define, measure, analyze, improve, control).

Sociability (Organizational)
The level of friendliness – or how well employees get along with each other.

Soft Objectives Objectives related to how people feel as a result of implementing a process (e.g., measured in terms of attitude, job satisfaction, etc.).

Solidarity (Organizational)
The level of alignment on common tasks, mutual interests, and shared goals within the organization.

Spirit
1. Compilation of wisdom creating the essential principle(s) influencing the thoughts and actions of an individual.
2. The life force within an organization.

Sponsor People having both the power and ability to allocate funds and/or resources to projects.

Sprinter Somebody who becomes totally immersed in a new activity for a short period of time, then wants to move on to something different.

Steward Person who takes on the good of the company as a whole and for its employees – willing to devote significant time and energy to help others and the company to grow.

Strategic Transfer Transfer of technology or knowledge from one point to another for the purpose of leveraging capabilities.

Stubbornness Being unreasonably obstinate, always insisting on your own way, being unable to admit the value of other viewpoints.

Sustained Innovation Continuous flow of new products, processes, and services that ensure an organization's competitive edge.

Synergy Effect that is greater than the simple sum of the parts.

T

Tame Problems
- Relatively well-defined and stable problem statement.
- Definitive stopping point.
- Objectively evaluated solutions as right or wrong.
- Similar to other problems and solution approaches.
- Solutions can be tried and abandoned or adopted.

Targeted Innovation Process for developing solutions to meet a specific need.

Transient Elements of Destruction
Elements that are recent and are usually associated with specific individuals. They are far less engrained into the organization than the genetic ones and are easier to overcome.

Transmitter (Communications)
One sharing internal thoughts (verbal or written) with another.

Trust Degree that one believes/entrusts another with sensitive thoughts to be used. Confidence in the integrity, ability, character, and truth of a person or organization, including both head and heart trust.

U

Unplanned Ideation Ideas generated without the influence of a formal process. Often they are bottom up driven.

V

Values Values are the impetus for generating results. Values provide the source of energy (or fuel) for turning a principle into action.

Vetting of Knowledge Nuggets
To make sure the nuggets have been reviewed to ensure accuracy and applicability.

W

"We be's"
Attitude of people who feel all they have to do is make it look like they are supporting an activity, knowing that it will go away before they really have to do anything or change. The mindset of "we be here before you and we be here after you."

Wicked Advocate
The person(s) charged with the accountability to represent the wicked team to the outside organization for the purpose of insuring that results of the team's efforts will be accepted and embraced by the rest of the organization or company.

Wicked Manager/Wicked Leader
The person(s) charged with the accountability to lead or direct all or part of an organization, often a business, through the deployment of resources (human, financial, material, intellectual or intangible).

Wicked Practitioner
The person(s) associated with an organization tasked with working on a wicked problem.

Wicked Problems
- No definite problem formulation.
- No stopping rules.
- Solution evaluation better or worse vs. right or wrong.
- Each problem is unique.
- Problem is symptom for other wicked problems.

Wicked Sponsor
The person(s) who has ultimate authority over the project and provides project funding, vision and scope. They approve major deliverables and also champion the project within their organization.

Wisdom — Compilation of knowledge to gain greater insights / discern relationships

X

Y

Yin/Yang Innovation Balance — Organizations need a balance of innovation along the entire innovation spectrum.

Z

Zero-Sum Game — The sum of activities remains constant. For everything added, something needs to be subtracted. For everything subtracted, something needs to be added.

Mosaic Partnership™ Questions

Mosaic Partnership Model

Idea Connection Systems' (*www.innovating.com*) research has shown that many of the skills required to be a good innovation partner are the same as those found in good friendships. Effective partnering combines aspects of business and technological skills as well as the skill of forming a deeper bond or friendship with another person.

Out of this research has come a process called Mosaic Partnerships™.[1] It is a process whereby two people can get to know each other, much like they do in a close friendship.

Friendship is about developing trust. And trust is developed by two things. First, by getting to know someone at a deeper level than you normally would an acquaintance. And second, by seeing that knowledge and deeper understanding come to life through committed action and service to each other – becoming Creativity Partners™.

The following describes the process and how it works. There are four sets of questions that go along with the process:

1. Getting to Know You
2. Planting the Seeds of Friendship
3. Deepening Our Trust
4. Reflections

In working through the process, you and your partner begin with the first set and only move to the next group when you are both comfortable with wanting to deepen the friendship and level of trust.

As part of the process we have found it useful to have a "formal" agreement with your partner. The purpose of the agreement to formally commit to each other to follow the guidelines of the process and, most importantly, not to violate the confidentiality commitment associated with not sharing information about your partner. The Partner's **Covenant** included in the appendix is an example of what we have used with many different organizations and communities. Feel free to modify it, or completely rewrite it, with your partner. But it is important to make the formal commitment to each other prior to proceeding.

Partner's Covenant

1. Confidentiality:
   Information shared between partners during the discussions, other than partner's name, is considered strictly confidential.

   The process can be shared with others, but not the specific information relayed by your partner.

2. Trust:
   Be open as much as possible with your partner. Accept a person not being willing to share – respect privacy.

3. Integrity:
   Always try to be honest with yourself and with your partner.

   It is OK to be unable or unwilling to answer any question, but say that to your partner.

4. Listen, listen, listen:
   Suspend internal judgment as much as possible.

   Do not interrupt when someone is speaking.

   Be honest in sharing your information with your partner. This includes stating:

   - "I don't want to answer that" or
   - "I prefer not talking about that right now" or
   - "I am not willing to share that information at this time."

5. Patience:
   The decision to share information about yourself is a human one and is based on many factors. The same is true for your partner – be patient.

______________________________ ______________________________

Signature of Partner A *Signature of Partner B*

______________________________ ______________________________

Date *Date*

Overview

This process is about asking meaningful questions, listening to your partner's responses, and telling your own story. For each of the sections we have included sample questions. For a complete list of questions, go to *www.innovating.com*. As you answer each question, consider using autobiographical stories as a way to help your partner get to know about your life and the path that has led you to be who you are today.

Start with the first set of questions, Getting to Know You. Once the two of you feel that you are ready, move on to the second set, Planting the Seeds of Friendship. As you move through the different sets of questions, feel free to go back to the prior lists if the questions are getting too personal. Remember, this is about developing a deep friendship, not about racing through the different questions.

Process

1. Look through all the questions attached. If you already know the answer to a question about your partner, place a check (✓) in the box to the right of that question.
2. Select a question to ask your partner which you would also be willing to answer.
3. Ask your partner if they are willing to answer the question. If yes, proceed to:
    a. Ask the question you selected and listen carefully to their response.
    b. Allow your partner to answer the question fully as you listen.
    c. Briefly paraphrase what you heard your partner tell you.
    d. Then answer the same question, with your partner listening carefully to your response.
    e. Have your partner briefly paraphrase what they heard you say.
4. Mark the question as "discussed" by placing a check in the box to the right of that question.
5. Now switch, so your partner picks a new question, and begin the process again.

Suggestions

Some people talk more than others. Try to balance the amount of time each person "has the floor."

Listen carefully! Give your partner your undivided attention, and try to really hear the heart of what they are telling you.

Avoid interrupting. This shows respect and appreciation for what your partner has to tell you. After your partner is finished, then you may ask questions for clarification.

Remember that all conversations between you and your partner are confidential!

Place a check (☐) in the box if you already know the answer to a question and after you have discussed a question with your partner.

Example Questions Only

Getting To Know You

- ☐ Who is the most important person in your life? Why?
- ☐ As a child, what did you want to be when you grew up? Why?
- ☐ Describe one of the most successful experiences you've ever had.

Planting The Seeds Of Friendship

- ☐ What do you look for in a person when first meeting them?
- ☐ How many children did you/would you like to have and why?
- ☐ What was the most difficult thing you had to overcome in school?

Deepening Our Trust

- ☐ When have you felt totally helpless?
- ☐ How have you been affected by divorce?
- ☐ Have you ever been arrested? What was it like?

Reflections

- ☐ What would it be like for you to invite me to your home with a group of your friends?
- ☐ What would it be like for you to be invited by me to my home with a group of my friends?
- ☐ Describe the person most different from you with whom you've maintained a long-term friendship.

Organization DNA Characteristics

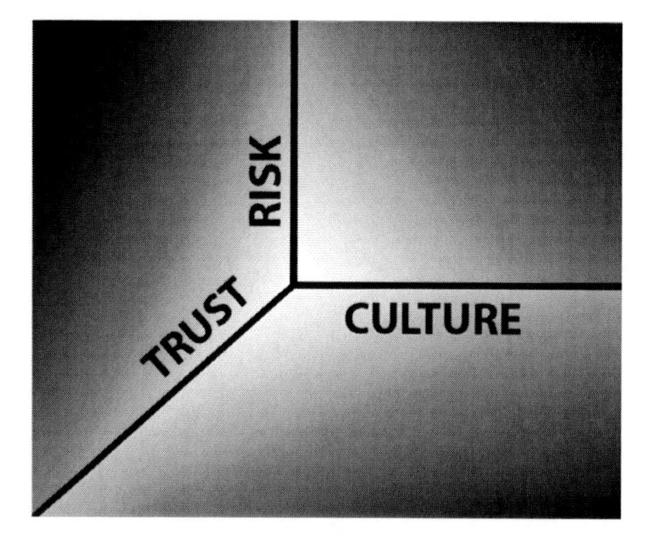

The following steps are used in analyzing your organization's DNA:

1. Assess your organization's:
   a. Culture (Past, Current and Desired): Chapter 12
   b. Trust Level (Past, Current and Desired) Chapter 13
   c. Risk Tolerance (Past, Current and Desired) Chapter 14
   d. Record your assessments in the table on the next page.
2. Look up the characteristics of the your past, current and desired organizations based on the characterization index tables.
   For example, the characterization for an organization that is fragmented and has low trust and low risk tolerance would be found on page 3 of this appendix.
3. Do they describe the past, current and desired organizations?

4. Note that different parts of your organization may have different DNA's. For example the leadership may be different from the individual contributors.

Organization Dna Table

Organization XYZ DNA Table

	Past	Current	Desired
Cultural Type FRAGMENTED NETWORKED MERCENARY COMMUNAL	**MERCENARY**	**FRAGMENTED**	**COMMUNAL**
Trust LOW TRUST MEDIUM TRUST HIGH TRUST	**LOW TRUST**	**MEDIUM TRUST**	**HIGH TRUST**
Risk LOW TOLERANCE MODERATE TOLERANCE HIGH TOLERANCE	**LOW**	**LOW**	**MODERATE**

Completed organizational DNA analysis table for use when looking at the characteristics of your organization

Characterization Index

Fragmented (f)

Mercenary (m)

Networked (n)

Communal (c)

f.1 Fragmented/Low Trust/Low Risk Organization

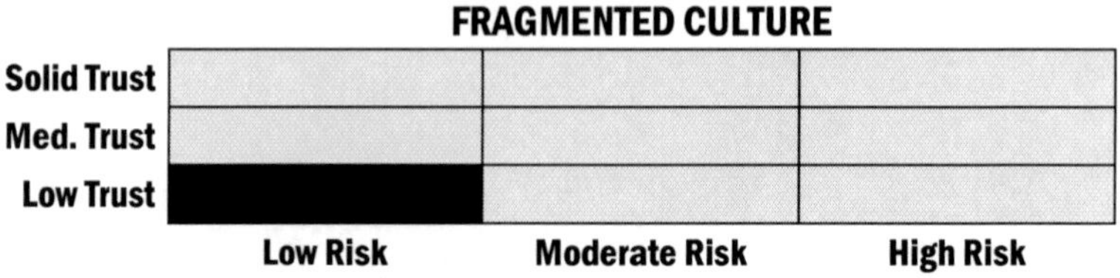

FRAGMENTED CULTURE

	Low Risk	Moderate Risk	High Risk
Solid Trust			
Med. Trust			
Low Trust	■		

OVERALL CHARACTERISTICS

- Independent professionals/focused on outside markets
- Individual creativity/"individual stars"
- Lack of teamwork/small "fiefdoms"
- Risks are taken only when there is a well-defined "safety net" in case of failure
- Organizational surprises occur frequently due to filtered or "spun" communication
- Growth through enhancements/productivity improvements to existing businesses/operations
- Predominantly focused on many near-term programs

LEADERSHIP CHARACTERISTICS

- High autonomy/strong sense of self
- Analytical vs. intuitive
- Minimum levels of sociability/failure to build relationships
- Execution adherence to established methodologies
- Well-established bureaucracy with policies and procedures covering most day-to-day activities
- Strict hierarchical organizational structure (if there is an organizational structure)

INDIVIDUALS CHARACTERISTICS

- Be valuable to organization/invest in one's self
- Focus on outputs/organization's reward system
- Try to get help without providing "reciprocity"
- Information/ideas are only readily shared with people the individual truly trusts – information/ideas guarded and/or filtered before sharing on a broader scale
- Examining of the motivation for challenging of ideas often

f.2 Fragmented/Low Trust/Moderate Risk Organization

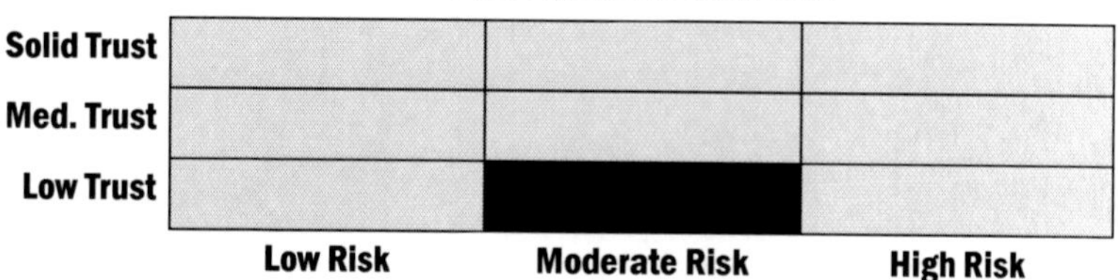

OVERALL CHARACTERISTICS

- Independent professionals/focused on outside markets
- Individual creativity/"individual stars"
- Lack of teamwork/small "fiefdoms"
- Risks are taken only when there is a well-defined "safety net" in case of failure
- Organizational surprises occur frequently due to filtered or "spun" communication
- Growth through balance of enhancements/productivity improvements to existing businesses/operations and creation of new businesses
- Focused on several near-term programs along with a few long-term new business programs

LEADERSHIP CHARACTERISTICS

- High autonomy/strong sense of self
- Analytical vs. intuitive
- Minimum levels of sociability/failure to build relationships
- Execution primarily guided by established methodologies
- Established bureaucracy with policies and procedures covering most day-to-day activities
- General adherence to hierarchical organizational structure

INDIVIDUALS CHARACTERISTICS

- Be valuable to organization/invest in one's self
- Focus on outputs/organization's reward system
- Try to get help without providing "reciprocity"
- Information/ideas are only readily shared with people the individual truly trusts – information/ideas guarded and/or filtered before sharing on a broader scale
- Examining of the motivation for challenging of ideas oftentimes gets greater focus than the content of challenge itself

f.3 Fragmented/Low Trust/High Risk Organization

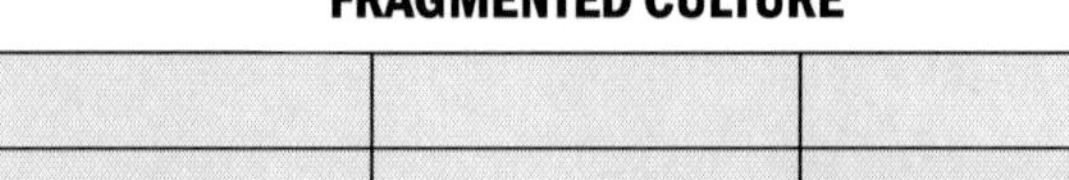

OVERALL CHARACTERISTICS

- Independent professionals/focused on outside markets
- Individual creativity/"individual stars"
- Lack of teamwork/small "fiefdoms"
- Risks are taken only when there is a well-defined "safety net" in case of failure
- Organizational surprises occur frequently due to filtered or "spun" communication
- Growth through ongoing creation of new businesses – limited focus on improving existing businesses
- Predominantly focused on a few long-term programs
- Continuously experimenting with new methods for development and commercialization

LEADERSHIP CHARACTERISTICS

- High autonomy/strong sense of self
- Analytical vs. intuitive
- Minimum levels of sociability/failure to build relationships
- Most likely having considerable flexibility relative to policies and procedures covering day-to-day activities
- Limited organizational structure – freedom to network as needed/desired

INDIVIDUALS CHARACTERISTICS

- Be valuable to organization/invest in one's self
- Focus on outputs/organization's reward system
- Try to get help without providing "reciprocity"
- Information/ideas are only readily shared with people the individual truly trusts – information/ideas guarded and/or filtered before sharing on a broader scale
- Examining of the motivation for challenging of ideas oftentimes gets greater focus than the content of challenge itself

f.4 Fragmented/Medium Trust/Low Risk Organization

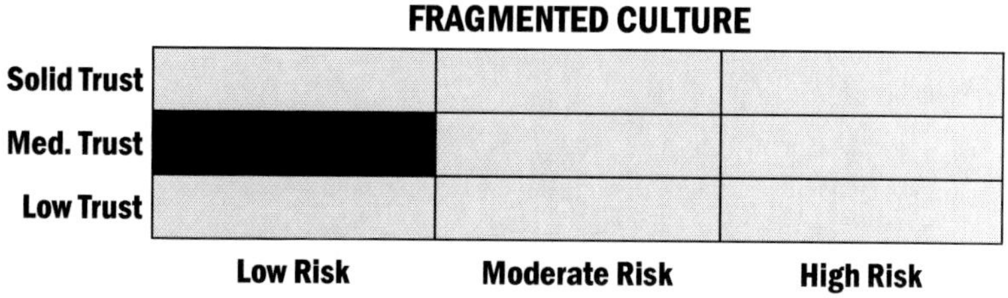

FRAGMENTED CULTURE

	Low Risk	Moderate Risk	High Risk
Solid Trust			
Med. Trust	■		
Low Trust			

OVERALL CHARACTERISTICS

- Independent professionals/focused on outside markets
- Individual creativity/"individual stars"
- Lack of teamwork/small "fiefdoms"
- Only moderate risks are taken with minimal concern for consequences of a failure – more significant risks need well-defined "safety net"
- Organizational surprises occur due to lack of open communication or filtering of the information
- Growth through enhancements/productivity improvements to existing businesses/operations
- Predominantly focused on many near-term programs

LEADERSHIP CHARACTERISTICS

- High autonomy/strong sense of self
- Analytical vs. intuitive
- Minimum levels of sociability/failure to build relationships
- Execution adherence to established methodologies
- Well-established bureaucracy with policies and procedures covering most day-to-day activities
- Strict hierarchical organizational structure (if there is an organizational structure)

INDIVIDUALS CHARACTERISTICS

- Be valuable to organization/invest in one's self
- Focus on outputs/organization's reward system
- Try to get help without providing "reciprocity"
- Individuals will generally share non-sensitive information/ideas without significant concern for negative consequences
- Sensitive information/ideas are only shared with the people the individual truly trusts
- Examining the motivation for challenging of ideas has equal weight as the challenge itself

f.5 Fragmented/Medium Trust/Moderate Risk Organization

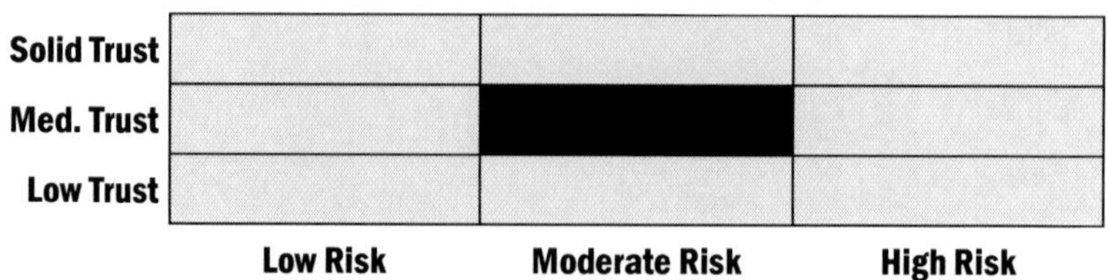

OVERALL CHARACTERISTICS

- Independent professionals/focused on outside markets
- Individual creativity/"individual stars"
- Lack of teamwork/small "fiefdoms"
- Only moderate risks are taken with minimal concern for consequences of a failure – more significant risks need well-defined "safety net"
- Organizational surprises occur due to lack of open communication or filtering of the information
- Growth through balance of enhancements/productivity improvements to existing businesses/operations and creation of new businesses
- Focused on several near-term programs along with a few long-term new business programs

LEADERSHIP CHARACTERISTICS

- High autonomy/strong sense of self
- Analytical vs. intuitive
- Minimum levels of sociability/failure to build relationships
- Execution primarily guided by established methodologies
- Established bureaucracy with policies and procedures covering most day-to-day activities
- General adherence to hierarchical organizational structure

INDIVIDUALS CHARACTERISTICS

- Be valuable to organization/invest in one's self
- Focus on outputs/organization's reward system
- Try to get help without providing "reciprocity"
- Individuals will generally share non-sensitive information/ideas without significant concern for negative consequences
- Sensitive information/ideas are only shared with the people the individual truly trusts
- Examining the motivation for challenging of ideas has equal weight as the challenge itself

f.6 Fragmented/Medium Trust/High Risk Organization

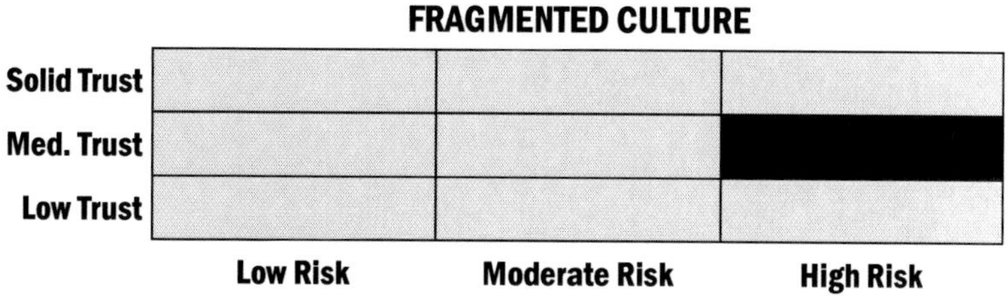

FRAGMENTED CULTURE

	Low Risk	Moderate Risk	High Risk
Solid Trust			
Med. Trust			■
Low Trust			

OVERALL CHARACTERISTICS

- Independent professionals focused on outside markets
- Individual creativity/"individual stars"
- Lack of teamwork/small "fiefdoms"
- Only moderate risks are taken with minimal concern for consequences of a failure – more significant risks need well-defined "safety net"
- Organizational surprises occur due to lack of open communication or filtering of the information
- Growth through ongoing creation of new businesses – limited focus on improving existing businesses
- Predominantly focused on a few long-term programs
- Continuously experimenting with new methods for development and commercialization

LEADERSHIP CHARACTERISTICS

- High autonomy/strong sense of self
- Analytical vs. intuitive
- Minimum levels of sociability/failure to build relationships
- Most likely having considerable flexibility relative to policies and procedures covering day-to-day activities
- Limited organizational structure – freedom to network as needed/desired

INDIVIDUALS CHARACTERISTICS

- Be valuable to organization/invest in one's self
- Focus on outputs/organization's reward system
- Try to get help without providing "reciprocity"
- Individuals will generally share non-sensitive information/ideas without significant concern for negative consequences
- Sensitive information/ideas are only shared with the people the individual truly trusts
- Examining the motivation for challenging of ideas has equal weight as the challenge itself

f.7 Fragmented/Solid Trust/Low Risk Organization

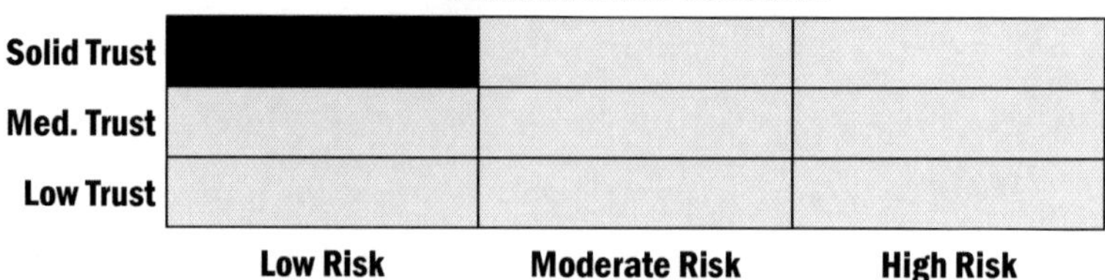

OVERALL CHARACTERISTICS

- Independent professionals/focused on outside markets
- Individual creativity/"individual stars"
- Lack of teamwork/small "fiefdoms"
- Risks can be taken with minimal organizational driven "fear of failure"
- Organizational surprises due to lack of open communication are minimal
- Growth through enhancements/productivity improvements to existing businesses/operations
- Predominantly focused on many near-term programs

LEADERSHIP CHARACTERISTICS

- High autonomy/strong sense of self
- Analytical vs. intuitive
- Minimum levels of sociability/failure to build relationships
- Execution adherence to established methodologies
- Well-established bureaucracy with policies and procedures covering most day-to-day activities
- Strict hierarchical organizational structure (if there is an organizational structure)

INDIVIDUALS CHARACTERISTICS

- Be valuable to organization/invest in one's self
- Focus on outputs/organization's reward system
- Try to get help without providing "reciprocity"
- Individuals readily share information/ideas without significant concern for negative consequences
- Challenging of ideas is accepted with minimal feelings of personal attacks or value judgments

f.8 Fragmented/Solid Trust/Moderate Risk Organization

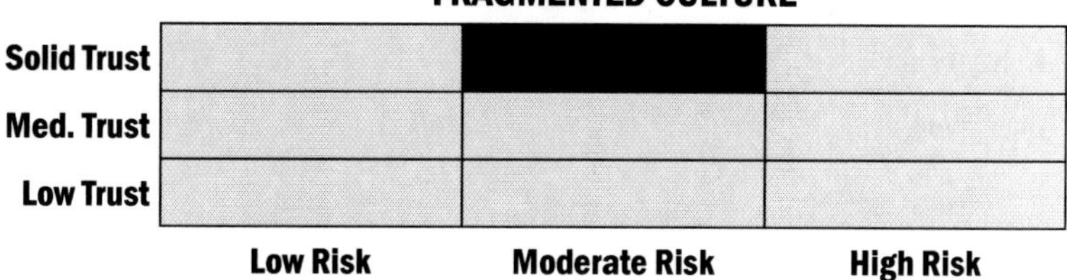

OVERALL CHARACTERISTICS

- Independent professionals/focused on outside markets
- Individual creativity/"individual stars"
- Lack of teamwork/small "fiefdoms"
- Risks can be taken with minimal organizational driven "fear of failure"
- Organizational surprises due to lack of open communication are minimal
- Growth through balance of enhancements/productivity improvements to existing businesses/operations and creation of new businesses
- Focused on several near-term programs along with a few long-term new business programs

LEADERSHIP CHARACTERISTICS

- High autonomy/strong sense of self
- Analytical vs. intuitive
- Minimum levels of sociability/failure to build relationships
- Execution primarily guided by established methodologies
- Established bureaucracy with policies and procedures covering most day-to-day activities
- General adherence to hierarchical organizational structure

INDIVIDUALS CHARACTERISTICS

- Be valuable to organization/invest in one's self
- Focus on outputs/organization's reward system
- Try to get help without providing "reciprocity"
- Individuals readily share information/ideas without significant concern for negative consequences
- Challenging of ideas is accepted with minimal feelings of personal attacks or value judgments

f.9 Fragmented/Solid Trust/High Risk Organization

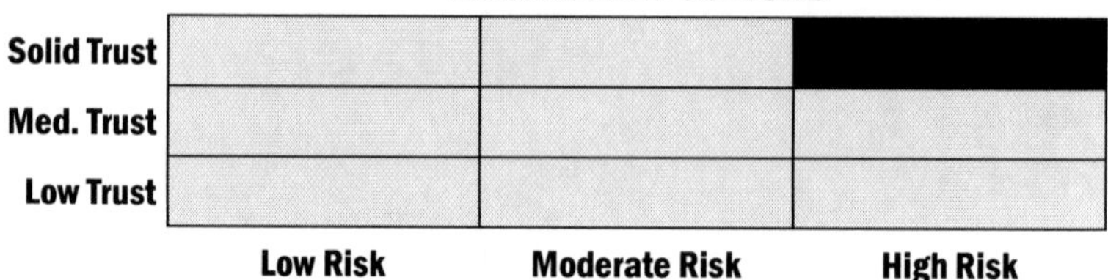

OVERALL CHARACTERISTICS

- Independent professionals/focused on outside markets
- Individual creativity/"individual stars"
- Lack of teamwork/small "fiefdoms"
- Risks can be taken with minimal organizational driven "fear of failure"
- Organizational surprises due to lack of open communication are minimal
- Growth through ongoing creation of new businesses – limited focus on improving existing businesses
- Predominantly focused on a few long-term programs
- Continuously experimenting with new methods for development and commercialization

LEADERSHIP CHARACTERISTICS

- High autonomy/strong sense of self
- Analytical vs. intuitive
- Minimum levels of sociability/failure to build relationships
- Most likely having considerable flexibility relative to policies and procedures covering day-to-day activities
- Limited organizational structure – freedom to network as needed/desired

INDIVIDUALS CHARACTERISTICS

- Be valuable to organization/invest in one's self
- Focus on outputs/organization's reward system
- Try to get help without providing "reciprocity"
- Individuals readily share information/ideas without significant concern for negative consequences
- Challenging of ideas is accepted with minimal feelings of personal attacks or value judgments

m.1 Mercenary/Low Trust/Low Risk Organization

MERCENARY CULTURE

Solid Trust			
Med. Trust			
Low Trust	■		
	Low Risk	**Moderate Risk**	**High Risk**

OVERALL CHARACTERISTICS

- Clear focus on business objectives/emphasis on profitability
- Rapid response to threats/quickly unified against an enemy
- Slavish adherence to numbers/intolerant of ambiguity
- Risks are taken only when there is a well-defined "safety net" in case of failure
- Organizational surprises occur frequently due to filtered or "spun" communication
- Growth through enhancements/productivity improvements to existing businesses/operations
- Predominantly focused on many near-term programs

LEADERSHIP CHARACTERISTICS

- Goal-oriented/obsessive desire to complete tasks once started
- Thrives on competitive energy/strong sense of ego
- Minimum levels of sociability/failure to build relationships
- Execution adherence to established methodologies
- Well-established bureaucracy with policies and procedures covering most day-to-day activities
- Strict hierarchical organizational structure (if there is an organizational structure)

INDIVIDUALS CHARACTERISTICS

- Calculate assistance and sharing based on "Negotiated Reciprocity"
- Hit individual targets/do only what is measured
- Information/ideas are only readily shared with people the individual truly trusts – information/ideas guarded and/or filtered before sharing on a broader scale
- Examining of the motivation for challenging of ideas oftentimes gets greater focus than the content of challenge itself

m.2 Mercenary/Low Trust/Moderate Risk Organization

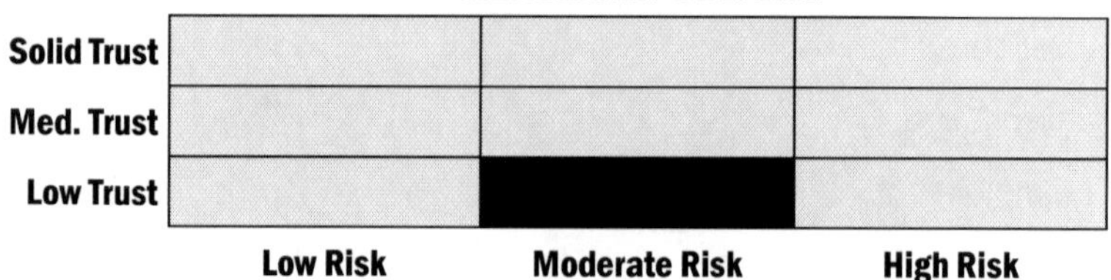

OVERALL CHARACTERISTICS

- Clear focus on business objectives/emphasis on profitability
- Rapid response to threats/quickly unified against an enemy
- Slavish adherence to numbers/intolerant of ambiguity
- Risks are taken only when there is a well-defined "safety net" in case of failure
- Organizational surprises occur frequently due to filtered or "spun" communication
- Growth through balance of enhancements/productivity improvements to existing businesses/operations and creation of new businesses
- Focused on several near-term programs along with a few long-term new business programs

LEADERSHIP CHARACTERISTICS

- Goal-oriented/obsessive desire to complete tasks once started
- Thrives on competitive energy/strong sense of ego
- Execution primarily guided by established methodologies
- Established bureaucracy with policies and procedures covering most day-to-day activities
- General adherence to hierarchical organizational structure

INDIVIDUALS CHARACTERISTICS

- Calculate assistance and sharing based on "Negotiated Reciprocity"
- Hit individual targets/do only what is measured
- Information/ideas are only readily shared with people the individual truly trusts – information/ideas guarded and/or filtered before sharing on a broader scale
- Examining of the motivation for challenging of ideas oftentimes gets greater focus than the content of challenge itself

m.3 Mercenary/Low Trust/High Risk Organization

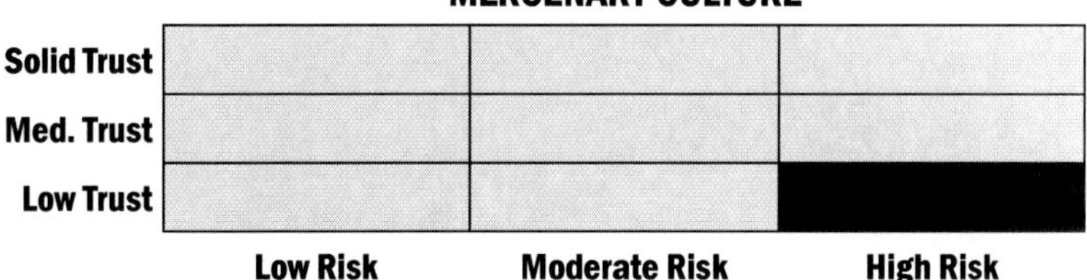

OVERALL CHARACTERISTICS

- Clear focus on business objectives/emphasis on profitability
- Rapid response to threats/quickly unified against an enemy
- Slavish adherence to numbers/intolerant of ambiguity
- Risks are taken only when there is a well-defined "safety net" in case of failure
- Organizational surprises occur frequently due to filtered or "spun" communication
- Growth through ongoing creation of new businesses – limited focus on improving existing businesses
- Predominantly focused on a few long-term programs
- Continuously experimenting with new methods for development and commercialization

LEADERSHIP CHARACTERISTICS

- Goal-oriented/obsessive desire to complete tasks once started
- Thrives on competitive energy/strong sense of ego
- Most likely having considerable flexibility relative to policies and procedures covering day-to-day activities
- Limited organizational structure...freedom to network as needed/desired

INDIVIDUALS CHARACTERISTICS

- Calculate assistance and sharing based on "Negotiated Reciprocity"
- Hit individual targets/do only what is measured
- Information/ideas are only readily shared with people the individual truly trusts – information/ideas guarded and/or filtered before sharing on a broader scale
- Examining of the motivation for challenging of ideas oftentimes gets greater focus than the content of challenge itself

m.4 Mercenary/Medium Trust/Low Risk Organization

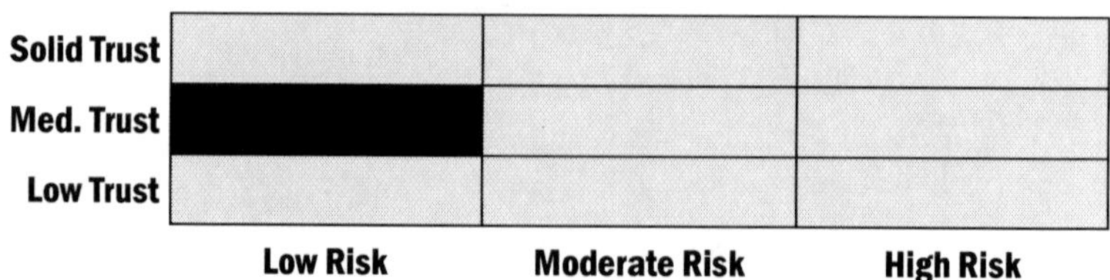

OVERALL CHARACTERISTICS

- Clear focus on business objectives/emphasis on profitability
- Rapid response to threats/quickly unified against an enemy
- Slavish adherence to numbers/intolerant of ambiguity
- Lack of teamwork/small "fiefdoms"
- Only moderate risks are taken with minimal concern for consequences of a failure – more significant risks need well-defined "safety net"
- Organizational surprises occur due to lack of open communication or filtering of the information
- Growth through enhancements/productivity improvements to existing businesses/operations
- Predominantly focused on many near-term programs

LEADERSHIP CHARACTERISTICS

- Goal-oriented/obsessive desire to complete tasks once started
- Thrives on competitive energy/strong sense of ego
- Execution adherence to established methodologies
- Well-established bureaucracy with policies and procedures covering most day-to-day activities
- Strict hierarchical organizational structure (if there is an organizational structure)

INDIVIDUALS CHARACTERISTICS

- Calculate assistance and sharing based on "Negotiated Reciprocity"
- Hit individual targets/do only what is measured
- Individuals will generally share non-sensitive information/ideas without significant concern for negative consequences
- Sensitive information/ideas are only shared with the people the individual truly trusts
- Examining the motivation for challenging of ideas has equal weight as the challenge itself

m.5 Mercenary/Medium Trust/Moderate Risk Organization

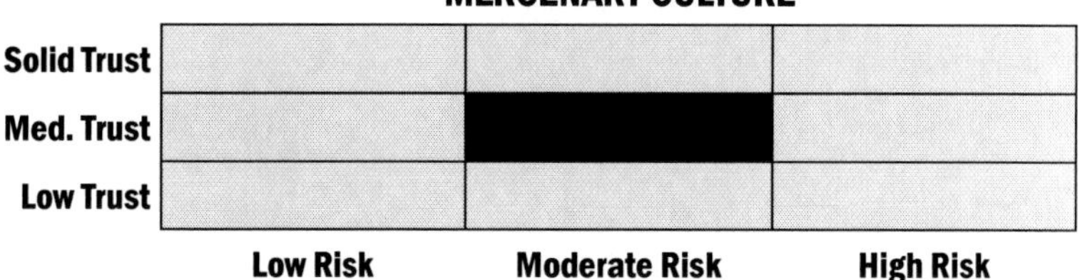

OVERALL CHARACTERISTICS

- Clear focus on business objectives/emphasis on profitability
- Rapid response to threats/quickly unified against an enemy
- Slavish adherence to numbers/intolerant of ambiguity
- Only moderate risks are taken with minimal concern for consequences of a failure – more significant risks need well-defined "safety net"
- Organizational surprises occur due to lack of open communication or filtering of the information
- Growth through balance of enhancements/productivity improvements to existing businesses/operations and creation of new businesses
- Focused on several near-term programs along with a few long-term new business programs

LEADERSHIP CHARACTERISTICS

- Goal-oriented/obsessive desire to complete tasks once started
- Thrives on competitive energy/strong sense of ego
- Execution primarily guided by established methodologies
- Established bureaucracy with policies and procedures covering most day-to-day activities
- General adherence to hierarchical organizational structure

INDIVIDUALS CHARACTERISTICS

- Calculate assistance and sharing based on "Negotiated Reciprocity"
- Hit individual targets/do only what is measured
- Individuals will generally share non-sensitive information/ideas without significant concern for negative consequences
- Sensitive information/ideas are only shared with the people the individual truly trusts
- Examining the motivation for challenging of ideas has equal weight as the challenge itself

m.6 Mercenary/Medium Trust/High Risk Organization

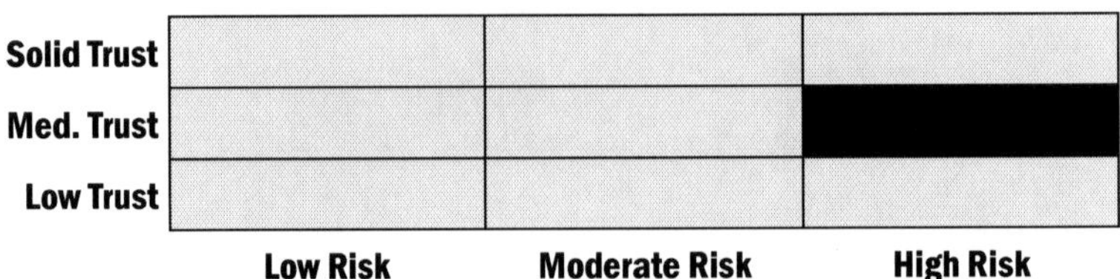

OVERALL CHARACTERISTICS

- Clear focus on business objectives/emphasis on profitability
- Rapid response to threats/quickly unified against an enemy
- Slavish adherence to numbers/intolerant of ambiguity
- Only moderate risks are taken with minimal concern for consequences of a failure – more significant risks need well-defined "safety net"
- Organizational surprises occur due to lack of open communication or filtering of the information
- Growth through ongoing creation of new businesses – limited focus on improving existing businesses
- Predominantly focused on a few long-term programs
- Continuously experimenting with new methods for development and commercialization

LEADERSHIP CHARACTERISTICS

- Goal-oriented/obsessive desire to complete tasks once started
- Thrives on competitive energy/strong sense of ego
- Most likely having considerable flexibility relative to policies and procedures covering day-to-day activities
- Limited organizational structure – freedom to network as needed/desired

INDIVIDUALS CHARACTERISTICS

- Calculate assistance and sharing based on "Negotiated Reciprocity"
- Hit individual targets/do only what is measured
- Individuals will generally share non-sensitive information/ideas without significant concern for negative consequences
- Sensitive information/ideas are only shared with the people the individual truly trusts
- Examining the motivation for challenging of ideas has equal weight as the challenge itself

m.7 Mercenary/Solid Trust/Low Risk Organization

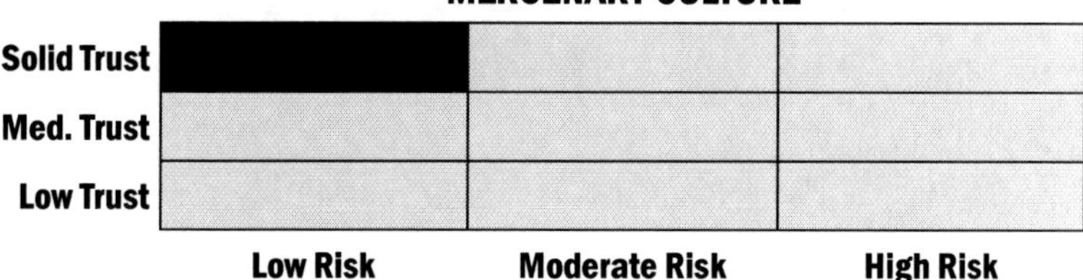

OVERALL CHARACTERISTICS

- Clear focus on business objectives/emphasis on profitability
- Rapid response to threats/quickly unified against an enemy
- Slavish adherence to numbers/intolerant of ambiguity
- Risks can be taken with minimal organizational driven "fear of failure"
- Organizational surprises due to lack of open communication are minimal
- Growth through enhancements/productivity improvements to existing businesses/operations
- Predominantly focused on many near-term programs

LEADERSHIP CHARACTERISTICS

- Goal-oriented/obsessive desire to complete tasks once started
- Thrives on competitive energy/strong sense of ego
- Execution adherence to established methodologies
- Well-established bureaucracy with policies and procedures covering most day-to-day activities
- Strict hierarchical organizational structure (if there is an organizational structure)

INDIVIDUALS CHARACTERISTICS

- Calculate assistance and sharing based on "Negotiated Reciprocity"
- Hit individual targets/do only what is measured
- Individuals readily share information/ideas without significant concern for negative consequences
- Challenging of ideas is accepted with minimal feelings of personal attacks or value judgments

m.8 Mercenary/Solid Trust/Moderate Risk Organization

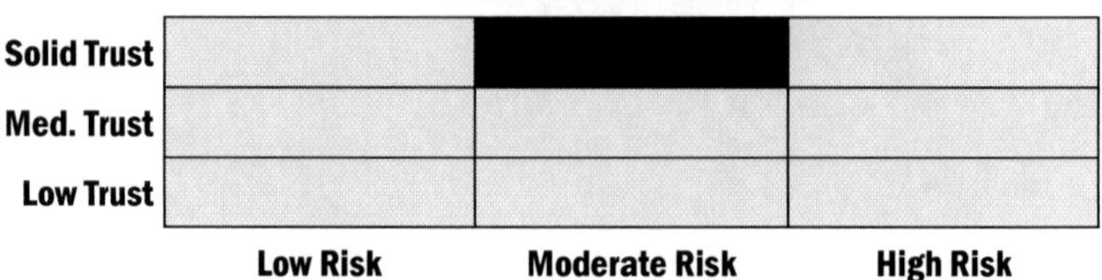

OVERALL CHARACTERISTICS

- Clear focus on business objectives/emphasis on profitability
- Rapid response to threats/quickly unified against an enemy
- Slavish adherence to numbers/intolerant of ambiguity
- Risks can be taken with minimal organizational driven "fear of failure"
- Organizational surprises due to lack of open communication are minimal
- Growth through balance of enhancements/productivity improvements to existing businesses/operations and creation of new businesses
- Focused on several near-term programs along with a few long-term new business programs

LEADERSHIP CHARACTERISTICS

- Goal-oriented/obsessive desire to complete tasks once started
- Thrives on competitive energy/strong sense of ego
- Execution primarily guided by established methodologies
- Established bureaucracy with policies and procedures covering most day-to-day activities
- General adherence to hierarchical organizational structure

INDIVIDUALS CHARACTERISTICS

- Calculate assistance and sharing based on "Negotiated Reciprocity"
- Hit individual targets/do only what is measured
- Individuals readily share information/ideas without significant concern for negative consequences
- Challenging of ideas is accepted with minimal feelings of personal attacks or value judgments

m.9 Mercenary/Solid Trust/High Risk Organization

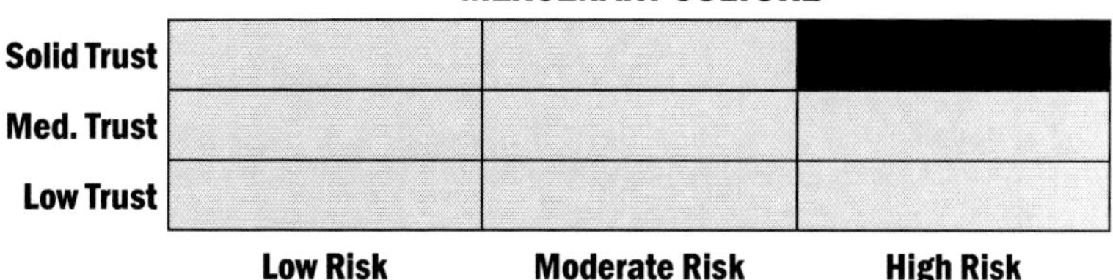

OVERALL CHARACTERISTICS

- Clear focus on business objectives/emphasis on profitability
- Rapid response to threats/quickly unified against an enemy
- Slavish adherence to numbers/intolerant of ambiguity
- Risks can be taken with minimal organizational driven "fear of failure"
- Organizational surprises due to lack of open communication are minimal
- Growth through ongoing creation of new businesses – limited focus on improving existing businesses
- Predominantly focused on a few long-term programs
- Continuously experimenting with new methods for development and commercialization

LEADERSHIP CHARACTERISTICS

- Goal-oriented/obsessive desire to complete tasks once started
- Thrives on competitive energy/strong sense of ego
- Most likely having considerable flexibility relative to policies and procedures covering day-to-day activities
- Limited organizational structure – freedom to network as needed/desired

INDIVIDUALS CHARACTERISTICS

- Calculate assistance and sharing based on "Negotiated Reciprocity"
- Hit individual targets/do only what is measured
- Individuals readily share information/ideas without significant concern for negative consequences
- Challenging of ideas is accepted with minimal feelings of personal attacks or value judgments

n.1 Networked/Low Trust/Low Risk Organization

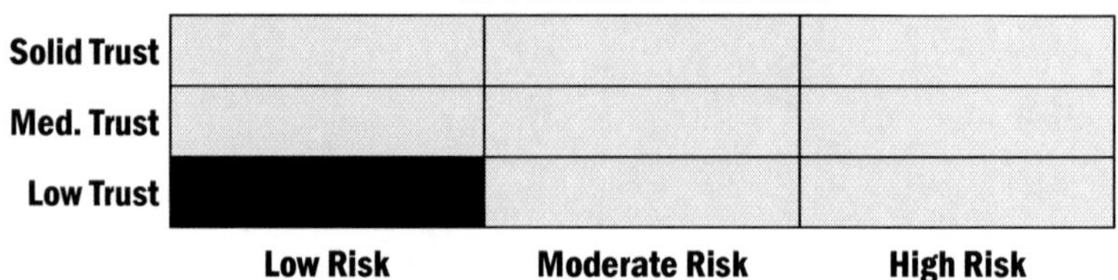

OVERALL CHARACTERISTICS

- Tacit knowledge available from internal networks/information moves quickly
- Consensus driven/lack of ability to adjust rapidly
- Risk avoidance/insidiously political
- Risks are taken only when there is a well-defined "safety net" in case of failure
- Organizational surprises occur frequently due to filtered or "spun" communication
- Growth through enhancements/productivity improvements to existing businesses/operations
- Predominantly focused on many near-term programs

LEADERSHIP CHARACTERISTICS

- Superb interpersonal skill/tolerant of differences and ambiguity
- Use emotional intelligence to manipulative ends
- Operate behind the scenes to get things done/can spot and stop "negative" politics
- Execution adherence to established methodologies
- Well-established bureaucracy with policies and procedures covering most day-to-day activities
- Strict hierarchical organizational structure (if there is an organizational structure)

INDIVIDUALS CHARACTERISTICS

- Freely provide assistance with no expectation of immediate return – eventually expect it
- Avoid risk – "keep your head down"
- Make friends/build relationships that last
- Information/ideas are only readily shared with people the individual truly trusts – information/ideas guarded and/or filtered before sharing on a broader scale
- Examining of the motivation for challenging of ideas

n.2 Networked/Low Trust/Moderate Risk Organization

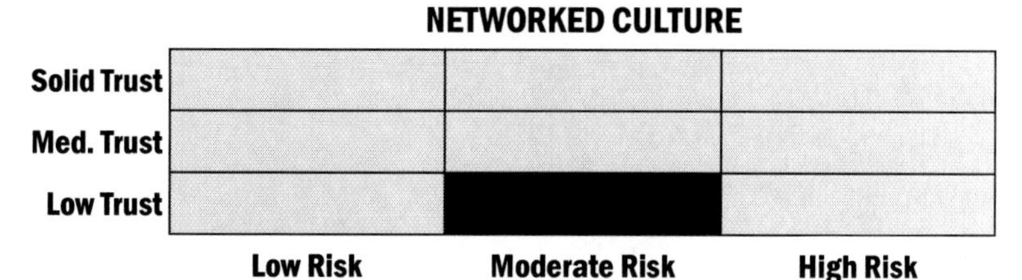

OVERALL CHARACTERISTICS

- Tacit knowledge available from internal networks/information moves quickly
- Consensus driven/lack of ability to adjust rapidly
- Risk avoidance/insidiously political
- Risks are taken only when there is a well-defined 'safety net' in case of failure
- Organizational surprises occur frequently due to filtered or 'spun' communication
- Growth through balance of enhancements/productivity improvements to existing businesses/operations and creation of new businesses
- Focused on several near-term programs along with a few long-term new business programs

LEADERSHIP CHARACTERISTICS

- Superb interpersonal skills/tolerant of differences and ambiguity
- Use emotional intelligence to manipulative ends
- Operate behind the scenes to get things done/can spot and stop 'negative' politics
- Execution primarily guided by established methodologies
- Established bureaucracy with policies and procedures covering most day-to-day activities
- General adherence to hierarchical organizational structure

INDIVIDUALS CHARACTERISTICS

- Freely provide assistance with no expectation of immediate return – eventually expect it
- Avoid risk – "keep your head down"
- Make friends/build relationships that last
- Information/ideas are only readily shared with people the individual truly trusts – information/ideas guarded and/or filtered before sharing on a broader scale
- Examining of the motivation for challenging of ideas oftentimes gets greater focus than the content of challenge itself

n.3 Networked/Low Trust/High Risk Organization

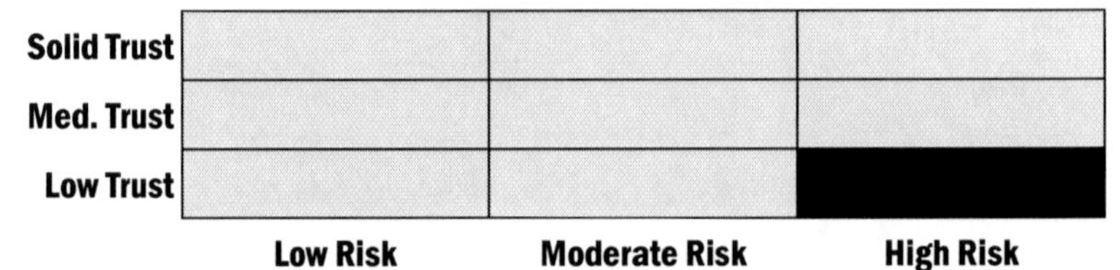

OVERALL CHARACTERISTICS

- Tacit knowledge available from internal networks/information moves quickly
- Consensus driven/lack of ability to adjust rapidly
- Risk avoidance/insidiously political
- Risks are taken only when there is a well-defined "safety net" in case of failure
- Organizational surprises occur frequently due to filtered or "spun" communication
- Growth through ongoing creation of new businesses – limited focus on improving existing businesses
- Predominantly focused on a few long-term programs
- Continuously experimenting with new methods for development and commercialization

LEADERSHIP CHARACTERISTICS

- Superb interpersonal skills/tolerant of differences and ambiguity
- Use emotional intelligence to manipulative ends
- Operate behind the scenes to get things done/can spot and stop "negative" politics
- Most likely having considerable flexibility relative to policies and procedures covering day-to-day activities
- Limited organizational structure – freedom to network as needed/desired

INDIVIDUALS CHARACTERISTICS

- Freely provide assistance with no expectation of immediate return – eventually expect it
- Avoid risk – "keep your head down"
- Make friends/build relationships that last
- Information/ideas are only readily shared with people the individual truly trusts – information/ideas guarded and/or filtered before sharing on a broader scale
- Examining of the motivation for challenging of ideas oftentimes gets greater focus than the content of challenge itself

n.4 Networked/Medium Trust/Low Risk Organization

NETWORKED CULTURE

Solid Trust			
Med. Trust			
Low Trust			
	Low Risk	**Moderate Risk**	**High Risk**

OVERALL CHARACTERISTICS

- Tacit knowledge available from internal networks/information moves quickly
- Consensus driven/lack of ability to adjust rapidly
- Risk avoidance/insidiously political
- Lack of teamwork/small "fiefdoms"
- Only moderate risks are taken with minimal concern for consequences of a failure – more significant risks need well-defined "safety net"
- Organizational surprises occur due to lack of open communication or filtering of the information
- Growth through enhancements/productivity improvements to existing businesses/operations
- Predominantly focused on many near-term programs

LEADERSHIP CHARACTERISTICS

- Superb interpersonal skills/tolerant of differences and ambiguity
- Use emotional intelligence to manipulative ends
- Operate behind the scenes to get things done/can spot and stop "negative" politics
- Execution adherence to established methodologies
- Well-established bureaucracy with policies and procedures covering most day-to-day activities
- Strict hierarchical organizational structure (if there is an organizational structure)

INDIVIDUALS CHARACTERISTICS

- Freely provide assistance with no expectation of immediate return – eventually expect it
- Avoid risk – "keep your head down"
- Make friends/build relationships that last
- Individuals will generally share non-sensitive information/ideas without significant concern for negative consequences
- Sensitive information/ideas are only shared with the people the individual truly trusts
- Examining the motivation for challenging of ideas has equal weight as the challenge itself

n.5 Networked/Medium Trust/Moderate Risk Organization

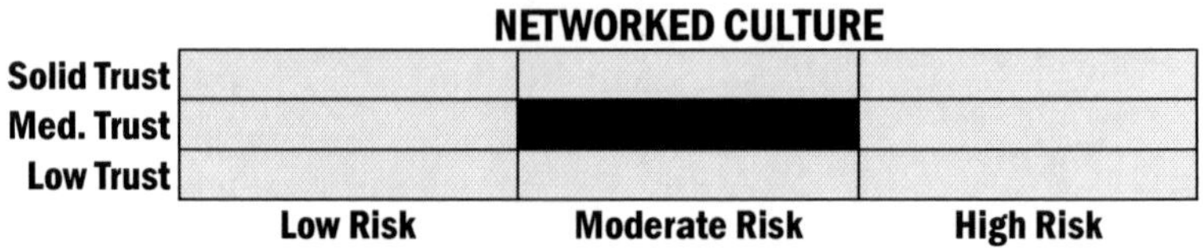

NETWORKED CULTURE

	Low Risk	Moderate Risk	High Risk
Solid Trust			
Med. Trust		■	
Low Trust			

OVERALL CHARACTERISTICS

- Tacit knowledge available from internal networks/information moves quickly
- Consensus driven/lack of ability to adjust rapidly
- Risk avoidance/insidiously political
- Only moderate risks are taken with minimal concern for consequences of a failure – more significant risks need well-defined "safety net"
- Organizational surprises occur due to lack of open communication or filtering of the information
- Growth through balance of enhancements/productivity improvements to existing businesses/operations and creation of new businesses
- Focused on several near-term programs along with a few long-term new business programs

LEADERSHIP CHARACTERISTICS

- Superb interpersonal skills/tolerant of differences and ambiguity
- Use emotional intelligence to manipulative ends
- Operate behind the scenes to get things done/can spot and stop "negative" politics
- Execution primarily guided by established methodologies
- Established bureaucracy with policies and procedures covering most day-to-day activities
- General adherence to hierarchical organizational structure

INDIVIDUALS CHARACTERISTICS

- Freely provide assistance with no expectation of immediate return – eventually expect it
- Avoid risk – "keep your head down"
- Make friends/build relationships that last
- Individuals will generally share non-sensitive information/ideas without significant concern for negative consequences
- Sensitive information/ideas are only shared with the people the individual truly trusts
- Examining the motivation for challenging of ideas has equal weight as the challenge itself

n.6 Networked/Medium Trust/High Risk Organization

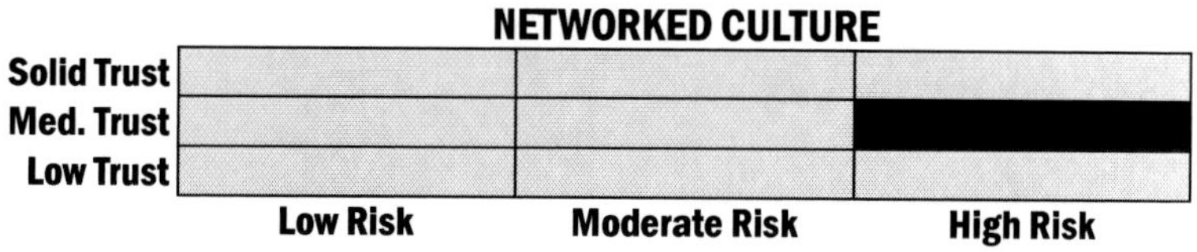

NETWORKED CULTURE

Solid Trust			
Med. Trust			
Low Trust			
	Low Risk	**Moderate Risk**	**High Risk**

OVERALL CHARACTERISTICS

- Tacit knowledge available from internal networks/information moves quickly
- Consensus driven/lack of ability to adjust rapidly
- Risk avoidance/insidiously political
- Only moderate risks are taken with minimal concern for consequences of a failure – more significant risks need well-defined "safety net"
- Organizational surprises occur due to lack of open communication or filtering of the information
- Growth through ongoing creation of new businesses – limited focus on improving existing businesses
- Predominantly focused few long-term programs
- Continuously experimenting with new methods for development and commercialization

LEADERSHIP CHARACTERISTICS

- Superb interpersonal skills/tolerant of differences and ambiguity
- Use emotional intelligence to manipulative ends
- Operate behind the scenes to get things done/can spot and stop "negative" politics
- Most likely having considerable flexibility relative to policies and procedures covering day-to-day activities
- Limited organizational structure – freedom to network as needed/desired

INDIVIDUALS CHARACTERISTICS

- Freely provide assistance with no expectation of immediate return – eventually expect it
- Avoid risk – "keep your head down"
- Make friends/build relationships that last
- Individuals will generally share non-sensitive information/ideas without significant concern for negative consequences
- Sensitive information/ideas are only shared with the people the individual truly trusts
- Examining the motivation for challenging of ideas has equal weight as the challenge itself

n.7 Networked/Solid Trust/Low Risk Organization

NETWORKED CULTURE

	Low Risk	Moderate Risk	High Risk
Solid Trust			
Med. Trust			
Low Trust			

OVERALL CHARACTERISTICS

- Tacit knowledge available from internal networks/information moves quickly
- Consensus driven/lack of ability to adjust rapidly
- Risk avoidance/insidiously political
- Risks can be taken with minimal organizational driven “fear of failure”
- Organizational surprises due to lack of open communication are minimal
- Growth through enhancements/productivity improvements to existing businesses/operations
- Predominantly focused on many near-term programs

LEADERSHIP CHARACTERISTICS

- Superb interpersonal skills/tolerant of differences and ambiguity
- Use emotional intelligence to manipulative ends
- Operate behind the scenes to get things done/can spot and stop “negative” politics
- Execution adherence to established methodologies
- Well-established bureaucracy with policies and procedures covering most day-to-day activities
- Strict hierarchical organizational structure (if there is an organizational structure)

INDIVIDUALS CHARACTERISTICS

- Freely provide assistance with no expectation of immediate return – eventually expect it
- Avoid risk – “keep your head down”
- Make friends/build relationships that last
- Individuals readily share information/ideas without significant concern for negative consequences
- Challenging of ideas is accepted with minimal feelings of personal attacks or value judgments

n.8 Networked/Solid Trust/Moderate Risk Organization

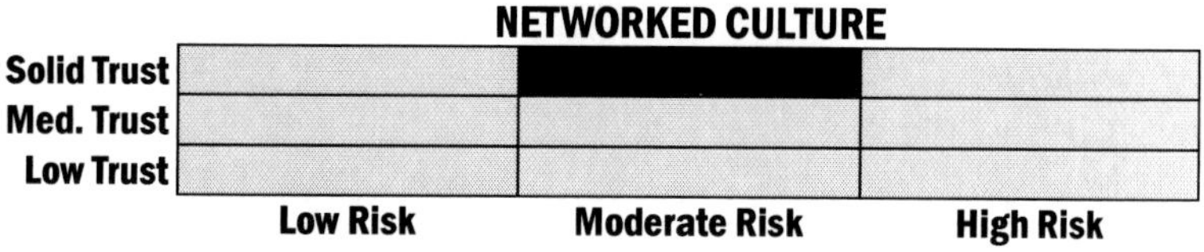

NETWORKED CULTURE

	Low Risk	Moderate Risk	High Risk
Solid Trust			
Med. Trust			
Low Trust			

OVERALL CHARACTERISTICS

- Tacit knowledge available from internal networks/information moves quickly
- Consensus driven/lack of ability to adjust rapidly
- Risk avoidance/insidiously political
- Risks can be taken with minimal organizational driven "fear of failure"
- Organizational surprises due to lack of open communication are minimal
- Growth through balance of enhancements/productivity improvements to existing businesses/operations and creation of new businesses
- Focused on several near-term programs along with a few long-term new business programs

LEADERSHIP CHARACTERISTICS

- Superb interpersonal skills/tolerant of differences and ambiguity
- Use emotional intelligence to manipulative ends
- Operate behind the scenes to get things done/can spot and stop "negative" politics
- Execution primarily guided by established methodologies
- Established bureaucracy with policies and procedures covering most day-to-day activities
- General adherence to hierarchical organizational structure

INDIVIDUALS CHARACTERISTICS

- Freely provide assistance with no expectation of immediate return – eventually expect it
- Avoid risk – "keep your head down"
- Make friends/build relationships that last
- Individuals readily share information/ideas without significant concern for negative consequences
- Challenging of ideas is accepted with minimal feelings of personal attacks or value judgments

n.9 Networked/Solid Trust/High Risk Organization

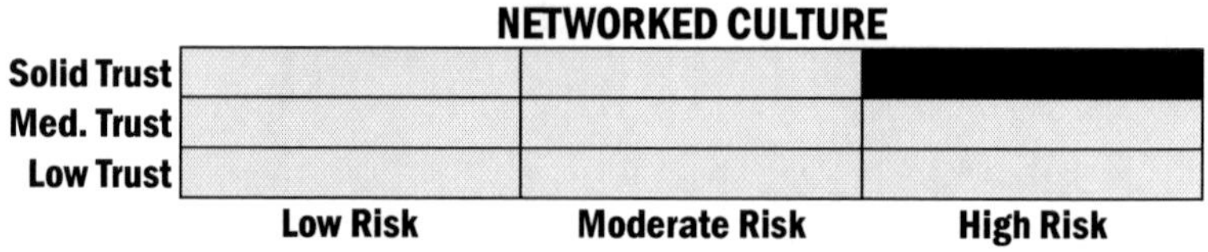

	NETWORKED CULTURE		
Solid Trust			■
Med. Trust			
Low Trust			
	Low Risk	**Moderate Risk**	**High Risk**

OVERALL CHARACTERISTICS

- Tacit knowledge available from internal networks/information moves quickly
- Consensus driven/lack of ability to adjust rapidly
- Risk avoidance/insidiously political
- Risks can be taken with minimal organizational driven "fear of failure"
- Organizational surprises due to lack of open communication are minimal
- Growth through ongoing creation of new businesses – limited focus on improving existing businesses
- Predominantly focused on a few long-term programs
- Continuously experimenting with new methods for development and commercialization

LEADERSHIP CHARACTERISTICS

- Superb interpersonal skills/tolerant of differences and ambiguity
- Use emotional intelligence to manipulative ends
- Operate behind the scenes to get things done/can spot and stop "negative" politics
- Most likely having considerable flexibility relative to policies and procedures covering day-to-day activities
- Limited organizational structure – freedom to network as needed/desired

INDIVIDUALS CHARACTERISTICS

- Freely provide assistance with no expectation of immediate return – eventually expect it
- Avoid risk – "keep your head down"
- Make friends/build relationships that last
- Individuals readily share information/ideas without significant concern for negative consequences
- Challenging of ideas is accepted with minimal feelings of personal attacks or value judgments

c.1 Communal/Low Trust/Low Risk Organization

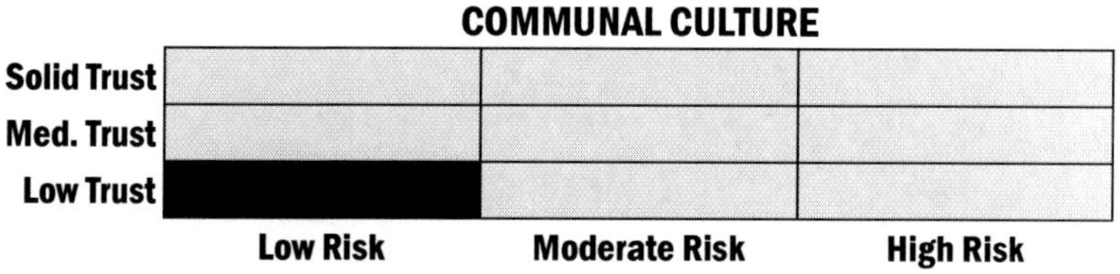

COMMUNAL CULTURE

	Low Risk	Moderate Risk	High Risk
Solid Trust			
Med. Trust			
Low Trust			

OVERALL CHARACTERISTICS

- Powerful sense of family/natural concern for coworkers
- Inward focus/potential lack of external awareness
- Clear focus/strong sense of urgency aligned with organization's mission
- Organizational surprises occur frequently due to filtered or "spun" communication
- Growth through enhancements/productivity improvements to existing businesses/operations
- Predominantly focused on many near-term programs

LEADERSHIP CHARACTERISTICS

- Create high degree of enthusiasm for organization's vision & values
- Building disciples/intimidating followers
- Fosters team work/loyal to those who perform well
- Execution adherence to established methodologies
- Well-established bureaucracy with policies and procedures covering most day-to-day activities
- Strict hierarchical organizational structure (if there is an organizational structure)

INDIVIDUALS CHARACTERISTICS

- Freely provide assistance with no expectation of return – it's good for the company/organization
- Trust your colleagues to know/follow the leader
- Identify with organization/invest time with peers talking about things important to the organization
- Examining of the motivation for challenging of ideas oftentimes gets greater focus than the content of challenge itself
- Risks are taken only when there is a well-defined "safety net" in case of failure

c.2 Communal/Low Trust/Moderate Risk Organization

COMMUNAL CULTURE

	Low Risk	Moderate Risk	High Risk
Solid Trust			
Med. Trust			
Low Trust			

OVERALL CHARACTERISTICS

- Powerful sense of family/natural concern for coworkers
- Inward focus/potential lack of external awareness
- Clear focus/strong sense of urgency aligned with organization's mission
- Organizational surprises occur frequently due to filtered or "spun" communication
- Growth through balance of enhancements/productivity improvements to existing businesses/operations and creation of new businesses
- Focused on several near-term programs along with a few long-term new business programs

LEADERSHIP CHARACTERISTICS

- Create high degree of enthusiasm for organization's vision & values
- Building disciples/intimidating followers
- Fosters team work/loyal to those who perform well
- Execution primarily guided by established methodologies
- Established bureaucracy with policies and procedures covering most day-to-day activities
- General adherence to hierarchical organizational structure

INDIVIDUALS CHARACTERISTICS

- Freely provide assistance with no expectation of return – it's good for the company/organization
- Trust your colleagues to know/follow the leader
- Identify with organization/invest time with peers talking about things important to the organization
- Information/ideas are only readily shared with people the individual truly trusts – information/ideas guarded and/or filtered before sharing on a broader scale
- Examining of the motivation for challenging of ideas oftentimes gets greater focus than the content of challenge itself
- Risks are taken only when there is a well-defined "safety net" in case of failure

c.3 Communal/Low Trust/High Risk Organization

COMMUNAL CULTURE

	Low Risk	Moderate Risk	High Risk
Solid Trust			
Med. Trust			
Low Trust			

OVERALL CHARACTERISTICS

- Powerful sense of family/natural concern for coworkers
- Inward focus/potential lack of external awareness
- Clear focus/strong sense of urgency aligned with organization's mission
- Organizational surprises occur frequently due to filtered or "spun" communication
- Growth through ongoing creation of new businesses – limited focus on improving existing businesses
- Predominantly focused on a few long-term programs
- Continuously experimenting with new methods for development and commercialization

LEADERSHIP CHARACTERISTICS

- Create high degree of enthusiasm for organization's vision & values
- Building disciples/intimidating followers
- Fosters team work/loyal to those who perform well
- Most likely having considerable flexibility relative to policies and procedures covering day-to-day activities
- Limited organizational structure – freedom to network as needed/desired

INDIVIDUALS CHARACTERISTICS

- Freely provide assistance with no expectation of return – it's good for the company/organization
- Trust your colleagues to know/follow the leader
- Identify with organization/invest time with peers talking about things important to the organization
- Information/ideas are only readily shared with people the individual truly trusts – information/ideas guarded and/or filtered before sharing on a broader scale
- Examining of the motivation for challenging of ideas oftentimes gets greater focus than the content of challenge itself
- Risks are taken only when there is a well-defined "safety net" in case of failure

c.4 Communal/Medium Trust/Low Risk Organization

COMMUNAL CULTURE

	Low Risk	Moderate Risk	High Risk
Solid Trust			
Med. Trust			
Low Trust			

OVERALL CHARACTERISTICS

- Powerful sense of family/natural concern for coworkers
- Inward focus/potential lack of external awareness
- Clear focus/strong sense of urgency aligned with organization's mission
- Lack of teamwork/small "fiefdoms"
- Organizational surprises occur due to lack of open communication or filtering of the information
- Growth through enhancements/productivity improvements to existing businesses/operations
- Predominantly focused on many near-term programs

LEADERSHIP CHARACTERISTICS

- Create high degree of enthusiasm for organization's vision & values
- Building disciples/intimidating followers
- Fosters team work/loyal to those who perform well
- Execution adherence to established methodologies
- Well-established bureaucracy with policies and procedures covering most day-to-day activities
- Strict hierarchical organizational structure (if there is an organizational structure)

INDIVIDUALS CHARACTERISTICS

- Freely provide assistance with no expectation of return – it's good for the company/organization
- Trust your colleagues to know/follow the leader
- Identify with organization/invest time with peers talking about things important to the organization
- Individuals will generally share non-sensitive information/ideas without significant concern for negative consequences
- Sensitive information/ideas are only shared with the people the individual truly trusts
- Examining the motivation for challenging of ideas has equal weight as the challenge itself
- Only moderate risks are taken with minimal concern for consequences of a failure – more significant risks need well-defined "safety net"

c.5 Communal/Medium Trust/Moderate Risk Organization

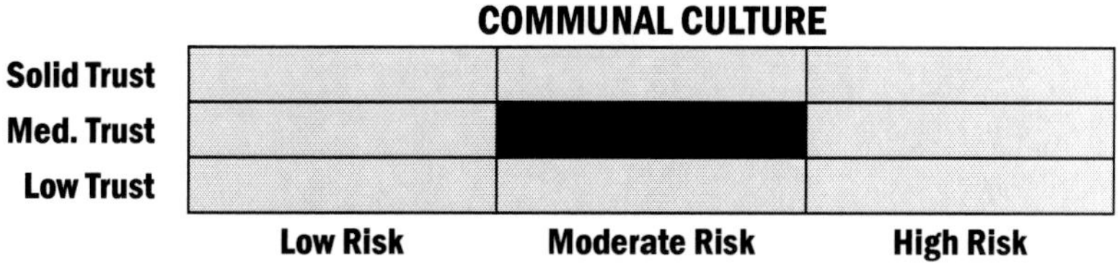

COMMUNAL CULTURE

	Low Risk	Moderate Risk	High Risk
Solid Trust			
Med. Trust		■	
Low Trust			

OVERALL CHARACTERISTICS

- Powerful sense of family/natural concern for coworkers
- Inward focus/potential lack of external awareness
- Clear focus/strong sense of urgency aligned with organization's mission
- Organizational surprises occur due to lack of open communication or filtering of the information
- Growth through balance of enhancements/productivity improvements to existing businesses/operations and creation of new businesses
- Focused on several near-term programs along with a few long-term new business programs

LEADERSHIP CHARACTERISTICS

- Create high degree of enthusiasm for organization's vision & values
- Building disciples/intimidating followers
- Fosters team work/loyal to those who perform well
- Execution primarily guided by established methodologies
- Established bureaucracy with policies and procedures covering most day-to-day activities
- General adherence to hierarchical organizational structure

INDIVIDUALS CHARACTERISTICS

- Freely provide assistance with no expectation of return – it's good for the company/organization
- Trust your colleagues to know/follow the leader
- Identify with organization/invest time with peers talking about things important to the organization
- Individuals will generally share non-sensitive information/ideas without significant concern for negative consequences
- Sensitive information/ideas are only shared with the people the individual truly trusts
- Examining the motivation for challenging of ideas has equal weight as the challenge itself
- Only moderate risks are taken with minimal concern for consequences of a failure – more significant risks need well-defined "safety net"

c.6 Communal/Medium Trust/High Risk Organization

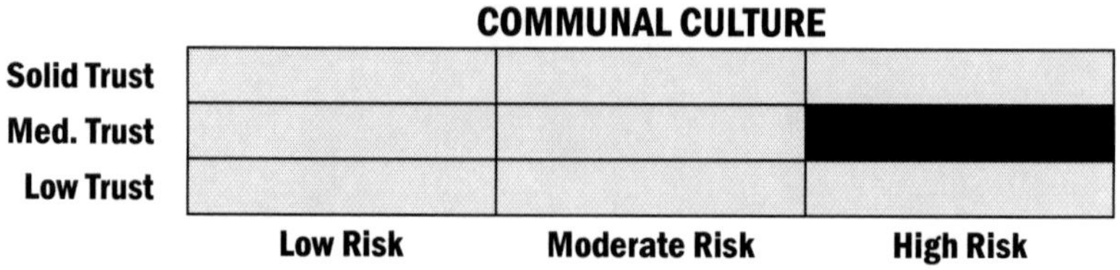

COMMUNAL CULTURE

	Low Risk	Moderate Risk	High Risk
Solid Trust			
Med. Trust			■
Low Trust			

OVERALL CHARACTERISTICS

- Powerful sense of family/natural concern for coworkers
- Inward focus/potential lack of external awareness
- Clear focus/strong sense of urgency aligned with organization's mission
- Organizational surprises occur due to lack of open communication or filtering of the information
- Growth through ongoing creation of new businesses – limited focus on improving existing businesses
- Predominantly focused on few long-term programs
- Continuously experimenting with new methods for development and commercialization

LEADERSHIP CHARACTERISTICS

- Create high degree of enthusiasm for organization's vision & values
- Building disciples/intimidating followers
- Fosters team work/loyal to those who perform well
- Most likely having considerable flexibility relative to policies and procedures covering day-to-day activities
- Limited organizational structure – freedom to network as needed/desired

INDIVIDUALS CHARACTERISTICS

- Freely provide assistance with no expectation of return – it's good for the company/organization
- Trust your colleagues to know/follow the leader
- Identify with organization/invest time with peers talking about things important to organization
- Individuals will generally share non-sensitive information/ideas without significant concern for negative consequences
- Sensitive information/ideas are only shared with the people the individual truly trusts
- Examining the motivation for challenging of ideas has equal weight as the challenge itself
- Only moderate risks are taken with minimal concern for consequences of a failure – more significant risks need well-defined 'safety net'

c.7 Communal/Solid Trust/Low Risk Organization

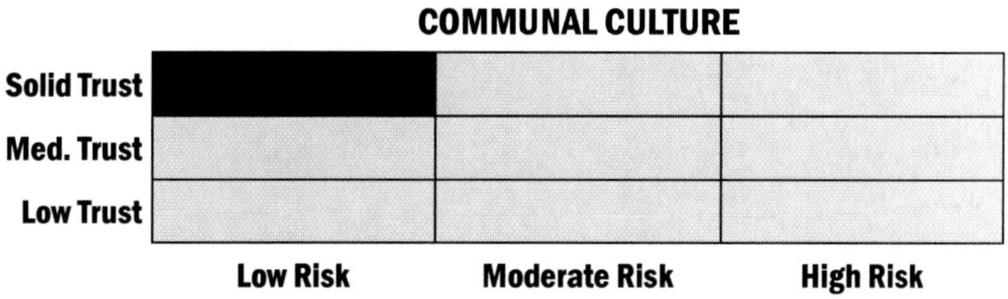

COMMUNAL CULTURE

Solid Trust	■		
Med. Trust			
Low Trust			
	Low Risk	**Moderate Risk**	**High Risk**

OVERALL CHARACTERISTICS

- Powerful sense of family/natural concern for coworkers
- Inward focus/potential lack of external awareness
- Clear focus/strong sense of urgency aligned with organization's mission
- Organizational surprises due to lack of open communication are minimal
- Growth through enhancements/productivity improvements to existing businesses/operations
- Predominantly focused on many near-term programs

LEADERSHIP CHARACTERISTICS

- Create high degree of enthusiasm for organization's vision & values
- Building disciples/intimidating followers
- Fosters team work/loyal to those who perform well
- Execution adherence to established methodologies
- Well-established bureaucracy with policies and procedures covering most day-to-day activities
- Strict hierarchical organizational structure (if there is an organizational structure)

INDIVIDUALS CHARACTERISTICS

- Freely provide assistance with no expectation of return – it's good for the company/organization
- Trust your colleagues to know/follow the leader
- Identify with organization/invest time with peers talking about things important to the organization
- Individuals readily share information/ideas without significant concern for negative consequences
- Challenging of ideas is accepted with minimal feelings of personal attacks or value judgments
- Risks can be taken with minimal organizational driven "fear of failure"

c.8 Communal/Solid Trust/Moderate Risk Organization

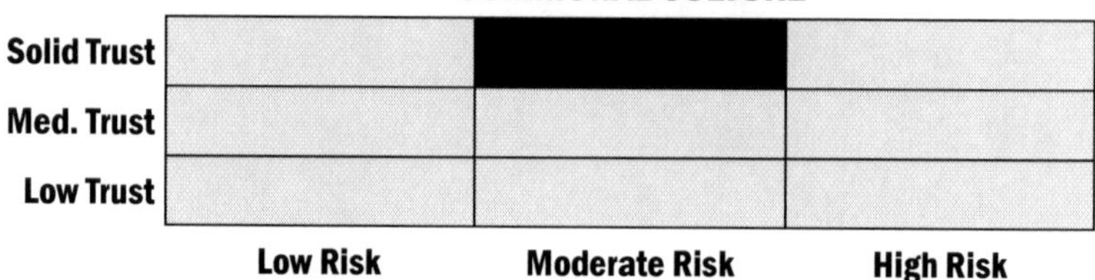

OVERALL CHARACTERISTICS

- Powerful sense of family/natural concern for coworkers
- Inward focus/potential lack of external awareness
- Clear focus/strong sense of urgency aligned with organization's mission
- Organizational surprises due to lack of open communication are minimal
- Growth through balance of enhancements/productivity improvements to existing businesses/operations and creation of new businesses
- Focused on several near-term programs along with a few long-term new business programs

LEADERSHIP CHARACTERISTICS

- Create high degree of enthusiasm for organization's vision & values
- Building disciples/intimidating followers
- Fosters team work/loyal to those who perform well
- Execution primarily guided by established methodologies
- Established bureaucracy with policies and procedures covering most day-to-day activities
- General adherence to hierarchical organizational structure

INDIVIDUALS CHARACTERISTICS

- Freely provide assistance with no expectation of return – it's good for the company/organization
- Trust your colleagues to know/follow the leader
- Identify with organization/invest time with peers talking about things important to the organization
- Individuals readily share information/ideas without significant concern for negative consequences
- Challenging of ideas is accepted with minimal feelings of personal attacks or value judgments
- Risks can be taken with minimal organizational driven "fear of failure"

c.9 Communal/Solid Trust/High Risk Organization

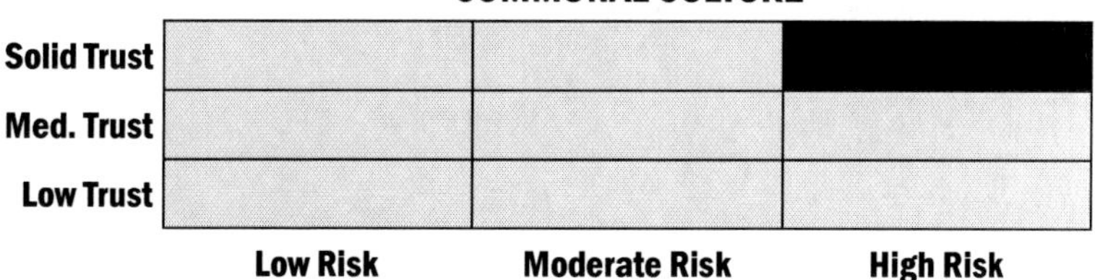

OVERALL CHARACTERISTICS

- Powerful sense of family/natural concern for coworkers
- Inward focus/potential lack of external awareness
- Clear focus/strong sense of urgency aligned with organization's mission
- Organizational surprises due to lack of open communication are minimal
- Growth through ongoing creation of new businesses – limited focus on improving existing businesses
- Predominantly focused on a few long-term programs
- Continuously experimenting with new methods for development and commercialization

LEADERSHIP CHARACTERISTICS

- Create high degree of enthusiasm for organization's vision & values
- Building disciples/intimidating followers
- Fosters team work/loyal to those who perform well
- Most likely having considerable flexibility relative to policies and procedures covering day-to-day activities
- Limited organizational structure – freedom to network as needed/desired

INDIVIDUALS CHARACTERISTICS

- Freely provide assistance with no expectation of return – it's good for the company/organization
- Trust your colleagues to know/follow the leader
- Identify with organization/invest time with peers talking about things important to the organization
- Individuals readily share information/ideas without significant concern for negative consequences
- Challenging of ideas is accepted with minimal feelings of personal attacks or value judgments
- Risks can be taken with minimal organizational driven "fear of failure."

Index

Bibliography

A

All About the Human Genome Project (HGP). Retrieved 2009, from National Human Genome Research Institute: http://www.genome.gov/10001772

A Quick Biography of Benjamin Franklin. Retrieved 2008, from US History.org: http://www.ushistory.org/franklin/info/index.htm

Allen, Oliver E. (1996). Kettering. Retrieved 2008, from *Innovation & Technology Magazine*, 12(1): http://www.americanheritage.com/articles/magazine/it/1996/2/1996_2_52.shtml.

A *Look Back ... Remembering the Cuban Missile Crisis, Oct., 2007.* Retrieved 2008, from Central Intelligence Agency: https://www.cia.gov/news-information/featured-story-archive/2007-featured-story-archive/a-look-back-remembering-the-cuban-missile-crisis.html

B

Bacon, Sir Francis. *Sir Francis Bacon Quote.* Retrieved 2008, from http://www.quotationspage.com/quote/2060.html

Bahá'u'lláh, The Hidden Words, No. P5. Retrieved 2009, from http://wilmetteinstitute.org/projects/hw.week4.html

Beals, G. (1999). *The Biography of Thomas Edison.* Retrieved 2008, from Thomas Edison.com: http://www.thomasedison.com/biography.html

Prospect Theory (Kahneman, D. and Tversky, A.). Retrieved 2008, from Behavior Finance: http://prospect-theory.behaviouralfinance.net/

Bellis, Mary. *The Invention of VELCRO® - George de Mestral.* Retrieved 2008, from About.com: http://inventors.about.com/library/weekly/aa091297.htm

Bellis, Mary. *Inventors of the Modern Computer.* Retrieved 2008, from About.com: http://inventors.about.com/library/weekly/aa051599.htm

Bellis, Mary. *The History of the Zipper.* Retrieved 2009, from About.Com: http://inventors.about.com/library/weekly/aa082497.htm

Benjamin Franklin: Glimpses of the Man. Retrieved 2008, from The Franklin Institue: http://www.fi.edu/franklin/

Bennis, Warren and Biederman, Patricia Ward (1997). *Organizing Genius.* Cambridge: Perseus Books.

Boeing B-17 Flying Fortress. Retrieved 2008, from http://www.acepilots.com/planes/b17.html

Bruneau, Stephen (2004). *Icebergs of Newfoundland and Labrador.* St. John's: Flanker Press.

C

Charles Kettering Quotes. Retrieved 2008, from BrainyQuote: brainyquote.com/quotes/authors/c/Charles_kettering.html

Chow, Ellesse. *Inspirational Stories II: The 3M Post-it® Notes Invention.* Retrieved 2008, from GoalSettingCollege: http://www.goal-setting-college.com/inspiration/inspirational-stories-ii-the-3m-post-it-notes-invention/

Christensen, C., & Raynor, M. (2003). *The Innovators Solution.* Boston: Harvard School Press.

Cialdni, Robert (1984). *Influence: The Psychology of Persuasion.* New York: William Morrow and Company.

Cofield, M (2009). *Creating Social Capital in Diverse Communities: The Formation Process and Relation Social Outcomes Exhibited by Executive Leaders* (Dissertation, Saint John Fisher College 2009).

Collison, Chris, & Parcell, Geoff. (2004). *Learning to Fly.* Chichester: Capstone Publishing Limited.

Conklin, Jeff (2005). *Dialogue Mapping: Building Shared Understanding of Wicked Problems.* Hoboken: John Wiley & Sons.

Collins, Jim and Porras, Jerry (2004). *Built To Last: Successful Habits of Visionary Companies.* New York: HarperCollins.

D

Dan's Cube (2009). *Retrieved* from NetApp.com: http://blogs.netapp.com/simple_steve/2009/06/dans-cube.html

Deal or No Deal (2008). Retrieved from NBC.com: http://www.nbc.com/Deal_or_No_Deal/

Decade of Innovation (2010). Retrieved 2010, from Ministry of Science & Technology: http://dst.gov.in/whats_new/press-release10/pib_10-3-2010.htm

Deci, E., Koestner, R. & Ryan, R. (1999). A Meta-Analytical Review of Experiments Examining the Effects of Extrinsic Rewards on Intrinsic Motivation. *Psychological Bulletin*, 125, 627-668.

Deci, E. & Ryan, R. (2000). The "what" and "why" of goal pursuits: Human needs and the self-determination of behavior. Psychological Inquiry, Vol 11, No.4, pages 227-268.

Dennison Consulting (2010): Retrieved from http://www.denisonconsulting.com/dc/

Dickens, E. (2005). *The Da Vinci Notebooks.* New York: Arcade Publishing.

Dinur, Adva (2006). *Knowledge Transfer: Stories from the Front.* Long Island University, Beyond the Classroom Lecture Series, Volume 2, Number 1.

DMAIC methodology. Retrieved 2010, from BusinessDictionary.com: www.businessdictionary.com/definition/DMAIC-methodology.html

Disraeli, Benjamin. *Benjamin Disraeli Quote.* Retrieved 2009, from Forbes: http://thoughts.forbes.com/thoughts/enthusiasm-benjamin-disraeli-every-production-of

Dobrzynski, Judith (1996). Chicken Done to a Golden Rule; Fast-Food Chain Treats Its Employees as Family. Retrieved 2009, from *The New York Times*: http://www.nytimes.com/1996/04/03/business/chicken-done-to-a-golden-rule-fast-food-chain-treats-its-employees-as-family.html

Drucker, Peter. *Peter Drucker on Knowledge Worker Productivity.* Retrieved 2008, from Knowledge Worker Performance.com: http://www.knowledgeworkerperformance.com/Knowledge-Worker-Management/Drucker-Knowledge-Worker-Productivity/default.aspx

Drucker, Peter. *Peter Drucker Quote.* Retrieved 2008, from BrainyQuote: http://www.brainyquote.com/quotes/authors/p/peter_drucker_2.html

E

Einstein's Lost Train Ticket. Retrieved 2008, from Snopes.com: http://message.snopes.com/showthread.php?t=11771

Embracing an Innovative Culture by The Wharton School (2010). Retrieved 2010, from Human Resource Executive Online: http://www.hreonline.com/HRE/story.jsp?storyId=373779461

F

Fishbein, Toby. *The legacy of George Washington Carver.* Retrieved 2008, from Iowa State University: http://www.lib.iastate.edu/spcl/gwc/bio.html

Fredholm, Lotta (2003). *The Discovery of the Molecular Structure of DNA – The Double Helix.* Retrieved 2008, from Nobelprize.org: http://nobelprize.org/educational/medicine/dna_double_helix/readmore.html

Friedman, Thomas (2005). *The World is Flat.* New York: Farrar, Straus, and Giroux.

G

George Washington Carver. Retrieved 2008, from Gale Cengage Learning™: http://www.gale.cengage.com/free_resources/bhm/bio/carver_g.htm

Gardner, Howard (1993). *Frames of Mind: The Theory of Multiple Intelligences.* New York: Basic Books.

Global Supersector Leaders (2010/2011). Retrieved 2011, from Dow Jones Sustainability Indexes: http://www.sustainability-index.com/07_htmle/reviews/review2010_1.html

Goffee, Rob and Jones, Gareth (1998). *The Character of a Corporation: How Your Company's Culture Can Make or Break Your Business.* New York: HarperCollins.

Grayson, C. and Baldwin, D.(2007). *Influence: Gaining Commitment, Getting Results.* Hoboken, John Wiley and Sons.

Greenleaf, Robert (2002). *Servant leadership: A journey into the nature of legitimate power and greatness.* New York: Paulist Press.

Grootaert, Robert (1998). *Social Capital: The Missing Link?* Retrieved 2008, from Social Capital Initiative: http://siteresources.worldbank.org/INTSOCIALCAPITAL/Resources/Social-Capital-Initiative-Working-Paper-Series/SCI-WPS-03.pdf

H

Harrington Institute, Inc., *Knowledge Management Methodology.* Retrieved 2010, from Harrington Institute, Inc: http://docs.google.com/viewer?a=v&q=cache:DkyQwmSCiggJ:www.harrington-institute.com/knowledge-objects/methodologies/harrington-institute-methodology-knowledge-management.pdf+Harrington+Institute,+Inc.,+%25+tacit+vs+%25+explicit+knowledge&hl=en&gl=us&pid=bl&srcid=ADGEESjE_ZsRxXCvQsba6-15psCUa7_9w19IFivwc4SKu9IiQDit7UIUSPKork_0VegDbI2S6GZBQMVnwXDcciifIsmwvavDpwcUYvFeGa2TQJNyrSaHljPmYgTmmrbBWjnRoitFtoA&sig=AHIEtbRoJGXTqc9Nnju8vgzih2NnbhAzUw

Hindo, Brian. *At 3M, A Struggle Between Efficiency And Creativity.* Retrieved 2008, from Businessweek, June 11, 2007: http://www.businessweek.com/magazine/content/07_24/b4038406.htm.

Holmes, Joshua (2008). *How Did You Do, Truett?* 2008. Retrieved 2009, from BumpShock: http://bumpshack.com/2008/08/01/chick-fil-a-founder-s-truett-cathy-punishes-vandals/

Hong, Lu and Page, Scott (2004). *Groups of diverse problem solvers can outperform groups of high-ability problem solvers.* Retrieved from The National Academy of Science: http://www.pnas.org/content/101/46/16385.full.pdf+html

How the Googleplex Works. Retrieved 2010, from http://computer.howstuffworks.com/googleplex3.htm

Huitt, William (2001). *The Mind.* Retrieved 2007 from Educational Psychology Interactive, Valdosta State University: http://chiron.valdosta.edu/whuitt/col/summary/mind.html

Huitt, William (2004). *Maslow's Hierarchy of Needs.* Retrieved 2006 from Valdosta State University: http://chiron.valdosta.edu/whuitt/col/regsys/maslow.html

Huitt, William (2001). *Motivation to learn: An overview.* Retrieved 2006, from Educational Psychology Interactive, Valdosta State University: http://chiron.valdosta.edu/whuitt/col/motivation/motivate.html

I

Isaacson, Walter (2005). *Kissinger: A Biography.* New York: Simon & Schuster.

J

Johansson, Frans (2006). *The Medici Effect.* Boston: Harvard Business School Press.

Johnson, Kimberly (2009). *Buick aims 2010 Allure at China market.* Retrieved 2009, from Wheels.ca: http://www.wheels.ca/article/494378

K

Kalervo Oberg (1901 – 1973) – anthropologist who introduced the term "culture shock." Retrieved 2010, from *Society and Culture*: http://society--culture.blogspot.com/2008/08/kalervo-oberg-1901-1973-anthropologist.html

Kim, W. Chan & Mauborgne, Renee (2005). *Blue Ocean Strategy.* Boston, Harvard School Press.

Kimmel, Leigh (1998). *Apple Computer, Inc.: A History.* Retrieved 2011, from http://webspace.webring.com/people/il/leighkimmel/applehistory.html

King, Martin Luther Jr. (1963, August). *I have a dream.* Speech. August 28, 1963. Retrieved 2008, from American Rhetoric: http://www.americanrhetoric.com/speeches/mlkihaveadream.htm

Kelly, Tom with Jonathan Littman (2001). *The Art of Innovation.* New York: Doubleday.

Koestler, Author (1964). *The Act of Creation.* New York: The Macmillan Co.

L

Lane, Carla. *Multiple Intelligences.* Retrieved 2009, from http://www.tecweb.org/styles/gardner.html

Lao-Tsu. *Lao-Tsu Quote.* Retrieved 2009, from InspirationalSpark.com: http://www.inspirationalspark.com/leadership-quotes.html

Carroll, Lewis. *Lewis Carroll Quote.* Retrieved 2008, from: http://www.brainyquote.com/quotes/authors/l/lewis_carroll.html

Lienhard, John H. *Inventing Benzene.* Retrieved 2009, from: http://www.uh.edu/engines/epi265.htm

Lloyd, Tracey (2009). *Triple Bottom Line Reporting: People Planet Profit Come Together to Give Full Picture of Business.* Retrieved 2010, from suite101.com: http://social-corporate-responsibility.suite101.com/article.cfm/triple_bottom_line_reporting

M

Marie Curie. Retrieved 2008, from Wikipedia: http://en.wikipedia.org/wiki/Marie_Curie

Marie Curie, The Nobel Prize in Physics 1903. Retrieved 2008, from: http://nobelprize.org/nobel_prizes/physics/laureates/1903/marie-curie-bio.html

Marion, R. and Uhl-Bien, M. (2002). Leadership In Complex Organizations. *The Leadership Quarterly*, Pergamon.

Twain, Mark. *Mark Twain Quotes.* Retrieved 2008, from: http://www.twainquotes.com/Ideas.html

McCarthy, Michael (2007). The fight game: NHL's rules of engagement. Retrieved 2009, from *USA Today*: http://www.usatoday.com/sports/hockey/nhl/2007-04-04-fighting_N.htm

Miller, John (2008). Service with a Smile. Retrieved 2009, from *Philanthropy Magazine*: http://www.philanthropyroundtable.org/article.asp?article=1553&cat=147

Mission Impossible (1, 2, & 3) [Motion Pictures]. (1996-2006). Paramount Pictures.

Mosaic Partnerships. Retrieved 2008, from Idea Connection Systems: www.innovating.com

N, O

P

Page, Albert L (1991). University of Illinois, "Presentation to Product Development & Management Association," Chicago, November 13, 1991.

Pang, Alex (2002). The Making of the Mouse. Retrieved 2009, from *Innovation & Technology Magazine*, Volume 17, Issue 3: http://www.americanheritage.com/articles/magazine/it/2002/3/2002_3_48.shtml

Pang, Alex (2002). *Mighty Mouse.* Retrieved 2009, from Stanford Magazine: http://www.stanfordalumni.org/news/magazine/2002/marapr/features/mouse.html

Perlmutter, Mark. *Cooperative Versus Competitive Strategies: Rewriting The Unwritten Rules Of Procedure.* Retrieved 2010, from http://www.bostonlawcollaborative.com/blc/202-BLC/version/default/part/AttachmentData/data/2005-07-perlmutter-article.pdf?branch=main&language=default

Personal communications: Thomas McGafee, PhD.

Personal communications: Jerry Belle, President, Aventis NA.

Personal communications: Col. Peter Engstrom, Ret.

Personal communications: Rocco Papalia, Sr. Vice President, Frito-Lay, Inc.

Plicht, Chris. *Herschel, F. Wilhelm.* Retrieved 2007, from http://www.plicht.de/chris/06hersch.htm

Post-it® Notes. Retrieved 2009, from http://www.ideafinder.com/history/inventions/postit.htm

President John F. Kennedy (1961). *The Decision to Go to the Moon: President John F. Kennedy's May 25, 1961 Speech before a Joint Session of Congress.* Retrieved 2008, from: http://history.nasa.gov/moondec.html

President Obama Lays Out Strategy for American Innovation (2009). Retrieved 2010, from The White House Office of the Press Secretary: http://www.whitehouse.gov/the_press_office/president-obama-lays-out-strategy-for-american-innovation/

Q

Quinn, James Brian (1992). *Intelligent Enterprise: A Knowledge and Service Based Paradigm for Industry.* New York: Simon & Schuster.

R

Renaissance Man. Retrieved 2006, from Museum of Science: http://www.mos.org/leonardo/bio.html

Reiss, Robert (2009). How NetApp Became A Great Place To Work. Retrieved from *Forbes*: http://www.forbes.com/2009/09/01/ceo-interview-workplace-ceonetwork-leadership-warmenhoven.html

Ritchey, Tom (2005). *Wicked Problems Structuring Social Messes with Morphological Analysis.* Retrieved 2006, from http://www.scribd.com/doc/9437975/Wicked-Problems-Structuring-Social-Messes-with-Morphological-Analysis

Rittel, Horst and Webber, Melvin (1973). Dilemmas in a General Theory of Planning. Retrieved 2006, from *Policy Sciences* 4 (1973), 155-169. Elsevier Scientific Publishing Company, Amsterdam: http://www.uctc.net/mwebber/Rittel+Webber+Dilemmas+General_Theory_of_Planning.pdf

Rosenfeld, R. and Servo, J. (1984). Business and Creativity: Making Ideas Connect. *The Futurist,* Vol. XVII, No. 4.

Rosenfeld, Robert with Kolstoe, John (2006). *Making the Invisible Visible: The Human Principles for Sustaining Innovation.* Bloomington: Xlibris.

Rules of engagement. Retrieved 2008, from BusinessDictionary.com: http://www.businessdictionary.com/definition/rules-of-engagement.html

Ryan, Richard and Deci, Edward (2000). Self-Determination Theory and the Facilitation of Intrinsic Motivation, Social Development, and Well-Being. *American Psychologist,* Vol. 55, No. 1, 68-78.

S

Schamel, John (2009). *How the Pilot's Checklist Came About.* Retrieved 2009, from http://www.atchistory.org/History/checklst.htm

SAIC (Science Applications International Corporation): http://www.saic.com/

Snow White and The Seven Dwarfs. Retrieved 2009, from Film Reference: http://www.filmreference.com/Films-Se-Sno/Snow-White-and-the-Seven-Dwarfs.html

Skousen, W. Cleon (2006). *5000 Year Leap: A Miracle That Changed the World.* National Center for Constitutional Studies.

T

Taylor, Peggy and Saey, Sara. *Herschel Club - Friedrich Wilhelm Herschel.* Retrieved 2006, from The Astronomical League: http://www.astroleague.org/al/obsclubs/herschel/fwhershs.html

The Apache Software Foundation: http://www.apache.org/

The Linux Foundation: http://linux.com/index.php

U

V

Vote for Triple Bottom Line Companies. Retrieved 2011, from http://drlorraine.blogspot.com/2010/03/vote-for-triple-bottom-line-companies.html

W

Wallas, Graham (1926). *The Art of Thought.* New York, Harcourt.

Walt Disney: A Biography. Retrieved 2008, from Disney Archives: http://disney.go.com/vault/read/walt/index.html

Wilson, Glenn and Lauer, Ken (2001). *Lessons from Boss Ket!* Communique retrieved 2007, from Volume 12, 2001, The Creative Problem Solving Group, Inc., Buffalo, NY: http://www.cpsb.com/cru/communique/#12

Wright, Robert (1999). "The Time 100: Scientist and Thinkers." Retrieved 2009, from *Time* March 29: http://205.188.238.109/time/time100/scientist/profile/watsoncrick.html

Wulf, Steve, Witkowski/Methuen, Tom (1996). "The Glow From A Fire." Retrieved 2008, from *Time Magazine*, January 8, 1996: http://www.time.com/time/magazine/article/0,9171,983916,00.html

X, Y

Z

Zipper. Retrieved 2008, from: http://www.ideafinder.com/history/inventions/zipper.htm

Endnotes

Introduction

1. *President Obama Lays Out Strategy for American Innovation (2009).* Retrieved 2010, from The White House Office of the Press Secretary: http://www.whitehouse.gov/the_press_office/president-obama-lays-out-strategy-for-american-innovation/
2. *Decade of Innovation (2010).* Retrieved 2010, from Ministry of Science & Technology: http://dst.gov.in/whats_new/press-release10/pib_10-3-2010.htm
3. *DMAIC methodology.* Retrieved 2010, from BusinessDictionary.com: www.businessdictionary.com/definition/DMAIC-methodology.html
4. Pang, Alex (2002). *Mighty Mouse.* Retrieved 2009, from Stanford Magazine: http://www.stanfordalumni.org/news/magazine/2002/marapr/features/mouse.html
5. Pang, Alex (2002). *Mighty Mouse.* Retrieved 2009, from Stanford Magazine: http://www.stanfordalumni.org/news/magazine/2002/marapr/features/mouse.html
6. 7½" by 3¼" card with 80 columns and 12 punch locations per column. The cards were used for inputting computer programs and data.
7. Kelly, Tom with Jonathan Littman (2001). *The Art of Innovation.* New York: Doubleday
8. Christensen, C., & Raynor, M. (2003). *The Innovators Solution.* Boston: Harvard School Press.
9. Kim, W. Chan & Mauborgne, Renee (2005). *Blue Ocean Strategy.* Boston: Harvard School Press.

10. Rosenfeld, Robert with Kolstoe, John (2006). *Making the Invisible Visible: The Human Principles for Sustaining Innovation.* Bloomington: Xlibris.
11. The ™ notation is only used the first few times a word or phrase is used. After that it is not used in order to make the text easier to read.
12. Rosenfeld (2006).

Part 1 (Chapters 1 – 10)

Chapter 1

1. Wilson, Glenn and Lauer, Ken (2001). *Lessons from Boss Ket! Communique* retrieved 2007 from Volume 12, 2001, The Creative Problem Solving Group, Inc., Buffalo, NY: http://www.cpsb.com/cru/communique/#12
2. Allen, Oliver E. (1996). *Kettering*. Retrieved 2008, from Innovation & Technology Magazine, 12(1): http://www.americanheritage.com/articles/magazine/it/1996/2/1996_2_52.shtml
3. Transcript of personal copy of Kettering's speech.
4. *Charles Kettering Quotes.* Retrieved 2008, from BrainyQuote: Brainyquote.com/quotes/authors/c/Charles_kettering.html
5. Rosenfeld (2006), pages 30-33.
6. Personal communications: Rocco Papalia, Sr. Vice President, Frito-Lay, Inc.
7. Key stakeholders are defined as those individuals who can directly affect or are accountable for establishing the direction of the organization. They are generally the key decision makers.

Chapter 2

1. To align with the Innovation House™, this principle has been renamed. The original principle in Rosenfeld (2006) is *"Trust Is the Means and Love the Unspoken Word,"* so that you can cross-reference it there.
2. Personal communications: Thomas McGaffey, Ph.D.
3. Grootaert, Robert (1998). *Social Capital: The Missing Link?* Retrieved 2008, from Social Capital Initiative: http://siteresources.worldbank.org/INTSOCIALCAPITAL/Resources/Social-Capital-Initiative-Working-Paper-Series/SCI-WPS-03.pdf

4. *Mosaic Partnerships.* Retrieved 2008, from Idea Connection Systems: www.innovating.com
5. Cofield, M (2009). *Creating Social Capital in Diverse Communities: The Formation Process and Relation Social Outcomes Exhibited by Executive Leaders* (Dissertation, Saint John Fisher College, 2009).
6. For a more detailed description of the Relationship Spectrum™, Rosenfeld (2006), pages 160-170.
7. Rosenfeld (2006).

Chapter 3

1. For a more detailed description, Rosenfeld (2006), pages 133-139.
2. Kimmel, Leigh (1998). *Apple Computer, Inc.: A History.* Retrieved 2011, from http://webspace.webring.com/people/il/leighkimmel/applehistory.html
3. Bellis, Mary. *Inventors of the Modern Computer.* Retrieved 2008, from About.com: http://inventors.about.com/library/weekly/aa051599.htm

Chapter 4

1. Holmes, Joshua (2008). *How Did You Do, Truett?* 2008. Retrieved 2009, from BumpShock: http://bumpshack.com/2008/08/01/chick-fil-a-founder-s-truett-cathy-punishes-vandals/
2. Miller, John (2008). *Service with a Smile.* Retrieved 2009, from Philanthropy Magazine: http://www.philanthropyroundtable.org/article.asp?article=1553&cat=147
3. Dobrzynski, Judith (1996). *Chicken Done to a Golden Rule; Fast-Food Chain Treats Its Employees as Family.* Retrieved 2009, from The New York Times: http://www.nytimes.com/1996/04/03/business/chicken-done-to-a-golden-rule-fast-food-chain-treats-its-employees-as-family.html
4. Huitt, William (2004). *Maslow's Hierarchy of Needs.* Retrieved 2006, from Valdosta State University: http://chiron.valdosta.edu/whuitt/col/regsys/maslow.html
5. Calving is when large pieces of an iceberg break away. It is similar to an organization becoming fragmented.
6. Bruneau, Stephen (2004). *Icebergs of Newfoundland and Labrador.* St. John's: Flanker Press.

7. Reiss, Robert (2009). *How NetApp Became A Great Place To Work.* Retrieved from Forbes: http://www.forbes.com/2009/09/01/ceo-interview-workplace-ceonetwork-leadership-warmenhoven.html

8. *Dan's Cube* (2009). Retrieved from NetApp.com: http://blogs.netapp.com/simple_steve/2009/06/dans-cube.html

9. If you create your own set of soft values, there must be an equal number of positive ones and negative ones. If you do not have seven of each, use the following to develop your own scoring grid:
   - The minimum number = 1 * total number of elements
   - The maximum number = 5 * total number of elements
   - High: maximum number to (3*max number + min number)/4 +1
   - Med: (3*max number + min number)/4 to (max number + min number)/2 +1
   - Low: (max number + min number)/2 to (max number + 3* min number)/4 +1
   - Seriously low: (max number + 3* min number)/4 to min number

10. Lao-Tsu Quote. Retrieved 2009, from InspirationalSpark.com: http://www.inspirationalspark.com/leadership-quotes.html

11. Bahá'u'lláh, *The Hidden Words, No. P5*. Retrieved 2009, from http://wilmetteinstitute.org/projects/hw.week4.html

Chapter 5

1. Bennis, Warren and Biederman, Patricia Ward (1997). *Organizing Genius.* Cambridge, Perseus Books.

2. *Walt Disney: A Biography*. Retrieved 2008, from Disney Archieves: http://disney.go.com/vault/read/walt/index.html

3. *Snow White and The Seven Dwarfs.* Retrieved 2009, from Film Reference: http://www.filmreference.com/Films-Se-Sno/Snow-White-and-the-Seven-Dwarfs.html

4. Hong, Lu and Page, Scott (2004). *Groups of diverse problem solvers can outperform groups of high-ability problem solvers.* Retrieved from The National Academy of Science: http://www.pnas.org/content/101/46/16385.full.pdf+html

5. Friedman, Thomas (2005). *The World is Flat.* New York: Farrar, Straus, and Giroux.

6. Knowledge work and knowledge worker were first used by Drucker. A knowledge worker is an individual valued for their ability to interpret information within a specific area.

7. Drucker, Peter. *Peter Drucker on Knowledge Worker Productivity.* Retrieved 2008, from Knowledge Worker Performance.com: http://www.knowledgeworkerperformance.com/Knowledge-Worker-Management/Drucker-Knowledge-Worker-Productivity/default.aspx

8. Huitt, William (2001). *The Mind.* Retrieved 2007, from Educational Psychology Interactive, Valdosta State University: http://chiron.valdosta.edu/whuitt/col/summary/mind.html

9. Plicht, Chris. *Herschel, F. Wilhelm.* Retrieved 2007, from http://www.plicht.de/chris/06hersch.htm

10. Taylor, Peggy and Saey, Sara. *Herschel Club - Friedrich Wilhelm Herschel.* Retrieved 2006, from The Astronomical League: http://www.astroleague.org/al/obsclubs/herschel/fwhershs.html

11. *Marie Curie.* Retrieved 2008, from Wikipedia: http://en.wikipedia.org/wiki/Marie_Curie

12. Marie Curie, The Nobel Prize in Physics 1903. Retrieved 2008, from http://nobelprize.org/nobel_prizes/physics/laureates/1903/marie-curie-bio.html

13. Fishbein, Toby. *The legacy of George Washington Carver.* Retrieved 2008, from Iowa State University: http://www.lib.iastate.edu/spcl/gwc/bio.html

14. *George Washington Carver.* Retrieved 2008, from Gale Cengage Learning™: http://www.gale.cengage.com/free_resources/bhm/bio/carver_g.htm

15. Beals, G. (1999). *The Biography of Thomas Edison.* Retrieved 2008, from Thomas Edison.com: http://www.thomasedison.com/biography.html

16. *A Quick Biography of Benjamin Franklin.* Retrieved 2008, from US History.org: http://www.ushistory.org/franklin/info/index.htm

17. *Benjamin Franklin: Glimpses of the Man.* Retrieved 2008, from The Franklin Institue: http://www.fi.edu/franklin/

18. *Renaissance Man.* Retrieved 2006, from Museum of Science: http://www.mos.org/leonardo/bio.html

19. Dickens, E. (2005). *The Da Vinci Notebooks.* New York: Arcade Publishing.

20. Embracing an Innovative Culture by The Wharton School (2010). Retrieved 2010, from Human Resource Executive Online: http://www.hreonline.com/HRE/story.jsp?storyId=373779461

21. Koestler, Arthur (1964). *The Act of Creation.* New York: The Macmillan Co.

22. Rosenfeld, R. and Servo, J. (1984). Business and Creativity: Making Ideas Connect. *The Futurist*, Vol. XVII, No. 4.

Chapter 6

1. Friedman (2005).
2. The Linux Foundation: http://linux.com/index.php
3. The Apache Software Foundation: http://www.apache.org/
4. For example, the design of the Buick Lacrosse's interior being done by a GM design team in China.
5. Johnson, Kimberly (2009). *Buick aims 2010 Allure at China market*. Retrieved 2009, from Wheels.ca: http://www.wheels.ca/article/494378
6. Dinur, Adva (2006). *Knowledge Transfer: Stories from the Front.* Long Island University, Beyond the Classroom Lecture Series, Volume 2, Number 1.

Chapter 7

1. *Post-it® Notes*. Retrieved 2009, from: http://www.ideafinder.com/history/inventions/postit.htm
2. Chow, Ellesse. *Inspirational Stories II : The 3M Post-it® Notes Invention*. Retrieved 2008 from GoalSettingCollege: http://www.goal-setting-college.com/inspiration/inspirational-stories-ii-the-3m-post-it-notes-invention/
3. Mark Twain Quotes: http://www.twainquotes.com/Ideas.html
4. For a more detailed description, see Rosenfeld (2006), pages 96-101.
5. Disraeli, Benjamin. Benjamin Disraeli Quote. Retrieved 2009, from Forbes: http://thoughts.forbes.com/thoughts/enthusiasm-benjamin-disraeli-every-production-of
6. Paradigm Creators™ are those people with both the passion and skills required to create new. They are the individuals who help mold the world around them and to whom others look for direction.
7. For a more detailed description, see Rosenfeld (2006), pages 96-101.

Chapter 8

1. Bellis, Mary. *The History of the Zipper*. Retrieved 2009, from About.Com: http://inventors.about.com/library/weekly/aa082497.htm
2. *Zipper.* Retrieved 2008, from http://www.ideafinder.com/history/inventions/zipper.htm

3. Bellis, Mary. *The Invention of VELCRO® - George de Mestral.* Retrieved 2008 from About.com: http://inventors.about.com/library/weekly/aa091297.htm
4. Lienhard, John H. *Inventing Benzene.* Retrieved 2009, from http://www.uh.edu/engines/epi265.htm
5. Rosenfeld (2006).
6. Wallas, Graham (1926). *The Art of Thought.* New York: Harcourt.
7. For a more detailed description see Rosenfeld (2006), pages 40-43.
8. For a more detailed description, see Rosenfeld (2006), pages 46-50.

Chapter 9

1. *Boeing B-17 Flying Fortress.* Retrieved 2008, from http://www.acepilots.com/planes/b17.html
2. Schamel, John (2009). *How the Pilot's Checklist Came About.* Retrieved 2009, from http://www.atchistory.org/History/checklst.htm
3. GPS: Global Positioning System used for navigation.
4. For a more detailed description, see Rosenfeld (2006), pages 52-81.
5. Taking market share from your organization, rather than from a competitor or growing the overall market segment.
6. Stakeholders will be discussed in greater detail in Part Two.
7. For a more detailed explanation see Rosenfeld (2006).

Part 2 (Chapters 11 – 23)

Chapter 11

1. Friedman (2005).

Chapter 12

1. *Kalervo Oberg (1901 – 1973) – anthropologist who introduced the term "culture shock."* Retrieved 2010, from Society and Culture: http://society--culture.blogspot.com/2008/08/kalervo-oberg-1901-1973-anthropologist.html

2. *How the Googleplex Works.* Retrieved 2010, from http://computer.howstuffworks.com/googleplex3.htm
3. Organizational Environment Survey. Retrieved from Idea Connection Systems, Inc., www.innovating.com
4. Dennison Consulting (2010): Retrieved from http://www.denisonconsulting.com/dc/
5. Goffee, Rob and Jones, Gareth (1998). *The Character of a Corporation: How Your Company's Culture Can Make or Break Your Business.* New York: HarperCollins.

Chapter 13

1. Huitt (2004).
2. Johansson, Frans (2006). *The Medici Effect.* Boston, Harvard Business School Press.
3. The approaches that we use to help you understand and be able to apply the ideas in the upper portion of the house are somewhat analytical at times. For those of you who are analytical by nature, this should be easy. For those of you who are not, it may be a bit confusing. For non-analytical readers, we suggest that you not worry about details and focus on understanding concepts. Once you understand them, you can develop your own ways to apply them.

Chapter 14

1. *Deal or No Deal* (2008). Retrieved from NBC.com: http://www.nbc.com/Deal_or_No_Deal/
2. *Prospect Theory (Kahneman, D. and Tversky, A.).* Retrieved 2008, from Behavior Finance: http://prospect-theory.behaviouralfinance.net/

Chapter 15

1. Fredholm, Lotta (2003). *The Discovery of the Molecular Structure of DNA – The Double Helix.* Retrieved 2008, from Nobelprize.org: http://nobelprize.org/educational/medicine/dna_double_helix/readmore.html
2. Ibid.
3. *All About the Human Genome Project (HGP).* Retrieved 2009, from National Human Genome Research Institute: http://www.genome.gov/10001772

4. Wright, Robert (1999). *The Time 100: Scientist and Thinkers, March 29, 1999*. Retrieved 2009, from Time: http://205.188.238.109/time/time100/scientist/profile/watsoncrick.html

5. Effect genes are those DNA segments that have been identified as being the key drivers of a particular trait or attribute of interest.

Chapter 16

1. *Rules of engagement*. Retrieved 2008, from BusinessDictionary.com: http://www.businessdictionary.com/definition/rules-of-engagement.html
2. Perlmutter, Mark. *Cooperative Versus Competitive Strategies: Rewriting The Unwritten Rules Of Procedure*. Retrieved 2010, from http://www.bostonlawcollaborative.com/blc/202-BLC/version/default/part/AttachmentData/data/2005-07-perlmutter-article.pdf
3. McCarthy, Michael (2007). *The fight game: NHL's rules of engagement*. Retrieved 2009, from USA Today: http://www.usatoday.com/sports/hockey/nhl/2007-04-04-fighting_N.htm

Chapter 17

1. *A Look Back ... Remembering the Cuban Missile Crisis, Oct., 2007*. Retrieved 2008, from Central Intelligence Agency: https://www.cia.gov/news-information/featured-story-archive/2007-featured-story-archive/a-look-back-remembering-the-cuban-missile-crisis.html
2. Isaacson, Walter (2005). *Kissinger: A Biography*. New York: Simon & Schuster.
3. For example:
    - Cialdni, Robert (1984). *Influence: The Psychology of Persuasion*. New York, William Morrow and Company.
    - Grayson, C. and Baldwin, D. (2007). *Influence: Gaining Commitment, Getting Results*. Hoboken: John Wiley and Sons.
    - Greenleaf, Robert (2002). *Servant leadership: A journey into the nature of legitimate power and greatness*. New York: Paulist Press.

Chapter 18

1. Bacon, Sir Francis. Retrieved 2008, from http://www.quotationspage.com/quote/2060.html

2. Drucker, Peter. *Peter Drucker Quote*. Retrieved 2008, from BrainyQuote: http://www.brainyquote.com/quotes/authors/p/peter_drucker_2.html
3. Personal communications: Col. Peter Engstrom, Ret.
4. Harrington Institute, Inc., *Knowledge Management Methodology*. Retrieved 2010 from Harrington Institute, Inc: http://docs.google.com/viewer?a=v&q=cache:DkyQwmSCiggJ:www.harrington-institute.com/knowledge-objects/methodologies/harrington-institute-methodology-knowledge-management.pdf
5. Collison, Chris, & Parcell, Geoff. (2004). *Learning to Fly*. Chichester: Capstone Publishing Limited.
6. Data is for illustration purposes only. It is based on observations and not on hard data.
7. Personal communications: Col. Peter Engstrom, Ret.
8. Note that there are different versions of Action Reviews. Here we have described the one that we have found most useful.
9. Collison, C. and Parcell, G. (2004).
10. That is, make sure the nuggets have been reviewed to ensure accuracy and applicability.
11. SAIC (Science Applications International Corporation): http://www.saic.com/
12. Collison, C. and Parcell, G. (2004), page 16.

Chapter 19

1. Rittel, Horst and Webber, Melvin (1973). *Dilemmas in a General Theory of Planning*. Retrieved 2006, from Policy Sciences 4 (1973), pages 155-169. Elsevier Scientific Publishing Company, Amsterdam: http://www.uctc.net/mwebber/Rittel+Webber+Dilemmas+General_Theory_of_Planning.pdf
2. ibid.
3. King, Martin Luther Jr. (1963, August). I have a dream. Speech August 28, 1963. Retrieved 2008, from American Rhetoric: http://www.americanrhetoric.com/speeches/mlkihaveadream.htm
4. Ritchey, Tom (2005). *Wicked Problems Structuring Social Messes with Morphological Analysis*. Retrieved 2006, from http://www.scribd.com/doc/9437975/Wicked-Problems-Structuring-Social-Messes-with-Morphological-Analysis
5. Conklin, Jeff (2005). *Dialogue Mapping: Building Shared Understanding of Wicked Problems*. Hoboken: John Wiley & Sons.

6. President John F. Kennedy (1961). *The Decision to Go to the Moon: President John F. Kennedy's May 25, 1961 Speech before a Joint Session of Congress*. Retrieved 2008, from http://history.nasa.gov/moondec.html
7. Conklin (2005).
8. That is, focus on novel or different solutions, as opposed to small modifications to those that offer only slight improvements to the existing system.

Chapter 20

1. Skousen, W. Cleon (2006). *5000 Year Leap: A Miracle That Changed the World.* National Center for Constitutional Studies.
2. Lane, Carla. Multiple Intelligences. Retrieved 2009, from http://www.tecweb.org/styles/gardner.html
3. Gardner, Howard (1993). *Frames of Mind: The Theory of Multiple Intelligences.* New York: Basic Books.
4. Marion, R. and Uhl-Bien, M. (2002). Leadership In Complex Organizations. *The Leadership Quarterly*, Pergamon.
5. ibid.
6. *Mission Impossible (1, 2, & 3)* [Motion pictures] (1996-2006). Paramount Pictures.

Chapter 21

1. Huitt, William (2001). *Motivation to learn: An overview*. Retrieved 2006, from Educational Psychology Interactive, Valdosta State University: http://chiron.valdosta.edu/whuitt/col/motivation/motivate.html
2. Fishbein, T. (2008).
3. Beals, Gerald (1999).
4. Ryan, Richard and Deci, Edward (2000). Self-Determination Theory and the Facilitation of Intrinsic Motivation, Social Development, and Well-Being. *American Psychologist, Vol. 55 No. 1,* 68-78.
5. Deci, E., Koestner, R. & Ryan, R. (1999). A Meta-Analytical Review of Experiments Examining the Effects of Extrinsic Rewards on Intrinsic Motivation. *Psychological Bulletin 125*, 627-668.
6. Deci, E. & Ryan, R. (2000). The "what" and "why" of goal pursuits: Human needs and the self-determination of behavior. *Psychological Inquiry, Vol 11, No. 4,* 227-268.

Chapter 22

1. Collins, Jim and Porras, Jerry (2004). *Built To Last: Successful Habits of Visionary Companies.* New York: HarperCollins.
2. Quinn, James Brian (1992). *Intelligent Enterprise: A Knowledge and Service Based Paradigm for Industry.* New York: Simon & Schuster.
3. *Lewis Carroll Quote.* Retrieved 2008, from http://www.brainyquote.com/quotes/authors/l/lewis_carroll.html
4. We have seen this story or versions of it for years. However, we haven't seen a credible reference to substantiate it.
5. *Einstein's Lost Train Ticket.* Retrieved 2008, from Snopes.com: http://message.snopes.com/showthread.php?t=11771
6. Hindo, Brian, *At 3M, A Struggle Between Efficiency And Creativity.* Retrieved 2008, from Businessweek, June 11, 2007: http://www.businessweek.com/magazine/content/07_24/b4038406.htm.
7. Lloyd, Tracey (2009). Triple Bottom Line Reporting: People Planet Profit Come Together to Give Full Picture of Business. Retrieved 2010, from suite101.com: http://social-corporate-responsibility.suite101.com/article.cfm/triple_bottom_line_reporting
8. *GLOBAL SUPERSECTOR LEADERS (2010/2011).* Retrieved 2011, from Dow Jones Sustainability Indexes: http://www.sustainability-index.com/07_htmle/reviews/review2010_1.html
9. *Vote for Triple Bottom Line Companies.* Retrieved 2011, from: http://drlorraine.blogspot.com/2010/03/vote-for-triple-bottom-line-companies.html
10. Mosaic Partnerships (2008).

Chapter 23

1. In this context, disruption is defined as the degree of impact to business as usual. A low level external disruption, such as a new flavor of breakfast cereal, will have minimal impact. Similarly, a low level of internal disruption will have minimal impact on the current organization. High levels of internal and external disruptions will have significant impact. Externally, they may even result in a new business category. Internally, they might require setting up a new business entity.

Epilogue

1. Rosenfeld (2006).

Appendix

Mosaic Partnership™ Questions

1. To read more about Mosaic Partnerships, go to: www.innovating.com.